W9-CCI-048

DATE DUE

MAR 1 1 2004		
GAYLORD		PRINTED IN U.S.A.

Modern Philosophies of Human Nature

MARTINUS NIJHOFF PHILOSOPHY LIBRARY

VOLUME 15

For a complete list of volumes in this series see final page of the volume.

Modern Philosophies
of Human Nature

Their Emergence from Christian Thought

by

Peter Langford
(La Trobe University)

1986 **MARTINUS NIJHOFF PUBLISHERS**
a member of the KLUWER ACADEMIC PUBLISHERS GROUP
DORDRECHT / BOSTON / LANCASTER

Distributors

for the United States and Canada: Kluwer Academic Publishers, 190 Old Derby Street, Hingham, MA 02043, USA
for the UK and Ireland: Kluwer Academic Publishers, MTP Press Limited, Falcon House, Queen Square, Lancaster LA1 1RN, UK
for all other countries: Kluwer Academic Publishers Group, Distribution Center, P.O. Box 322, 3300 AH Dordrecht, The Netherlands

Library of Congress Cataloging in Publication Data


```
Langford, Peter (Peter E.)
   Modern philosophies of human nature.

   (Martinus Nijhoff philosophy library ; v. 15)
   Includes bibliographies and index.
   1. Man--History.  2. Man (Christian theology)--
History of doctrines.  I. Title.  II. Series.
BD450.L325  1986        128'.09        86-12659
ISBN 90-247-3370-7
ISBN 90-247-3371-5 (pbk.)
```


ISBN 90-247-3370-7 (hardback)
ISBN 90-247-3371-5 (paperback)
ISBN 90-247-2344-2 (series)

Copyright

PRINTED IN THE NETHERLANDS

Table of Contents

Chapter 1 : Introduction

General Argument

My aim is to survey some of the most influential philosophical writers on
human nature from the time that Augustine codified Christian belief to the present.
During this period philosophical opinions about human nature underwent a
transformation from the God-centered views of Augustine and the scholastics to
the human-centered ideas of Nietzsche, Freud and Sartre.

While one aim has simply been to provide a handy survey, I do have three
polemical purposes. One is to oppose the notion that the modernism of more recent
writers was produced by methodological innovations. According to both Freud
and Sartre, as well as other key figures like Lacan and Heidegger, their views
were the product of new methods of investigating human nature, namely those
of psychoanalysis and the phenomenological reduction. Psychoanalysis claimed
to use the interpretation of both dreams and the relationship between analyst and
patient to penetrate the unconscious. Phenomenology has claimed that trained
philosophers are able to obtain a privileged view of consciousness by a special
act of thought called the phenomenological reduction which enables them to view
consciousness without preconceptions.

On many issues my sympathies are with Nietzsche rather than with Freud or
phenomenology. This is also the case regarding methodology. Nietzsche saw quite
clearly that the possibility of popularising the views he himself held came from
the decline of Christianity.

My rejection of exclusive reliance upon the methodologies of psychoanalysis
and phenomenology is based on two lines of argument. Firstly that thinkers using
similar methodologies arrived at different conclusions, while those using different
methodologies sometimes arrived at the same conclusions. Thus Heidegger,
Sartre and Jaspers all claimed to use the method of phenomenological reduction,
but they arrived at widely differing views of human nature. Nietzsche and Jaspers
arrived at very similar conclusions, though Nietzsche did not use phenomenology
and Jaspers did.

Secondly it will be shown that there is always a jump in the line of argument,
departing from the strict use of methodology in order to adopt unproven
assumptions. I have no hesitation in saying that this is the real moment of
inspiration, while the methodology is partly window-dressing.

My second polemical purpose is to comment upon the best known descriptions
of the historical shift in ideas about human nature. Here my aim is to offer a
treatment based on a return to educated commonsense, in opposition to the
excessively daring theses of some other writers. Goldsmith is reported to have
said of Hume that as all sensible positions had been occupied by previous writers
a young person was obliged to adopt wrong ideas to make a name for themselves.[1]

Very much the same can be said for many available treatments of the present topic. A fuller analysis of these writers is given in a later section of this introduction.

My third polemical aim has been to oppose the views of the so-called post-structuralists, particularly their call for a return to irrationalism. This is closely linked to the problems of excessive novelty just discussed, but as it involves a distinct group of authors it can be separated for purposes of exposition. Discussion of this issue will be more conveniently postponed until the concluding chapter when the necessary background will have been supplied.

The Christian view of human nature contained seven general problems. By selecting answers to these the theorist built up a position, which usually expressed a generalised attitude to human life and historical events. This structure developed as the early church fathers selected certain lines of philosophical inquiry as permissible for Christian thinkers. The chief line ultimately closed to inquiry was nihilist metaphysics. This is the belief that non-existence or not-being is somehow more real or more powerful than existence or being. Other specific doctrines were prohibited after Augustine but later slipped back into the fold.

The seven problems were as follows:
1. Can we develop ourselves by our own efforts or do we need divine grace? 2. Can we understand God with the human intellect? 3. What is the relative influence of motives in human affairs, particularly those for good and evil? 4. How does God communicate to human beings? 5. How are symbols formed and how can we interpret them? 6. How are particular motives moulded by society? 7. How do we acquire knowledge about human nature?

Of these problems the positions adopted on the first five define the Christian view as such. These answers are as follows:
1. Either we can develop ourselves by our own efforts or we need the assistance of divine grace. 2. We understand God by the human intellect, either fully, partially or not at all. 3. Either evil or good motives predominate in human affairs. This is linked with the debate on human rationality. If human beings are fundamentally rational then a just society will be able to arrange things so that in seeking personal good the individual will achieve social good. 4. God communicates with us either by revelation, by symbols or we know God, at least in part, by the intellect. 5. Symbols are an expression of divine truth and are to be interpreted either by revelation or by some kind of rational method.

This definition of the Christian view is least applicable to the British empiricist philosophers, for most of whom the religious orientation implied in the above description was kept rather separate from their view of human nature. This movement is the point at which the Christian view begins to alter, but as yet the shift is relatively slight. Most of the empiricists retained their Christian faith. Their discussion of human nature usually excluded a discussion of points 4 and 5 as these were thought to belong to the sphere of religious faith and revelation. This was quite explicitly stated by Bacon and seems implied in much of the later writing.

The most important issue that divided Christian thinkers was rationality and linked with it the relative importance of social as opposed to antisocial motives.

Augustine thought that most people were fundamentally irrational and activated by the evil desires for power, sex and possessions. Scholasticism, empiricism, metaphysical rationalism and Kant all believed most people capable of becoming sufficiently rational that if laws were framed to penalise wrongdoing and reward doing good, people would choose their own self-interest. In addition, most of these writers believed that altruistic and social tendencies had some influence in human affairs, while some like Hume thought them actually predominant. There were exceptions to these general statements, particularly the scholastic philosophers Bradwardine and Gregory of Rimini, both of whom leaned towards Augustine.

The main issues approached by modernism have been an expansion of the concerns of traditional thinkers. Two factors produced this expansion: the relaxation of restrictions placed by Christianity upon certain lines of inquiry and the increasing interest in causal mechanisms produced by modern science. The issues approached are as follows: 1a. Do we consider primarily the problem of socialisation, or redemption or both? 1b. Do we admire stability and safety or change and fascination? 1c. Do we consider experienced or abstract freedom? 1d. Should we engage in deep or only in minimal interpretation? 1e. Is there a drive towards completion of the human personality? 2. Can we become conscious of the instincts and the unconscious? 3a. What is the relative strength of motives? 3b. Which repressed motive is most important for the production of culture? 3c. What are motives like and how do they work? 3d. How do defence mechanisms mediate the interaction of motives? 4. How does the unconscious communicate with consciousness? 5. How are symbols formed and how may we interpret them? 6. What attitudes may be taken to the personal management of pleasure and pain? 7. How do we acquire knowledge about human nature?

Of all these issues it is 1a and 1b that are most neglected by commentators. Christianity is like all religions redemption-oriented. It wants to know how adults can be saved from this vale of tears. Among the modern mythologists it was Freud who focussed most clearly and most exclusively on the problems of socialisation: how do infants become social and how can adults remain social? One of Freud's many errors was to try to explain redemption, that is the religious impulse, through socialisation, in the guise of the wish to become childish again.

The issue of stability and safety versus change and fascination was also prejudged by Christianity at least so far as its official philosophers were concerned. Stability and unchangingness were the ideals of the Christian philosopher; change and decay belonged to the world of sense from which the philosopher was trying to escape.

During the nineteenth century Christianity, along with secular philosophers, began to reverse this direction, admiring change and spontaneity more than unchangingness. This alteration in the Christian attitude is found in both Maine de Biran and Hegel, though the swirling drama of the Hegelian dialectic is somewhat negated by the timeless essences of the *Logic* that lie behind the shifting scenes. Bergson, who radicalised this attitude towards the end of the nineteenth century, was probably right in saying that Christian mystics had always been hostile to the unchanging God of Augustine and the scholastics.

We can perhaps better appreciate this by considering the difference between our own typical contact with the spontaneity of nature and that of people in the medieval and early modern period. It has been said that the main association of woods in the minds of the medieval population was wolves. Woods and commons were dangerous places containing wolves, bears and robbers. Agricultural land, particularly that of the owner, would have posed less danger. When we come to the period of romantic pastoral paintings by such painters as Claude in the eighteenth century, it is the agriculturalist who is frequently the centre of attention. It was agricultural life, not life in the woods, that excited admiration. Twentieth century admiration for wildernesses partly stems from the fact that our own experience of such places is limited and usually undertaken from the safety of human habitation and modern transport. Equally the attitude of the medieval thinker to the abstract, unchanging and eternal must have been conditioned by fairly limited contact with it.

Having decided to concentrate on stability and redemption Christianity ruled out a whole number of approaches that were to become important in the modernist movement. Freud developed an emphasis on social stability and socialisation; Nietzsche admired in the main redemption through change; in his earlier writings Sartre stressed the quicksilver evanescence of a metaphysical nothingness barely able to come into being. Sartre's close connection with traditional metaphysics and his concentration upon the adult psyche show that his chief interest was in redemption rather than socialisation.

If these are some of the dominant chords in these three modernist writers, there are certainly others, stated in a more restrained manner but nonetheless present. Christianity played off the dynamic vision of its mystics against the timeless God of the philosophers. Modernism has often managed to express its ambivalence in a single individual. Nietzsche's myth of the eternal recurrence, stated in *Thus Spake Zarathustra*, looking forward to a time when all events now occurring will be precisely repeated, reveals a hidden longing for the unchanging eternity of the Christian philosophers. While Freud admired social stability his myth of the primal horde allowed for the time in each generation when the younger generation overthrows the old. In his later writing, particularly *Critique of Dialectical Reason*, Sartre makes the human longing for being dominate the power of nothingness.

Both Nietzsche and Sartre also cross over to deal with socialisation as well as redemption. Nietzsche's *The Genealogy of Morals* offers us an analysis of the morality of communities, while Sartre's descriptions of being include stable social arrangements as a special case. Both Nietzsche and Sartre seek salvation through social change. Freud on the other hand tried to explain salvation through socialisation: we look to God the Father for a lost parent.

Something more positive should also be said about the epistemological views of Nietzsche and Jaspers, as these writers did both practice and preach a reasonably distinctive method of arriving at knowledge about human nature. This can be broadly described as perspectivism.[2] This takes at least two forms in

Nietzsche. According to the more moderate version we should look at a problem from as many viewpoints as possible in order to avoid one-sidedness. This is extended in Jaspers to include the process of synthesising the viewpoints into a coherent whole, something Nietzsche appears sometimes to have intended but doesn't say much about explicitly. According to a more extreme version of perspectivism found particularly in *The Genealogy of Morals* there is less emphasis on finding a synthesis and more on the permanently subjective nature of individual perspectives. It is of course the case that the second version of perspectivism must within its own terms remain a permanently subjective viewpoint. The view then collapses unless we give the overall approach a privileged status. Leaving aside the problems of the second approach I will concentrate on the first, which seems to offer more promise.

The moderate version of perspectivism cannot in itself be considered a cast-iron guarantee of success. Other things will obviously go to make a successful theorist, particularly ability in conceptual thinking, openness to experience and breadth of experience. There are also other systematic elements at work. Both Nietzsche and Jaspers were distinguished from other modern theorists by their politics. Both were more sympathetic to elites and aristocratic attitudes than others. This is obviously linked to their tendency to view the will to power as the most significant motive in social life. Those sympathetic to the exercise of power can afford to admit the widespread influence of the motive. Those like Sartre who are unsympathetic to the exercise of power will naturally be unwilling to admit to the inevitability of such a striving.

This argument can be turned around. Perhaps those who realise themselves through power tend to justify this by giving the striving for power an inevitable quality it does not possess. The difficulty with this is that it cannot apply in detail unless we assume, with Sartre, that all human actions are motivated by metaphysical striving. This is impossible to square with the regularity with which human beings seek the satisfaction of certain natural wants. The proponents of the will to power are quite willing to admit a large admixture of strivings for transcendence as an important additional source of the will to power. Thus it is Sartre and not Nietzsche who is flying in the face of obvious facts and common experience.

There is, it seems, a real connection between the balanced and all-round view of human personality taken by Nietzsche and the moderate version of perspectivism. It is not the case however that we should simply see the adoption of this method as leading to a correct result. The theory of perspectivism itself suggests we look at other interpretations of the connection between method and result. A real clue here is given by Nietzsche's claim that one-sided and simplistic viewpoints are characteristic of the oppressed. It seems likely that the aristocratic attitude, moderate perspectivism and a certain view of human nature are linked into a kind of self-reinforcing syndrome, each part of which tends to prop up the others.[3] It remains true that this new constellation of thought could only come into existence as a result of the decline of Christianity.

It is worth enquiring briefly as to the meaning of the terms 'aristocratic' and 'elite' within this formulation. Both the Augustinian and scholastic versions of human nature as well as their successors within the Christian tradition provided relatively rounded views of human personality that were considerably less one-sided than the extreme exaggerations of Sartre or the behaviourists. Thus we must consider the term 'elite' here to include the intellectual elite promoted by both the church and the church-dominated universities. Nietzsche complained about the bad aroma emanating from the gospels of the New Testament, but this low origin was later overtaken by the influx of highly trained intellectuals into the church. Augustine himself provides the perfect example of this, having been trained by and having taught in the Roman education system. If the devotional life of the majority of Christians was confined to listening to the Bible and a creed, the activities of philosophers were far removed from these sources, being limited chiefly by the dangers of heresy.

Christianity as it evolved was strongly elitist. The Catholic Church believed as a matter of principle that its teaching ministry involved the superior authority of the teacher. This was undermined by the reformation but the ultimate result was a long time coming. The more extreme protestants advocated reading the bible in the vernacular, but to finally undermine authority it was necessary to write new books. For a long time this was the privilege of the privileged or intellectuals very close to them. For thoroughly one-sided ideas to finally enter the highest reaches of the academic disciplines of philosophy, psychology and sociology several centuries of gradually increasing democratic influence were necessary. The writing had been long on the wall in this regard. La Mettrie's *L'Homme Machine* had signaled the possibilities available and several of his successors in eighteenth century France were every bit as extreme. Their ideas never however gained wide acceptance, unless we count their period of official favour during the revolution.

The rise of political democracy and the emergence of a mass public of the semi-educated provided a general precondition for the widespread acceptance of very exaggerated ideas within the academic disciplines. The specific details of their emergence highlights the complexity of the process.

Watson's crude propaganda writings were succeeded within behaviourism by the more subtle, complex and academic work of Tolman and Hull. It was Skinner who entrenched the most laughable simplifications within American academic psychology. He was able to do this partly by appealing, like Watson, to the mentality of a non-academic public, partly through the desire of his own profession to establish itself as something distinctively different from philosophy. The underdog mentality of psychology in regard to philosophy was in the 1930s one of the most obvious features of the profession in the United States. This led it to embrace some distinctively underdog ideas.

Sartre also had an underdog mentality, though in his case it was one with larger horizons. His own struggle for power and recognition within philosophy was conducted quite outside the normal confines of an academic career. He never held a teaching post in a university, gaining wide recognition through his novels and philosophical books. Such a combination was not new in French philosophy, but the breadth of the public to which he appealed in his novels was. In a newspaper interview he described how after the second world war he deliberately set out to exploit the new mass market for paperback books dealing with the everyday life of ordinary people.[4]

This path was not one fore-ordained to Sartre. Unlike some of the less subtle behaviourists he was both knowledgeable and gifted. It was his choice, motivated by distaste for his background, perhaps even distaste for life. There was a clear space within the problems opened up by the decline of Christianity for the development of the Sartrian philosophy. It was not entirely accidental that a person with Sartre's distinctively underdog mentality should have pushed this choice to the extreme that he did. The very obscurity of *Being and Nothingness* carries the suspicion of a high priest celebrating rites in front of a baffled audience of the ignorant and uninitiated.

The case of sociology is also instructive. Both psychology and sociology had established themselves as respectable academic disciplines in Germany by the first world war. While some of the work of Wundt and Ebinghaus was narrow and stultifying, the disciplines appeared to be developing in a reasonably balanced manner. The early achievements of German sociology were particularly impressive. In the United States the acceptance of sociology occurred later and once again the underdog mentality became prominent, not just in the attitude of the discipline to other disciplines, but also in the close connections established between some kinds of sociology and various movements for social reform. Allied with this arose a tradition that came to believe that individuals are simply the products of the desire for social conformity. This extends from Moreno and Kardiner down to Berger and Luckmann. This was neither the most radical nor the most conservative trend within American sociology, but became a counterpart to an unthinking and intellectually lazy middle America.

In short, behaviourism and conformity theory both emerged within newly-accepted disciplines in the United States, a country where democracy has often been suspected of corrupting academic standards.[5] The flagrant exaggerations of Sartre's philosophy are hard to separate from his Marxist sympathies.

Two qualifications should be included here. The United States has attempted to offer higher education to a greater proportion of its population than any other Western country. It is probably true that the standards of the elite sections of this system are as high as anywhere; it is however the presence of the remaining portion of the system that allows ideas to gain academic respectability that might elsewhere be considered simply as the simplifications of popular writing. In addition, it is certainly true that the dividing line between popular and academic writing has always been somewhat blurred. Popular philosophy has always existed and has often irritated the professional. My submission is only that certain kinds of exaggeration found within recent writing are peculiarly suited to a popular audience and that we are rather more inclined to blur this distinction than previous centuries.

Another factor that has probably contributed to the development of exaggerated views has been a lack of attention to the philosophy of classical antiquity. Nietzsche and Jaspers were both interested in Greek philosophy, which had already devised several relatively balanced views of the relation between our higher and lower natures. Heidegger and Sartre both began chiefly from Christian philosophy - particularly that of Duns Scotus and Descartes - and thus were left failing to reinvent the wheel. Freud and most of his Marxist disciples were activated by the traditional radical liberal hostility to religion and metaphysics and so had a definite motive for neglect of our higher nature, but their lack of attention to classical philosophy certainly contributed to their exaggerations. Ironically Marx himself was interested in classical philosophy - his doctoral thesis was on Epicurus and Democritos - and his early philosophical writings provide a fairly balanced picture of the interaction of lower and higher nature; or at least a sketch that could have been developed into one. This was neglected by Marxists until after the second world war and even at that time Fromm was one of the few to develop a balanced interpretation of their implications. Sartre provides the worst example of a one-sidedly metaphysical approach to the notebooks of Marx in his later work, where, as throughout his career, it is hard not to detect the influence of a secret resentment at work in the form of hostility to human pleasures.

Finally a word is in order on the slippery term 'instinct'. One central use of this in the nineteenth century was to denote certain actions of animals, like the nest building of birds, that might appear to be the result of foresight and intelligence but which on closer examination contain elements of inborn and automatic mechanism that do not involve these. Buffon's attempts in the eighteenth century to minimise the intelligent aspect of animal behaviour had led to controversy about how far non-intelligent instinctive mechanisms could explain such behaviour. Interest in animal instincts was revived by Darwin's writings and the last three decades of the nineteenth century saw the observational and quasi-experimental studies of Spalding and Romanes in Britain, Schneider in Germany and Fabre in France.[6]

The central meaning of the term as applied to animals was thus a non-intelligent mechanism guiding animal actions that in human beings might be thought as the result of intelligence. This applied to 'instinct' in French and English and 'instinkt' in German. As applied to human activity the term 'instinct' had acquired a different denotation, though sometimes the connotations merged. This was to indicate the traditional idea of inborn motive or natural human end. The term 'instinct' in English and French comes from the Latin *instinctus*, meaning an instigation or impulse.[7] Cicero uses the phrase '*instinctu divino*', meaning divine inspiration. In the nineteenth century the term retained this meaning, but began to have a more biological connotation.

In *The Descent of Man* Darwin goes out of his way to emphasise that human beings are distinguished from other animals by their vastly greater intelligence and foresight. He uses the term 'social instinct' to apply to sympathy, fidelity, courage and love of social admiration, all of which he says have been improved by natural selection.[8] Wallace follows this usage in his *Darwinism* (1905), though he disagrees with the emphasis upon natural selection. The looseness with which even such a rigorous thinker as Darwin used the term is shown by his inclusion of 'courage', which is really a quality of character, rather than a motive.

In Britain the term instinct was further redefined by McDougall in his *Introduction to Social Psychology* (1908). Here the human nervous system is said to have a 'psycho-physical disposition' to react in three ways in certain kinds of situation. First we naturally 'perceive and pay attention to objects of a certain class'; second we 'experience an emotional excitement of a particular quality' on perceiving these objects; third we react to such objects with an inborn pattern of actions.[9] This in effect spells out more clearly than traditional writers had the meaning of 'natural human end'. At the same time McDougall greatly multiplied the number of such natural ends or instincts, including such things as the 'instinct of acquisition'. Traditional writers, particularly those influenced by British empiricism, had tended to assume that we like acquiring things because when we get them into our possession we can use them in pleasurable ways. Acquisition was at first a means, though it might later become an end in itself. McDougall was much criticised along these lines, particularly in the United States.[10] This academic criticism has not prevented a number of more recent popularisers of human ethology from extending the term instinct in this way. Desmond Morris in *The Naked Ape*, for instance, suggests that it may be 'instinctive' for mothers to hold their babies on the left side of the body so they can hear the heart.[11] Morris is however at pains to provide a rather suggestive argument for this idea, where McDougall and some human ethologists have been less cautious.[12]

I have adopted the term 'instinct' despite the fact that only one group of the writers dealt with in what follows, the Freudians, used the term prominently and that only when translated into English. Freud uses the term *Trieb* extensively which his English translators have usually rendered as 'instinct', though it might be more directly rendered into English as 'drive'.[13] *'Trieb'* has the idea of a push towards a goal as part of its meaning, better conveyed by the English 'drive'. However his translators were not wrong in their translation: the English word 'instinct' can have this meaning too. Darwin's use of 'social instinct' includes in effect both the end and the push towards it. Freud's emphasis on the drive aspect of instinct is however far from accidental, for it is the drive of the instinct for expression that produces the need for repression. Nietzsche, the other and greater of the biologically oriented theorists, preferred the term 'passion' *(Leidenschaft)* rather than instinct, though he does on occasion use the German *Trieb* (drive).[14]

Alternative Views of these Developments

The most obvious line of counter-argument to the one put forward in this chapter is that advanced by Bertrand Russell in his *History of Western Philosophy* (1946). He labels all those influenced by Nietzsche and Schopenhauer as 'irrationalists', who have contributed to the undermining of the traditional liberal ideals of prudence and rationality. This supposes that the rise of irrationalist philosophy had little or no roots in everyday social life. Russell himself, unlike eighteenth century liberal writers, is at pains to stress that too much prudence can be deadening and that we may need the Dionysan moment in life. His discussion of Greek culture centers on this point, taken straight from *The Birth of Tragedy* by Nietzsche, though Russell attributes it to the Cambridge school of classical philology. A leading member of this school, F.M. Cornford, has acknowledged Nietzsche's priority here.[15]

On a more abstract level Russell has argued that philosophical ideas reflect a social cycle. At first strong, unified government is accompanied by belief in dogma. The material success of the government brings moderate individualism, accompanied by rational debate and scientific inquiry. Ultimately however this degenerates into extreme individualism and irrationalism in which the rules of inquiry and debate are themselves called into question. In modern European history we have seen a shift from dogmatic Catholicism, through Descartes, Berkeley and Kant to the ultimate subjectivist, Fichte. 'This was insanity, and, from this extreme, philosophy has been attempting, ever since, to escape into the world of everyday common sense.'[16] The difficulty of applying this to more recent ideas about the individual is that it is only Nietzsche who really fits the bill, with his denial of scientific objectivity. Most writers flying the flags of psychoanalysis, phenomenology and semiotics have aimed at objectivity. We might put this down to a revolt against subjectivity, but that doesn't take us very far with an analysis of their conceptions of the individual. Russell's theory in fact suggests that 'irrationalism' as an interest in the irrational side of human nature always goes along with 'irrationalism' as subjectivist epistemology. This is plain untrue. It is probably true that subjective epistemology does reflect Russell's social cycle, but modern interest in the irrational has persisted through considerable shifts in political orientation and has more plausibly been produced chiefly by the decline of Christianity rather than by relations between the population and the state.

A second influential study of our subject matter is Parsons' *The Structure of Social Action* (1949).[17] This is primarily a study of human action as viewed by economists and sociologists, but it also overlaps widely with the subject matter discussed here. The study begins from a peculiar and in my view incorrect characterisation of the views of 'utilitarianism'. By this Parsons means any theory of human action that concentrates upon finding increasingly rational means for ends that are accepted as given and treated as a random factor for purposes of analysis.[18] This scheme is most typical of utilitarian economists who consider 'aggregate demand' while not wishing to inquire why a particular person bought a particular thing on a particular day. It also appears in Hobbes' political theory.[19]

This description of utilitarianism is misleading as it implies that those who held to it adopted this as their view of individual action, which is untrue. Both Hobbes and the economists quite deliberately adopted the aggregate view as a legitimate kind of abstraction when dealing with the actions of large numbers of people. When dealing with individuals they were quite aware that an analysis of the actual motives of the individual was required.[20]

Because of his misconstruction of utilitarianism, Parsons thinks that it led to a number of contradictions. One was that in attempting to apply scientific rationality to the choice of ends a problem arose: 'If ends were not random, it was because it must be possible for the actor to base his choice of ends on scientific knowledge of empirical reality.' This leads to the difficulty that with both ends and means chosen scientifically action becomes completely predictable.[21]

The truth was that the problem of total predictability had long arisen in the Christian tradition in another context, that of an individual with a certain amount of rationality, a certain kind of character and given strengths of various motives. Parsons refers to an original theory of 'Christian voluntarism'; but in the Christian tradition this was always in tension with the problem of determinism, the latter arising out of theological as well as psychological analysis.[22]

Another difficulty said to emerge from utilitarian theory was that any failure of actors to behave with rational choice of means had to be attributed to ignorance or error.[23] If the causes of such ignorance or error could be located in the physical environment or heredity of the actor then complete predictability could be ensured. Once again this problem was of much longer standing than Parsons implies.

A third difficulty for both utilitarianism and those more generally 'positivistic' systems that developed from the above mentioned contradictions was as follows. Both the scientific rationality and the individualistic, self-interested outlook of these systems came to be seen, particularly through the work of Pareto, Durkheim and Weber, as expressing values rather than eternal truths about human nature.[24] To give an example, Weber claimed that the development of Calvinist theology in England emphasised individualism for theological motives. Voluntarism, for Parsons, has thus now become choice of values rather than choice of course of action. In choosing values we reach outside what can be predicted.

In his conclusions Parsons points to one factor above all as having occasioned the convergence of such disparate thinkers on this one central conclusion: that their views were in accord with the facts.[25] Their conclusion thus stands as a genuine advance in understanding, rather than, say, an intellectual fashion.

In this second part of his argument Parsons is on much stronger ground than in the first. Yet there is still room for disagreement, particularly over his choice of the term 'voluntarism' to describe the analysis of values present in these sociological writers. For in both Durkheim and Weber the aim is quite clearly to understand the causal origins of values. In this sense their views are not voluntaristic. Parsons makes them appear so by his repeated insistence that utilitarianism, in his sense, lies at the heart of deterministic, causal analysis. Once we abandon this quite false assumption Durkheim and Weber are just as determinist and anti-voluntarist as Hobbes.

The process Parsons is talking about really seems much better described in the terms used by Weber. Western culture has progressively rationalised, that is reflected upon and made relative, both means and ends.[26] The difficulty of this process for causal analysis is that once the individual has rationalised and made self-conscious the choice of values there may remain only an act of arbitrary choice. This is a problem that was much-canvassed by the phenomenological and semiotic movements but remains in the background for Durkheim and Weber, both of whom remained personally committed to broadly 'liberal' values.

The next major contribution to our topic comes from the American historian

H. Stuart Hughes. In his book *Consciousness and Society* (1958) he puts forward a number of arguments that are close to those advanced here. The 1890s are described as a period of revolution in European social thought that led to an unprecedented interest in the unconscious.[27] The reasons he gives for this new interest centre however on a release from the stifling of speculation and imagination in the preceding decades rather than on the decline of Christianity.[28] In one sense these two things are bound up with one another, but it would be impossible to understand the central issues that divided the modernist writers without introducing a whole range of issues as well as their attitudes to repression.

Ambiguity is also introduced to Hughes' treatment by the circumstance that he borrows some of Parsons' terminology and refers key points to *The Structure of Social Action*.[29] He takes from this source the terms 'utilitarian' and 'positivism' and talks about the 1890s as a revolt against positivism. Yet neither Parsons' misdescription of utilitarianism nor his arguments about its supposed contradictions are introduced. The Parsonsian vocabulary is introduced when Hughes' explanation for the changes is far more cultural than that advanced by Parsons, for whom an advance in understanding produced by internal contradictions in previous intellectual stances is the key process. For Hughes it is the 'stuffy decade' of the 1880s with its 'smugness' and 'philistinism' that creates the explosion. He mentions Egon Friedell's description of 'the art of the upholsterer, the confectioner, the stucco decorator...'[30]

These are minor blemishes on an often brilliant study of Freud, Sorel, Croce, Troeltsch, Alain, Weber and a number of literary intellectuals. That the same problem of cultural crisis can be discerned in the largely different cast of authors dealt with in what follows is an indication of the general scope of the revolution in thought. Hughes' comments on the German and Austrian intellectual scenes in the decade of the 1890s are worth including at this point because of the key role played by these countries on the international stage.[31]

One problem in Germany was created by the success of the universities, which had come to dominate the cultural scene. Professors in the universities were hardworking, highly paid and enjoyed a good standing with the public. Their problem was that they had become too specialised, had modelled themselves too closely on the natural sciences and had become too closely integrated into the political establishment. This was most marked at Berlin, the leading university, still living off the reputations of Dilthey, Ranke, Drousen, Sybel and Trietschke, and still addicted to a Prussian sense of duty that had earned it the nickname 'First Guards Regiment of Learning'.

In opposition to Berlin were the southern universities of Munchen, Heidelberg, Freiburg, Strassburg and, in Switzerland but often mentioned with them, Basel. Here a spirit of bohemianism sometimes prevailed, symbolised by the Munchen satirical review *Simplizissimus*. At the same time the intellectual climate was influenced by the anti-positivism of Windelbandt and Rickert, who in their turn were to influence those stars of the rising generation Meinecke, Weber and Troeltsch, all at one time resident in the South. Though Hughes does not have occasion to mention it, Husserl and Heidegger were both associated with the university of Freiburg, while Sartre was later a student there.

This cultural opposition was reinforced by political division. Under Bismark German democracy had been sacrificed on the twin altars of national unity and craving for empire. After Bismark the progress of German liberal democracy was most notable in the Grand Duchy of Baden, governed as a parliamentary democracy, and least so in Prussia. Baden included the two university towns of Heidelberg and Freiburg.

If Berlin was the official centre of German intellectual culture, the new trends emerged on the periphery. The same tendency was also noticeable in Freud's relation to Viennese society. As both a Jew and a medical man he was removed from the mainstream of intellectual and social life. At the same time Vienna showed some of that Bohemianism and 'decadence' sometimes associated with the Southern German universities.

Peters' *The Concept of Motivation* (1960) deals with Christian as well as more recent views of human nature. The two views for which Peters has most respect are the rule-following view and the hedonistic view. The former says that we follow the rules of behaviour we were brought up to follow. We may appear to seek certain ends but 'norms enter into and often entirely define the end. Ends like passing an examination, getting married, becoming a professor, and reading a paper, explain quite adequately a great deal of the goings on in the precincts of a university...'[32] This, he claims, is the viewpoint of common sense.[33]

In my view this is simply false. Common sense would say that often behind these ends lie the further ends to which these goals are only means, namely such common human frailties as desire to get a job to obtain money, and vanity. Common sense would furthermore say that we like doing these things because they are pleasurable. Common sense, like most traditional theorists, is a hedonist.

The truth behind Peters' claim is that some twentieth century theorists of human nature have argued in the way that he does, namely that rule-following is the predominant mode of human social action. What Peters fails to explain, though he is clearly aware of the relevant facts, is why this view gained at least a foothold in the twentieth century when it had virtually no currency before. Peters seems to see the emergence of the rule-following view as an advance in our understanding of motivation. A more plausible view is that rule-following has been a more widespread form of social action in the twentieth century. It is not the students of human nature who have produced the alteration in viewpoint but rather the manifestations of human nature now studied. Some factors that further exaggerated the role of desire for social conformity have already been mentioned.

Peters ably documents the revival of hedonism within modern psychology, which has come to realise the strength of traditional doctrine here.[34] He feels however that states of pleasure don't have enough in common for there to be a common experience of pleasure: 'the pleasure of tasting sugar is specific to tasting sugar; the pleasure of sexual activity is specific to sexual activity; the pleasure of finding out things is specific to finding out things. It is difficult to see what properties the alleged hedonic states have in common if they are thought of as species under a genus.'[35] Again I can only meet this with flat denial. We do often compare the pleasure or advantage we will obtain from different activities and decide which to undertake. We are going to the cinema and someone says 'I prefer horror movies to comedies.' The experiences of watching the two are very different, yet somehow we decide which is preferable.

Peters' view of the 'revival of hedonism' in modern academic psychology is itself a quite partial one, partly produced by his own career as a philosophical critic of such psychology. He would however be well aware that the hedonist doctrine of Freudian psychoanalysis has always remained part of academic psychology in Britain and the United States since the 1930s. The other main trend in motivation theory within academic psychology in these countries in the period 1930-1950 was behaviourism. The reason this denied hedonism was more for reasons of philosophical principle than because it wished to deny the facts involved. Pleasure, as a mental state, was out of bounds to a science bent on describing behaviour. The movement however never denied that faced with a conflict of motives both humans and animals somehow decide which is preferable and opt for the most powerful combination of motive and habit.

The problem of pleasure has certainly become an acute one in modern views of human nature, but for rather different reasons than those suggested by Peters. In Freud the problem is precisely that in his day the repression of instincts by modern civilisation had also repressed pleasure and erected duty ('rule-following') as the all-important end. This, he thinks, is unnatural to us and we strive, through psychoanalysis, art and other means, to reduce our dependence on duty.

Another opposition dealt with by Peters is also of importance in traditional theories, namely that between theories that focus on end-states and those that focus on pleasure.[36] Nearly all Christian theorists thought the search for pleasure was of great importance. Augustine viewed this as the chief guide to human action. In scholasticism a concomitant emphasis also appeared on the natural ends of life, such as maintaining health and producing and caring for children. Because the search for pleasure was now thought to be constrained by reason, it provided the mechanism by which we are impelled to the natural ends of life. We like eating and sex and this ensures we will maintain health and produce children. In general the ideas of explanation by pleasure and explanation by final causes (we tend to certain ends because they are appointed for us) were able to coexist quite happily until Hobbes. He began the tendency for later British empiricist writers to look to pleasure as the chief explanation and to downplay explanation by final causes. This followed the general enthusiasm for mechanistic explanation which appeared in Britain in the seventeenth century. Peters is right to stress that the attempts by Hobbes and later writers to produce purely mechanistic explanations for motivation were largely play-acting at physics.[37] Hedonism is not a mechanical explanation involving nerves, muscles, electrical charges and so forth. It is an explanation that assumes we can weigh up general courses of action and then instigate the specific movements necessary to carry them out. It doesn't explain the second part of this process, but leaving that aside it is a very useful way of looking at human action.

Recent sociological writing on the history of psychoanalysis has been dominated by Rieff and his school. Rieff argues, following Durkheim, that religion is in some sense a worship of society: 'Behind shaman and priest, philosopher and physician, stands the great community as the ultimate corrective of personal disorders.'[38] Rieff's extension of the Durkheimian thesis is however clear from this sentence. It is not only the shaman and priest who worship society: in traditional Christian society it is also the philosopher and physician. Both philosophy and therapy were traditionally sacred activities - they placed social interdicts on the free expression of impulse by means of cultural symbols.

Rieff would hardly have achieved the success he has were there not some truth here, particularly in the American context. Yet it is hard to disentangle this from the confusion of Rieff's writings. Thus we learn: 'From Plato and Aristotle, through Burke and de Toqueville, the therapeutic implication of social theory is remarkably consistent: an individual can exercise his gifts and powers only by participating in the common life.'[39] What nonsense! Rieff himself knows better than this. In an earlier work he writes - 'In the immediately pre-Christian period, when the antique world was suffering its own exhaustion, the utopian yearning had been toward something higher, for it was a period of erotic satiety and the needs of the flesh were only too well attended.'[40] Even this statement is overgeneralised, hardly being true of slaves or the army, for.instance. But perhaps Rieff means us to skip the Hellenistic, Roman and Augustinian periods, none of which fit the former statement: particularly not Augustine for whom fulfilment lies in the relation of the individual to God. Scholasticism of the Aquinas-Scotus type and the chivalry of the court fit this generalisation. Catholicism after the Counter-Reformation fits it, as do certain kinds of revisionist Protestantism. The rest of Western intellectual and devotional history has been read out of the record. Luther, Calvin, militant Protestantism generally saw the relation of the individual to God as the avenue to fulfilment. The state was for them a necessary evil.

The element of truth in Rieff's analysis is that the official nineteenth century dominance of Catholicism (France) and a kind of state absorbed Protestantism (Britain, Germany, United States) has given way to the official dominance of varieties of secular hedonism. The element of falsity is that he ignores the anti-state and individualist Protestantism of the lower middle class in the nineteenth century (found for instance in Methodism) and the atheism of the nineteenth century European working class. He also reads back his simplified picture of unified Christian culture onto previous centuries. When doubt threatens he can always suggest that facts contradicting his overall picture are transitional forms. Marxism is a faith of the traditional type, though atheistic. It spans the traditional and the modern therapy-dominated culture.

The placing of Freud is an important topic for sociology of knowledge, but to read him as the expression of a new 'therapeutic culture' is to overgeneralise Freud's significance. Crucial here are Rieff's repeated references to the culture of 'the hospital and the theatre'. At least four separate intellectual and cultural movements are promiscuously implied by this phrase: the scientific manipulators of behaviourism, welfare sociology and a certain kind of 'physical treatment' psychiatry; the various styles of psychotherapy ranging from Freud to Jung; the 'acting out' of 'psychodrama' (another favourite Rieffian word); and dramas appearing in the theatre and on television (themselves infinitely various). Had he thrown in metaphysics, existentialism and the novel we could just call 'therapeutic culture' 'modern non-religious culture'.

Now crucial to Freudian therapy is its appeal to the intellect rather than the heart, to dispassionate analysis rather than ambiguous cultural symbolism. Theatre and television - purveyors of ambiguous anti-intellectual cultural symbolism - sit oddly here. Rieff calls them 'remissive culture' - the theatre of sex and violence that allow the lifting of restraints through 'psychodrama'. One of Rieff's many ambiguities is that he is unclear whether modern culture is becoming more intellectualised or less. That different sectors of the population may be moving in different directions is something he finds hard to encompass. Freudian therapy is intellectualised - television psychodrama anti-intellectual. The two have obviously different audiences, but Rieff ignores this.

Turning to metaphysics, a subject Rieff seldom mentions, we apparently see a similar transformation at work - from the traditional metaphysics of being to the Sartrean nothingness of absolute spontaneity. Yet such a conclusion would be thoroughly misleading. Sartre's spontaneity is not the freedom to do what one wants but rather a blind spontaneity that wells up out of nothingness. The emergence of belief in such spontaneity in Heidegger and Sartre reflects the lifting of intellectual constraints on considering a certain kind of metaphysical salvation. The quite varied ways in which Heidegger and Sartre develop this idea certainly reflect sociological factors but the very possibility of discussing such an idea stems from the relaxation of intellectual not of motivational prohibitions.

Rieff's view can certainly have some success with Nietzsche's release of the will to power, but here again this is not the only aspect of Nietzsche's thinking and cannot explain the overall structure of his ideas.

Rieff's book on Freud contains several excellent chapters, particularly on the resemblance between the Freudian methods of interpreting symbolic meaning and religious hermeneutics. But we cannot read Freud as the 'crux' of modern cultural change, its inner spirit; rather as a writer who addressed himself first to psychotherapists, later to the world. 'Therapeutic culture' is a highly misleading term. Properly speaking it applies only to the culture of psychotherapists - those who offer 'talking cures' for mental discontents. Much modern Western culture is a culture of attempted release from constraint. Rieff's writings have the great merit of questioning the wisdom of this mania. Like a mature roué, he wonders if sin wasn't more romantic before it was permitted. To harvest the full meaning of this question we need to abandon his perspective. We may also reflect that release from all constraints but those necessary for war and contract is an ideal whose mass diffusion owes much to the triumph of the capitalist economy. Rieff's determination to see societies generally as 'culture-dominated' tends to blind him to the truth that economic change can and has driven Western culture in directions no unfolding of its various 'spirits' would have dared to suggest.

Another book that bears on our topic is *The Discovery of the Unconscious* (1970) by H.F.Ellenberg. The main emphasis here is on changes in methods of treating mental disorders and in the theories to which such methods have given rise. He moves from a discussion of magical and religious methods of cure through eighteenth and nineteenth century magetism, mesmerism and hypnotism to Freud, Janet, Adler and Jung. Because the psychotherapist has always been in close and sympathetic contact with patients, often drawn from a distinctive social class, Ellenberger emphasises the importance of the social relations of that class in influencing the relation between therapist and patient. Thus Mesmer's *Sociefé de l'Harmonie* adopted the 'paternalist and symbiotic' relationship of the nobility and their subjects.[41] The hypnotism of the nineteenth century 'reflected the authoritarian attitude of the bourgeois master towards his dependents.'[42] At the end of the nineteenth century the upper classes became discontented with the application of such methods to themselves and demanded a more participatory method, provided by Freud. The latter metamorphosed into an ideology for 'the hedonistic-utilitarian world of mass consumption'.[43] Though not specifically mentioned it seems that Adler and the ego-psychologists are intended here.

Ellenberger is intent on coming to grips with the several factors impinging on the developments he describes. Psychoanalysis is rightly described as partly reflecting the romantic revival at the end of the nineteenth century, while the divergent views of Freud, Janet, Adler and Jung are related to their personalities and personal difficulties.[44] The portrait of Freud is particularly illuminating and has been used in a later chapter.

It is interesting to compare the history of psychotherapy with that of formal studies of human nature before Freud. Authors of the latter type tended to belong to what we might call the Olympian intellectuals. They usually had a very high level of formal education and were usually also professionals. The professions from which they were drawn shifted from the clergy to the traditional professions and from thence to more recently emerging professions like sociology and psychology in the nineteenth century. These writers were quite separate from psychotherapists who made a living by treating patients.

One of the peculiar features of recent writings about human nature is that so many of them have come from psychotherapists. While Ellenberger rightly makes some case for the influence of theories of animal magnetism on general culture in the eighteenth century, the real impact of psychotherapy in discussions of human nature begins with Freud.[45] Once it became accepted that there was a problem of reaching the elementary or 'animal' nature masked by civilising tendencies, it became plausible to look to neurosis and psychosis as providing cases of either a partial regression to an original state or the over-civilisation that Freud detected in compulsion neurosis.[46]

The psychotherapist has often been more closely in touch with a particular social class than the Olympian intellectuals, who were more in touch with general social problems. V. Thweatt has made a good case for connecting the writings of de la Rochefoucauld with the rise of a mercantile aristocracy in the seventeenth century, replacing the older more warlike nobility in France.[47] This is however a relatively unusual case.

With the advent of psychoanalysis it is reasonable to detect the influence of problems related to particular social classes in discussions of human nature, particularly those relating to the middle and upper classes. Classical psychoanalysis with its daily one hour sessions was an expensive undertaking. Undoubtedly the forces of propriety and repression bore down more heavily on these classes, particularly the middle class, than on other sectors of society. Yet with the extensive mechanisation of labour, bureaucratisation of social life, the coming of universal education and the 'gentling' of the working class, they were certainly not immune from these problems. Considerations of social class are relevant to understanding psychoanalysis as well as to understanding modern writings on human nature by professional academics, many of whom live a quite specialised lifestyle. They do not however 'explain away' the problems with which these writers dealt, which were far from being confined to particular classes and have become even less so with the passage of time.

The last item on our agenda is Kaufmann's trilogy *Discovering the Mind* (1980). Here he proposes that what is novel in recent views of human personality was due to Goethe rather than Nietzsche. The substance of this novelty is first and foremost Goethe's denial that there is an inner core or essence to the human individual.[48] We are in a position, for Goethe, to choose our actions and our lives in complete freedom and autonomy.[49]

Kaufmann is well aware that this position appears sharply at variance with the depth psychologies of Nietzsche and Freud.[50] They were intent on penetrating behind the superficial masks of consciousness to the realities of instinctual life beneath, a process of unmasking explicitly disapproved by Goethe. The solution, says Kaufmann, lies in another of Goethe's discoveries, that we are our deeds.[51]

At this point a considerable sleight of hand appears. Having credited Goethe with the solution to the problem, this solution fails as yet to address the difficulty at hand. Goethe is now rounded out by saying that 'We are what we have done, written and dreamed. But our consciousness shuts out most of this...'[52] The question must surely arise as to how consciousness does this. 'Third, we tend not to take in what we would very much rather not see of hear. This is the insight Nietzsche formulated succinctly in *Beyond Good and Evil*: 'I have done that', says my memory. 'I could not have done that', says my pride and remains inexorable. Finally, my memory yields.' Freud, as we have seen, applauded and developed this suggestion.'[53]

Nothing more is said about the glaring contradiction that has now opened up. The force that shuts our actions and dreams from consciousness is said to be our wants. But what are these if not the forbidden core of the personality, the heart of depth psychology and something quite in opposition to Kaufmann's reading of Goethe?

This is not an isolated mistake. Further on he asks what is of most value today among the discoveries of Nietzsche and Freud. His answer is the exploration of sublimated aggression; an answer with which I thoroughly concur.[54] Yet aggression is precisely part of that hidden core of personality that at other moments Kaufmann decries. We cannot have the autonomy of the self and no inner core together with the instincts of depth psychology. In reality both exist as major currents within modern writing.

Limitations of Coverage

This book is chiefly concerned with philosophical writers and my aim has been to show how the central concerns of European philosophy in regard to human nature have shifted. For this reason three groups of writers who have dealt with human nature in the twentieth century have been omitted. These are philosophical writers who have developed the work of writers from the Christian era; primarily psychological writers; primarily sociological writers.

Among the first group I include the large number of Augustinian, neoscholastic, empiricist and neoKantian writers. It is rather more difficult to defend my exclusion of psychological writers. Having admitted so clearly psychological a writer as Freud the gates might well be open to others. However Freud is an author who has attracted more attention from philosophers than most other psychologists. Three other groups of psychological writers might be considered: behaviourists, human ethologists and cognitive developmentalists. None of these have attracted the same amount of interest from philosophers as Freud and this is my main reason for leaving them out. It is however of interest to inquire if their inclusion would alter my overall argument about the nature of modernism.

Behaviourism as a movement arose from empiricism. Its chief novelty was that some of its proponents, notably B.F. Skinner, downgraded the power of human reason while maintaining that wise application of rewards and punishments could result in a workable social order. On the other hand many, notably Tolman, Cantor and Osgood, stayed close to traditional empiricist positions.

The best explanation for the emergence of writers like Skinner was I think given by Nietzsche in relation to some nineteenth century empiricists:

'These English psychologists whom one has also to thank for the only attempts hitherto to arrive at a history of the origin of morality - they themselves are no easy riddle; I confess that, as living riddles, they even possess one essential advantage over their books - they are interesting! These English psychologists - what do they really want? One always discovers them voluntarily or involuntarily at the same task, namely at dragging the shame of our inner world into the foreground and seeking the truly effective and directing agent, that which has been decisive in its evolution, in just that place where the intellectual pride of man would least desire to find it (in the vis inertiae of habit, for example, or in forgetfulness, or in a blind and chance mechanistic hooking-together of ideas, or in something purely passive, automatic, reflexive, molecular, and thoroughly stupid) - what is it really that always drives these psychologists in just this direction? Is it a secret, malicious, vulgar, perhaps self-deceiving instinct for belittling man? Or possibly a pessimistic suspicion, the mistrustfulness of disappointed idealists grown spiteful and gloomy? Or a petty subterranean hostility and rancor toward Christianity (and Plato) that has perhaps not even crossed the threshold of consciousness? Or even a lascivious taste for the grotesque, the painfully paradoxical, the questionable and absurd in existence? Or finally - something of each of them, a little vulgarity, a little gloominess, a little anti-Christianity, a little itching and need for spice.'[55]

Empiricism had threatened to lapse into the vulgarity of behaviourism before it did. The French empiricists, whom Nietzsche calls English in style, had developed extreme vulgarisations of British empiricism in the emphasis upon association and habit found in Condillac and Taine.[56] Here we may well suspect that it is the 'rancor toward Christianity' that impelled these writers to scandalise their contemporaries with such materialistic monsters.[57]

This motive can hardly, however, be regarded as significant for American behaviourism, unless one assumes an unconscious wish to scandalise the American establishment was at work. A reading of Watson's *Psychology from the Standpoint of a Behaviourist* (1919) shows this was certainly very far from their founder's conscious intentions.[58] These were to recommend himself to industrial, military and educational leaders as a man of sound common sense who was developing, along with others, a new scientific approach to human beings that would solve their management problems. Here lay the secret of behaviourism: it mirrored the assumptions of the managers of large bureaucracies and sanctified their cynicism and concern for reliable unthinking work habits as science. As work had become atomised into the trivial skills used on the assembly line and in routine office work, this viewpoint could naturally develop a following. Ironically the later development of the movement turned towards laboratory experiments with rats, which helped management little, if at all.[59]

Human ethology is a view of human nature that emphasises instincts in the sense of blind and mechanical inborn sequences of actions. This is a continuation of a minority interest during the Christian period which originated in Plutarch's writings. The social meaning of ethology appears to be rather different from that of behaviourism. Behaviourism originated in the promise of academic bureaucrats to assist their beleaguered fellows in other walks of life. Human ethology gained most of its popularity from the discovery by two students of animal instinct - Lorenz and Morris - that they could write bestselling books applying the animal metaphor to human beings.[60] The most plausible explanation for the success of these books is that they provide an intellectual defence of conservatism in relation to the family and property rights. Human ethology continues a trend already apparent in the Christian period.

The cognitive developmental view of personality of Lawrence Kohlberg is acknowledged both by himself and by other writers as a development of the ideas of Kant and thus also finds a clear place in my scheme.[61]

Before turning from psychological writers it will be necessary to defend my choice of post-Freudian writers for treatment. Here I have chosen chiefly those who seem to be of greatest current interest to philosophers: Marcuse, Lacan and Fromm. This choice can also be defended as exemplifying those post-Freudian writers who were themselves most influenced by philosophy. I have also included Reich as a writer who while more 'sociological' continues to arouse great interest.

The inclusion of the large number of post-Freudians who were most successful in America - Adler, Horney, Sullivan, Ausubel - would mainly serve to provide further examples of how Freud's ideas were adapted to other approaches, notably those of empiricism and the philosophy of history.

The decision not to include Jung was less easy to make, but taken on the grounds that he falls outside the three major modern traditions covered here. Jung broke more completely with Freud than most of the other ex-disciples. The main features of his thinking are an emphasis on the richness of innate ideas and on the tendency of the personality to strive for all-round development, particularly during the mid-life crisis. In Jung getting in touch with instincts means getting in touch with inherited ideas ('archetypes'), many of which point the direction to be taken in achieving wholeness of the personality. Jung believed that the study of cultural history was one of the best ways to get in touch with archetypes and he himself wrote widely on the relation between alchemy and his own theory of archetypes.[62] His system is in effect a fourth possibility among attitudes to the instincts and our genetic inheritance. Jung was profoundly conservative in believing that we find ourselves more fully in the past than in the future. Two good ways of learning about Jungian psychology are to read either his autobiography *Memories Dreams and Reflections* or *Psychology and Alchemy*.

Sociological views of human nature have often been derived from those already discussed: Kantian, behaviourist and Freudian writers have been particularly prominent. In recent years the phenomenology of writers like Schutz, Goffman and Berger and Luckmann has also been popular.[63] Perhaps the only novel feature of this movement was the idea found in Berger and Luckmann that we do what we know to be the done thing.[64] This general idea was found earlier in American social psychology in 'conformity theory'. Sartre was undoubtedly right when he attributed the popularity of such ideas in the United States to the importance of conformity in American social life.[65]

The view that we do what we know is the done thing can only arise in an affluent society in which there is little social conflict. Under such circumstances more fundamental motives are either satisfied or effectively repressed and the desire for social approval is able to appear as the only significant motive. As an attitude this is quite similar to that found in other varieties of phenomenology: the role of 'base' instincts is denied and the social instinct for approval is emphasised.

Three other sociological views of human nature should be mentioned: those of the Durkheimian school, of Weber and of semiotics. Durkheim and Weber were thoroughly traditional thinkers and differed little from empiricism in fundamentals, though their view of social ethics was of course novel.[66] Semiotics, as I shall argue later, is a methodological slogan rather than a theory. Like psychoanalysis and phenomenology it includes thinkers with very diverse views on human nature as well as on other topics. Semiotics claims that we can achieve a special insight into human affairs by looking at human communication through signs and symbols, after the manner of linguistics. Lacan and Baudrillard are both writers who fly the flag of semiotics and are dealt with in what follows. Their views about human nature are quite divergent, supporting my claim that methodology is not the key to views on this topic. Lacan follows Freud, while Baudrillard makes use of a kind of amalgam of Sartre and Freud in which Sartre definitely has the upper hand. Consideration of other semiotic writers like Morris and Levi-Strauss would only reinforce the general conclusion that they are 'divided by a common method'. Levi-Strauss is unusual in the emphasis he gives to intellectual motives among tribespeople, but his overall view of human nature is more traditional than modern.[67]

Further Reading

The following are all informative general surveys; some of their biases have been noted in the text:

H.F. Ellenberger, *The Discovery of the Unconscious*, Allen Lane, London, 1970.
H. Stuart Hughes, *Consciousness and Society*, J.C.B. Mohr, Tubingen, 1958.
W. Kaufmann, *Discovering the Mind*, 3 Vols., McGraw-Hill, New York, 1980.
A.O. Lovejoy, *Reflections on Human Nature*, John Hopkins Press, Baltimore, 1961.
J. Passmore, *The Perfectibility of Man*, Duckworth, London 1970.

Chapter 2 :
Unreason and Self-Destruction

Main Assumptions

Augustine's ideas regarding the irremediable evil of fallen human nature were able to exert their wide influence because of the position of the church in the ancient world. The church had become, in 380 A.D., the official religion of the Roman Empire. But it could not hope to exert more than a moderating effect upon a secular world that was both long-established and disintegrating through a dynamic the church had no power to check. This situation determined the three directions of Augustine's theory: the flight from an inherently evil world into mysticism; the attempt to divine a mysterious providence in the apparently downward path of secular society; and the belief that the masses are possessed by a fundamentally evil and ineradicable nature.

In relation to the seven main issues approached by Christian thinkers Augustine's views were as follows: 1. He believed we are unable to develop ourselves by our own efforts to any significant degree, requiring the gift of God's grace to do so; 2. With the assistance of grace the human intellect is capable of dimly apprehending divine matters, provided it can overcome its inveterate tendency to think using pictures modelled on physical reality; 3. Evil motives are predominant and human rationality weak; 4. God may communicate to us through visions, dreams, inner voices and divine scripture, all of which require extensive interpretation; 5. Symbols are pictures used by God to make his message more comprehensible to human beings; 6. Society makes little impact on human pride or other passions; 7. We acquire knowledge about human nature, as about other significant issues, through divine guidance.

Augustine (345-430 A.D.)

Augustine's writings fall into two distinct groups: those from before and during his conversion and those written later in life. At the end of his life Augustine published a book of *Retractions* in which he disavowed some early doctrines. The following account is based chiefly on his later writings, taking into account the *Retractions*.

Lower Nature

The origin of all sin is pride. It was the pride of Satan that turned him away from God and the pride of Adam that caused him to disobey God's commandment not to eat the fruit of the tree of knowledge of good and evil. 'Pride is the commencement of all sin because it was this which overthrew the devil, from whom arose the origin of sin; and afterwards, when his malice and envy pursued man, who was yet standing in his uprightness, it subverted him in the same way in which he himself fell. For the serpent, in fact, only sought for the door of pride whereby to enter when he said, 'Ye shall be as gods'.'[1]

Pride is not only the origin of all sin, but always accompanies it, except 'among the ignorant, the infirm, the weeping and the sorrowful'.[2] Pride is turning away from God, which is sin.

The three main forms of lust are the desire for material possessions, the desire for power over others and sexual desire. There is no limit to the human desire for material possessions: 'And it (the world) does not make good what it promises, it is a liar, and deceiveth. Therefore man never ceases hoping in this world, and who attains to all he hopes for? But whatever he attains, that is immediately considered worthless. Other things begin to be desired, other fond things are hoped for; and when they come whatever it is that comes to you, is considered worthless. For this reason are these things considered worthless, because they cannot stand, because they are not what He is. For nought, O soul, suffices you, save he who created you.'[3]

Avarice, this boundless desire for possessions, knows no limit: 'You at first desired a farm; then you would possess an estate; you would shut out neighbours; having shut them out, you set your heart on the possessions of other neighbours; and extended covetous desire till you reached the shore: arriving at the shore, you coveted the islands: having made the earth your own, you would haply seize upon heaven.'[4]

The avaricious man leaves no stratagem untried in his lust for possession: 'Like the shrewd man you are, you leave nothing untried, whereby you may pile coin upon coin; and may store it up more carefully in a place of secrecy. You plunder others; you guard against the plunderer; you are afraid lest you should yourself suffer the wrong that you yourself do; and even what you suffer does not correct you.'[5] This picture is not only applied to the rich; it also applies to the poor.[6] Furthermore, the wicked and cruel actions that stem initially from the insatiable desire for possessions acquire a momentum and dynamic of their own. Some eventually pursue cruelty for its own sake. The means to acquiring possessions has become an end in itself.[7]

Yet despite the unending striving for possessions, such worldly people are never happy.[8] They have a 'hunger' that can never be satisfied. Reading Augustine on the lust for possessions we are inevitably reminded of modern objections to the consumer society.

The second major lust is the passion for domination over others. While God created all equal and kin with Adam, the soul of fallen humanity, tainted with original sin, shows 'a reach of arrogance utterly intolerable', seeking to imitate God by aspiring 'to lord it even over those who are by nature its equals - that is, its fellow men.'[9]

It is in the nature of things for God to have power over man, but through the sin of pride men seek to imitate God. And like avarice, the lust for power is found in almost everyone: 'There is hardly anyone who is free from the love of rule, and craves not human glory.'[10]

The greatest example of the love of power and glory is the sacrifice of the Roman soldiers on behalf of their city and empire. Perhaps swayed by the favour showed by the Roman Empire to Christianity, which was declared the official religion of the Empire by Theodosius the Great in 380 A.D., Augustine sometimes sees the Roman love of conquest and glory as superior to other vices: 'Such men as, for the sake of honour, and praise, and glory, served their country well, in whose glory they sought their own, and whose safety they did not hesitate to prefer to their own, suppressing the desire of wealth and many other vices for this one vice, namely the love of praise.'[11]

The fratricide committed by Cain was repeated by Romulus, the founder of Rome, for glory and power: 'Romulus and Remus desired to have the glory of founding the Roman republic, but both could not have as much glory as if one only claimed it; for he who wished to have the glory of ruling would certainly rule less if his power were shared by a living consort...by this crime the empire was made large indeed, but inferior, while otherwise it would have been less, but better.'[12]

The worst crimes are committed by those who lust for power but do not at the same time seek praise and glory. The desire for praise and glory saved the Romans of the republican period from the worst excesses, because the desire for glory encourages individuals to act for the common good, rather than purely out of the lust for domination. The later empire saw the love of power and luxury submerge the desire for glory:

'He who is a despiser of glory, but is greedy for domination, exceeds the beasts in the vices of cruelty and luxuriousness. Such, indeed, were certain of the Romans, who lacking the love of esteem, did not lack the thirst for domination. But it was Nero Caesar who was the first to reach the summit, and, as it were, the citadel of this vice; for so great was his luxuriousness, that one would have thought there was nothing manly to be dreaded in him, and such his cruelty, that, had not the contrary been known, no one would have thought there was anything effeminate in his character.'[13]

The third lust of fallen humanity is sexual desire. His treatises on marriage and concupiscence - *De Bono Coniugali, De Virginitate, De Nuptiis et Concupiscentia* - make it clear that marriage is second best to virginity. Even within marriage sexual activity is best confined to its real purpose - the procreation of children. But he follows St. Paul in allowing that sexual intercourse between husband and wife for the satisfaction of sexual desire may be permitted, even though sinful, to reduce the risk of the greater sin of adultery.

Before the fall sexual desire and the sexual members were under the control of the will. But since Adam's sin of disobedience the sexual organs have acted through the compulsion of lust rather than through the will:

'When it comes to man's great function of the procreation of children, the members which were expressly created for this purpose will not obey the direction of the will, but lust has to be waited for to set these members in motion, as if it had legal rights over them, and sometimes it refuses to act when the mind wills, while often it acts against its will. Will this not bring the blush of shame over the freedom of the human will that by contempt of God, its own Commander, it has lost all proper command over its own members?'[14]

Some worldly men are dominated by their sexual appetites, while others restrain the sexual appetites to further their lust for material possessions or for power and glory. Compared to the avaricious or power-hungry, the sexual profligate is the most wretched of all, whose satisfactions are even more transitory and whose sufferings and frustrations more profound.

The lusts of avarice, domination and sex are transmitted to each new generation by the very nature of the sexual act, which cannot occur without sexual desire and so taints those conceived by such sin. This is how the original sin of Adam is visited on all his descendants in the form of original sin. The infant is conceived in sin and is born sinful. In his descriptions of himself as an infant in his *Confessiones*, Augustine notes the selfish egoism inherent in the infant.

'Nor was it good, even at that time, to strive to get by crying what, if it had been given to me, would have been hurtful; or to be bitterly indignant at those who, because they were older - not slaves either, but free - and wiser than I, would not indulge my capricious desires. Was it a good thing for me to try, by struggling as hard as I could to harm them for not obeying me, even when it would have done me harm to be obeyed?...I have myself observed a baby be jealous, although it could not speak; it was livid as it watched another infant at the breast'.[15]

The basic characteristic of the infant is self-centerdness. From this the other sins of avarice, domination and sexual desire will follow. It is interesting to see how closely Augustine anticipated Freud in his remark that the baby desires even harmful things. In Freudian terms, the baby acts according to the 'pleasure principle' rather than the 'reality principle'. The baby does not yet understand how to restrain capricious desires even if these will lead to harmful consequences.

Unlike Freud, however, Augustine does not give sexual desire an important place in early childhood. He first mentions sex in his *Confessiones* as arising in adolescence: 'Bodily desire, like a morass, and adolescent sex welling up within me exuded mists which clouded over and obscured my heart, so that I could not distinguish the clear light of true love from the murk of lust.'[16]

So much for the basic characteristics of fallen nature. We now turn to Augustine's treatment of the law and civil powers that temper and restrain these insatiable drives to steal, dominate and injure.

Law and the State

While Augustine believed that even those not elected to salvation retained a natural knowledge of God's Law to 'love thy neighbour as thyself', this small voice of conscience was ineffective in the mass of fallen humanity. This fallen mass is only restrained by the fear of punishment by earthly courts and rulers. This restraint is made possible by a 'law of nature' which, Augustine says, 'has never been violated, and which is common to us with the beasts'. This is the instinct for self-preservation, by which 'we love ourselves, and what is beneath us but connected with us'.[17] While the knowledge of the moral law is only reached by a recollection of the state of the soul before the fall, knowledge of this law of self-preservation is instinctual and part of fallen human nature.

Human law and the power of the state have been providentially arranged by God as a punishment and remedy for our fallen nature. While private property, private wealth and slavery are not 'natural' and have no sanction from the divine law of love, they must be upheld by Christians as necessary for the correction of fallen nature. Better laws cannot be hoped for and worse may easily follow if they are disregarded. Yet if an earthly ruler takes and gives property this is also a result of divine providence and must be obeyed.[18]

Augustine is utterly cynical as regards the origins and motives of the human state and its ruler: 'The (robber) band itself is made up of men; it is ruled by the authority of a prince; it is knit together by the pact of the confederacy; the booty is divided by the law agreed on. If, by the admittance of abandoned men, this evil increases to such a degree that it holds places, fixes abodes, takes possession of cities, and subdues peoples, it assumes the more plainly the name of a kingdom because the reality is now conferred on it not by the removal of covetousness, but by the addition of impunity.'[19] The law of the kingdom is likened to the pact of association whereby the robber band divides up its spoils among its members. The only difference between the robber band and the state is that the robbers may be punished by the state, while there is no superior power to restrain the actions of the state. Augustine hammers this point home with an anecdote about Alexander the Great: 'Indeed there was an apt and true reply that was given to Alexander the Great by a pirate who had been seized. For when the king had asked the man what he meant by keeping hostile possession of the sea, he answered with bold pride, 'What do you mean by seizing the whole earth; but because I do it with a petty ship, I am called a robber, whilst you who do it with a great fleet are styled emperor.''[20]

Yet even the most brigand-like sovereign should be obeyed as an expression of the working of divine providence. The best that can be hoped for from the earthly state is that it restrain human lusts through the fear of punishment. It is true that there are Christian princes and kings who have tried to rule in accordance with God's law of love, but this manifestation of the heavenly city within an earthly kingdom can never be more than partial and fleeting. Likewise, some pagan rulers were activated by their remembrance of the divine law of love and also endeavoured to rule wisely. But as the mass of humanity is inevitably fallen and beyond redemption this can never be the general rule.

The Higher Life: Augustine's Metaphysics

Until Kierkegaard Christian metaphysics sought the answer to two questions: What attitude should I take to my existence and that of the world? How can I ascend from the everyday world of sense and change to a better state? Its answers have naturally been constrained by Christian doctrine, which insists that God created the world and that the world is not evil. Christianity has also often encouraged the ideal of active contemplation as the means to union to God. These answers differ from those of Eastern mysticism, which is prepared to consider that the world is evil and that the goal of spiritual striving should be non-existence, the loss of self in *nirvana*.

Augustine gave Christian beliefs a decisive formulation at a time when the Catholic church in the West was congealing into a unified organisation. The Council of Nicea had begun codifying theological doctrine in A.D. 325. Augustine was to be a key figure in further fixing Catholic doctrine on human nature, divine grace and the sacraments. His metaphysical doctrines aimed at combining NeoPlatonist metaphysics with the new Christian synthesis in an acceptable manner.

In doing this Augustine was strongly influenced by his antipathy to the Manicheans, who in his youth had been one of the most powerful religious opponents of Christianity among the Romans. He had himself been a Manichean while in Rome. They held that evil exists as a real principle in the world, struggling against good on an equal footing. Augustine approached the problem of evil through his doctrine of the fall: God had given human beings and angels free will as part of their perfection. Their pride in turning away from God had not created a real principle of evil, but was the product of free will.[21]

On the positive side Augustine was strongly influenced by Plotinus and probably also his pupil Porphyry.[22] Both master and pupil had stressed 'emanationism', though in Plotinus this was often combined with the contrary approach of 'omnipresence'. Omnipresence denies the spatial metaphor of grades of reality emanating from a source, emphasising the simultaneous existence of all grades everywhere. In his emanationist metaphysics Plotinus tried to answer the question of how the world came into existence. This had been a difficulty for all Platonist and NeoPlatonist philosophy. We begin by contemplating the everyday world and ultimately ascend to the One - the mystical consciousness that there is something beyond all predicates and existence, something utterly transcendent.[23] The difficulty then arises: How to explain the production of the impermanent and imperfect world we know from the perfect and unchanging One. Plato had asked 'How then do things proceed from the first principle? If the primal be perfect, and the most perfect of all things, and its power be fundamental, it must be the most powerful of all things that are, and other powers must imitate it as far as they can. Now, when anything comes to perfection we see that it procreates, that it cannot endure to remain as it is by itself, and so creates another being.'[24] This overflowing of perfection was also involved in the emanations of Plotinus' three hypostases. In the beginning was the One. The perfection of the One (the first hypostasis) overflowed into Ideas and Being (the second hypostasis). That overflowed into the World-Soul (the third hypostasis). The World-Soul in its turn overflows to produce the material world and human beings.[25]

A similar process of emanation is involved in nearly all systems of Christian metaphysics. Its function is to explain why perfection should leave its unchanging state and flow over into the world. It also shows the contemplative how to reverse this process - how to reascend the ladder of perfection and achieve once again unchanging peace. Involved in all such metaphysics is a difficulty . If the world results from a superabundance of perfection then why do we need to leave the world to achieve perfection?[26]

Emanationist metaphysics are fundamentally arbitrary. The process involved in producing metaphysical categories, often called dialectics, is used in an arbitrary way to produce whatever sequence is required by the metaphysician. The production of the categories is really determined by the various problems the metaphysician is attempting to find answers to, which are often the products of official doctrines adopted for reasons that have nothing to do with metaphysical categories.

The arbitrary nature of metaphysical deductions is seen in the alterations that Augustine made to Plotinus. In Augustine some categories, like the One, disappear entirely and a new organisation appears.[27] This organisation is determined by theological positions. The church had settled upon a Creator-Father God who made a good world, a Son God who was the incarnation of the Logos (Word) and the Holy Ghost who dispenses divine grace and salvation. Evil is not a fundamental principle. For Augustine it results from pride.

Augustine made the category of being primary. This decision decisively influenced all later Christian metaphysics. God is fullness of being and all lesser emanations have a lesser participation in being. This had the effect of fixing the quest for immortal bliss in a formal metaphysical doctrine. To seek for being was to seek continued existence. This guarded against the ambiguities inherent in the Platonic and NeoPlatonic quest for the One as the ultimate metaphysical state of consciousness. The One involved a loss of existence - being appears in Plotinus only as an emanation of the One. Thus NeoPlatonism was in effect questing for that loss of existence and release from being that Christianity had so firmly set itself against.[28]

Augustine and Freud

Augustine and Freud are two of the great pessimists of the Western tradition and the similarities between them are interesting. In his controversy with Pelagius, who attributed more good to human nature than Augustine would allow, Augustine argued that not all evil wishes find a fully conscious expression. He gives the very Freudian example of a slip of the tongue betraying the 'desire of sin'.[29]

The parallel between Augustine's method of interpreting the bible as a text hiding a secret inner meaning and Freud's method of interpreting dreams has often been noted by scholars.[30] Augustine's view of biblical interpretation was that as a result of the fall human beings have become distant from God; their intellects are clouded by original sin and their inveterate tendency to think about divine matters in a physical and pictorial manner. The language of the bible is the language God has been obliged to use to communicate across this chasm of understanding. Augustine believed this justified his often extraordinarily tenuous interpretations of the bible. Just as we often feel Freud is reading what he wants to find into a dream, so Augustine habitually distorts the bible to fit in with his own NeoPlatonist preconceptions.[31]

While the style of interpretation may be similar, the explanation for the origin of the distorted message is not. For Freud the 'dream work' is an attempt by an agency of the human mind to 'scramble' the message of the dream so other mental agencies, particularly the conscience, cannot read it. In Freud the content of the message is too sexual, too instinctual and too primitive to be allowed direct expression. For Augustine the real message of the bible is too abstract and too sublime for human ears. It has been recoded to be less sublime and more human.

In his attempts to decipher the hidden meanings of the bible Augustine was of course only a particularly notable exponent in a long tradition of such exposition, Jewish as well as Christian. Freud himself was influenced by the Jewish as well as the Christian strand of this tradition.[32]

Influence

The social situation in which Augustinism arose persisted and to some extent intensified during the seventh and eighth centuries in which the Mohammedan invasions of territories adjoining the Mediterranean added to the decline of trade produced by the previous invasions.[33] Despite initial resistance to Augustine's view that human nature was so corrupt it could play no part in its own improvement, his doctrine of grace became official doctrine in 529 A.D. at the Council of Orange. It persisted as such until the Carolingian renaissance of the ninth century.

In this period the empire of Charlemagne offered a brief respite from the continual ravages of war as well as a demonstration that a new and more stable economic and social system was possible - feudalism.[34] Unlike the money economy of the ancient world feudalism encouraged a more settled personality type based on the feudal notions of status and obligation. The church had by this time assumed a more dominant social role. These two changes meant the church could begin to hope for a Christian commonwealth, a society actively inspired by a version of the Christian ideal.[35]

This lead to the ultimately unsuccessful efforts of Hincmar in the ninth century to change official church doctrine. Hincmar wanted to revise two aspects of the Augustinian doctrines of grace and human nature. The first was the doctrine of 'double predestination'; that God had predestined the elect to salvation and the damned to damnation. It is easiest to understand Hincmar's rather obscure revision of this doctrine by considering an assertion of the Council of Quiercy, controlled by Hincmar, in 853 A.D. This was that 'God, the good and just, elected, on the basis of his foreknowledge, those from the mass of perdition who he by grace predestined to life.'[36] This according to a contemporary commentator, Florus, meant that God had foreknown who would perform good actions and who would commit evil actions and had alloted grace on this basis. This was tantamount to saying that grace was a reward merited by good actions. For Augustine good actions were only possible as a result of grace. So to attribute God's distribution of grace to his foreknowledge of actions was a roundabout way of attributing the power to do good to human nature. In more developed versions of his doctrine Hincmar, following the pseudo-Augustinian treatise *Memorandum against the Pelagians and Celestians*, asserted that God had predestined salvation but foreknown damnation. This effectively softened the statement of the Council of Quiercy, while still insisting that it had some validity.[37]

Hincmar's doctrine of the sacraments was a more direct assault on Augustinism. Here he maintained that there are three kinds of human being, rather than the two assumed by Augustine - the saved and the damned. Between the saved and the damned are those who have received the sacraments but are not predestined to salvation. The receipt of the sacraments has washed away original sin in such people, who could be reckoned as the vast majority in a predominantly Christian society. Human nature was transformed from evil to good by receipt of the sacraments, though this did not guarantee election to salvation.

Two years after Quiercy a synod at Valence reversed its decisions and reasserted a fundamentalist Augustinism. But in his controversy with the Augustinians Hincmar had shown that his own views commanded considerable support. Eventually even more radical revisions of Augustine were to emerge victorious.

Augustine's view was widely rejected by the scholasticism of the thirteenth century, though it was revived by some in the fourteenth.[38] A major Augustinian revival occurred in the Reformation of the sixteenth century and in a temporary revival of Augustinism within the Catholic church at that time. The breakdown of feudal conditions had reached a point at which there were two alternatives. One was to remain in opposition to the personality type produced by the revival of trade. As in Augustine's day the personality produced by the new political and economic conditions was dominated by an egoistic desire for possessions, power and pleasure. To oppose this type in the name of the moral injunctions and mystical sensibilities of Christianity was to become Augustinian once again. That was the way of Luther and Calvin and of Augustinism within the Catholic church.[39]

The alternative, adopted by the majority within the Catholic church, was to accept that human nature was naturally perfectible, at least after baptism. The followers of Aquinas argued that original sin was moderated by baptism, while those of Duns Scotus tended, by means of hair-splitting arguments, to say that human nature was intrinsically good.[40]

The whole of the Reformation, beginning from Wyclif and lasting through to Luther and Calvin, used a kind of 'return to Augustine' to attack the worldliness of the church and its claim that everyone, or at least nearly everyone, could be saved if they would just engage in good works and receive the sacraments of the church. The reformers argued that the mass of humanity was under the sway of radical evil, including even large sections of the church.

Wyclif himself did not give great attention to the doctrine of original sin. Both Luther and Calvin revived a kind of super-Augustinian pessimism about human nature in its fallen state. In his lectures on the early books of Genesis, written in 1535-6, Luther condemns Augustine for his excessively rosy view of fallen human nature.

In *Genesis*, 1:26 God said: 'Let us make a man according to our image and likeness'. Luther comments as follows: 'What is that image of God according to which Moses says that man was made? Augustine has much to say in his explanation of this passage, particularly in his book *On the Trinity*. Moreover, the remaining doctors in general follow Augustine, who keeps Aristotle's classification: that the image of God is the powers of the soul - memory, the mind or intellect, and will. These three, they say, comprise the image of God which is in all men... These very dangerous opinions of the fathers were discussed in all the churches and schools, but I really do not see what the fathers intended to achieve by them... I am afraid that since the loss of this image through sin we cannot understand it to any extent. Memory, will, and mind we have indeed; but they are most depraved and seriously weakened, yes, to put it more clearly, they are utterly leprous and unclean. If these powers are the image of God, it will also follow that Satan was created according to the image of God, since he surely has these natural endowments, such as memory and a very superior intellect and a most determined will, to a far higher degree than we have them.'[41]

In commenting on the disobedience of Adam and Eve, Luther says it was not pride that led to eating the fruit, as Augustine asserted, but lack of faith in God's assurance that to eat the fruit would be certain death. This leads to a typically Lutheran dissertation on the importance of faith.

The initial impact of original sin was, says Luther, just as stated in Genesis: pain to the woman in childbirth and the man to live by the sweat of his brow. It was only in the course of millenia of sinning that God's punishment for sin, in the form of a greater depravity in human nature, reached its present nadir. Even at the time of the gospels, people were comparatively 'respectable', compared with Luther's own time.[42]

The inveterate sinfulness of mankind led to a second punishment in the great flood, from which only Noah and his family were saved. Once again the sinfulness was initially in the following of false gods, that is a loss of true belief. This then led, according to Luther, to the sins of 'tyranny, bloodshed and injustice'.

He makes great play with the two verses in *Genesis* (6:5, 8:21) that describe the evil of the human heart and imagination. Unfortunately for his theory that people were more wicked after the flood than before, the two verses, one referring to the time before the flood and one to the time after the flood, describe human evil in similar phrases: 'every imagination of the thoughts of his heart was only evil continually' (6:5); 'For the imagination of man's heart is evil from his youth' (8:21). But the eye of piety is able to discover convincing evidence in less obviously relevant passages, such as that in which it is said that Noah did not beget children until he was five hundred years old: 'This in itself shows that at that time (i.e. before the flood) the nature of man was far stronger and better, and that the Holy Spirit was more active and more abundant to the holy men of the original world than he is today in us, who are, as it were, the dregs of the world.'[43]

Luther's general description of the evils that are lately within the world follows closely Augustine's doctrine of original sin: the lusts for domination, possession and sex. Added to these is a new evil - the appearance of the pope as antichrist.

Calvin's view of original sin and its correction is in general very similar to that of Luther, from whom it was largely taken, with the exception of Calvin's generally more favourable attitude towards humanistic and scientific learning and his more optimistic view of the perfectibility of human institutions.[44] Calvin at all times betrays his early attraction to the doctrines of Erasmus and other humanist scholars. So while he can expound a doctrine of original sin every bit as extreme as those of Augustine and Luther, he attributes scientific and humanistic learning, as well as the ability of people to perform moral and just actions, to God's grace. He also thinks it possible to instal Christians in enough key positions of power to ensure Christian government.

'Whenever we come upon these matters (arts and sciences) in secular writers, let that admirable light of truth shining in them teach us that the mind of man, though fallen and perverted from its wholeness is nevertheless clothed and ornamented with God's excellent gifts... Shall we deny that the truth shone upon the ancient jurists who established civic order and discipline with such equity? Shall we say that the philosophers were blind in their fine observation and artful description of nature? Shall we say that those men were devoid of understanding who conceived the art of disputation and taught us to speak reasonably?'[45]

Luther wanted to go back to Augustine because he feared the secular arts and sciences and the fever for wealth as hostile to true religion and the true church. The medieval church had become closely connected with secular society and when this society changed the church was drawn in. Popes and bishops became secular potentates, to some extent corrupted by secular wealth.[46]

Calvin asserted the possibility of combining certain aspects of the secular changes - particularly secular learning - with the reassertion of a 'true', Augustinian religion, which kept its distance from the world in other respects. Other early reformers were obliged to correct the Lutheran excesses in corresponding ways. The Swiss reformer Zwingli (1484-1560) diluted the Lutheran doctrine of original sin and asserted that human nature was more perfectible than Luther imagined.[47] Melanchthon (1497-1560), together with Luther the chief founder of Lutheran theology as it was later found in the Lutheran churches, like Calvin stressed that the secular sciences contained an element of divine inspiration.[48]

German universities were much influenced by the reformation in its earliest phase, Catholic teachers being expelled from Tubingen in 1535 and Lutheranism imposed on Leipzig in 1539. These changes were however later moderated by the influence of Melanchthon in the Lutheran church.[49]

In 1518 the previous gallicanism of the French church, or relative independence from both king and pope, was replaced by the 'royal gallicanism' of the Concordat of Francis I. The King now had the effective right to nominate archbishops, bishops and abbes. This situation encouraged theories of the divine right of the French King and gave him very effective control over the church.[50]

Luther found a response in France, particularly among those opposed to the growth of royal absolutism. From 1541, with the publication of a French edition of Calvin's *Institutes* he too became a force in the thinking of French protestants.[51] The protestant Huguenots were suppressed with intermittent vigour until 1562 when the first of the Wars of Religion broke out, to end in the Pacification of Amboise in 1563. The Massacre of Saint Bartholomew (1572) further increased the gulf between Huguenot and Catholic. The Edict of Nantes (1598) granted the Protestants 150 cities of refuge. Having revoked this Edict, Louis XIV, after nearly ninety years of uneasy truce, published the Edict of Fountainbleau in 1685, under which all protestant places of worship were destroyed, public and private worship prohibited and all ministers forced to leave the country. French protestantism was defeated.

Lutherans were to be found in both Oxford and Cambridge from the 1520s.[52] Lutheran doctrine however found less response in England than in many other European countries. The universities were also comparatively little disturbed by the Henrician reformation.[53] Under Edward VI there was a thorough purge organised by the Calvinist Peter Martyr, which was duly reversed under the Catholic Mary.[54] The Anglicanism that emerged as a political compromise from the reigns of Elizabeth and James took a compromise theoretical position, emphasising loyalty to the 'protestant' Anglican church, but in its view of human nature much closer to scholasticism.[55] Its greatest exposition was by Richard Hooker in *The Laws of Ecclesiastical Polity* (1594-1597). This so called 'Arminian movement' was particularly prominent at Cambridge University.

Further Reading

Augustine

J.F. Anderson, *St. Augustine and Being*, Martinus Nijhoff, The Hague, 1965.
P. Brown, *Augustine of Hippo*, Faber, London, 1967.
E.H. Gilson, *The Christian Philosophy of Saint Augustine*, Random House, New York, 1960, trans. L.E.M. Lynch.
A.W. Matthews, *The Development of Augustine from Neoplatonism to Christianity*, Uni. Press of America, Washington, 1980.
R.E. Meagher, *An Introduction to Augustine*, New York Uni. Press, New York, 1978.

The Augustinian Tradition

N. Abercombie, *Saint Augustine and French Classical Thought*, Russell and Russell, New York, 1972.
R.H. Bainton, *Here I Stand; A Life of Martin Luther*, Abingdon-Cokesbury, New York, 1950
H. Bornkamm, *Luther's World of Thought*, Concordia, St.Louis, 1965.
G.W. Bromiley, *An Introduction to the Theology of Karl Barth*, Eerdmans, Grand Rapids, 1979.

H.G. Haile, *Luther: A Biography*, Sheldon, London 1980.

E. Iserloh et al, *Church History, Vol. 5*, Burns and Oates, London, 1980, chaps 5 and 41.

G. Leff, *Bradwardine and the Pelagians*, CUP, Cambridge, 1957.

G. Leff, *Gregory of Rimini*, Manchester University Press, Manchester, 1961.

T.H.L. Parker, *John Calvin, A Biography*, Dent, London, 1975.

B.B. Warfield, *Calvin and Augustine*, Presbyterian and Reformed, Philadelphia, 1956.

F. Wendel, *Calvin: The Origins and Development of his Religious Thought*, Collins, London, 1965.

Chapter 3 :
Reason and Self-Interest

Main Assumptions

This tradition took its cue largely from Aristotle. During the twelfth and thirteenth centuries the renewed attention to Aristotle by scholastic philosophy led to numerous attempts to incorporate the ideas of that philosopher into the fabric of Christian belief. Aristotle believed human beings were fundamentally rational and that if wise laws were enacted to punish wrongdoing and reward right then people would follow them. This view fitted in with the optimism about the human condition that gained ground in the periods of stability in medieval society, particularly during the thirteenth century.

The main assumptions of the scholastic version of Aristotle and its successors in empiricism, rationalism and Kantian philosophy were: 1. Human development can rise part of the way towards perfection by its own efforts; 2. Some scholastics thought God could be partly understood by reason, others as well as some later empiricists were sceptical about this; 3. Most philosophers in this category thought human motives fairly well balanced, though Hume actually believed altruistic impulses outweighed selfish desires; 4. Opinion was also divided regarding communication with God, but most would have agreed that inspiration as to God's purposes could be derived from meditation on divine scripture; 5. Opinion was also divided regarding the nature of divine symbols but many continued to agree with Augustine that concrete symbols allow God to appeal to the limited human intellect; 6. It was widely believed that once good actions were repeated they became habitual; 7. We can find out about human nature through common observation, reading the classics and the application of human reason, rationalist philosophers as well as Hobbes giving more weight to the last.

1. Scholasticism

Bonaventure (1217 - 1274)

Bonaventure's work is of interest both because he was the chief founder of a distinctively Franciscan current in theology and because he was one of the first important theologians to propose an original synthesis of the newly-discovered Aristotle and traditional Christian doctrine. Albert the Great (1206 - 1280) showed a compiler's interest in Aristotle and Alexander of Hales (1186 - 1245) had used the Philosopher to deal with philosophical topics, while largely citing orthodox theologians on theological topics. Bonaventure not only thoroughly absorbed the teachings of Aristotle, but propounded an original synthesis of these ideas with Christian tradition.

He became a Franciscan about 1243 and taught at Paris after 1248, succeeding to the chair reserved for the Franciscans in 1253. He was involved in the conflict between the masters of the university and the Franciscans and Dominicans, though he died before this conflict was finally resolved.

The movement to integrate Aristotle with theological tradition was more than the rediscovery of an eminent philosopher. Aristotle represented the new secular learning, while the new learning in its turn reflected an increasing faith in human capacity to understand the natural world and to order human society in a rational and harmonious manner. Augustine had confronted a world that was falling apart socially and politically. Bonaventure could see an emerging European order that held some promise of peace, security and orderly advance. So while Bonaventure is fond of citing Augustine, he really thinks, with Aristotle, that human beings in their natural state incline towards God and towards moral actions. Grace is required to perfect these inclinations, but not to initiate them. Augustine had emphasised that human beings are inherently immoral and ungodly, though he sometimes refers to dim memories of the law of love lingering in the hearts of fallen men.

In his theory of the intellect, Bonaventure accepts the Aristotelian distinctions between the agent intellect and the possible intellect. The agent intellect is responsible for deriving universals like 'man' or 'four' from sensory experience, while the possible intellect considers possible combinations of universals. Both these departments of the intellect belong to the soul and are immortal. In defending this thesis against the views of other commentators, particularly Avicenna, Bonaventure becomes involved in a typically scholastic discussion of substances and accidents that need not detain us here.[1]

The use of the intellect in studying sciences draws us upward to contemplate God. Aristotle had identified four kinds of cause, among them the efficient and the formal. Efficient causation is by direct contact, as when we cause a door to open by pushing it. Formal causation gives objects shape, organisation and their characteristic form of development. Thus an acorn grows into an oak because it contains the form of the oak. Bonaventure argues, with Aristotle, that in reflecting on efficient causes we are led back through a chain of causes to the first cause, which is God, an immutable and uncaused being. Likewise in reflecting on formal causes, philosophy moves back to the ultimate form of forms, or God.[2]

In his *Sentences* Bonaventure also argues that human beings desire to be happy and engage in rational action directed to this end.[3] This is to be achieved by following a middle course between extreme indulgence of sensual desires and complete abstinence. Both these sentiments are Aristotelian. Augustine denied that natural men could devise a rational and temperate moral order. Bonaventure is willing to borrow from Augustine the idea that human beings have an innate knowledge of 'natural law' which inclines them towards moral action.[4] But the effect of adding this to Aristotle's prudential theory of morality is to strengthen the moral capabilities of the unredeemed individual, so making Bonaventure's view even less Augustinian.

Bonaventure distinguishes between moral knowledge and the will to perform moral acts. It is obvious that we may know what is right without actually willing it and so doing it. Knowledge of what is right is given by the conscience, which has innate knowledge of the moral law. However, in applying the moral law in a particular instance, there may be an error of judgement. We may, for instance, judge that someone committed a murder when they did not and so punish them unjustly.

The use of reason to decide upon moral courses of action involves a conflict between the superior reason, which is able to consult the innate moral law, and the inferior reason, which considers how best to satisfy the bodily and sensuous appetites. Bonaventure agrees with Aristotle, against Augustine, that the superior reason governs the inferior reason.

The will is also split between the God-given tendency to will the right, which Bonaventure calls synderesis, and 'deliberative appetite' which can lead the individual to wrong actions. He pictures the process of willing an action as taking place in two stages. In the first stage of intention the good is always willed, guided by synderesis. In the second stage of deliberative choice the animal appetites are brought into play, which may over-rule initial good intentions.

This is a highly simplified picture of Bonaventure's view of human nature in its fallen state. A fuller consideration would include the several interactions that occur between the intellect and the will in the course of moral action.[5] It is however sufficient to show the enormous gulf that already separated scholasticism from the views of Augustine. This change extended to, and partly originated from, changes in religious practice. Considerable emphasis is now placed upon the need for human effort in preparing the soul to receive grace. Bonaventure can write about the ascent of the soul in his *The Soul's Journey into God*:

'Our soul is also marked with nine levels and within it the following are arranged in orderly fashion: announcing, declaring, leading, ordering, strengthening, commanding, receiving, revealing and anointing. These correspond level by level to the nine choirs of angels. In the human soul the first three levels pertain to human nature; the next three, to effort and the last three, to grace.'[6]

We should not take the mention of 'nine levels' too literally here as the overall structure of *The Soul's Journey* provides for only six stages in the ascent to God, and these six stages are to be conceived more as a devotional aid than as an intellectual system. It is significant, however, that it is not until we reach the fourth stage that the soul requires the gift of grace to aid it on its journey. The six stages are: contemplation of God's reflection in nature; in sensation; in the natural faculties of the soul; in these faculties transformed by grace; finally turning to God as manifested in Being and the Good; and on to mystical ecstasy. The first three stages can be traversed by unaided human capacity.

But Bonaventure was unwilling to revise the Augustinian doctrine of grace as freely given by God. He needed a doctrine to reconcile the new emphasis on effort with the freely given grace of God.[7] This was that human effort prepared the individual for the receipt of grace, but grace itself was a free gift from God and not received simply through sacraments. Sacraments, like merit, prepare the soul for grace, but the actual gift of grace comes freely from God, who may give or withhold according to his inscrutable purposes. This doctrine appealed to individuals with strong religious and moral sensibilities at a time of social optimism. Human effort was encouraged and an orderly society declared possible. At the same time, the importance of the church in dispensing sacraments was safeguarded and the omnipotence and unchangeability of God protected. The religious and the moral elite was inevitably sceptical about the possibility of saving the majority of the population, who have little capacity for religious or mystical experience and are at best morally lax. This had been the view of Augustine and is perhaps the inevitable view of religious elites. Given that only a minority of the population are to be saved, the unchangeability of the Christian God requires that the elite are already decided. Belief in the unchangeable nature of God is a central component of NeoPlatonic and Christian mysticism and was maintained by all medieval Christian theologians of importance. Stress by the religious elite that salvation cannot be guaranteed by merit gained strength from the common observation that in cases like Paul and Augustine great sinners could, following a dramatic revelation, become great saints almost overnight. True mystical experience, even for the already devout, is hard to foresee. In the last years of his life Aquinas experienced a revelation that called into question all his previous writings and caused him to give up composition. Bonaventure's meditations on the vision of St. Francis, which occasioned his writing *The Soul's Journey into God*, are distinctively different from and in some ways incompatible with, his earlier academic writing.

With the exception of the assumption that a stable and progessive social order is possible, these factors have been relatively constant in the experience of theologians throughout the history of Christianity, until recently. The views of the laity and parish clergy arose from other sources, notably the commonsense belief that God operates like the social order in punishing wrong and rewarding right and the belief in the magical power of the sacraments which, as Weber pointed out, is characteristic of the laity throughout the whole history of Catholicism, particularly in the countryside.[8]

Aquinas (1225 -1274)

A contemporary of Bonaventure, Aquinas was the founder of a distinctively Dominican current in Scholasticism. The outstanding feature of this was reliance on Aristotle to an even greater extent than in Bonaventure and the Franciscans. Yet perhaps because of this greater swing away from Augustine, Aquinas is at pains to guard one central point of Augustinian orthodoxy with even greater vehemence than Bonaventure: the doctrine of grace.

Aristotelian doctrine had a fundamental defect from the point of view of a Christian theologian. Aristotle assumed that men can know God through their own efforts. Any such assertion by a Christian theologian would have been dangerously heretical as it undercut the role of the church in dispensing grace, the chief means recognised by Christians for achieving knowledge of God. So Aquinas corrects Aristotle by saying that while people do naturally strive for knowledge of God, the human intellect is constructed in such a way that it cannot by its own efforts achieve this knowledge. This is only possible through grace.

By making this move Aquinas was able to propose an optimistic view of human nature relating to earthly matters while retaining the purest Augustinian orthodoxy on the questions of predestination and grace. Grace is necessary to achieve knowledge of God and eternal life. God has predestined by his will those who will receive this grace and those who will not. This is because, in the Thomistic theory, the human intellect is too weak to grasp the infinity of God.

But as far as earthly affairs are concerned there is a complete break with Augustinian pessimism. Human nature has a tendency to seek certain ends. For Aristotle everything, from stones to human beings, is a process, described as a 'form', that tends to a certain end. Stones tend to fall earthwards as this is their natural end. Human beings pursue the end of happiness within rationally ordered social life. Man, as Aristotle had defined him, is a rational animal.

Appetites or desires are divided by Aquinas into the concupiscible and irascible. For Augustine concupiscence was another term for sexual lust, one of the three great motives (possession, power and sex) that drive human beings into the mad irrationality that is social life. To Aquinas concupiscence, or the desire for pleasure, is, at least in those cleansed by baptism, a benign manifestation of the human animal striving to achieve its natural and divinely appointed ends. The irascible appetite is the natural anger and frustration that occur when our aims are frustrated. This too is good because it helps us to achieve our natural ends.

'The sense appetite is one generic power, and is called 'sensuality'; but it is divided into two powers, which are species of the sense appetite, viz., the irascible and the concupiscible.

'In order to make this clear, we must consider that in natural, perishable things there is needed an inclination not only to the acquisition of what is suitable and to the avoiding of what is harmful, but also to resistance against corruptive and contrary forces which are a hindrance to the acquisition of what is suitable, and are productive of harm. For example, fire has a natural inclination, not only to rise from a lower place, which is unsuitable to it, towards a higher place, which is suitable, but also to resist whatever destroys or hinders its action. Therefore, since the sense appetite is an inclination following upon sense cognition (just as natural appetite is an inclination consequent to the natural form), there must be in the sensory part of the soul two appetitive powers: one, through which the soul is inclined simply to seek what is suitable, according to the 'concupiscible'; and another, whereby an animal resists the attacks that hinder what is suitable, and inflict harm, and this is called the 'irascible' - whose object therefore is said to be something 'arduous', because its tendency is to overcome and rise above obstacles.'[8]

While in Augustine the human will in its natural state is perversely oriented toward sin, for Aquinas the human will is simply the executive officer of the rational intellect, carrying out its wishes and successfully subduing any resistance offered by the appetites.

'In two ways do the irascible and concupiscible powers obey the higher part, in which are the intellect or reason, and the will: first, as to the reason, and secondly, as to the will. They obey the reason in their own acts, because in other animals the sense appetite is naturally moved by the estimative power; e.g. a sheep, esteeming the wolf as an enemy, is afraid. In man the estimative power, as was said above, is replaced by the cognitive power, which is called by some the 'particular reason', because it compares individual notions. Hence in man the sense appetite is naturally moved by this particular reason. But this same particular reason is in man naturally guided and moved according to his power of universal rationality; and that is why in syllogisms particular conclusions are drawn from universal propositions. Clearly, therefore, this universal reasoning power directs the sense appetite, which is divided into the concupiscible and the irascible, and this appetite obeys it. But because to draw particular conclusions from universal principles is not the work of the intellect, as such, but of the reason, so it is that the irascible and concupiscible appetites are said to obey the reason rather than the intellect. Anyone can experience this in himself; for by applying certain universal considerations, anger or fear or the like may be lessened or increased.

'The sense appetite is also subject to the will as to the execution (of action), which is accomplished through the motive power. For in other animals movement follows at once the concupiscible and irascible appetites. Thus the sheep, fearing the wolf, flies at once, because it has no superior counteracting appetite. On the contrary, man is not moved at once according to the irascible and concupiscible appetites; but he awaits the command of the will, which is the superior appetite. For wherever there is order among a number of motive powers, the second moves only by virtue of the first; and so the lower appetite is not sufficient to cause movement, unless the higher appetite consents. And this is what the Philosopher says, viz., that 'the higher appetite moves the lower appetite, as the higher sphere moves the lower'. In this way, therefore, the irascible and concupiscible appetite are subject to reason.'[10]

Law and the State

For Augustine human law had in effect four sources. One was our inborn knowledge of right and wrong, which is however only a dim remembrance of our state before the fall and has a negligible impact on human affairs. The second is the power of divine grace, which lights on a small minority; it too has a negligible impact on human affairs. The third source is the instinct to self-preservation, which can sometimes maintain an uneasy peace in the war of all against all. The fourth source is divine providence, which often acts through the violence of the state to chastise the ungodly.

Aquinas manages to amalgamate the words used by Augustine into a totally different view. The rational intellect has been providentially given to us so we can tell right from wrong, which is our own rational self-interest.

'Now among all others the rational creature is subject to divine providence in the most excellent way, in so far as it partakes of a share of providence, by being provident both for itself and for others. Wherefore it has a share of the eternal reason, whereby it has a natural inclination to its proper act and end: and this participation of the eternal law in the rational creature is called the natural law.'[11]

The domination of one person over another is also a natural and divinely appointed state, which is Thomas' explanation of monarchical rights: 'The control of one over another who remains free, can take place when the former directs the latter to his own good or to the common good. And such dominion would have been found between man and man in the state of innocence for two reasons. First, because man is naturally a social animal; and in consequence men would have lived in society, even in the state of innocence. Now there could be no social life for many persons living together unless one of their number were set in authority to care for the common good. Many individuals are, as individuals, interested in a variety of ends. One person is interested in one end. So the Philosopher says (in the beginning of the Politics): 'Whenever a plurality is directed to one object there is always to be found one in authority, giving directions'. Secondly, if there were one man more wise and righteous than the rest, it would have been wrong if such gifts were not exercised on behalf of the rest...'[12]

Common possession was right and good in the state of nature, but after the fall natural law no longer applied. To prevent quarreling and discord it is now right to accept private ownership. The rich must nonetheless give away all their superfluous wealth to the poor.

Aquinas' Metaphysics

Aquinas denies the reality of Platonic forms. Ideas have no existence or reality apart from their realisation in 'substances' which are individual entities like 'Socrates'.[13] The man Socrates is a 'substantial form'; he is a form realised as an entity. For Aquinas there are no forms that do not have existence as entities. The substantial form of Socrates involves the definition that he is a rational animal. There is no ideal form of 'rationality' or 'animal' existing apart from individual entities like Socrates.

The notions of 'rationality' and 'animal' are not, however, static definitions, rather they express the tendency for every process and creature in the universe to seek certain ends. One of the ends of animals is, for instance, to satisfy their appetites. We apprehend this as part of the 'essence' of an animal when we perceive one by an act of direct apprehension vouchsafed us by God. Scholars disagree as to whether this direct insight into substantial forms is given for Aquinas by the understanding or by the judgement.[14]

The potency of any process of end-seeking is channelled into the act by which the end is sought. In animals and people there is a poor realisation of potency within the act of living and seeking the ends of life because human beings are material creatures. It is only in immaterial substances like angels and God that potency is perfectly realised in act. This should make both angels and God unchanging. The full realisation of potency in an act leads to fullness of being. Due to Thomas' refusal to admit, as Bonaventure had, that angels are material beings, he was hard put to it to explain how it was that angels are reputed in the Christian tradition to change. The chief example of this is the turning away from God of Lucifer and the rebel angels. This led to an enormous elaboration of the theory of angels by Aquinas and thus to his medieval name *Doctor Angelicus*.

Human knowledge involves sensation, as when we perceive Socrates and receive, through the agent intellect, a direct apprehension of his substantial form as 'human and animal'. Sensation is the way we, as creatures, tune into other substantial forms. When we are in heaven we will be directly tuned into God and will receive a direct apprehension of the divine form or 'essence'. We will know that God is the highest being, all powerful, all wise, all good, unchanging and so forth by a direct spiritual vision. Sometimes in contemplation we are able to remove the soul sufficiently from worldly things to do this even now.[15] Normally, however, we have to rely upon a number of indirect routes to know that God exists and what he is like.

These routes are of two main kinds: proofs that God exists and proofs about what he is like. An example of an argument that God exists is based on the potency-act theory of change: 'It is characteristic of things in process of change that they do not yet have the perfection towards which they move...Now the same thing cannot at the same time be both actually and potentially ... Of necessity therefore anything in process of change is being changed by something else. Moreover, this something else, if in process of change, is itself changed by yet another thing; and this last by another. Now we must stop somewhere, otherwise there will be no first cause of the change, and, as a result, no subsequent causes.'[16]

God must be the ultimate cause of potency. Four other arguments are also given to prove that God exists.[17]

We know by natural knowledge only what God is like, not his essence or substantial form: 'God is known to the natural reason through the images of his effects.'[18] The higher we rise in the scale of being on this earth the closer creatures approximate to God. In human beings we find a greater degree of perfection, of the realisation of potency in act, than in lower creatures. 'But things are likened to God, first and most generally in so far as they are; secondly in so far as they are alive; thirdly and lastly in so far as they have discernment and intelligence.'[19] The image of God is found primarily in human activities, and only secondarily in human attitudes and powers. This is because while God is the first cause of potency in the world, He himself 'has no potentiality but is pure actuality, in Him intellect and what is known must be identical in every way; thus He is never without the knowledge-likeness, as our intellect is when it is only potentially knowing...'[20] So all knowledge is eternally present to the mind of God. He is not like human beings who must acquire knowledge by use of their powers.

It is the going forth of human beings to actualise themselves in the world that bears the stamp of the divine likeness. Aquinas is critical of Lombard's claim in his *Sentences* that the likeness of the Trinity is found in the faculties of memory, understanding and will, as these terms were used by Augustine in his *On the Trinity*.[21] Such a likeness is rather to be found in the activities of memory, understanding and will. Because, however, he disagrees with Augustine's theory of memory, which involves a vision of forms not realised in substances, Aquinas emphasises understanding and will, playing down memory.[22]

Aquinas' metaphysics would make the creation of the world in the normal sense a problem. God is pure actuality with no potency. The world contains potency partially realised through matter. Why should God create a world so unlike himself?

According to Aquinas God didn't create the world. Creation is an idea we have because we are temporal creatures and think in terms of time.[23] God caused the world and did not create it. 'In the case of things produced without process of change, to become and to be are simultaneous regardless of whether the production marks the term of a change (thus there is no interval of time between becoming lit and being lit), or whether it does not, as when a concept is at once being formed and is formed in the mind.'[24] Here we see how the activity of the mind in forming a concept stands closer to the activity of God than the material process of lighting a lamp. (The mind for Aquinas is not a material substance.) God caused the world but not in time. Thus from the standpoint of God what to us is potency is already realised in act; God's activity in creating the world was a pure act. Temporal creatures normally fail to appreciate this, though they can guess at it through the image of God found in their own mental activity.

Baptism

For Augustine baptism meant the forgiveness of previous sins, rather than the washing away of original sin, or the tendency to sin. Under his inspiration the Synod of Carthage (418 A.D.) had resolved to anathematise anyone who declared that infants 'do not bear anything of the original sin from Adam which is expiated by the washing of regeneration.' This was directed against the Pelagians and was interpreted to mean that original sin was little diminished by baptism.[25]

Aquinas attempted to find a place within Aristotelian psychology for the Christian concept of original sin. He distinguishes two aspects of original sin: 'turning inordinately to mutable good' or concupiscence and the removal of original justice.[26] The effect of original sin is to cause the appetite for sensuous enjoyment to cloud the reason. Baptism weakens this dominance of the sensuous appetites, but never entirely removes the possibility that the reason will be overwhelmed by them. 'Though the stain of original sin passes, its effect remains.'[27] But Aquinas is not consistent in his application of this principle. His discussion of prudence clearly implies that it can be obtained without the aid of sacraments.[28]

At the same time, the natural human intellect is unable to grasp the infinity of God and thus unable to bend itself completely to his will; it requires to be assisted by grace. Here the part played by the various sacraments is less clear. True knowledge of God appears to be given to the few who are elect by God rather than the many who receive baptism.

Duns Scotus (about 1265 - 1308)

The first major opposition to Aquinas came from the Franciscan scholastic, Duns Scotus. His opposition did not however extend to Aquinas' view of original human nature. For Scotus, this nature is Aristotelian, acting by rational principles to achieve its natural ends. In Question Eighteen of his *God and Creatures* Scotus describes moral goodness:

'The source of moral goodness or badness. The moral goodness of an act consists in its having all that the agent's right reason declares must pertain to the act or the agent acting ... Just as the primary goodness of a being ... implies that there is no imperfection ... so the being's secondary goodness ... consists in its being perfectly suited to or in complete harmony with something else ... As an example of the first, health is said to be good for man because it suits him. As an example of the second food is called good because it has an appropriate taste ... Now an act is by nature apt to be in agreement with its agent as well as to have something suited to itself.'[29]

It is ironic that Scotus refers the example of health, though not, significantly, that of food, to Augustine. The sentiments could scarcely be less Augustinian.

In his doctrine of baptism Scotus, by means of subtle distinctions, comes close to denying the existence of an original sin that must be washed away by baptism.[30] It was for arguments of this sort that Scotus acquired the title *Doctor Subtilis*; though in the sixteenth century his followers were attacked by the reformers as Dunses, meaning cavilling sophists. This later passed into the English word 'dunce', or blockhead.

Scotus' Metaphysics

Scotus taught both at Oxford (1300-4) and at Paris (1304-7). He developed many of the metaphysical arguments of Aquinas. He taught that we can know more about God with the aid of natural reason than Aquinas was prepared to admit. This is the meaning of his doctrine of the univocity of being. When we extrapolate from the will and intellect of creatures to those of God this extrapolation leads to exact knowledge of God's essence, not just a dim intimation.[31]

Another feature of Scotus' doctrines is his insistence that God causes everything that happens in the world directly, not indirectly. God did not set the universe up with matter, forms and efficient and final causes and then let things run their own course. He is always everywhere causing everything. Here we return to an argument often taken up by Augustine but never fully integrated into his doctrine - the omnipresence of God. Scotus thinks that this omnipresence of God as cause is only known by revelation, not by natural reason.[32]

In his doctrine of the human individual, Scotus laid great emphasis on the freedom of the will. In God, however, we know that the divine intellect constrained the action of the divine will.[33] The divine intellect provided ideas, such as the impossibility of two things being at the same place at the same time, that the divine will could not over-rule. Beyond this, however, the divine will was free to create as it saw fit - more heavenly bodies or less, more angels or less and so forth.

Ockham (died 1349)

Scotus was in his turn criticised by another Franciscan, William of Ockham, but again the criticisms did not extend to Scotus' Aristotelian conception of human nature. Ockham lays great emphasis upon acts of will in his interpretation of Aristotle.

Aristotle had himself stressed the importance of will in defining a moral action, as distinct from actions performed by habit. Habits of moral or immoral action, in Aristotle's view, generally result from deliberate choices to do good or evil. But as such choices are made repeatedly they build up habits that are increasingly difficult to alter. 'And thus in the beginning it was in the power of the unjust and the intemperate man not to become such; and therefore they are so voluntarily; but when they have become so, it is no longer in their own power to avoid being so.'[34] Both Scotus and Ockham devote considerable attention to this question of the relation between the will and habits.

Ockham also outlines a hierarchy of moral virtue beginning from natural virtue and ending with the love of God. The first three gradations of this hierarchy relate to the natural tendency to seek certain ends, particularly happiness, in accordance with the dictates of right reason. The fourth and fifth degrees relate to theological as opposed to natural morality and require grace for their attainment.[35]

Ockham defines original sin as the inclination of the sensuous appetites to overcome the use of right reason and thus cause immoral actions.[36] We can partly understand the significance of this from Aristotle's comment in the *Ethics* that 'there is such a character as takes less delight than he ought in bodily pleasures, and does not abide by reason ...'[37] Excessive desire or anger also act like a madness to deprive people of their reason. Again the contrast with Augustine's asceticism is striking.

Ockham's Metaphysics

Ockham takes metaphysics in the opposite direction from Scotus, denying that we can have any knowledge of God by natural reason and generally restricting its claims to a minimal level.[38] His metaphysics is one of individual substances that have forms and are acted upon by efficient causes. There are no final causes. In so far as we have a concept of being it is derived by abstraction from our experience of individual substances, chiefly material ones.[39] Our knowledge of God is by revelation. As the world that God has created is a world of individual substances we are tempted to say that God created all these substances and their particular contingent relations by arbitrary acts of will. If Ockham's God were the God of another philosopher this might be so. But for Ockham the divine intellect is the plan of what is created, contingent though it is. Thus Ockham is led to say that the divine will and intellect are the same thing.[40]

Ockham's philosophy is similar to the later protestant division between the realm of theological faith and the realm of empirical reason. There is however little likelihood that Ockham's influence was transmitted to the reformation. The later development of scholasticism in England during the fourteenth century was dominated by the radically anti-Ockhamist teachings of Bradwardine and Wyclif, while Paris also reacted against him.[41]

Later Developments

During the medieval period the philosophical and theological disciplines were treated in only an elite group of universities of which Paris and Oxford were the most important. Their impact was however disproportionate as these universities provided both theory and bishops for the church. In the twelfth century philosophy was hardly yet a recognised discipline.[42] With increasing interest a problem arose as to its place in the framework of university studies. The initial impulse was Averroist - philosophy and theology offered independent forms of truth that could stand side by side. At Paris Averroism was, rightly, suspected of pantheism and in 1210 both Averroism and certain works of Aristotle, including *Metaphysics, On the Heavens* and *Physics*, were banned following papal intervention.[43] At Oxford papal supervision seems to have been less strict at the beginning of the century and Averroist tendencies survived there somewhat longer.

The Averroist theory of 'double truth' was in effect an expression of the purely academic tendency to allow the disciplines to pursue their objects and methods in isolation from religion. Following the anathematisation of those who treated of God or creation in other than Christian terms in 1277 there was considerable confusion. Even Aquinas was sometimes suspected of Averroism and no general consensus appeared at Paris until the Ockhamist movement, which became dominant in Paris in the 1330s.[44] This revived the ideal of separating reason and religion.

Oxford tended to closer adherence to Augustine's views in philosophy at this time, though these were not always extended to human nature. The Oxford tradition stemming from Grosseteste and Bacon and emphasising experimental research in natural science often showed a faith in human capacities that was not entirely Augustinian.

The events of the fourteenth century, particularly the Hundred Years War and the Black Death, were not conducive to optimism and the optimistic assessment of human nature borrowed from Aristotle by the majority of scholastic philosophers was not without its critics in this period, particularly Bradwardine and Gregory of Rimini. Both accused Ockham in particular of semi-Pelagianism.[45] This is significant as Bradwardine was the major influence on Wyclif.[46] While Wyclif himself does not appear to have written against the Aristotelian view of human nature, we may take it that he sympathised with Bradwardine's critique, though Luther was later to accuse Wyclif of underestimating the depravity of original sin.[47]

The sixteenth century again found Duns Scotus and Aquinas established as the leading theological influences within the Catholic church, though there was also a temporary minority current sympathetic to the Augustinism of the Reformation. At the Council of Trent (1543 - 1563) theoretical strategy to counter the protestant Reformation was discussed. Decisions of the Council later became the recognised Catholic authority on matters of faith.

In its decree on original sin the Council adopted roughly the view of Aquinas:

'Concupiscence or slumbering passion remains in the baptised; when this is exposed to conflict it cannot do injury to those who do not yield, but strenuously resist it through the grace of Christ Jesus ...'[48]

This was qualified by the explanation that while concupiscence is the inclination to sin, it is not the inevitability of sin. There is in the council's statement a suggestion of Augustine's idea that sin can only be resisted by grace and never by human effort. This was counteracted by the immediate and subsequent campaigns against Augustinism in the Catholic Church. As early as 1567 Pope Pius V condemned the Augustinian propositions of the French university professor Bajus regarding original sin.[49] When Jansen later assailed the Jesuits in his book *Augustine* (1640), contrasting Jesuit belief unfavourably with the views of Augustine on original sin and other topics, Pope Urban VIII promptly prohibited the book as heretical. This was the beginning of a long and bitter struggle within the French church between Jansenists and Jesuits that lasted well into the eighteenth century and ended with the triumph of the Jesuits.[50]

While the Dominican and Franciscan orders still possessed their medieval inheritance, the Jesuits, that special order of the Counter- Reformation whose chief reason for existence was to oppose the Protestants, were eclectic.[51] This was elevated to a principle in their doctrine of probabilism, first stated by the Spanish Dominican de Medina in 1577: 'If an opinion is probable, it is lawful to follow it, though the contrary opinion is more probable.'[52] This conveniently enabled the Dominican lion, Aquinas, to lie down with the theological lambs (Scotus and the later conceptualism of Ockham continued to be popular). It also allowed for considerable laxity in the moral sphere. The fierce attacks of Pascal and several censures by popes during the seventeenth century combined to curb the more extreme manifestations of the doctrine; only for it to rise again more vigorous than before in the writings of Alphonso Liguori (1699 - 1787), the most influential Catholic theologian of the eighteenth century.[53]

2. Metaphysical Rationalism

In the seventeenth century the philosophers of the European continent leaned towards metaphysical rationalism, while the British inclined to empiricism. The chief characteristics of the rationalist view were the stress on innate ideas and the belief that conscience is part of unredeemed human nature and is distinct from prudence. There was also a tendency to think of human nature as divided into two, lower and higher. The origin of this division between British and continental philosophy lay in different methods of coping with the impact of science on scholasticism. This can be seen from the careers of Locke and Descartes. In the content of their philosophical education they differed surprisingly little. When Locke attended Oxford from 1652 -1660 his course of philosophical studies was based chiefly on the work of Aristotle, as was that of Descartes at the Jesuit Collège la Flèche in 1611 and 1612.[54] The difference lay in the directions in which the two men rebelled against Aristotelianism. In 1623 Francis Bacon had been officially complimented by the University of Oxford as 'a mighty Hercules who had by his own hand greatly advanced those pillars in the learned world which by the rest of the world were supposed immovable'.[55] Bacon's advance was to stress observation over reverence for the ancients. This attitude of Bacon was already widespread in England, which became in Locke's day the leading country in Europe in the field of experimental science.[56] Bacon had also voiced a growing English sentiment that 'to seek divinity in philosophy is to seek the living among the dead' and that 'the scope or purpose of the spirit of God is not to express matters of nature (i.e. science) in the scriptures'.[57] The four main branches of divinity are for Bacon: faith, manners, liturgy and church government. A strict separation is to be made between religion and science, and the two not allowed to interfere with one another. This is possible because in his Protestantism faith is in a personal God.[58]

The study of the natural world had been sanctioned by both Aquinas and Scotus as leading to knowledge of God through his creation. By the seventeenth century the advance of physics and the widespread use of machines began to threaten this comfortable coexistence between science and religion. In scholastic terminology, machines worked by efficient causality, through one wheel or lever pushing on another. Aquinas' end-directed potencies and the general scholastic interest in final causes were not needed in the new science.

For Descartes and the other rationalist philosophers part of the solution lay in a re-emphasis on Platonic contemplation of the abstract concepts of mathematics as an aid to knowledge of God.[59] Aquinas and Scotus had both incorporated this aspect of Augustine's teaching in their work. Francisco Suarez, the most influential Catholic interpreter of scholastic doctrines in Descartes' youth, had emphasised this important function of abstract concepts or real universals and Descartes was now led to re-emphasise this and to down-play the role of end-directed potencies.[60]

The other major problem created by the success of the machine metaphor was the unpleasant thought that animals and human beings might be nothing more than complicated machines.[61] Descartes had a more original solution for this problem, as we shall see.

The seventeenth and eighteenth centuries saw the development of a largely middle class and aristocratic reading public in Britain and France.[62] In the seventeenth century this public retained a strong religious commitment, but was already prepared to receive the opinions of savants like Bacon and Descartes whose chief claim to a hearing was secular learning. The savants who wrote for this market were often supported by noble patrons. In England the empiricist philosophy of Bacon, Hobbes and Locke appeared. Shaftesbury and Clarke opposed them with a rationalist ethics at the close of the seventeenth century, while France remained under the domination of the great rationalist metaphysicians - Descartes, Mallebranche and Leibniz.[63]

The savants of the seventeenth and eighteenth centuries were nearly all drawn from the traditional professions - the clergy, physicians, lawyers, physical scientists and mathematicians. The clergymen like Mallebranche and Berkeley were naturally particularly concerned with the defence of religion, but they made their appeal to the public as savants rather than as clergymen. There was a tendency for empiricist philosophers to be trained as lawyers (Bacon, Hume) or physicians (Locke) while the greatest metaphysical rationalists were both physical scientists and mathematicians (Descartes and Leibniz). Legal and medical research both contain an element of inductive reasoning, building up generalisations from the gradual accumulation of cases. The method of mathematics, on the other hand, involves the isolation of 'clear and distinct ideas' leading to chains of deductive reasoning. Both Descartes and Leibniz thought that physics was rather closer to this method than we would allow today.

Descartes continued the Catholic traditions of scholasticism. While Leibniz was a Lutheran, the Lutheran church after Luther had rapidly moved to a reconciliation with scholastic philosophy. Leibniz himself, who was a prominent diplomat as well as a savant, was interested in effecting a reconciliation between the Lutheran and Catholic churches and engaged in some political manoeuvers to this end.[64] It is not surprising to find that Leibniz, who studied under the Lutheran scholastic philosopher Calov and lived for a time in Paris, adopted an approach similar in broad outline to Descartes.

It is sometimes said that the seventeenth century was a century of dawning 'individualism' in philosophy because many of its philosophers concentrated upon theory of the individual.[65] This can lead to quite loose thinking. Augustine and the scholastics were also mainly interested in the theory of the individual, for the same reason as Descartes: they sought as inner salvation. The British empiricist philosophers of the seventeenth century, Bacon and Locke, were again much concerned with the theory of the individual, but in their case this was partly due to an interest in developing a theory of knowledge that would protect and advance science. This was coupled with a division of labour between theorists of the individual and theorists of politics and economics like Hobbes, Harington and Petty.

There is a genuine sense in which the British empiricists reflected middle class individualism, but this was largely to stress the possessive individualism that guaranteed the rights to ownership and contract.[66]

Descartes (1596-1650)

Descartes held that the soul and the body are distinct substances. The body interacts with the soul, but neither completely determines the other. The body is our lower nature and is likened to a machine. This body-machine includes certain lower 'mental' functions as well as automatic physiological processes like respiration, digestion and circulation. The soul contains only pure thought, including the pure moral intuitions that make up the conscience and pure mathematical, logical, physical and theological intuitions.

This doctrine is diametrically opposed to the Thomistic theory that the soul is the form of the body.[67] Thomas had taken this doctrine straight from Aristotle.

The danger of the Aristotelian doctrine was that it could imply that when the body disintegrates so does the soul. Aquinas had skated on thin ice in avoiding this implication and others were afraid they might fall in.

With the improvement of knowledge about physiology during the fifteenth and sixteenth centuries this danger became more acute.[68] Just being fairly certain, as Descartes was, that the brain is the seat of the mind brought the problem into sharper focus.

We need concern ourselves solely with the psychological functions of the body-machine, taking it for granted that respiration, circulation and digestion pursue their automatic course. In describing the operations of the body-machine Descartes uses a now antiquated view of the transmission of nervous impulses.[69] He thinks the nerves are tubes. Messages are taken from the sense organs to the brain by threads contained in the tubes being pulled by the sense organs. So when light falls on a particular part of the retina of the eye particular threads are pulled.[70] Messages are taken back along the tubes to the muscles by the movement of particles called 'animal spirits'. Descartes thinks, wrongly, that the same nerves that carry messages from senses to brain take them back from brain to muscle. We are often astonished at the details given of the circulation of these animal spirits. Surely, we think, he should be expressing some doubts about all this, saying 'probably' and 'possibly' in the manner of the modern scientist. But Descartes is so sure of his method, which is to begin from clear and distinct ideas, that he gives scarcely an inkling of doubt.

Despite the often fantastic details given, Descartes actually hits upon the main point about nervous transmission; that the nerves take impulses from the various organs of sight, hearing, touch, taste and smell and transmit them to the brain. Here they are received, evaluated and, if necessary, appropriate impulses are then sent out from the brain to the muscles.

Inside the brain is 'a gland H', generally identified as the pineal gland.[71] This is the seat of the soul. When the senses are stimulated, a particular set of nerve-threads are pulled. The ends of the nerve tubes containing these threads are pointed at gland H. When a thread is pulled the end of the tube pointed at gland H opens and fires animal spirits at the surface of H. For every pattern of threads pulled there will be a corresponding pattern of tubes blowing on H.[72] This means that animal spirits can pass both ways along any particular nerve tube; towards gland H when the nerve thread is pulled and away from gland H when instructions are being carried to the muscles.

Depending upon the particular source of the sensation, the pattern of tubes blowing on H will alter:

'And note that, by these patterns, I don't just mean things which represent in some way the position of lines and the surfaces of objects, but also everything which, as I have just said, might allow the soul to feel movement, size, distance, colours, sounds, odours, and other such qualities; and even those which can make it feel happiness, sadness, hunger, thirst, joy, despair, and other such passions.'[73] So sensations and feelings are coded up into patterns of nervous impulses and blown against the surface of gland H 'where they must be taken for ideas, that is to say for forms of images that the reasonable soul will consider immediately.'[74]

In his explanation of the feelings of comfort and discomfort, Descartes anticipates an idea that became popular in the nineteenth century and continued in behaviourism; that pleasure is the sign of a well-functioning body-machine:[75]

'First, if these little threads, which make up the centre of the nerves, are pulled with such force that they break and are separated from the place (i.e. the sense organ) to which they are attached, such that the structure of the whole machine is disturbed: the movement which they cause in the brain (i.e. the opening of the tube-ends) will cause the soul, to which it (normally) carries the message that its resting place is secure, to feel discomfort *(douleur)*.

'And if they are pulled with a somewhat smaller force, which does not quite break them, nor separate them from their points of attachment: they will cause a movement in the brain, which, by showing that all is well with the other parts of the body, will cause the soul to feel bodily voluptuousness, which we call bodily well-being *(chatouillement)*…'[76]

Descartes also assigns the association of ideas to the body-machine and hazards a physiological explanation for the observation that events occurring at the same time tend to recall one another (the eyes and nose of a face recall the mouth).[77]

He also anticipates the notion of physiological arousal that was to become popular with 20th century behaviourists.[78] A stimulus like fire burning the skin or hunger would, for a behaviourist, create arousal whose function is to assist in carrying out actions to avoid the fire or obtain food. So it is for Descartes. In any movement, part of the outgoing animal spirits are diverted to the interior organs 'which serve to dispose the heart and the liver, and all other organs that influence the state of the blood and so that of the (animal) spirits, in such a way that the (animal) spirits that result are suitable for causing the external movements that should follow.'[79] These animal spirits are thus produced in readiness for further nervous activity.

We now come to Descartes' ideas about the soul. These can be conveniently divided into his general doctrine of innate ideas, which is used to provide us with a correct method of reasoning, and his doctrines about what innate ideas we actually have in the areas of theology, physics and morals. This is largely the organisation Descartes adopts in his *Discourse on Method* and is the most natural one. Before going into details, it is worthwhile remembering that Descartes is urging us to follow our higher nature and turn away from the senses and bodily pleasures towards a world of pure thought and intellectual satisfaction. Scholasticism had substituted Aristotelian man as the natural man, unvisited by grace, for Augustinian natural man, mad with the folly of pride. But it had always retained a fundamentally Augustinian view of the higher life as a turning away from the world towards the pleasures of pure contemplation. Particularly in Aquinas, the form of contemplation was often not fully Augustinian or NeoPlatonist. But the ideal of contemplation is still present. It is this contemplative ideal that Descartes is trying to protect by using mathematics, particularly geometry, as his ideal of method. He is emphasising the mathematical and conceptual side of scientific inquiry to turn science from being a threat to Catholic religion to its ally. The atmosphere of the Catholic retreat pervades his description, probably fictitious and therefore idealised, of how he came to the ideas contained in the *Discourse*:

'I was then in Germany, brought here by the wars that are still continuing; and when I returned from the emperor's coronation to the army, the beginning of winter stopped me in a district where, with no conversation to divert me, and by good fortune having neither cares nor passions to trouble me, I stayed shut up all day in a room with a stove, with complete leisure to give myself up to my thoughts.'[80]

Yet scholasticism was altered in the process. For it was the natural man, 'giving himself up to his thoughts', who entered the heaven of contemplation without the assistance of grace. God has so ordered the human mind that it contains true ideas about God and the world. It is up to human beings, by their own efforts, to turn into themselves and take possession of this knowledge. Naturally as a Catholic Descartes would have to pay lip service to the role of grace, but as a philosopher he pays it little attention.

In bringing scientific method to the assistance of religion, Descartes was also adopting a strategy of attack as the best means of defence. Christian belief in general had been disturbed by the Reformation. Could religious or scientific beliefs that were so much disputed be certain? In philosophy these two difficulties had made sceptical humanism popular. The newly discovered work of the classical sceptical philosopher Sextus Empiricus, *Hypotyposes*, published in 1569, provided a focus for these humanist discussions.[81]

Descartes complains that in contemporary philosophy 'there is nothing about which there is not dispute, and which is not therefore doubtful'.[82] The sceptics had doubted not only religion, but the possibility of attaining scientific knowledge of the world. In adapting science to religion Descartes also hoped, by his doctrine of innate ideas, to secure the reliability of science. It could be argued, as the sceptics did, that a malicious God might have given us unreliable knowledge both about God and about the world. But that was a chasm Descartes was unwilling to look into.

Descartes gives four rules for right thinking:

'The first was to never take anything as true, unless I knew it to be obviously so: that is to say, to carefully avoid haste and prejudice; and to include nothing in my judgements, which did not present itself so clearly and so distinctly to my spirit, that I could have no occasion to doubt it.

'The second, to divide each difficulty that I would examine, into as many parts as I could, and which would be required to resolve them better.

'The third, to so order my thoughts, beginning from objects that are simplest and easiest to know, to rise little by little, by degrees, to knowledge of the most complicated: and even supposing order among those which do not at all naturally follow one another.

'And the last, to make throughout such complete enumerations, and such general reviews, that I could be assured of leaving out nothing.

'The long chains of reasoning, each simple and easy, which geometers are accustomed to use, to achieve their difficult demonstrations, caused me to imagine that everything which could be known by men, follows along in the same way and that, given only that one abstains from taking something for true that may not be, and that one keeps to correct order of deduction, there could be nothing so distant one could not come to it, nor so hidden that one would not discover it.'[83]

Descartes says here 'supposing order among those (ideas) that do not at all naturally follow one another.' This seems to be bound up with his insistence on enumeration. Thus in geometry we have to enumerate certain initial assumptions or axioms. It does not matter which order we enumerate them in, so long as they are all present, but to ensure this they must be placed in some order.[84]

In his theology Descartes proceeds using the first rule above all: only believe that which you cannot doubt. Now doubt, in the sceptical humanism of the day, had reached epidemic proportions. With this in mind, Descartes begins by doubting the existence of his own body, of the world, and his existence at a place. The only thing he cannot doubt is that he thinks: it is he who is having these doubts. This gives rise to the formula: 'Je pense, donc je suis' (I think therefore I am). Here is a firm point of departure also used by Augustine in *The City of God*.[85]

His next certain intuition is that he doubts and therefore he is not perfect, because to know is more perfect than to doubt. This implies that he has some innate knowledge of perfection by which to judge the difference between doubting and knowing. So he must have an innate idea of 'some nature that would be in effect more perfect'. This idea of God must have been put into him by God. God must thus possess every perfection of which he has an idea. One of the perfections of God is existence. This is then used to argue back that a perfect God would not deceive his creatures and has placed in our minds clear and distinct ideas by which to know the world. Descartes sees the chief obstacle to knowledge as our tendency to turn towards the senses rather than towards these clear and distinct ideas.

In dealing with physics, Descartes makes use of the clear and distinct ideas that God has given us about the world. We have innate ideas of the geometry of space and a concept of matter extended in space. As in his physiology, his faith in clear and distinct ideas extends to the details of the sciences. So he tells us:

'Even, to adumbrate my ideas somewhat, and to be able to say what I think about things more freely, without being obliged to follow nor refute the received opinions of the doctors, I resolved to leave this world to its disputes, and to speak only of what would occur in a new world, if God created now somewhere, in imaginary space, enough matter for it, and if he agitated diversely and without order the various parts of this matter, so that it formed a chaos as confused as the poets were ever able to feign, and that, after he did nothing other than give his ordinary concurrence to nature, leaving it to act according to the laws he has established.'[86]

Needless to say, Descartes' physics is as speculative as his physiology, and was soon to be discredited by the success of Newton.

Moral philosophy is an absent presence in the writings Descartes published in his lifetime. In his *Discourse on Method* he fobs us off by saying he will live in the existing house of moral and social arrangements while he is building the new one.[87] Nor does *Passions of the Soul*, which describes how to avoid the passions and turn to the moral life, tell us much about the latter. It is in his correspondence about the moral life with the Protestant Princess Elizabeth that he finally deals with this topic. The correspondence with Elizabeth and a later letter to Chanut containing similar sentiments were published by Clerselier in 1664-67. And here we discover that Descartes has not been building a new house, but rather shoring up the old one - the Christian Law of Love. We are able to look inside ourselves and find God's decrees written in our souls. Explaining to Elizabeth his disagreement with Seneca, he gives the 'first and principal' thing we need to know: 'that there is a God, on whom everything depends, whose perfections are infinite, whose power is immense, whose decrees are infallible: because that teaches us to suffer with a good spirit everything that happens to us, as being sent expressly by God: and because the true object of love is perfection...'[88]

This contains the two elements of Descartes' moral philosophy: submission to divine providence and the love of perfection in others. For as Descartes explains in his next letter, our need to love perfection leads to our love for others.

'In my last letter I have already given my opinion regarding the difficulty your highness suggests (in fact he had not): namely, whether those who relate everything to themselves are more right than those who torment themselves too much for others. For if we only think about ourselves, we can only enjoy those goods that are particular to ourselves; instead of which, if we think of ourselves as part of some other body, we participate also in those goods it holds in common, without for that reason being deprived of any of our own.'[89] So we love God to participate in his perfection. He goes on to explain that:

'I admit it is difficult to measure exactly the extent to which reason orders us to act for the public good; but there again, we don't have to be too precise about this: it is enough to satisfy one's conscience, and that can be left up to one's inclination. For God has so ordered things, and joined men together in such close association, that even if each related everything to himself, and had no charity for others, he would not ordinarily omit to conduct himself on their behalf by every means in his power, given that he employed prudence, especially if he lived in a century when the customs were not corrupted.'[90]

This is the scholastic belief that prudence allied to wise laws and customs can guarantee a stable and reasonably equitable society without the intervention of charity. Conscience is nonetheless real and important for the individual. It commands us to love perfection in others.

Finally we come to the passions, which involve the interaction of body and soul and are described in *Passions of the Soul*. In the case of withdrawing a hand from fire, when the tubes pointing at gland H fire animal spirits following stimulation of the sense organs, the animal spirits, either passing directly or bouncing off H, may pass into the tubes leading to the muscles without the intervention of the soul. In this case they pass through the brain by purely mechanical action without the influence of the soul. Some people, confronted with a frightening face, automatically turn and run. At the same time the heart is automatically set pounding.

So far we have assumed that gland H remains stationary, except for its movements to attend to different senses. But in fact any voluntary movement involves gland H being moved by the soul in order to direct its streams of animal spirits into the correct motor nerve tubes. This voluntary movement of H is continually deflected by the mechanical action of the animal spirits being sprayed at it. Thus the soul finds it difficult to control the passions of the body. It also finds that the passions are acting upon it, causing it to want things it has not decided upon. Wanting is an inclination of gland H.

To prevent these two undesirable effects it is necessary for the soul to regain control over the body. This does not mean the elimination of the passions, which are often helpful in accomplishing necessary actions, as when pounding of the heart assists in running away. It means the correction of bad effects of the passions.

Here Descartes' advice is less than novel. We should beware those passions to which we are most prone and delay decisions when under the influence of passion until a calmer frame of mind ensues. When delay is not possible give particular attention to reasons favouring the course of action not indicated by the passionate impulse to fight, insult or flee.[91]

Later Developments

Descartes left one great problem. How does the soul influence the body and vice versa? His own solution was plausible, but generated a number of difficulties.

Three notable solutions were proposed. Spinoza (1632-1677) took the extreme way out and proposed to abolish spirit-body dualism altogether, substituting a comprehensive monism.[92] The universe was one substance. Because of its radical break with traditional theology and philosophy Spinoza refused to publish his magnum opus, *Ethics*, during his lifetime, fearing public reaction. When it was published posthumously his name quickly became a by-word for atheism and unacceptable speculation. His works were rarely mentioned except to execrate them and some even refused to describe their dangerous contents.[93] So Spinoza, despite his interesting psychology, did not immediately enter the cultural heritage of European rationalism. By the time materialism became fashionable in France among the philosophers of the eighteenth century enlightenment, metaphysics had gone out of fashion.

Mallebranche (1638-1715) proposed the solution of 'occasionalism'. On every occasion that soul-body interaction occurs God intervenes to cause it.[94]

This is a clumsy solution. Leibniz' view is not far removed from it in spirit, but is more elegant. Leibniz (1646-1716) was also able to use his own discoveries in physics to make Mallebranche seem dated.

His solution is based on a synthesis of certain aspects of Aristotelian logic, his own version of the new physics and his theory of pre-established harmony. The last named states that real interactions between physical substances and real interactions between the soul and physical substances do not take place. They appear to take place, but this is an illusion. The body was pre-ordained by God to lift an arm at exactly the moment a decision was taken to move the arm. When two bodies collide or influence one another by gravity, there is no interaction but the perfectly synchronised acting out of a pre-ordained plan. What is real is the process by which each body unfolds its destiny, or entelechy.[95] At first sight this appears mere sophism. Leibniz was able to raise it above this level by his sophistication in mathematics and physics.[96]

If the soul-body problem was seen at the time as the central philosophical issue in both French and German eyes, other aspects of Leibniz' philosophy were ultimately to survive longer in the rationalist and critical traditions. These were largely beliefs that he shared with Descartes, particularly in innate ideas, in real universals and in the distinct nature of conscience. For while the English Protestants of the seventeenth century tended to separate science and faith, the Lutheran church, to which Leibniz belonged, was drifting closer to Catholicism. Leibniz was far from alone in his hopes of reuniting the two churches.

After Luther's death the Lutheran churches were under the influence first of Melanchthon and then of Chemnitz. Both men encouraged the study of Aristotle and weakened Luther's condemnation of secular learning. Human beings could begin to glimpse God through the study of Aristotelian philosophy. Soon it was realised that the medieval scholastics had been considerable adepts in the reconciliation of Aristotle and the Christian faith. What had begun as a humanistic admiration for Aristotle ended as enthusiasm for the scholastics.[97] Leibniz himself was taught by Scherzer and Jakob Thomasius and Abraham Calov, all Lutheran scholastics.

These doctrinal tendencies were undoubtedly assisted and partly caused by more mundane events. Germany remained economically backward and removed from the scientific awakening of the seventeenth century. She was also effectively under the political domination of Catholic France following the Treaty of Westphalia in 1648. Until the late 1680s this resulted in cultural subservience, while after that time German intellectual nationalism succeeded in encouraging Germans to adopt their native philosophers, but not in turning those philosophers away from French and quasi-Catholic habits of thought.[98] Leibniz himself spent the years 1672 to 1676 in Paris and regarded French cultural life as the centre of the intellectual world.

Following his scholastic background, Leibniz emphasised the use of real universals in attaining a contemplative knowledge of God.[99] Descartes had persuaded him that such universals and the fundamental principles of logic are known innately. He wrote against Locke on this issue, while acknowledging that Locke himself allowed some room for innate ideas within his own system.[100] He agrees with both Locke and Descartes that the association of ideas disrupts true reason, especially in children and animals.[101] It can even turn the head of a great philosopher: 'Descartes, having in his youth quite an affection for a squint-eyed person, could not prevent himself from having all his life an inclination towards those who had this defect.'[102]

However, unlike Descartes and traditional Platonism, Leibniz did not think it necessary to assume that mathematics contains innately known propositions (axioms). While branches of mathematics like geometry and arithmetic begin from axiomatic propositions, Leibniz thought these could be reduced to the assumptions of logic, which are all similar to the statement that something is itself (A is A).[103] Thus the axiom 'The whole is greater than its part' could be reduced to the definition of the term 'greater' and the principle 'A is A'.[104]

Leibniz' view of the moral order is at first sight surprising and was later to become notorious through Voltaire's satire on it in his character Dr. Pangloss. Leibniz did indeed assert that we live in the best of all possible worlds.

Yet this was not a novel view. The scholastic philosophers had declared that natural human appetites, regulated by just laws and customs, would lead to the good society; Leibniz simply followed them in this.[105] From the time of Augustine, to declare that evil was a creation of God or equal with God was heresy. For Augustine and more orthodox Christianity, whether Protestant or Catholic, it was the rebellion of Lucifer and the fallen angels followed by the rebellion of Adam that produced evil in the world. God had made the world good and to perfect his creatures had given them free will. It was the abuse of this perfection that created evil. So even for the pessimists evil had a derived character, while in the scholastic tradition from which Leibniz emerged, society could be perfected.

Leibniz became a spokesman for the scholastic position on evil in a controversy with Bayle, who argued from a position close to that of the later *philosophes* of the French enlightenment. In his dictionary Bayle had spoken favourably of the Manichean argument that the world contains two equal and opposing principles: good and evil.[106] Bayle and later Voltaire argued that this was in accordance with facts.[107] The world is just as full of evil as it is of good. To say that the evil is not as real or as fundamental as the good is a metaphysical hoax. There is a conflict between metaphysics, which claims to gloss the facts with their real meaning, and empiricism, which takes the facts as they are.

Against Bayle, Leibniz puts the argument of the scholastic philosophers: that evil is the lack of perfection in creatures. Augustine had also used this argument, but placed more weight on the rebellion of the angels and Adam.[108] The scholastics, following their general tendency to stress good rather than evil, emphasised lack of perfection. Leibniz says: 'For God could not give a creature everything without making it a God; so there must be different degrees in the perfection of things, and limitations also of every kind.'[109]

Leibniz' view of the moral conscience is identical with that of Descartes: 'Love (i.e. spiritual love) is that mental state which makes us take pleasure in the perfections of the object of our love ... One directs all one's intentions to the common good, which is no different from the glory of God; one finds that one has no greater individual interest than to espouse the general good, and one satisfies oneself by having the pleasure of procuring benefits for others.'[110]

Finally an aspect of Leibniz' philosophy must be mentioned that derived neither from the scholastics nor from Descartes: his doctrine of confused perceptions. This introduced an interest in unconscious mental processes into German psychology that eventually issued, much magnified and altered, in Freudian psychoanalysis. No doubt Freud would have been horrified to learn of this connection; though Leibniz might have been rather pleased with the mysterious flavour of Freud's investigations of the unconscious.

Leibniz, like Aquinas, was interested in whether a finite human creature could achieve knowledge of an infinite world. This was the motive for his creation of and interest in the infinitistic methods of differential calculus. This calculus appeared to provide a bridge between the truths of reason and truths of fact.[111] He saw in the combined action of physical forces upon bodies to produce curves of motion this combination of divine laws and facts, a combination that could only effectively be studied through the differential calculus.

Leibniz conceived of the human soul on an analogy with the motion of physical bodies in space. The analogy was also worked in the opposite direction to claim that physical bodies have perception and are able to perceive other physical bodies and even souls. In his later work Leibniz replaced the traditional ideas of physical bodies and souls with his own metaphysical concept of the monad. Monads are metaphysical substances responsible for the existence and movement of physical bodies. In inanimate bodies the monads are capable of perception. Animals have perception and memory, but only the monad of the human soul has perception, memory and reason, containing innate knowledge of certain ideas and of the principles of reason.[112] These monads are similar to Aristotle's notion of entelechy - they are an inner dynamic principle of the body, animal or person which enables it to develop successive states according to its nature.

While he would not believe in Newton's view that gravity acts at a distance, Leibniz did think that every monad in the universe influences every other one - or rather that the universe is constructed as if they did. In Leibniz' metaphysics real influence is not allowed. So the contemporary view of physics - that the world is a vast interdependent machine - is applied by Leibniz, with his passion for synthesis, to the soul monads as well. Every monad perceives every other monad in the universe. Perception is a mode of connection that exists between all monads, physical and spiritual.[113]

We are not ordinarily aware of this connection with every other monad in the universe - it only breaks through at times of heightened awareness. To explain this, we must assume that our perception of other monads is largely unconscious. Leibniz also argues that such unconscious perceptions exist while we are asleep, even when not dreaming.[114]

Leibniz was able to successfully publicise his monadology and at the time of his death in 1716 it held about equal esteem with the Cartesian system in the minds of the French public.[115] Success in Germany was slower in coming and when it did so was largely through the success of Wolff, who achieved a *succés de scandal* following his dismissal from a professorial post at Halle by the King of Prussia, for allegedly delivering an impious lecture on Chinese philosophy, in 1723. From the mid-1740s until the time of Kant, Wolff remained the most prominent influence in German philosophy.

While Wolff (1697-1754) reached some of his conclusions independently of Leibniz, he also borrowed much from him and the two systems are remarkably similar.[116] He chiefly differed from Leibniz in denying perception to the monads contained in inanimate bodies. He was however more concerned to provide a systematic psychology than Leibniz and in his vast tomes on empirical and rational psychology and moral philosophy provides a detailed synthesis of Leibniz' metaphysics with scholastic faculty psychology.[117] Here the personality is divided into senses (imagination and memory), representation (attention and reflection) and intellect (sensual desire and aversion).

Wolff makes much play with the power of the mind, through sensation, imagination and intellect, to represent the surrounding world. This power of representation he makes the basic driving force of the personality and in this respect provides an enlarged notion of the guiding entelechy of Leibniz' soul monads. It is noteworthy that there is no separate faculty of will. Like Aquinas, Wolff thinks that once we know the course of action that will best fulfil our bodily and sensual needs we will take it, just as when we know the course that will lead to the greatest perfection in others we will take that course.

The two kinds of need seldom conflict. Yet there is at this point a curious alteration to Thomistic theory. For Aquinas slumbering concupiscence could still cloud the reason. Wolff has to hand a new model of clouded reason, provided by Leibniz' idea that the soul monad is at all times confusedly perceiving every other monad in the universe. Like a radio listener suffering interference from other stations, the individual must continually tune up their set, forming clear ideas of the world and of the good and using clear logic. It is this buzz of interference that creates confused perception and this can produce conflicts between the sensory and rational appetites:

'If we represent a distinct good with respect to ourselves which is seen confusedly as a perceived evil and vice versa; the superior part of the faculty of desiring fights with the inferior.'[118]

Only clarity in reason can avoid this stirring up of the *sensitiva* and the rebellion of the senses.

After the death of Leibniz in 1716 the French reading public, which had done so much for the success of Descartes, Mallebranche and Leibniz, turned quite rapidly to the philosophers of the French enlightenment, who admired all things English, including empiricist philosophy and suspicion of the Catholic church. French Catholicism responded with revivals of scholasticism sometimes indistinguishable from the views of the enlighteners, except regarding Catholicism![119]

In the nineteenth century the restored French Catholic church was once again able to exert a vital influence in French intellectual life. At the end of the century it was even able to produce such an undoubtedly important social philosopher as Bergson. By this time, however, French religious metaphysics had become radically transformed.[120]

3. British Empiricism

This differed from scholasticism chiefly in that religion and metaphysics were considered to be primarily matters of faith and thus not to be discussed in rational or scientific discourse.

Hobbes (1588-1679)

For all Hobbes' talk of a scientific and rational approach, he is clearly expressing a view of how things ought to be, rather than of how they invariably are. We may be surprised that Hobbes thought human nature everywhere was as he describes it; but it is understandable for philosophers to generalise conditions of their own time and place to human life generally. What is more surprising is Hobbes' claim that human beings inevitably decide to protect themselves from one another by adopting a strong ruler to keep law and order. The aim of Hobbes' Leviathan is to persuade people to do this, which implies a clear consciousness that they may not.[121]

Hobbes' view of human motives is disarmingly simple and is based on his idea that true sciences, like those of ballistics and astronomy, deal first and foremost with the motion of bodies. So human action is to be considered as either towards an end or away from an object or result. Such movements are always the result of thoughts:

'Going, speaking and the like voluntary motions depend always upon a precedent thought of *whither*, *which way*, and *what*; it is evident that the imagination is the first internal beginning of all voluntary motion...These small beginings of motion, within the body of man, before they appear in walking, speaking, striking and other visible actions, are commonly called endeavour.'[122]

Endeavour leads to action. When the endeavour is towards something it is called 'appetite' or 'desire'; when away from something 'aversion'. Hobbes was not much interested in the question of why it is that some people desire one thing and others another; some people fear one thing and others another. He is content to note that everyone desires some thing or things and that this is bound to lead to a conflict over scarce resources. In an interesting passage he sketches the differences between his political analysis, based on this assumption, and individual psychology, which delves into the desires and fears of the particular individual:

'I say the similitude of passions, which are the same in all men, desire, fear, hope, etc; not the similitude of the objects of the passions which are the things desired, feared, hoped, etc: for these constitution individual, and particular education, do so vary and they are so easy to be kept from our knowledge, that the characters of man's heart, blotted and confounded as they are with dissembling, lying, conterfeiting, and erroneous doctrines, are legible only to him that searcheth hearts. And though by men's actions we do discover their design sometimes; yet to do it without comparing them with our own, and distinguishing all circumstances, by which the case may come to be altered, is to decypher without a key, and be for the most part deceived, by too much trust, or by too much diffidence; as him that reads, is himself a good or evil man.

'But let one man read another by his actions never so perfectly, it serves him only with his acquaintance, which are but few. He that is to govern a whole nation, must read in himself not this or that particular man; but mankind: which though it be hard to do, harder than to learn any language or science yet when I shall have set down my own reading orderly, and perspicuously, the pains left another, will be only to consider if he also find not the same in himself. For this kind of doctrine admitteth no other demonstration.'[123]

As well as the desire for material possessions, Hobbes, like Augustine, also emphasises the desire for glory. Together these are the causes of a third need which arises out of them: diffidence, or the desire for security, which arises when the individual considers how much he may suffer at the hands of others who, like himself, will 'deprive him, not only of the fruit of his labour, but also of his life, or liberty'.[124]

Love of power arises from this common sense of insecurity:

'And from this diffidence of one another, there is no way for any man to secure himself, so reasonable, as anticipation that is, by force, or wiles, to master the persons of all men he can, so long, till he see no other power great enough to endanger him: and this is no more than his own conservation requireth, and is generally allowed. Also because there be some, that taking pleasure in contemplating their own power in the acts of conquest, which they pursue farther than their security requires; if others, that otherwise would be glad to be at ease within modest bounds, should not by invasion increase their power, they would not be able, long time, by standing only on their defence, to subsist. And by consequence, such augmentation of dominion over man being necessary to a man's conservation, it ought to be allowed him.'[125]

Hobbes, however, also uses power in another sense: 'The power of man, to take it universally, is his present means; to obtain some future apparent good...'[126] While it is often unclear which kind of power Hobbes is talking about, both are clearly described as originating in the desire to obtain pleasures; one from the fear of this desire in others and one from the wish to obtain them ourselves.

The love of glory or of a great reputation arises from the desire to have power in the second sense, which is power to obtain pleasures:

'Reputation of power, is power; because it draweth with it the adherence of those that need protection.

'So is reputation of love of a man's country, called popularity, for the same reason.

'Also, what quality soever maketh a man beloved, or feared of many; or the reputation of such quality, is power; because it means to have the assistance, and service of many.'[127]

These passions result in a natural condition of war, each against all:

'So that in the nature of man, we find three principal causes of quarrel. First competition; secondly, diffidence; thirdly glory.

'The first, maketh men invade for gain; the second, for safety; and the third, for reputation. The first use violence, to make themselves masters of other men's persons, wives, children, and cattle; the second, to defend them; the third, for trifles, as a word, a smile, a different opinion, and any other sign of undervalue, either direct in their persons, or by reflection in their kindred, their friends, their nation, their profession, or their name.

'Out of civil states, there is always war of every one against every one. Hereby it is manifest, that during the time men live without a common power to keep them all in awe, they are in that condition which is called war; and such a war, as is of every man, against every man. For war, consisteth not in battle only or the act of fighting; but in a tract of time, wherein the will to contend by battle is sufficiently known; and therefore the notion of time, is to be considered in the nature of war; as it is in the nature of weather. For as the nature of foul weather, lieth not in a shower or two of rain; but in an inclination thereto of many days together; so the nature of war, consisteth not in actual fighting; but in the known disposition thereto, during all the time there is no assurance to the contrary.'[128]

Hobbes lays considerably less stress upon sex as a human motive than Augustine. Though he routinely mentions it as a common passion, he does not stress it in the way that Augustine did. Augustine regarded all worldly lusts as compulsions, which, far from bringing happiness, dragged those who fell within their power further and further into a state of wretched misery. Hobbes too was aware that there is no end to the desires of mankind, no final point of satisfaction: 'For while we live, we have desires, and desire presupposeth a further end. Seeing all delight is appetite, and presupposeth a further end, there can be no contentment but in proceeding...Felicity, therefore, by which we mean continual delight, consisteth not in having prospered, but in prospering.'[129] For Augustine the process of 'prospering' was a cycle of hellish torment, punctuated by fleeting episodes of pleasure. For Hobbes, the delight of anticipated pleasure lights up the whole process of 'prospering' and gives to worldly life the possibility of perfection. Hobbes' natural man has the problem that he is always at his neighbour's throat, but if this can be overcome then earthly life can in principle be made pleasant, even 'delightful'.

Hobbes had a remedy for the natural state of war between individuals. This was the human desire for self-preservation. Observing that the natural state of war threatens their existence, people cast about for a solution. Furthermore, Hobbes says, they have a right to do this: 'The right of nature, which writers commonly call *jus naturale*, is the liberty each man hath, to use his own power, as he will himself, for the preservation of his own nature; that is to say, of his own life; and consequently, of doing anything, which in his own judgement, and reason, he shall conceive to be the aptest means thereunto.'[130]

This is an example of Hobbes' tendency to move from supposedly descriptive, scientific statements (people do preserve themselves) to moral judgements (they have a natural right to preserve themselves). This is followed by the argument that the right to self-preservation can produce the law of love of the Christian gospels:

'From this fundamental law of nature, by which men are commanded to endeavour peace, is derived this second law; that a man be willing, when others are so too, as far-forth, as for peace, and to all things; and be contented with so much liberty against other men, as he would allow other men against himself...This is the law of the Gospel; whatsoever you require that others should do to you that do ye to them.'[131]

This process of 'laying down this right to all things' is called a contract or covenant:

'If a covenant be made, wherein neither of the parties perform presently, but trust one another; in the condition of mere nature, which is a condition of war of every man against every man, upon any reasonable suspicion, it is void: but if there be a common power set over them both, with right and force sufficient to compel performance, it is not void. For he that performeth first, has no assurance the other will perform after; because the bonds of words are too weak to bridle men's ambition, avarice, anger, and other passions, without the fear of some coercive power; which in the condition of mere nature, where all men are equal, and judges of the justness of their own fears, cannot possibly be supposed. And therefore he which performeth first, does not betray himself to his enemy; contrary to the right, he can never abandon, of defending his life, and means of living.'[132]

'The force of words, being, as I have formerly noted, too weak to hold men to the performance of their covenant; there are in man's nature, but two imaginable helps to strengthen it. And those are either a fear of the consequence of breaking their word; or a glory, or pride in appearing not to need to break it. This latter is a generosity too rarely found to be presumed on, especially in the pursuers of wealth, command, or sensual pleasure; which are the greatest part of mankind. The passion to be reckoned upon, is fear; whereof there be two very general objects; one, the power of spirits invisible; the other, the power of those men they shall therein offend. Of these two, though the former be the greater power, yet the fear of the latter is commonly the greater fear.'[133]

We have now the necessity for the sovereign power to enforce contracts through fear of the law. To complete his analysis Hobbes describes the various ways in which this power may be exercised:

'The difference of commonwealths, consisteth in the differences of the sovereign, or the person representative of all and every one of the multitude. And because the sovereign is either in one man, or in an assembly of more than one; and into that assembly either every man hath right to enter or not every one, but certain men distinguished from the rest, it is manifest, there can be three kinds of commonwealth. For the representative must needs be one man, or more; and if more, then it is the assembly of all, or but of a part. When the representative is one man, then is the commonwealth a MONARCHY; when an assembly of all that will come together, then it is a DEMOCRACY, or popular commonwealth; when an assembly of a part only, then it is called an ARISTOCRACY. Other kind of commonwealth there can be none: for either one, or more, or all, must have the sovereign power, which I have shown to be indivisible, entire.'[134]

He follows these observations with a list of the pros and cons of the three types of sovereignty and concludes that monarchy is the most efficient, least corruptible and least prone to encourage civil war.

Hobbes' pessimism about human nature was not absolute. He worried that the new phenomenon of political democracy would undermine established law and order and lead to chaos. He had seen the ravages of civil war in England in the period 1640-1650 and this provided a confirmation of his fears. *Leviathan* was not published until 1651, though Hobbes had been thinking along similar lines since before 1640. The monarch is required to keep in check the potentially disruptive forces of human nature, but given appropriate government a relatively contented life is possible for all.

In an earlier work, *Elements of Law* (1650), Hobbes had expanded on his theory of individual motivation in greater detail. Charity is explained as a gift designed to demonstrate to the giver their own power.[135] The remembrance, present experience and future expectation of pleasures and pains is also discussed, as well as pleasure derived from the harmony of musical notes or colours.[136] Despite his generally low regard for sympathy, Hobbes thinks that in lust there is, in addition to sensual pleasure, 'the delight men take in delighting...consisting in the imagination of the power they have so much to please'.[137]

Hobbes is removed from the optimism of writers like Locke and Hume by his low regard for sympathy. He continues however to maintain a powerful respect for rationality. Though people will tend to seize the possessions of others if unchecked, they are reasonable enough, removed from the heat of the moment, to assent to a sovereign power that will safeguard contract. We are therefore still at some distance from the pessimism of Augustine that denies even this measure of reasonableness in human nature.

John Locke (1632-1704)

Although Locke disliked the Aristotelianism he studied at Oxford in the years 1652-60, his objection was more to the form of proof used by the Aristotelians of the day, than to the content of their doctrines. Just as Hobbes had earlier produced a modernised pessimism, which justified itself by appeal to self-evident truths rather than divine revelation, so Locke now set about constructing a modernised Aristotelianism, justified by an appeal to sound factual common sense rather than by a joint appeal to self-evident principles and opinions derived from authority. Another feature of Locke's writing was its secular basis. Locke was a religious man, but he declined to bring a specific theological position to bear on political science. Medieval Aristotelianism assembled such a huge apparatus of terms and distinctions at least partly because even quite mundane matters contained important metaphysical and religious implications. In Locke's time this injection of doctrine into the discussion of logic in particular was continued in the controversy between the followers of Ramus, who tended to be Huguenots, and the anti-Ramists.[138]

Like Aristotle and his followers, Locke supposed that human social life was naturally orderly and just, due to the operation of natural reason, which showed that such a life was a form of enlightened self-interest; though those lacking in natural reason often required punishment:

'And thus, in the state of Nature, one man comes by a power over another, but yet no absolute or arbitrary power to use a criminal, when he has got him in his hands, according to the passionate heats or boundless extravagancy of his own will, but only to retribute to him so far as calm reason and conscience dictate, what is proportionate to his transgression, which is so much as may serve for reparation and restraint. For these two are the only reasons why one man may lawfully do harm to another, which is that we call punishment. In transgressing the law of Nature, the offender declares himself to live by another rule than that of reason and common equity, which is that measure God has set to the actions of men for their mutual security, and so he becomes dangerous to mankind; the tie which is to secure them from injury and violence being slighted and broken by him, which being a trespass against the whole species, and the peace and safety of it, provided for by the law of Nature, every man upon this score, by the right he hath to preserve mankind in general, may restrain, or where it is necessary, destroy things noxious to them, and so may bring such evil on any one who hath transgressed that law, as may make him repent the doing of it, and thereby deter him, and, by his example, others from doing the like mischief. And in this case, and upon this ground, every man hath a right to punish the offender, and be executioner of the law of Nature.'[139]

While Locke appeals in this passage and in many others to the ordinance of God, these appeals are of a general kind, intended to be acceptable to any Christian. Locke believes that sound common sense is in accord with a generalised Christianity, but has quite lost the medieval passion for introducing particular doctrinal premises into his description of human nature.

Hobbes had used his arguments about the state of nature to reason that all society presupposes a social contract and that of such contracts monarchy is best.

Hobbes was not however popular in seventeenth century England, which disliked both his pessimism and his monarchism.[140] Locke continued the more dominant tradition of Hooker in his *Two Treatises on Civil Government* (1689), though with less emphasis on theology. He argues that the state of nature had its 'inconveniences', especially in the legal sphere. This led to agreement upon a civil government responsible to the people. Here Locke merely echoes Hooker's adaptation of scholasticism.

Locke argues from his optimistic premises that periodic election of the legislators is the best way for the people to maintain control over them. Absolute government of any kind tends to foster rebellion and revolution, which are then the only available means for the people to redress their grievances.[141] Under absolute government the people are quite justified in such rebellion, given due cause, particularly infringement of their right to property. For these views Locke was forced into exile under James II, only to return to England with the revolution of 1688. This overthrew the Stuarts and brought William of Orange to the throne. Locke, needless to say, thoroughly approved of this Glorious Revolution.[142]

Hume (1711-1776)

The Scottish writer David Hume found himself ranged against the current rationalistic ethics of Clarke and Shaftesbury: 'Those who affirm that virtue is nothing but a conformity to reason; that there are eternal fitnesses and infitnesses of things which are the same to every rational being that considers them; that the immutable measures of right and wrong impose an obligation: not only on human creatures but on the Deity himself: All these systems concur in the opinion, that morality, like truth, is discerned merely by ideas and their juxtaposition and comparison.'[143]

Locke, still a conventional Christian, had drawn back from the rigorous application of the empirical method to human affairs and human morality. For Hume circumstances that produce pleasure for the individual are good and those that produce pain are evil. There is no longer a supernatural moral order.

Hume's view of motivation is clouded by his use of the term 'passion'. Having defined the term to include any experience that brings pleasure or pain rather than just violent emotion he is forced to conclude that all actions depend upon passion, as all action tends to seek pleasure and avoid pain. He upbraids previous writers for neglecting this truth when it is he himself who has created the difficulty.[144] Hume really agrees with previous Aristotelians that we seek pleasure and avoid pain except when reason is clouded by extreme emotion.

Hume does however have a reason for redefining the term 'passion'. This is because he wants to separate 'original impressions' from 'secondary impressions'. Original impressions are 'such as, without any antecedent perception, arise in the soul, from the constitution of the body, from the animal spirits, or from the application of objects to the external organs'.[145] Secondary impressions are built up by association with original impressions. All passions are secondary impressions. Thus the passion of thinking someone beautiful is the result of our associating the pleasant impression gained by looking at them with the idea of that person.[146]

Hume wants to make this distinction between original and secondary impressions because he is interested in breaking the human mind down into its original parts. Passions apply to objects; we love or hate primarily other people; we feel pride or humility in ourselves. But the ideas of objects must themselves be built up by the laws of association. Thus what is inborn in us cannot be the link between emotion and object, but that between emotion and original impression. He goes so far as to apply this to passions whose object is ourselves, such as pride, humility and the love of fame. Here, however, a difficulty appears. We perceive a pleasant quality like beauty in ourselves and obtain a feeling of pride; but why should this be any different from the simple pleasure we experience from the pleasant quality?[147] It must therefore be an inborn tendency that 'Anything that gives a pleasant sensation, and is related to self, excites the passion of pride, which is also agreeable, and which has self as object.'[148]

Hume's achievement here is that he makes traditional theory more precise. The real novelty that this produces is his theory of pride, which he places first in his discussion of passions. We become aware that others are like ourselves. If they think well of us, then we 'convert an idea into an impression' and this new pleasant sensation, once again related to the self, produces a further source of our pride. This transfer of feelings will be assisted if the other people involved resemble us 'in our manners, or character, or country, or language'.[149]

By this means Hume is able to use his theory of pride to explain the great influence that the opinion of others and the love of fame have upon us. The analysis of fame and reputation that began to be so noticeable in Hobbes has been refined by Hume. It was also to be of concern to his contemporary Adam Smith. Hume's view appears the most successful of the three in explaining the force with which 'mere' opinion affects us. A sociologist might object that a reputation is of unusual importance to those people who must live by them. Hume, however, was no sociologist. His view of sympathy allowed him to conclude that we consider meeting the expectations of others and even acting to promote their interests as part of our own self-interest.

Hume also points to the attraction between the sexes as encouraging sociability.[150] Sympathy and sexual attraction between them make human beings inherently altruistic:

'So far from thinking, that men have no affection for any thing beyond themselves, I am of the opinion, that tho' it be rare to meet with one, who loves any single person better than himself; yet 'tis as rare to meet with one, in whom all the kind affections, taken together, do not over-balance all the selfish.'[151]

Sympathy and sexual attraction are not, however, the origin of our idea of justice, which Hume relates even more clearly to the institutions of private property and fair trade than any of the writers we have previously examined. The main problem for Hume is to explain the origin of these institutions, which he feels to lie in a convention 'which is only a general sense of common interest; which sense all the members of the society express to one another, and which induces them to regulate their conduct by certain rules.'[152] It is not that these institutions are the most important thing in human life, far from it: 'There are three different species of goods, which we are possess'd of; the internal satisfaction of our mind, the external advantages of our body (i.e. health), and the enjoyment of such possessions as we have acquired by our industry and good fortune.'[153] Only the third may be stolen from us by others, so that while not in itself more important, it is the 'species of goods' most liable to promote social discord.

The 'general sense of common interest' causes people to develop a convention that punishes violations of the law. Only in this way can the strong desire to rob others of their possessions be overcome. Avarice, Hume believes, is a much stronger motive than sympathy for the difficulties of others.

Hume also developed a view of the will that was to become prevalent among later empiricists. As with so many other aspects of Hume's doctrine, his view of this had been anticipated by the medieval Aristotelians, particularly Aquinas and the Dominicans. They had argued, as Hume did, that given a choice between different courses of action leading to happiness or unhappiness, reason would decide upon the the best one. Once reason had decided, the will was bound to follow reason. Thus the will was subordinate to decisions based on reason and had little independence. Hume even tends to reduce the will to a mere by-product of this process of choice: 'by the will, I mean nothing but the internal impression we feel and are conscious of, when we knowingly give rise to any new motion of our body, or new perception of our mind.'[154]

In his theory of the intellect Hume followed Berkeley in arguing that universals are formed by abstraction from the properties of individual bodies.[155]

Hume's treatment of the association of ideas in his *Treatise* differs quite sharply from that offered by Locke, though the apparent divergence is increased by a difference in terminology. Locke contrasts the 'natural correspondence' of ideas that generates logic and the unnatural associations that generate illogic, or, as he puts it, 'madness'.[156] To Hume 'the qualities from which this association (of ideas) arises ... are three, viz. resemblance, contiguity in time or place, and cause and effect'.[157] Cause and effect is different from contiguity because it involves one object producing 'motion or action' in another. So Hume includes 'resemblance' as a kind of association, while Locke excludes such 'natural correspondence'.

Hume tries to explain three kinds of 'complex ideas' from his three principles: relations, modes and substances. In modern language we more easily recognise 'mode' as the 'manner' in which something is done. Relations are all to be explained through seven kinds of resemblance: simple resemblance (as one apple resembles another); identity (a particular apple retains its identity as an object); space and time (two objects are distant, close together, etc.); quantity (comparison of different colours or shapes); opposites (large is connected with small); resemblance by causes (two letters are similar because written by the same person).

The substance 'gold' may be explained as a collection of qualities that are always found together. So when we find 'yellow colour, weight, malleableness, fusibility, soluble in aqua regia' we say 'gold'; this is our name for this combination of qualities.

A mode is simply another kind of resemblance. A certain sequence of dance steps is called a 'jig'. The 'mode' is the resemblance itself, the definition of the steps.

The stress in Hume and in later British and American empiricism is on these operations of reasoning, which are those involved in empirical study. Emphasis is on biological, legal and medical studies, with their classification and study of causes (Locke was trained as a physician and Hume as a lawyer). In his own analyses of 'natural correspondence' Locke had argued in a similar way to Hume. But Hume, following his bent for sublime optimism, could not think that any habitual operations of the mind promoted irrationality. Association by 'contiguity in time and place' conspired with the other two principles to promote reason and learning.

Ironically, this principle of contiguity was to prove the cuckoo in the nest of the doctrine of associations, eventually displacing its fellow fledglings, the principles of similarity and causation. Hume's doctrine was adopted in the nineteenth century by writers like John Stuart Mill.[158] In twentieth century behaviourism, association by contiguity, particularly as manifested in conditioning, took over as the major principle of association, the others being seldom mentioned. The reason for this was the stress upon habit as against rational deliberation which was characteristic of behaviourism.

Adam Smith (1723-1790)

Smith's *The Theory of Moral Sentiments* appeared in seven editions from 1759 to 1792 and was one of the most influential books on moral philosophy in this period. Smith borrows much from his predecessors Hume and Hutcheson, but he also refines.[159]

He begins from a wide knowledge of traditional views of morality, and he particularly admires Stoicism. Passions, he believes, may be unsocial, like excessive anger or jealousy; social, like kindness and benevolence; and, 'holding a sort of middle place between them', the selfish passions of grief and joy.[160] What interests him is how others judge us when we feel such passions. His view of them is a subtle one. They are passions of the imagination and he says: 'The frame of my body can be but little affected by the alterations that are brought about upon that of my compassion: but my imagination is more ductile, and more readily assumes, if I may say so, the shape and configuration of the imaginations of those with whom I am most familiar.'[161] Thus, he claims, we would not base a tragic play on the loss of a limb, but we would base one on the loss of a mistress. The passions of sexual love, jealousy and revenge belong to the imagination and are thus more easily sympathised with.

This line of argument is actually quite dubious. The bodily torture of Christ and the blinding of Oedipus are commonly taken to be tragic in the extreme. Smith seems to have been led to emphasise imagination partly through a refinement which declared bodily matters to be of less dignity than the life of the imagination. His distrust of the imagined successes conjured by unfettered ambition is also an important motive.

Smith next proposes that 'It is because mankind are disposed to sympathise more entirely with our joy than with our sorrow, that we make parade of our riches and conceal our poverty.'[162] This is chiefly the reason we pursue riches and avoid poverty. It also explains why people admire the wealthy and powerful so much. Sympathy for kings is also seen as a powerful political force: 'The strongest motives, the most furious passions, fear, hatred, and resentment, are scarce sufficient to balance this natural disposition to respect them: and their conduct must, either justly or unjustly, have excited the highest degree of all those passions, before the bulk of the people can be brought to oppose them with violence, or to desire to see them either punished or deposed. Even when the people have been brought to this length, they are apt to relent every moment, and easily relapse into their habitual state of deference to those whom they have been accustomed to look upon as their natural superiors. They cannot stand the mortification of their monarch. Compassion soon takes the place of resentment, they forget all past provocations, their old principles of loyalty revive, and they run to re-establish the ruined authority of their old masters, with the same violence with which they had opposed it. The death of Charles I brought about the Restoration of the royal family. Compassion for James II, when he was seized by the populace in making his escape on ship-board, had almost prevented the Revolution, and made it go on more heavily than before.'[163]

This passage is notable as an early expression of the theory of identification with authority that was further developed during the nineteenth century and has assumed such importance in twentieth century sociological writing. Smith sensibly advises people not to taste the apple of high ambition themselves lest they be unable to rise, or having risen fall. This passion of the imagination is one that he sees all around him, even in 'place, that great object which divides the wives of aldermen'.[164] His remedy is the Stoic philosophy: 'Our primary appetites directed us to the pursuit of health, strength, ease, and perfection, in all the qualities of mind and body; and of whatever could promote or secure these, riches, power, authority: and the same original principle taught us to avoid the contrary. But in chusing or rejecting, in preferring or postponing, those first objects of original appetite and aversion, nature had likewise taught us, that there was a certain order, propriety, and grace, to be observed, of infinitely greater consequence to happiness and perfection, than the attainment of those objects themselves.'[165]

Smith's moral philosophy turns on the distinction between 'preferring' or 'postponing' our natural appetites and the vices of imagination. We should learn the Stoic self-command that will enable us to weigh up a present against a future pleasure, decide which is the more exquisite and lasting and act accordingly. The vices of imagination lead not only to lechery and gluttony, but also to the peculiar hell of ambition.

While Smith on the whole sees our admiration for wealth and rank as a positive, stabilising social influence, he warns that foppish, flattering but amusing courtiers may become an object of public emulation. We should rather admire the 'masculine virtues of a warrior, a statesman, a philosopher, or a legislator.'[166]

He is aware of the important role played by reward and punishment in social life. However unlike some later utilitarians he regards the physical aspects of these as secondary.[167] What really counts is the social meaning of rewards and punishments: we are swayed chiefly when these originate from people we admire and respect.

His views on conscience and the sense of duty altered somewhat in the course of the editions of *Moral Sentiments*. Earlier editions had appeared to make the sense of duty a simple reflection of public opinion: we think we ought to do what other people think we should do. Here was an early version of the emphasis on social conformity found in some American social psychology of the 1940s and 1950s. Smith's description of how we learn to see ourselves reflected in others is however more reminiscent of the metaphor of the mirror used by Jacques Lacan:

'Our first ideas of personal beauty and deformity, are drawn from the shape and appearance of others, not from our own. We soon become sensible, however, that others exercise the same criticism upon us. We are pleased when they approve of our figure, and are disobliged when they seem to be disgusted. We become anxious to know how far our appearance deserves either their blame or approbation. We examine our persons limb by limb, and by placing ourselves before a looking-glass, or by some such expedient, endeavour, as much as possible, to view ourselves at the distance and with the eyes of other people.'[168]

Following criticisms of his earlier emphasis, Smith added a discussion of how we separate praise from praiseworthiness in later editions. Here he adds that the impartial spectator who sits inside us and judges our actions is not simply a residue of actual people: they have been placed there by 'the all-wise Author of Nature' to give us a higher tribunal than mere human opinion.

He continues with an analysis of the influence of custom and mode of life. These, he thinks, have a great effect upon our ideas of beauty, but less upon our ideas of morality, which are born with us. One of his remarks about character and mode of life is worth repeating. Military men, he thinks, are prone to a levity, cheerfulness and 'a degree of dissipation', to prevent themselves from dwelling on the awful nature of their profession. The book concludes with a discussion of the virtuous, Stoic, character, whose outline has already been given.

To fully appreciate Smith's view of human nature it is helpful to add something about his view of history. Enlightenment historians were above all activated by the fear that the rise of manufacture and trade, having brought in its wake individualism, luxury and loss of contact with the land, would lead to a new age of historical dissolution and social decline. Montesquieu had warned of this in his book on the grandeur and decline of the Roman empire.[169] The English historian Gibbon backed him up with his massive six volumes on *The History of the Decline and Fall of the Roman Empire (1776-88)*.

After Montesquieu, however, the most original and influential historical theory was that proposed by Adam Smith in *The Wealth of Nations*. Through his expertise in economics he was able to suggest some detailed mechanisms operating in the process of economic development. Smith's message was a comforting one. Contrary to the prophets of doom, who foresaw an increase in luxury and individualism, decline of military virtues and, by implication, ruin amid new barbarian invasions, he saw economic growth as a self-limiting process.

The accumulation of capital cut out opportunities for new investments, ultimately reducing the rate of profit to a point where investment remained static and a steady state society was achieved.[170] Thus while *The Theory of Moral Sentiments* says little about social change, Smith in company with many enlightenment thinkers, was implicitly concerned that the passions for physical pleasure, fame and social advancement would come to dominate in a capitalistic society devoted to economic expansion. The Stoicism expounded in *The Theory of Moral Sentiments* has the additional implication that with its aid and the benevolent law of the falling rate of profit social ruin can be avoided.

Later Developments

British empiricist philosophy has continued down to the present through the writings of Bentham, James and John Stuart Mill, Bertrand Russell and A.J. Ayer.[171] Its dominance in British philosophy was overturned in the second half of the nineteenth century by the popularity of German philosophers, particularly Kant and Hegel. While it has never recaptured its dominant position of the early nineteenth century, Russell and Ayer have certainly re-established it as a leading force. Their version of the philosophy is however substantially different from the earlier writers. While Bentham and the Mills as well as the Scottish school of Reid and Stuart continued to use versions of the association of ideas as a theory of knowledge, both Russell and Ayer have moved away from this.[172] What continues to mark them out as distinctively empiricist philosophers is their belief that rationality allied to the development of prudence and the framing of wise laws can result in a rational and liberal form of society.[173]

4. The Kantian Synthesis

Kant (1724-1804) watched the events in France of 1789-92 from his academic post in Germany and enthusiastically supported the revolution. Yet he was not a participant and his philosophy was in sharp contrast to the materialism of the *idéologues*. While he sympathised with the ideal of progress, he was deeply concerned that both religion and morality were being eroded by materialist philosophy and individual self-seeking. His philosophy concentrates on the traditional problems of reconciling science with religion and of finding a secure foundation for morality. He also outlines a philosophy of history.

L.W. Beck has described the following six major influences on Kant: the rise of science, particularly Newtonian physics; the Pietist religion of his parents; the rationalist philosophy of Leibniz and Wolff; German popular philosophy; British psychological ethics; Rousseau. Of these, it must be said, German popular philosophy was chiefly a negative influence - Kant detested it.[174]

German intellectuals had, from the time of Leibniz, assumed the role of synthesisers. Leibniz and Wolff played this role within a revived scholasticism made possible by the rapprochement of Lutheranism and Catholicism. By Kant's time, a new matrix of cultural influences had appeared in Europe. Foremost among these was the now clearly visible opposition between science and religion. Another important impulse was the desire for a cosmopolitan European religious culture. The French philosophers had, since about 1740, increasingly deserted rationalism for materialism and empiricism. The desire of many with strong religious sensibilities was for a corresponding international religious philosophy that could halt the disastrous inroads of the materialist-empiricist philosophy.

Kant was well-placed to undertake the task of synthesis. His Pietist background provided a belief in a transcendent and personal God, while his training in Wolffian philosophy enabled him to sympathise with the impersonal and knowable God of rationalism and the Catholics. His commitment to Newtonian science was matched by his immersion in the Wolffian philosophy. One of the scandals of rationalist philosophy was the failure of its physics. Having boldly set out to deduce the laws of the physical world from first principles, Descartes and Leibniz had arrived at 'metaphysical' systems that contrasted unfavourably with Newtonian physics.[175] This boded ill for the doctrine of innate ideas. Yet with his training in rationalist philosophy Kant was unwilling to jettison all vestiges of innate ideas.

Added to these influences, was the contemporary discussion of evil, symbolised by Voltaire's satire on Leibniz in his play *Candide*. Kant's Pietist background had emphasised the evil of human nature, while his formal philosophical training had claimed that we live in the best of all possible worlds.[176]

Kant's critical system is certainly the most complex work of cultural synthesis ever to use the concept of human nature as its foundation. Succeeding generations have inhabited various wings of the Kantian castle at different periods. The whole edifice is not only inconvenient in size but also draughty in construction. To avoid both exhaustion and influenza my tour will be as rapid as possible, concentrating on two aspects of the system only: its size and its leaning towards rationalism on some key issues.

Kant manages to house his baroque edifice within a relatively conventional groundplan. This groundplan is the division between intellect, motive and feeling.[177] With intellect and motive we are on familiar ground - the whole of the Western tradition uses them, and in Kant's period this applies as much to Hume, by whom Kant was greatly influenced, as to Leibniz and Wolff. In his understanding of feeling, however, Kant makes some significant departures.

Kant's mature philosophy is most easily approached through consideration of his three critiques: *The Critique of Pure Reason* (1788) - corresponding to the intellect; *The Critique of Practical Reason* (1788) - corresponding to motives, particularly moral impulses and rules; and *The Critique of Judgement* (1790) - containing his analysis of feelings. The investigations undertaken in these works all relate to 'metaphysics', that is to the pure forms of knowledge, morality and feeling, rather than to facts about them. This is particularly important in dealing with motives, as bodily and even culturally determined motives lie outside the scope of pure forms.[178]

The metaphysics Kant is undertaking is however not that of Descartes and Leibniz. Their methods went too far in the use of innate ideas and innate logical principles. Rather than attempting to show that we have innate knowledge that can actually be used to construct sciences, Kant argues that pure thought can only lead us to the presuppositions of sciences. The sciences themselves must be sought by empirical methods. He further limits the claims of metaphysics by arguing that pure thought cannot lead to knowledge about an underlying reality, or 'thing-in-itself'.[179] We see the world and our own conduct in a certain way because of our nature. We can investigate our knowing and acting, but not any underlying reality. Yet in the study of human personality, the investigations of pure thought turn out to yield very substantial results, just because they are directed to discovering the structure of human nature.

In the *Critique of Pure Reason* Kant is chiefly concerned to investigate the 'synthetic *a priori*'. Leibniz had denied that we have innate knowledge of propositions, like the axioms of geometry and arithmetic. Given innate ideas, the laws of logic and the right definitions, we can, he thought, produce these axiomatic propositions without any appeal to innateness.

Leibniz was now discredited by Newtonian physics. The Newtonian doctrines of absolute space and time and of the correspondence of Euclidean geometry with reality continued to suggest innate forms of knowledge. So Kant went back to the traditional idea that as well as innate ideas and innate knowledge of logic, we also have innate knowledge of propositions. These propositions provide us with the 'synthetic *a priori*', which are not just tautologies but give actual knowledge about our world.

His investigation proceeds in four parts: first the structure of the world of sensation is examined (called aesthetic); then of the understanding; of judgements; and of reason.

Sensations are given to us represented in space and time, which are the *a priori* forms of sensory representation. Such sensations give only subjective space and time 'in here'; not objective space and time and objects existing 'out there'. The business of the understanding is to provide such objectivity. Kant is not saying that an objective world structured by real space and time exists; merely that we are led by our very nature to think it does. The categories that the understanding uses to construct this supposedly objective world are those of Quantity, Quality, Relation and Modality (the latter including possibility, existence and necessity). That we use these categories is simply a fact, but that we relate them to an outside world of objects can be ascribed to our psychological makeup. By comparing sensations we derive cognitions, such as that of a line. This is derived from a comparison of the various parts of the line, which at the same time must be held together by 'the synthetic unity of apperception'. Apperception was a term used by Leibniz to denote the clarity of purely intellectual ideas. In his phrase Kant is stressing that such apparently basic ideas are really derived from activities performed on sensations which synthesise the sensations into cognitions that are more than simply the sum of their constituent sensations. In particular these cognitions refer to a world 'out there' which was in no wise implied in the original sensations. We might say that when we carry a body we feel the pressure of its weight. This is a subjective judgement. But we normally say that the body is heavy, implying that it would always, since it came into existence, have felt heavy; and will always continue to do so until it goes out of existence.[180] This extra unity that we give to experience arises from the synthetic unity of apperception. We may note at this point in passing, though Kant does not, that what we normally mean by 'this body is heavy' is a generalisation not only to our own possible experiences, but also to those of others. Kant in effect denies that we normally make this leap. For him the intellect is quite individualistic.

The activity that the understanding performs upon the senses is often physical: to understand a line we draw it, in reality or in our imagination.[181] In this doctrine Kant anticipates Piaget and other modern views of intellectual development that stress activity. Piaget has written of the influence that Kant had upon him.[182] This kind of reproduction in imagination is assisted by the association of ideas, which causes us to associate the successive perceptions involved in drawing a line with one another.[183] Like Hume, Kant thinks the association of ideas is benevolent and assists correct reasoning.

The understanding is brought to bear on sensations by the faculty of judgement. This involves an initial problem as sensations are fundamentally different from the categories of the understanding. To relate them we need *transcendental schemata*, which are rules for passing between the two. The schema for quantity for instance is number, which in the procedure of counting gives us a rule to decide what quantity of things is present.[184]

Having surmounted this problem we pass to synthetic *a priori* judgements whose possibility is given by *a priori* sensory manifolds of time and space and by the *a priori* categories of the understanding. Such judgements include: the axioms of Euclidean geometry and certain parts of arithmetic; that all phenomena are continuous quantities; the permanence of substance, that every effect has a cause, that all substances are in a state of reciprocal interaction; certain general criteria for what is possible, real or necessary, notably that anything evidenced by sensation is real. These four kinds of synthetic *a priori* judgements correspond, respectively, to the four main groups of categories: Quantity, Quality, Relation and Modality. In his discussion of the synthetic *a priori* Kant tries not to claim too much for a priori reasoning. Thus in discussing continuity he excludes the notion that all change is continuous, which was a metaphysical principle Leibniz had attempted to use in physics.[185]

The products of the understanding are then further operated on by reason: 'If the understanding is a faculty for producing unity among phenomena, by means of rules, reason is the faculty for producing unity among the rules of the understanding, according to the principles.'[186] The chief activity of reason is to reach back from the judgements and rules of the understanding to find ultimate premises. But, Kant warns us, this search for more and more general principles is the proper function of reason. To think that we have found them is an illusion of metaphysics that leads on to all sorts of mental disorders.

The search of reason for ultimate principles takes place in three areas: psychology and the soul; cosmology and metaphysics (in the sense of physics carried out by *a priori* methods); ontology or the investigation of absolute being. All these areas could be subsumed under the title metaphysics, conceived in a broad sense. Kant's discussion of them is a warning: if you proceed too far in this direction you will arrive at false conclusions and may become enmeshed in contradictions, as happened to the Greek philosopher Zeno when he tried to prove that nothing really changes.[187] Yet Kant is not a positivist. So long as its investigations are kept within bounds, reason has a right to investigate these matters. The principles of reason must be used 'regulatively' rather than absolutely. The principles must not be thought to correspond to real objects, like absolute being, but to principles of inquiry. Examples of such valid principles of inquiry are the unity of science, that is the search for more and more general scientific laws; and the distinctness (variety) of science, which is the study of more and more detail.

These general regulative principles find their expression in the above three areas of psychology, cosmology and ontology.[188] The ego is assumed, by a regulative principle, to form a unified whole. The universe is assumed, by a similar principle, to form a whole. Finally ontology accepts as a regulative principle the existence of a being of the highest perfection, namely God. The wise governance of God in the universe is seen in his assignment of ultimate ends to most, if not all, processes in the universe, which are thus governed by teleological (end-seeking) causes, in addition to the physical and mechanical laws of nature. God is to be worshipped primarily for his assignment of ultimate ends to processes, rather than for his imposition of natural laws. This is at variance with scholastic and rationalist theology, which worship God in both manifestations, though the Kantian search for physical and mechanical laws may admittedly assist in the investigation of teleology. The important thing for Kant is to resist the temptation of dogmatic mysticism to think that we have a real insight into natural and psychological phenomena without making a detailed investigation of them.[189]

In his *Critique of Practical Reason* Kant investigates the moral faculty. His discussion here has generally been related to that of Rousseau, for whom Kant had a profound admiration.[190] Kant said he was more deeply moved by Rousseau than by any other writer. Yet he felt Rousseau accepted as given important matters requiring proof. Put another way, Rousseau could revolt emotionally against the philosophers of the French enlightenment; against their admiration for *le despotisme éclairé* (enlightened despotism) and for enlightened selfishness; against their incipient atheism (stronger in Diderot than in Voltaire). Kant wanted to prove them wrong beyond doubt. His method was naturally a continuation of his investigations of the *a priori* forms of knowledge begun in the *Critique of Pure Reason*.

The possibility of God, freedom and immortality had been shown in the *Critique of Pure Reason*. In the *Critique of Practical Reason* Kant sets out to show that there exists, besides pure reason, a realm of practical reason that has as much, in fact more, claim to reality than pure reason. This is the moral realm. For unlike most previous Western thinkers, with the ambiguous exception of Rousseau, Kant thinks that God and immortality are to be proved by appeal to moral knowledge, rather than the other way round. Machiavelli and Montesquieu argued that fear of punishment in the afterlife acts as an incentive to maintain political order and thus moral order, imperfect though it may be.[191] This cynical view of religion justified it in terms of its beneficial political and moral effect. Rousseau, and following him Kant, did not share this scepticism about religion, but did share the assumption that the moral and political order on earth is a more certain starting point for reason than God and immortality.

Given his approach in the *Critique of Pure Reason*, Kant must argue from the inevitable forms of our moral thinking, rather than from inevitable contents. As space and time are the forms of our sensation, so the forms or our moral thinking are:
1. 'Act so that the maxim guiding your will could always be taken as the principle of a universal law.'
2. 'The autonomy of the will is the sole principle of all moral laws and of the duties conforming to them; determination of choice by others, on the other hand, does not establish any obligation and is opposed to the principle of duty and the morality of the will.'[192]

Unlike other moral systems, that take the happiness of all or the Christian injunction to love one's neighbour as their starting point, this approach contains no initial reference to such aims. For like Rousseau Kant wants to establish that moral obligation stems from the fact that there is a social order with laws, not from how people feel. An additional motive for moral formalism is that laws and feelings are dramatically variable in different peoples.[193] Formalism can establish an unassailable and intelligible moral realm that lies outside such local variation and beyond the corrupting influence of selfishness and enlightenment.

That there is a moral law, places us under the obligation to strive to obey it. But as selfish creatures with sensuous appetites we are unable to acquire this perfection. So our ability to obey the moral law requires an endless progress towards moral perfection.[194] This in turn requires immortality.

The idea of moral perfection, or the highest good, also leads us to God. Our striving towards such perfection assumes its existence. Moral perfection is not possible in a being that is part of nature and thus dependent upon it. Such a being is unable to determine all its actions purely by wishes derived from the moral law. An example of such an imperfect being is ourselves, who are prevented from always carrying out moral wishes by our sensuous inclinations. But, Kant says, any being that is part of nature must be determined in some way by the rest of nature, thus acting according to natural laws, not according to moral laws. A morally perfect being must be the cause of nature. This being's moral intentions are translated into natural laws, which prevents there being any conflict between its will and natural laws. This being therefore has the attributes of God, at least as Kant conceives them.[195] God as conceived in this way is a subjective need, rather than a 'thing'. But as knowledge of 'things' is ruled out in the Kantian system, a need is as real, indeed more real, than the constructions of theoretical reason.

This argument appears to contain a flaw, as it is not proved that the morally perfect being has any connection with nature. God might, like the God of Epicurus, take little interest in the world, either to make it or to interfere in it.

We might be tempted to overcome this problem by jumping the gap to theoretical or 'pure' reason, where it had already been proved that God has a connection with nature. This is a temptation to which Kant partly succumbed in his *Critique of Judgement*, where a synthesis of pure and practical reason is attempted.

Another ernest of this coming synthesis is found in the *Critique of Practical Reason* in Kant's discussion of respect for the moral law. This is a feeling that acts to bridge the gap between morality and motivation. It provides a moral motive for obeying the moral law. To cooperate with the moral law in the hope of obtaining rewards or avoiding punishments is nothing other than self-interest and is thus not moral at all. But by striking at our self-conceit, the moral law make us feel respect for it, which is thus a truly moral feeling.[196]

Apart from the differences between self-interest and self-conceit we are not told much about the non-moral motives in the *Critique of Practical Reason*. In his *Anthropology* Kant describes the desires for freedom, sex, revenge and the love of mastery (of the physical world) as inborn human passions.[197] In emphasising the inborn nature of the human desire for freedom, he points out that both young children and nomadic peoples show great ferocity when their freedom is restricted.[198]

The inclusion of mastery over the physical world seems at first sight paradoxical, because he defines passions as pertaining to people, not things. Yet the passion for mastery of things (technical-practical reason) easily extends itself to people, who become thereby the instruments of this desire for mastery. In the *Critique of Practical Reason* Kant had already warned us against this tendency in his injunction, derived from his two major moral premises, always to treat people as ends, not as means.[199] As ends the freedom of human beings must be respected, while in a system of technical-practical reason such freedom cannot be so respected. Technical-practical reason recognises only laws of nature and not freedom.

It is this desire for mastery, stemming from the faculty of technical-practical reason (the empirical reason dealt with in the *Critique of Pure Reason*) that leads on to the three culturally induced passions - for glory, power and possessions.[200] These passions begin as attempts to find the means to obtain technical-practical power over people. Kant says that the attempt to control other people through their opinions becomes eventually a passion for glory as an end in itself. The attempt to control others through fear becomes the passion for power. The attempt to control them by manipulating their self-interest becomes the passion for possessions.[201]

Finally we come to the *Critique of Judgement*. Here pure reason is reconciled with practical reason. This synthesis produces a world of real, intelligible and supersensible objects that unite both the realm of freedom and the realm of scientific reason. As an introduction to this world we can recall Samuel Johnson, who was annoyed by Berkeley's assertion that the world might not really exist. 'I refute it thus', said Johnson, kicking a large stone.[202] We may imagine that the pain in his toe gave him good evidence for the reality of the world. This is a common sense refutation of solipsism, the philosophical doctrine that nothing exists outside our immediate experience.

Kant too had been sailing near the reefs of solipsism. He argued in the *Critique of Pure Reason* that the world really exists, but we cannot know what it is like by reason. Reason tells us about our private world of experience, not about an 'outside' world. A way of establishing that our reason does tell us about the world would be to argue that reason enables us to successfully seek pleasure and avoid pain, so giving a kind of proof that it does deal with the world. But Kant, significantly, does not take this line. Instead he argues that pleasure and pain provide us with a proof of the reality of the products of reason in another way. For when we find a principle that enables us to subsume two empirical laws of nature under it, this gives us 'marked pleasure, even admiration'.[203] This gives us an inkling that the laws we discover really provide knowledge about the world.

We might also expect Kant to go on to say that our admiration for purposive teleological explanations shows their real validity. He had told us that the faculty of pleasure and pain stands between the faculty of knowledge (pure reason) and the faculty of desire (practical reason) and has compared this to the way in which judgement, in his new and expanded sense, stands between understanding and reason.[204]

Yet he doesn't take either line. The reason, I think, is that this would take him back to basing moral and rational-scientific reality on what people feel about them. That is something he wants to avoid at all cost. It threatens a collapse of his whole system, which is based upon a separate realm of moral knowledge lying outside the reach both of science and of what people feel about it.[205]

Instead, Kant prefers a more cautious course. After dark hints in the introduction he sets out to discuss beauty and the sublime in a way that hints at both the Johnson and the feeling-for-teleology arguments, but does not contain the same dangers. Then he gives a discussion of teleology that virtually repeats the analysis contained in the *Critique of Pure Reason*, reiterating that we cannot know whether teleology belongs to the real world or is just an *a priori* way of looking at the world with no basis in reality.[206] Teleology is now assigned to judgement rather than reason.

The *Critique of Judgement* is written in a more cautious way than the earlier critiques. Matters are said to be pending further investigation. We are finally left with the impression that the internal contradictions of his system have become too much even for Kant's immense capabilities.

Kant's ideas about history are most clearly stated in the 1784 essay 'Idea for a Universal History from a Cosmopolitan Point of View'. The first thesis of this says 'All natural capacities of a creature, are destined to evolve completely to their natural end.'[207] He argues from this that as reason is a prominent natural capacity in human beings, we are therefore destined to evolve a rational society. The selfish competition between individuals is the mechanism through which this perfection is destined to arise. The chief obstacle to this development is war between nations and the remedy that will eventually cure this is a league of nations. One important force tending to promote international cooperation is improvement in popular education.

Later Developments

In the first half of the nineteenth century German philosophers like Fichte, Hegel and Schopenhauer attempted to go beyond Kant. The years after 1860 saw the 'back to Kant' movement and from that point on his direct following in Germany has remained considerable.[208] The NeoKantian sociology of Simmel (1858-1918) and the early works of Scheler re-established the Kantian conception of human nature as the foundation for sociology.[209] This movement itself lost influence after the first world war, largely because it had identified itself with the optimistic side of Kant's thinking. Its most brilliant younger representative, Scheler, turned first to phenomenology then to a pessimism rooted in Freud.[210] After the second world war many of the most prominent German sociologists continued to develop the more pessimistic strand in Kant's thinking. This was particularly clear in the work of Horkheimer, whose *Habilitationschrift* had earlier been on the topic *Kant and the Bourgeois Philosophy of History*.[211] Horkheimer and Adorno developed Kant's emphasis on the dangers of treating people as if they were things. They argued in *The Dialectic of the Enlightenment* that Western society had been overtaken by the principle of technical rationality and that this had overwhelmed human values.[212] Habermas also uses a distinctively Kantian philosophy of human nature, though in his case it is emphasised that the process of scientific inquiry itself requires certain human values, such as freedom of opinion and information.[213]

Further Reading

Scholasticism

R.E. Brennan, *Thomistic Psychology; A Philosophic Analysis of the Nature of Man*, MacMillan, New York, 1941.

F. Coppleston, *Thomas Aquinas*, Search Press, London, 1976

C.R.S. Harris, *Duns Scotus*, Humanities Press, New York, 1959, 2 vols.

G. Leff, *William of Ockham*, Manchester University Press, Manchester, 1975.

R.M. McInerny, *St. Thomas Aquinas*, Twayne, Boston, 1977.

H. Meyer, *The Philosophy of Thomas Aquinas*, Herder, Freiberg, 1944, trans. F. Eckhoff.

J.F. Quinn, *The Historical Constitution of St. Bonaventure's Philosophy*, Pontifical Institute of Medieval Studies, Toronto, 1973.

Metaphysical Rationalism

W.H. Barber, *Leibniz in France, from Arnauld to Voltaire: a Study in French Reactions to Leibnizianism 1670-1760*, Clarendon, Oxford, 1965.

C.D. Broad, *Leibniz: an Introduction*, CUP, London, 1975.

R.A. Brooks, *Voltaire and Leibniz*, Droz, Genève, 1964.

E.M. Curley, *Descartes Against the Skeptics*, Blackwell, Oxford, 1978.

J. Hostler, *Leibniz's Moral Philosophy*, Duckworth, London, 1975.

S.V. Keeling, *Descartes*, OUP, London, 1968, 2nd ed.

A. Kenny, *Descartes: A Study of his Philosophy*, Random House, New York, 1968.

L. Pearl, *Descartes*, Twayne, Boston, 1977.

R.H. Popkin, *The History of Skepticism form Erasmus to Descartes*, Van Gorcum, Assen, 1960.

J. Rée, *Descartes*, Allen Lane, London, 1974.

N. Rescher, *Leibniz*, Blackwell, Oxford, 1979.

L.D. Rosenfield, *From Beast-Machine to Man-Machine; animal soul in French letters from Descartes to La Mettrie*, Octagon, New York, 1968.

R.L. Saw, *Leibniz*, Penguin, Harmondsworth, 1954.

B. Williamson, *Descartes: The Project of Pure Enquiry*, Harvester, Hassocks, 1978.

M.D. Wilson, *Descartes*, Routledge, London, 1978.

84

Empiricism

R.F. Anderson, *Hume's First Principles*, Uni. of Nebraska Press, Lincoln, 1966.
P.S. Ardal, *Passion and Value in Hume's Treatise*, Edinburgh Uni. Press, Edinburgh, 1966.
A.J. Ayer, *Hume*, OUP, Oxford, 1980.
J.F. Bennett, *Locke, Berkeley, Hume: Central Themes*, Clarendon, Oxford, 1971.
C.J. Berry, *Hume, Hegel and Human Nature*, Nijhoff, The Hague, 1982.
T.D. Campbell, *Adam Smith's Science of Morals*, Allen and Unwin, London, 1971.
V.C. Chappell, *Hume*, Doubleday, Garden City, 1966.
C.E. Dankert, *Adam Smith; Man of Letters and Economist*, Exposition Press, Hicksville, 1974.
M.W. Cranston, *John Locke*, Arno, New York, 1979.
D.P. Gauthier, *The Logic of Leviathan*, Clarendon, Oxford, 1969.
C.H. Hinnant, *Thomas Hobbes*, Twayne, Boston, 1977.
R.M. Kydd, *Reason and Conduct in Hume's Treatise*, Russell and Russell, New York, 1964.
J. Laird, *Hume's Philosophy of Human Nature*, Methuen, London, 1932.
J.R. Lindgren, *The Social Philosophy of Adam Smith*, Nijhoff, The Hague, 1973.
J.L. Mackie, *Problems from Locke*, Clarendon, Oxford, 1976.
P.C. Mercer, *Sympathy and Ethics*, Clarendon, Oxford, 1972.
M.J. Oakeshott, *Hobbes on Civil Association*, Blackwell, Oxford, 1975.
J.A. Passmore, *Hume's Intentions*, Duckworth, London, 1968, rev. ed.
R.S. Peters, *Hobbes*, Penguin, Harmondsworth, 1967, 2nd ed.
D.D. Raphael, *Hobbes: Morals and Politics*, Allen and Unwin, London, 1977.
W.S. Sahakian, *John Locke*, Twayne, Boston, 1975.
W.L. Taylor, *Francis Hutcheson and David Hume as Predecessors of Adam Smith*, Duke Uni. Press, Durham, 1965.
S. Tweyman, *Reason and Conduct in Hume and his Presecessors*, Nijhoff, The Hague, 1974.

Kant

H.B. Acton, *Kant's Moral Philosophy*, MacMillan, London, 1970.
L.W. Beck, *A Commentary on Kant's Critique of Practical Reason*, Uni. of Chicago Press, Chicago, 1960.
L.W. Beck, *Studies in the Philosophy of Kant*, Bobs-Merrill, Indianapolis, 1965.
L.W. Beck, *Early German Philosophy; Kant and his Predecessors*, Belknap, Cambridge, 1969.
C.D. Broad, *Kant; An Introduction*, CUP, Cambridge, 1978.
J. Kemp, *The Philosophy of Kant*, OUP, London, 1968.
C.N.G. Orsini, *Coleridge and German Idealism*, Southern Illinois Uni. Press, Carbondale, 1969.
F.P. van de Pitte, *Kant as Philosophical Anthropologist*, Nijhoff, The Hague, 1971.

R. Scruton, *Kant*, OUP, Oxford, 1982.
H.J. Vleeschauwer, *The Development of Kantian Thought*, Nelson, London 1962, trans. A.R.C. Duncan.
R.S. Walker, *Kant*, Routledge, London, 1978.
K. Ward, *The Development of Kant's View of Ethics*, Blackwell, Oxford, 1972.
J. Watson, *Kant and his English Critics*, Garland, New York, 1976.

The Neo-Kantians

T. Abel, *Systematic Sociology in Germany*, Columbia University Press, New York, 1929.
D.A. Martindale, *The Nature and Types of Sociological Theory*, Houghton Miflin, Boston, 1960.
J. Passmore, *A Hundred Years of Philosophy*, Duckworth, London, 1966, 2nd ed., Chap.3.
F.J. von Rintelen, *Contemporary German Philosophy*, H. Bouvier, Bonn, 1970.
K.F. Wolff, *The Sociology of George Simmel*, Free Press, Glencoe, 1950.

Chapter 4 :
The Origins of Modernism

Some of the material in this chapter is more difficult than that in others and the whole chapter could be omitted at a first reading. I have concentrated on writers who were immediately and directly influential on the thinking of the most important founders of the modernist movement: Nietzsche, Freud, Heidegger and Sartre. It is however of interest to look at the earlier development of the ideas of unconscious motives and of investigations of human nature through consciousness.

The conceptions of unconscious motivation found in Nietzsche and Freud had their origins in four traditions. One was a kind of political thought which argued that politics often involves the use of rationalisations and ideologies to cloak self-interest. The most influential early writer in this tradition was La Rochefoucauld in the seventeenth century, whom Nietzsche often cites.[1] This idea was generally more distasteful to later liberal tradition, though Bentham coined the term 'sinister interest' to refer to this hidden action of motives.[2] In the nineteenth century it was taken up most forcefully by Marx and Engels.[3] As German Marxism began to exert an important influence on German society in the 1880s we must count this as an influence in creating the European climate for Freud's thinking. Nietzsche developed his ideas somewhat earlier and if any one writer can be counted as having fertilised his imagination it would be La Rochefoucauld.

A second influence that helped create a climate receptive to the idea of unconscious motivation was that philosophy of history which saw individual action as unconsciously under the direction of an all-embracing historical spirit. This was in effect a partially secularised version of the Christian idea that history is controlled by a divine plan. The German philosophers Herder, Hegel and von Hartmann were most influential in popularising this conception in the nineteenth century.[4] Von Hartmann even emphasised the use of the term 'the unconscious' to describe the activities of this spirit in *The Philosophy of the Unconscious* (1868).

A third influence was through aesthetic and literary writers, many of whom in the eighteenth and nineteenth centuries were beginning to think that aesthetic feelings were the manifestation of unconscious processes. Such processes might either be thought of as motives or a historical spirit; it is often not clear which is intended. Writers in this group included Rousseau, Schelling, Goethe, Schiller, Coleridge, Wordsworth and Schopenhauer.[5]

The fourth influence came from the study of hypnotism, which leapt into prominence in the eighteenth century through the activities of Mesmer and was very influential in the work of both Freud and Janet.[6] Mesmer himself argued that the phenomena of hypnotism could be explained through the passage of 'animal magnetism' between the hypnotist and the subject, which was not an explanation via unconscious motives. In the nineteenth century interest in hypnotism was often associated with ideas of the universal mind along the lines suggested in Hegel's discussions of the world-spirit.[7] Again this kind of speculation probably helped prepare a favourable reception for the ideas of Freud and Janet.

The idea that the investigation of human nature should begin with consciousness is almost as old as Christian philosophy, being prominent in both Augustine and Descartes. All along this had been seen as a kind of defence against both materialism and scepticism. A renewed emphasis on the defence against materialism appeared in French philosophy with Maine de Biran, who reacted against the materialist excesses of Condillac and the *idéologues* of the revolution of 1789.[8] His work was popularised by Cousin in the mid-nineteenth century and extended by Bergson towards the end of the century, undoubtedly preparing a favourable climate for Sartre's atheistic version of the philosophy of consciousness.[9]

In Germany the line of influence ran from the emphasis on consciousness in the neoscholastic philosopher Brentano, through his pupil Husserl to Heidegger. As Sartre and later French tradition referred their own work to this German tradition rather than to de Biran and Bergson I have chosen to concentrate in what follows on the writings of Brentano and Husserl.

1. Before Nietzsche

Schopenhauer (1788-1860)

Schopenhauer presented his doctoral thesis at Jena University in 1813 with the title *On the Fourfold Root of the Principle of Sufficient Reason*.[10] He argues that in perception we do not just passively take in knowledge about the outside world. From sensations the intellect builds up 'representations' of the world that are partly projections of intellectual ideas.

Such representations are divided into four kinds: causal processes, logic, space and time and the realisation of motives in actions. The principle of sufficient reason states that all our knowledge in these spheres is governed by *a priori* forms of connection of the kind investigated by Kant.

The *a priori* form of causality is the connection between cause and effect and the means for establishing this. The form of logic entails the movement from premises to conclusions. For space and time it is that one relation implies another, as happens in Euclidean geometry. The last and for our purposes most interesting form is that from the strength of motives in a person and their character, which may be for instance reflective or steadfast, a course of action inevitably follows.

In 1819 Schopenhauer published his greatest work, *The World as Will and Representation*. He was a failure as a teacher, usually failing to attract sufficient students to his classes, and finally gave up academic life.[11] *The World as Will and Representation* was initially a failure as a book. In the preface to the second edition in 1844, Schopenhauer attributes this to the fear it aroused in philosophy professors by failing to propose a speculative theology in accordance with 'modern, Judaising, optimistic Christianity'.[12] Actually it went rather further than this and condemned optimism as something actively wicked, while holding true Christianity to be a symbolic presentation of the idea that life is predominantly suffering. Only by overcoming the will to life can we find release from suffering. To round out the marketability of his text, Schopenhauer makes no effort to disguise his admiration for Buddhism and its quest for release from life. When we consider that the defeat of Napoleon in 1815 had signalled the defeat of liberalism in Europe and that freethinking and materialism were tantamount to professional suicide in German universities at this time, we may wonder at the boldness of making such views known.[13]

Schopenhauer, however, belongs to that distinguished tradition which regards philosophy as a more serious matter than professional careers. If the world is as black as he says it is, then we urgently need to fortify ourselves to meet it. Such fortification is not to be found in the applause of professors and the 'corybantic shouting with which the birth of the spiritual children of those of the same mind is celebrated.'[14] It is to be found in the right mental outlook, in a philosophy of life. While a pessimistic view of the human condition had been quite common in eighteenth century literary circles - Samuel Johnson, Sydney Smith and Voltaire are all outstanding examples - it had never found expression in what we might call a technical philosophy, except in the case of Hobbes, whose pessimism is in any event relatively moderate.[15] Spinoza had developed a philosophy of resignation in the seventeenth century, which Schopenhauer often refers to, but since that time an academic philosophy of pessimism had been lacking.

We have seen that the four divisions of sufficient reason leave human action governed by precisely that scheme of determinism found in scholasticism, minus any interference from free will. *The World as Will and Representation* sets out to go further than this by attempting to penetrate beyond appearances ruled by *a priori* forms into the thing-in-itself. Kant had regarded this as unknowable, but Schopenhauer believes he can penetrate into it by using consciousness. We can never know the inner being of other bodies, but we are conscious of our own inner being and have direct knowledge that this inner being is the will.

Our body can be considered as a representation. It then falls under the *a priori* appropriate to it, which is that its movements are wholly determined by character and motives. But our body has the additional peculiarity that we see these movements from the inside, in consciousness, where we observe that the essential precondition for any action is will. This is not one of the causes of acting, which lie in motive and character. Will is something that accompanies all actions and may therefore be called the presupposition of action.[16]

So far there is I think irrefutable logic in Schopenhauer's argument. We may wonder what the point of selecting will as the invariable conscious accompaniment of action is, rather than say perception or motive or intellect. But there can be no argument that it does accompany at least deliberate actions. Schopenhauer says it does not accompany non-deliberate actions, so we are to understand action here as deliberate action.[17]

The remainder of the argument in *The World as Will and Representation* is devoted to stepping off, in rather doubtful ways, from this unobjectionable beginning to reach spectacular conclusions. The first such branching out is described as follows: 'We shall judge all objects which are not our own body, and therefore are given to our consciousness not in the double way, but only as representations, according to the analogy of this body. We shall therefore assume that as, on the one hand, they are representation, just like our body, and are in this respect homogeneous with it, so on the other hand, if we set aside their existence as the subject's representation, what still remains over must be, according to its inner nature, the same as what in ourselves we call will. For what other kind of existence or reality could we attribute to the rest of the material world? From what source could we take the elements out of which we construct such a world? Besides the will and the representation, there is absolutely nothing known or conceivable for us.'[18]

Another expansion of the argument, more relevant to our present purposes, occurs as follows: 'On the other hand, it must not be overlooked that in all Ideas, that is to say, in all the forces of inorganic and in all the forms of organic nature, it is one and the same will that reveals itself, i.e., enters the form of representation, enters objectivity. Therefore, its unity must make itself known also through an inner relationship between all its phenomena. Now this reveals itself at the higher grades of the will's objectivity, where the whole phenomenon is more distinct, and thus in the plant and animal kingdoms, through the universally prevailing analogy of all forms, namely the fundamental type recurring in all phenomena. This has therefore become the guiding principle of the admirable zoological systems begun by the French in the nineteenth century, and is most completely established in comparative anatomy as l'unité de plan, l'uniformité de l'elément anatomique. To discover this fundamental type has been the main concern, or certainly at any rate the most laudable endeavour, of the natural philosophers of Schelling's school. In this respect they have much merit, although in many cases their hunting for analogies in nature degenerates into mere facetiousness. However, they have rightly shown the universal relationship and family likeness even in the Ideas of inorganic nature, for instance between electricity and magnetism, the identity of which was established later; between chemical attraction and gravitation, and so on.'[19]

It is apparent here that will as precondition for the phenomena of the body has passed over into the realm of causality and is threatening to become a force like those in physics and chemistry. To be more precise the fact that will is a common denominator of certain phenomena is being used to imply that this unity will be expressed in unifying forces. It later becomes quite clear that the principle of will is to be used as just such a unifying force. The struggle for survival, which Schopenhauer speaks of in remarkably Darwinian terms, is seen as an expression of a vital force or urge running through nature. 'Thus from the contest of lower phenomena the higher one arises, swallowing up all of them, but also realising in the higher degree the tendency of them all.'[20]

One relation between lower and higher forms of life had been discussed by the scholastic philosophers under the title *Principium Individuationis*. The sixteenth century compiler Suarez had summarised their doctrines and

Schopenhauer refers to this summary.[21] This principle states that higher forms of life are more distinctive in their individual manifestations and more various than lower forms. Schopenhauer also speaks of higher forms attaining a greater degree of 'objectification', by which he means a greater degree of participation in Platonic *Ideas*, just as some scholastic philosophers conceived them to.[22]

These two relations of individuation and objectivity are important for Schopenhauer. Individuation, he says, occurs in space and time and is thus a matter of representation, not of will, which is uniform and indivisible throughout nature.[23] Here he goes back to the valid use of the principle of will as precondition with which he began. Strictly speaking, however, will should never have left this sphere of precondition at all. Individuation is, he later tells us, an illusion and we must 'see through' it to reality.[24] The grades of Ideas are not, however, illusory: 'Not themselves entering into time and space, the medium of individuals, they remain fixed, subject to no change, always being, never having become.'[25]

In the second book of *The World as Will and Representation* Schopenhauer sets out to examine these Ideas more fully. They are, he has told us, the grades of objectification of will in representations.[26] This already involves a third illegitimate extension of the notion of will as precondition. The proposition that will is a precondition for the movement of living bodies, if we accept it, does not imply that this homogeneous precondition is realised in various grades. Schopenhauer's enthusiasm for Platonic philosophy leads him to this extension. It does not however lead him, with Hegel, to identify the grades of Ideas with the passage of human history. The Idea of the human race is always the same. 'Consequently, the history of the human race, the throng of events, the change of times, the many varying forms of human life in different countries and centuries, all this is only the accidental form of the phenomena of the Idea.'[27]

Ideas are most completely revealed in works of art, which are 'the way of considering things independently of the principle of sufficient reason', that is independent of causality and mathematics. The genius of the artist enables us to see directly into the reality of the Ideas contained in will.[28] The acts of genius by which artists perceive reality lead them into a state close to madness, a condition noted by Pope, Goethe, Cicero and Plato and attested to by the biographies of Rousseau, Byron and Alfieri.[29]

The intuitions of genius show us Ideas under two aspects, the beautiful and the sublime, both topics extensively dealt with by Kant in the *Critique of Judgement*. The predominance of knowing over willing in the act of genius produces the beautiful, as in Dutch still life paintings. This kind of creation is closely linked to light, geometry, colours and the perception of space.[30]

In the sublime, we apprehend something, like a storm or other natural force, that threatens our will. This natural feeling of terror is converted to the sublime when we are able to tear ourselves away from the threat posed to us and achieve a state of disinterested reflection.[31] Thus a real storm might produce terror, but a painting of a storm enables us to recollect the terror in tranquility. Terror never leaves us, but we overcome it in the sublimity of the painting. Architecture and landscape gardening are then discussed in the light of the tension between the beautiful and the sublime. Greek sculpture captured the Idea of human beauty in a perfect form, while Shakespeare represents to us Ideas of different kinds of human character.[32] Historical painting has the particular merit of attempting to unite both.[33] Allegory in the visual arts is however condemned as a clumsy attempt to show concepts directly, as when Nemesis is depicted glancing into her bosom to indicate that she sees what is hidden![34] Poetry and its ability to convey human character are selected for a concluding section that once again emphasises Shakespeare's pre-eminence in this sphere. In his tragedies we experience the sublime in its highest manifestation, as the human will meets its boundaries and collapses under the weight of self-contradiction. In the characters of Richard III and Iago Shakespeare shows that wickedness leads to its own downfall. In *Romeo and Juliet* it is blind chance that frustrates human will, while *Hamlet* exemplifies the most perfect kind of tragedy, where it is simply the incompatibility of ordinary characters and their situations that brings about ruin.[35] The 'ordinariness' of the characters here is their human constitution, not their social station. While Schopenhauer does not say as much, we may infer that their high station shows us how even in a favourable situation that many envy, character leads to ruin. The works of Euripides, Sophocles, Voltaire and Goethe are also commended as displaying these varieties of tragic downfall.

Music, which seems to have touched Schopenhauer more closely even than other arts, does not depict Ideas but is a purely abstract art. As such, he confesses it finds no clear place in this theory. He is nonetheless prepared for a leap in the dark to grasp the essence of its power over us.[36] Music, he speculates, does not copy Ideas, but the will itself.[37] Low notes in some sense depict the Ideas of lower life forms and our planet, while higher notes depict the Ideas of higher animals and human beings. Chords represent species, discords miscegenations.[38] A number of other analogies between music and the grades of objectivity are also canvassed.

In the fourth book we come to Schopenhauer's portrait of human nature. He begins by disclaiming any intention of propounding ethical precepts or a doctrine of duty.[39] His doctrine of human nature, as now revised, begins from 'the-will-to-live', or as we might now say the will to survive.[40] He claims that we can deduce from the will as precondition for action the will to survive. As with previous deductions from this principle, there is something of a jump here as the will to survive is a motive and thus belongs to the sphere of causality.

Leaving this aside, what Schopenhauer actually tells us of the will to survive is of great interest. Much of his philosophy here is taken from Buddhism and Hinduism. 'The basis of all willing, however, is need, lack, and hence pain, and by its very nature and origin it is therefore destined to pain. If, on the other hand, it lacks objects of willing, because it is at once deprived of them again by too easy a satisfaction, a fearful emptiness and boredom come over it; in other words, its being and its existence itself become an intolerable burden for it. Hence its life swings like a pendulum to and fro between pain and boredom, and these two are in fact its ultimate constituents. This has been expressed very quaintly by saying that, after man had placed all pains and torments in hell, there was nothing left for heaven but boredom.'[41]

Later thinkers built systems in which the repression of sex or the will to power provided the energy for culture. In Schopenhauer the energy for popular culture is produced by boredom. The high culture of the beautiful and the sublime is inaccessible to the mass, who follow only active pursuits that either involve action or engage sympathy for action.[42] The pursuits of the masses are public circuses and animal-baiting.[43] Only the philosophical individual can, through the contemplation of the eternal in the beautiful and sublime, achieve anything more than diversion. 'The essential purport of the world-famous monologue in *Hamlet* is, in condensed form, that our state is so wretched that complete non-existence would be decidedly preferable to it.'[44]

The will to live is manifested both in the urge for personal survival and in the urge to have children. The true object of the religions of Christianity, Hinduism and Buddhism is to teach that sexual reproduction condemns future generations to the cycle of suffering. In condemning the sin of Adam, so widely identified as lust, the Christian churches urged people to turn their backs on life.[45]

This is followed, at first sight surprisingly, by a discussion of right and justice. It turns out, however, that this is premised on the earlier pessimistic discussion of human nature. The struggle of wills that manifests itself in the folly of egoism can be met in two ways. From natural justice, which is immediately evident to all, we learn that harm to another person's body and by extension to their wellbeing are wrong.[46] This leads the state to set itself up as the arbiter in conflicts of interest, as Hobbes suggested, and 'to place beside every possible motive for committing a wrong a more powerful motive for leaving it undone, in inescapable punishment.'[47]

Beyond such temporal justice there lies eternal justice, which originates from the activity of willing itself. To desire and to will the achievement of the objects of desire leads us back into the cycle of suffering. We must kill this desire and the will to life within us to escape from suffering by withdrawal from the world. Eternal justice metes out to those who will life their deserts by condemning them to further suffering, a moral doctrine encapsulated in the Hindu belief that wrongdoing is punished by rebirth.

2. Before Freud

Fechner (1801-1887)

In his *Interpretation of Dreams* Freud refers to Fechner's work on dreams and the unconscious. Fechner's idea was that consciousness is like a 'swell'. When we are wide awake the swell is high. When we sleep the swell recedes. Experiences, images and memories are called 'waves'. When the waves reach above the swell they become conscious. All the time below the swell there are little waves that are not conscious but can become so when the swell recedes, as it does in sleep. Fechner is uncertain, however, whether we are actually conscious of dreams when asleep or only become so later:

'So in the experience of a walk, the sunshine, green, bird-song appear as an unconscious accompaniment; one sees and hears nothing of all that, but feels something and will have quite a different train of thought when one reflects in a darkened room... Each appearance of things that we know in life, a house, a person, forms through association an amalgam with other images that remain in the unconscious. So the meaning of a house or a person is formed unconsciously, without which these things would appear to our eyes as mere blobs of colour... One can think that the dreams we have in the night are unconscious in the same sense as a word overheard when awake but distracted. Right afterwards while still awake we recollect the event and the word is consciously produced in the recollection. One can also think, and I hold this more likely, that we have already consciously experienced the dream in the night...'[48]

The Concept of Identification before Freud

Identification is central to Freud's social psychology and to most social psychology after him. Through personal identification the masses experience the enjoyments of the wealthy and powerful as their own. Curiously enough this idea, that now seems so obvious and everyday, is hard to trace earlier than Adam Smith. We come close in a passage in Descartes' correspondence with Elizabeth already cited: 'if we think of ourselves as part of some other (social) body, we participate also in those goods it holds in common'.[49] Descartes is however uncertain what part this plays in social life as a whole and falls back on the idea that prudence will ensure a well-ordered society.[50]

The place where the traditional political theory of Aristotle might have dealt with identification was in its analysis of demagogues and tyrants. It was well known that the demos often developed such adulation for demagogues that they were allowed to become tyrants. Aristotle, however, invariably puts this down to the ability of demagogues and tyrants to flatter the people. He advises tyrants not to indulge in 'pleasures of the sense' in public, lest they incur too much envy.[51] Aristotle thought an imposing and rather reclusive demeanour suited a tyrant. The people were to love the tyrant for his dignity rather than gain a vicarious experience of power.

Throughout the long discussions of the dangers of individualism during the seventeenth and eighteenth centuries we find little reference to the idea of personal identification with power. Morality, religion, republican spirit, community spirit are the chief means sought to oppose the rising egoism.

This was changed by the French revolution of 1789, which had one outcome that was quite unexpected by enlightenment thinkers: the rise of Napoleon and the adulation given him by the masses. Another aspect of the revolution - the bloodthirsty vengeance of the *sansculottes* - had been partially foreseen, but no one imagined the propertied classes would be rescued from this vengeance by a kind of republican king.

These events were perceived in various ways. To some radicals, particularly Fourier and his followers, the irrationality of the masses was to be removed by changes in the family and education.[52] For the radical right represented by Carlyle, Hegel and later Nietzsche, history required that the masses be given heroic leadership. It is in this second group that we find the first clear discussions of identification - in Hegel's *The Phenomenology of Spirit* (1807) and Nietzsche's *The Genealogy of Morals* (1887), the latter a work that greatly influenced Freud.[53,54]

What prevented the enlightenment from analysing so obvious a phenomenon as identification? The king was the chief object of mass adulation within an absolute monarchy.[55] The king, unlike a hero risen from the people like Napoleon, was not a figure the masses could identify with. They revered him. Such reverence was ascribed by the *philosophes* to the influence of priests in encouraging worship of the monarch.[56] The population was generally wildly enthusiastic about victories by the national army, but the road to top command posts was usually reserved for the nobility and gentry.[57] In the new society that emerged with Napoleon it was possible for anyone, at least in theory, to rise up in the army, politics or business. Identification now became a potent source of social cohesion that liberalism could not afford to ignore.

Adam Smith's discussion of this topic in *The Theory of Moral Sentiments* is a blend of the new theory of identification with the old reverence for monarchy. He is sensitive to the dangers of unfettered ambition and the identification that this brings with the rich and powerful. At the same time he reads this back onto the reverence for the monarchy experienced during the English Civil War.[58]

3. Before Heidegger and Sartre

Brentano (1838-1917)

Brentano, like Kant, sets out to rescue our idea of ourselves from the viewpoints of empiricism and materialism. He begins by contrasting physical and mental phenomena in his widely successful *Psychology from an Empirical Standpoint* (1874). Mental phenomena are distinguished by two characteristics: intentional in-existence and by being the object of inner perception.[59] In saying that mental events are the objects of inner perception Brentano is claiming mental events are all conscious. This is in opposition to those many thinkers from Aquinas and Leibniz to James Mill, Herbart, Beneke, Fechner, Wundt, Helmholtz and von Hartmann who say there are unconscious mental events.[60] Because that which is perceived in consciousness and that which perceives are 'fused' we avoid running into an infinite regress by having to continually assume that each perceiver of consciousness is himself perceived.[61]

Intentional (or mental) inexistence is a scholastic term that Brentano takes to mean that in a mental event the object of thought, judgement or emotion, is included in the mind, but does not actually exist in the mind.[62] While the term is rather barbaric, there is nothing odd about thinking this. When we think the idea 'an apple' there is something apple-like in our mind. Even more obviously if we make a judgement about an apple or we desire to eat a particular apple these apples have entered our mind in some way; though they don't exist in the mind - they exist in the world.

These three kinds of mental phenomena - ideas (sometimes, using a Herbartian term in an unHerbartian way Brentano calls these 'presentations'), judgements and emotions or wishes - are very important for Brentano. They comprise the three departments of the mind. By carefully examining the phenomena of consciousness we are driven to realise that it is these three that are basic, not the division of thought and appetite suggested by Aristotle, nor that made by 'most modern authors' into presentation, feeling and will.[63] Brentano says this latter has been 'dominant in psychology since Kant'.[64] This ought to be read 'after Kant'. Kant's division is primarily the Aristotelian and scholastic one between intellect (pure reason) and appetite-will (practical reason). Those 'intimations of the sublime' contained in the *Critique of Judgement* are more like the apex of a pyramid than an equal partner in a triumvirate.

The comparison with Herbart can also be misleading as for him it is the laws governing presentations that determine everything else - feeling and will are virtually epiphenomena in the Herbartian scheme.

Brentano has something different again in mind: every judgement, wish or emotion contains ideas.[65] There is nothing epiphenomenal about judgements, wishes or emotions. They are in effect fuller versions of ideas. Brentano's technical term for this 'containing' is 'referring'. Judgements and wishes both 'refer' to ideas as their objects.

To complete his evaluation of judgements and wishes Brentano examines what it is for judgements to be true and what it is for wishes to be 'correct' or good. For a judgement to be true in his earlier view it is only necessary that 'if it asserts of some object that is, *that* the object is, or if it asserts of some object that it is not, *that* the object is not'.[66] This is in effect scholastic realism pushed to an extreme degree. Aristotle is criticised for saying that true judgements merely correspond to things or states of affairs. In a true judgement the object of the judgement is in the mind and that makes the judgement true.[67]

At first sight this gives rise to the problem of accounting for mistakes. I may judge, in the twilight, 'There is a bull'. Further examination shows it was a cow. In his later writing Brentano answers this by saying that truth is correct judgement, the judgement of 'the person who judges about a thing in the way in which anyone whose judgements were *evident* would judge about the thing'.[68] An evident judgement is one about which everyone agrees.[69] The cow-bull in the twilight occupies a hazy area, but we can rescue it by saying that after a torch was shone on the bull anyone present could tell it was a cow. Everyone would agree that bulls rarely change into cows in the twinkling of an eye. So everyone will agree there is a high probability the animal was a cow. It is likely that Brentano would want to go further and say it was certainly a cow. He hoped that if we shone the light of clear thinking on human consciousness, this too could be a matter for general agreement.[70]

Just as the true came to be defined as that which was evident to everyone, so the good was defined as that which appeared correct to everyone. Rational creatures will inevitably agree on what this is.

'Our observations about the different cases of preference that are experienced as being correct have this important consequence. The sphere of the highest practical good is the whole area that is affected by our rational activities insofar as anything good can be brought about within it. Thus one must consider not only oneself, but also one's family, the city, the state, every living thing upon the earth, and one must consider not only the immediate present but also the distant future. All this follows from the principle of the summation of good. To further the good throughout this great whole so far as possible - this is clearly the correct end in life, and all our actions should be centred around it. It is one supreme imperative upon which all the others depend. It is thus a duty to give of oneself and even on occasion to sacrifice oneself. Any given good, whether in ourselves or in others, is to be loved in proportion to its value and it is to be loved equally wherever it may be found. Envy, jealousy, and malice are ruled out.'[71]

One of the results of Brentano's theory of truth and good was that he could retain Aquinas' proofs of the existence of God and Thomistic theology virtually unchanged.[72] These are matters that, for Brentano, are at least potentially evident and correct for everyone.

His hope was dashed by historical events. For centuries the view of Aristotle, backed by the authority of Aquinas, had appeared as evident to many. Just as certainly it became, during the eighteenth and nineteenth centuries, less and less evident. People had changed and when they looked into themselves they saw something different. The difficulty of continuing the analysis of consciousness along lines laid down by Aristotle was shown by the fate of Brentano's pupils. Those, like Husserl, Freud and Scheler, who abandoned the master's teaching found fame in the new century. Those, like Oscar Kraus, who adhered strictly to Brentano could not comprehend their own isolation.[73]

Husserl (1859-1938)

Husserl's philosophy reached its mature and widely influential form in his *Ideas: A General Introduction to Pure Phenomenology* (1913). This philosophy has often been characterised as a kind of modern Platonism.[74] This is true insofar as Husserl called himself an idealist.[75] He also recommended the philosopher to turn away from the everyday world towards the transcendental-phenomenological realm of Ideas that exists within us. This is however a Platonism in transition.

In *Ideas* Husserl begins by considering the 'natural standpoint' according to which there is a taken-for-granted world of everyday experience that everyone accepts. Science is a refinement of this everyday viewpoint. He then suggests that to achieve the viewpoint of transcendental phenomenology we must 'bracket' the world of everyday experience - 'disconnect' ourselves from it.[76]

The model for this bracketing is given by Descartes' method of doubt. Descartes had set out on his metaphysical quest by attempting to doubt everything in the 'natural standpoint' we take for granted, such as the existence of space and material bodies.

The Cartesian doubt carries right through to imagining, for the sake of argument, that the world does not exist. Descartes then searches around for something that cannot be doubted - our own existence - from which to build back the world of everyday experience. Husserl's method is not to negate the world or various aspects of the natural viewpoint, but rather to suspend this viewpoint. In effect we retain experience while suspending the natural viewpoint, thus looking at experience from a new transcendental-phenomenological viewpoint. So if we examine a tree from the Cartesian viewpoint we consider that the tree does not exist. Subjectively we adopt the attitude that the sight of the tree is 'just a sensation' or, which amounts to something similar, we think we might be dreaming. In Husserl's new viewpoint we 'bracket' all scientific knowledge about the tree and also all 'natural' understanding of the tree. This, Husserl claims, will reveal a new realm if carried out consistently with every kind of content. What is 'left over' will be 'transcendental consciousness'.[77]

The first thing we find about our experience is that it is always experience of something. In Husserl's terminology, experience is always intentional.[78] This term is taken over from Brentano. In the case of seeing a tree, we do not see sensations, we see the tree. We don't experience this as 'seeing shapes and colours', but as seeing a tree. Like Brentano, Husserl is a realist. We experience the world directly, not indirectly.

From the viewpoint of empirical psychology we might say that 'seeing the tree' is the end result of an unconscious identification of certain kinds of shapes and colours as indicating the presence of a tree. Husserl is, however, attempting to bracket out any such scientific considerations in favour of direct experience. Directly we experience 'a tree'. But what, disconnected from the scientific and natural viewpoints, does that mean?

The most general characteristic of transcendental-phenomenological discoveries is that they are eidetic, that is they concern the meaning of experiences. Husserl has the modern conviction that the scientific-natural viewpoint somehow obscures our view of the meaning of experience. In Brentano's Aristotelian-Thomistic philosophy meaning is given to experience by God. We discover God through the scientific-natural viewpoint. One of the proofs of God's existence is the scientific-natural principle that every effect needs a cause, thus leading us back to a first cause. Meaning is particularly to be found in the teleology of the world as revealed by the scientific-natural viewpoint, supplemented by revelation.

Husserl, on the contrary, suspects the scientific-natural viewpoint of imposing a certain kind of meaning upon the world that he is not entirely happy about. It may be very well as one viewpoint among many, but we must suspend this viewpoint to investigate the meaning of experiences more generally.

In considering the experience of a tree, this develops through distinct phases. In the immediate perception of the tree there is a 'presentation' of the tree.[79] What here holds good for perception is likewise true of memory, expectation and imagination. Each of these contains direct presentations of objects accompanied by a 'noematic meaning' which is different for each realm.[80] Thus a 'blossoming tree' perceived, remembered, expected and imagined has a different meaning in each case.

Next we consider attention, which Husserl calls the 'glance' of the Ego, playing over the various realms of perception, memory, expectation and imagination. Attention is a 'free essence' that carries along with it the various attitudes of the Ego, particularly those of being free or being conditioned.[81]

Layered on top of the presentation of objects within perception, memory, expectation and imagination we find the three 'higher spheres of consciousness', judgement, sentiment (feeling) and will.[82] Each of these in turn add their own modification of noematic meaning. Judgements, for instance, might be suppositions, questions or doubts. Such judgements can be applied to the realms of perception, memory, expectation and imagination: 'the noema of the presenting act becomes part of the judging act taken in its full concreteness'.[83]

In all the various types of presentations - memory, fancy, perception, anticipation and signs particularly - we find that repeated application of the modes of presentation leads to a complicated structure of levels within certain kinds of experience. There can be 'memories of memories' and 'signs of signs' as well as 'memories of signs' and so forth.[84]

We experience varying degrees of belief in the objects of consciousness. As compounded by the other complexities of consciousness this degree of belief is able to generate a kind of transcendental metaphysics of being. The compounds of degree of belief are called the 'modalities of being'.[85] Such modifications of being are particularly produced by the affirmation and negation of beliefs.[86]

Consciousness can also undertake the neutrality-modification, which is not a positive disbelief, but rather a suspension of all questions of belief or disbelief. Here Husserl seems to be describing something close to the consciousness of drifting through a meaningless existence:

'An arbitrary doing of some kind is everywhere included in the meaning indicated, whereas there should be no hint of this in the meaning we are seeking to fix. We therefore set it aside. The result of doing this has certainly a distinctive content, which, apart from the fact that it 'springs from' the doing (which would of course *also* be a phenomenological datum), can be considered in itself, in detachment from all such arbitrariness as something both possible and actual within the sphere of experience. Let us then exclude all volitional elements from the 'leaving postponed', and also avoid interpreting it in the sense of what is doubtful or hypothetical, and there remains a certain having 'postponed' something, or, better still, a 'having let it stand', where we have not in mind anything that has been 'really' let stand. The positing characteristic has become powerless. The belief is no longer seriously a belief, the presumption not seriously a presumption, the denying not seriously a denying. It is *'neutralized'* belief, presumption, denial, and the like, and their correlates repeat those of the unmodified experiences though in a radically modified way: the simply being, the being possible, probable, questionable, likewise the non-being, and all that has been previously negated or affirmed - this is all consciously there, but not in the 'real' way, only as 'merely thought', as 'mere idea'.'[87]

It is characteristic of the neutrality-modification that while for other types of presentation we can experience reflexion - as in forming 'memories of memories' - in the neutrality-modification there can be no repetition.[88] There is no 'neutralising of neutralising'. This accounts for the peculiar flatness of neutralised experience.

Consciousness based on belief or disbelief is termed 'positional', that based on indifference to belief 'natural'. These two types of consciousness are implicitly contained in every act of consciousness.[89]

Next follows a brief but important acknowledgement that there are both 'acts of consciousness' and 'acts in the broader sense', which are the actions of the body. The distinction between positional and neutral attitudes applies to acts in the broader sense as well as to acts of consciousness. Beyond this, however, little attention is given to bodily action.

From presentation we can proceed in two directions. The first is that of 'noetic syntheses', that is of a purely intellectual logical linking of experience. The second leads to 'secondary positings', which are complications of our belief or disbelief in given propositions or theses. This process produces a kind of synthesis of belief that contains both feeling and will. Feeling and will are to be shown as analogous to belief. Yet this belief is not of a purely intellectual type.[90] There is a kind of 'logic of experience', called the logic of positing, that applies to intellect, feeling and will:

'Therein are grounded in the last resort those analogies which have at all times been felt to hold between general logic, general theory of value and ethics...'[91]

Earlier we were introduced to the notion of belief in an intellectual idea. Now Husserl extends this to belief (or disbelief) in feeling and willing. The 'positing' of each experience means a kind of belief or disbelief in it. Thus when consciousness is neutralised it is not only belief in intellectual ideas that is neutralised, but belief in feelings and decisions as well.

The actual elaboration of the 'syntactic forms' of consciousness is suggested by an example of the universal 'logic of positing'. This makes an analogy between pure logic and the logic of feeling. Pure logic connects its theses or propositions by 'and', 'or', 'if', 'because', 'thus'. A mother looking at her children feels not just love for one child and not just love for her whole flock. She feels love for 'Jimmy and Johnny and Jane'. The proposition 'Here is Jimmy and Johnny and Jane' contains within itself the syntax of the mother's love for her children.[92]

In the fourth and final part of *Ideas* Husserl provides a further elaboration of the logic of positing. He is evidently conscious that such a 'syntax of positing' might seem like a 'syntax of experience' and thus be merely a repetition of Kant's a priori forms of experience. Husserl is careful to distinguish our scientific-natural ideas from those of transcendental phenomenology. In scientific-natural thinking we know only appearances, as Kant had said. But in transcendental phenomenology we intuit 'a connexion of endless processes of continuous appearing, absolutely fixed in its essential type'.[93]

In dissociating himself from both science and neutralisation by constructing a phenomenology of pure essences, Husserl undertakes this task in a very different manner from Bergson. In Bergson's philosophy intuition will always reveal the new and mysterious that is emerging through creative evolution.[94] Husserl was, by contrast, a mathematician by training and a logician by vocation. His world of essences is timeless and secured from change. Yet his logic is not solely that of mathematics. He continues to make considerable use of Aquinas' potentiality-act metaphysics for describing the end-directedness of processes within both history and consciousness.[95]

In *Cartesian Meditations* Husserl extends his analysis to a level not reached in the first volume of *Ideas*, though also treated in the posthumously published second volume. This is the level of intersubjectivity. He asks how we can know that we experience things, which present themselves to us directly, in the same way as other people experience them. The answer, quite consistently, is that we experience the presentations of others directly. When we see someone looking at something we experience this 'as if I were standing over there, where the other's body is'.[96] We can object: the person could experience them as experiencing a house when looking at a tree. Here Husserl summons the shade of Leibniz to his aid. We live in a community of monads. There is, between our Ego and the Ego of the other person, a harmony that makes us both see the object as a tree.

This harmony is not quite the pre-established harmony of Leibniz. It appears rather that seeing into the other person's mind presupposes 'perception proper', that is a direct sight (or at least some direct and independent knowledge) that what the other person is looking at is a tree. That is also the viewpoint of common sense.

The problem of intersubjectivity is clearly of considerable importance for phenomenological investigation. In the case of the tree we may share our experience fairly directly with someone else. But in areas of experience more strongly influenced by culture there are problems involved in understanding 'alien' worlds. This is a valid sphere for phenomenological research.[97]

In Husserl's lifetime his own attempts to approach these problems remained unpublished and had little direct influence. After his death his notion of the 'lifeworld' became known through the writings of Landgrebe, Merleau-Ponty and Schutz.[98] In 1954 a complete German edition of *The Crisis of the European Sciences and Transcendental Phenomenology* appeared.[99] Previously only two sections of this had been published in the Belgrade journal *Philosophia*.

Here the term 'lifeworld' is used to explain the 'forgotten foundations of the meaning of the natural sciences'.[100] While *Crisis* concentrates explicitly on the history of European philosophy and psychology since Galileo we are to understand that the inner meaning of the transformations of these disciplines is a transformation of the lifeworld of entire peoples.

The first period dealt with, between Galileo and Kant, shows a sharp division between the sciences of physical objectivity, particularly physics, and transcendental subjectivity. With their mathematical methods, Galileo and the physicists strove for a formal mathematical description of the world. Geometry, the chief mathematical method of this new science, had begun as ideal concepts inherited from the ancients, but was soon reduced to a mere technique.[101] It was this emptying out of noematic meaning from mathematics and its conversion into a mere technique that emptied the objective, physical world of meaning: 'We take for real Being, what is a method ...'.[102]

For the transcendental subjectivist 'the meaning of the Being of the given lifeworld is a subjective idea, it is the achievement of coming to know life and of life prior to knowledge'.[103] Descartes is the paradigm for this opposition between the meaningless world of nature and the inner meaning of subjectivity. Berkeley and Hume attacked the objectivity of the world because they found it intolerable in the form it had taken.

Kant correctly saw the need to overcome the dualism between the meaningless objective and the meaningful subjective, but he was unsuccessful. However he paved the way for phenomenology by posing the problem and by stressing the difference between 'flat life' and 'profound life'. This insight, however, was not properly integrated into his system.[104] This was left to Husserl's own philosophy, with its emphasis on noematic meaning.

Other posthumous publications of Husserl include the second and third volumes of *Ideas* in 1952 and three volumes titled *On the Phenomenology of Intersubjectivity* in 1973.[105] None of these volumes has so far had the impact of *Crisis*.

Husserl's influence, like that of Freud, has been so widespread that any full sampling of it would be impractical. Apart from his effect on the tradition of existential phenomenology stemming from Heidegger, Husserlian influence has been felt in sociology, particularly in America, where the Husserlian antipathy to the direction of modern science as well as the religious possibilities inherent in his metaphysics have won him many disciples. This influence in America was originally transmitted through the writings and teaching of Husserl's pupil Alfred Schutz. These writings are highly generalised and partly philosophical. The application of his teaching to the more concrete problems of sociology is particularly well illustrated by the writings of Berger.[106]

Feuerbach (1804-72)

While both Feuerbach and Marx lived considerably earlier than Husserl I have dealt with them after him as their influence on conceptions of human nature was much delayed. Feuerbach was forgotten during the second half of the nineteenth century while Marx's manuscripts dealing with his early view of human nature were not generally available in European languages until the 1940's.

Feuerbach studied at the universities of Heidelberg (1824) and Berlin (1825-6). At the latter he came under the influence of Hegel. Shortly he obtained a post as *Privatdozent* at Erlangen but ruined his career with the publication of an attack on the idea of personal immortality. In 1841 he published *The Essence of Christianity* which established him as a leader among the liberal left-Hegelians, including at that time Marx and Engels.[107] His period of popularity lasted only until the revolutions of 1848, when the defeat of liberalism made radical critics of Christianity unpopular.

The Essence of Christianity states its main thesis as follows: 'The religious object of adoration is nothing but the objectified nature of him who adores.'[108] God is nothing more than a projection of human nature onto an imaginary outside being. This nature is also clearly defined: 'To a complete man belong the power of thought, the power of will, and the power of the heart. Intellect, love and will are perfections, the perfections of the human being, nay more, they are the absolute and ultimate perfections of being: the very purpose of human existence.'[109] From these human powers we project the attributes of perfect knowledge, love and will onto the deity.

The two theses so far considered are easily understood. *The Essence of Christianity* however begins with a third proposition that is by no means as transparent: 'What distinguishes man from the brutes is the awareness of a distinctive human nature transcending individuality... Consciousness in the strictest sense is present only in a being to whom his species, his essential nature, is an object of thought.'[110] Thus in objectifying themselves in activity and religious speculation human beings do not objectify themselves as individuals. They do not labour for or worship the greater glory of themselves as individuals but the greater glory of the human race.

It is easy to see how this might be true of religion, but Feuerbach asserts it also for the activity of individuals: 'Man is nothing without some 'objective'. The great models of humanity, such men as reveal to us the essence of man, have attested the truth of this proposition with their lives. They had only one dominant passion - the realisation of the aim which was the essential object of their activity.'[111]

Historical change does not play a very large role in *The Essence of Christianity*. The main historical problem pinpointed is the Christian separation of believers from unbelievers. This kind of faith, Feuerbach thinks, stands in the way of the realisation of universal human love because believers are enjoined to love other believers and to hate unbelievers. From the materialist standpoint Marx and Engels were later to adopt this clearly marks Feuerbach out as an idealist who directs his criticism at the ideas of Christians rather than at the living conditions of the population.

While Feuerbach published a number of other interesting later works these did not have the influence of *The Essence of Christianity* and can be passed over here.[112]

Marx (1818-83)

Marx (1818 - 1883) and Engels (1820 - 1895) were both strongly influenced by Feuerbach in the 1840s. Both the *Economic and Philosophical Manuscripts of 1844* of Marx and the jointly written *German Ideology* of 1846 contain polemics against Feuerbach aimed at establishing a new conception of human nature and its relation to social conditions.

The critique directed at Feuerbach is however only aimed at certain aspects of his work, mainly its abstraction and its emphasis upon philosophy and religion as opposed to the material conditions of life in producing the estrangement of human beings from their species being. In *Economic and Philosophical Manuscripts* Marx uses the two kinds of objectification discussed by Feuerbach - activity and religion - but reverses their significance. It is the frustration of the desire for objectification through activity - now described more specifically by the economic category of labour - that produces other estrangements. In describing the human urge to self-objectification through labour Marx still uses very Feuerbachian terms: 'The object of labour is, therefore, the *objectification of man's species life*: for he duplicates himself not only, as in consciousness, intellectually, but also actively, in reality, and therefore he contemplates himself in a world that he has created. In tearing away from man the object of his production, therefore, estranged labour tears from him his *species life*, his real objectivity as a member of the species and transforms his advantage over animals into the disadvantage that his inorganic body, nature, is taken away from him.'[113]

The estrangement of man from man is held to be a consequence of the estrangement of labour: 'Hence within the relationship of estranged labour each man views the other in accordance with the standard and the relationship in which he finds himself as a worker.'[114]

Intellect objectifies itself in labour. Our contemplation of other individuals objectifying themselves produces our love of others. The third element of the Feuerbachian scheme of human nature is will. Marx brings this in in a rather forced way by saying that 'in degrading spontaneous, free, activity, to a means, estranged labour makes man's species life a means to his physical existence.'[115] This seems to assume that at some point human beings were in a Utopian state of deciding their form of labour by free will, rather than being compelled by circumstances to work to produce food and shelter.

This kind of criticism is partly anticipated by Marx himself later in the *Manuscripts* in a polemic against Hegel. Here he discusses natural human needs and instincts: 'That is to say, the *objects* of his instincts exist outside him, as *objects* independent of him; yet these objects are objects that he needs - essential objects, indispensable to the manifestation and confirmation of his essential powers.'[116] What remains unclear here is whether such objects are primarily necessary for the satisfaction of natural needs like hunger and warmth or for the expression of the powers of making and understanding. It appears that Marx really means both, for he goes on to say that 'man is not merely a natural being: he is a *human* natural being. That is to say he is a being for himself. Therefore he is a *species being*, and has to confirm and manifest himself as such both in his being and his knowing.'[117]

Human nature as revealed in the passage on Hegel therefore has two aspects: the animal nature that requires the satisfaction of natural needs and the human nature that requires the objectification of species being. This picture is really an adaptation of parts of the scholastic and empiricist views, with the addition of an emphasis on the realisation of human potentialities through labour rather than, as in scholasticism, intellect.

Marx is very conscious in the *Manuscripts* that human nature has been radically altered by the passage of history. 'Under private property .... every person speculates on creating a new need in another, so as to drive him to a fresh sacrifice, to place him in a new dependence and to seduce him into a new mode of *gratification* and therefore economic ruin.'[118] These new, artificial needs are fantasies, caprices and whims.

If natural needs are perverted to become whims, so the ability of the individual is perverted by the division of labour. According to Say this is 'a skilful deployment of human powers for social wealth; but it reduces the *ability of each person* taken *individually.*'[119]

In 1845 Marx wrote, in exile in Brussels, a series of theses on Feuerbach that were later edited by Engels and published in 1888 as an appendix to 'Ludwig Feuerbach and the End of Classical German Philosophy'. As neither *The German Ideology* nor the *1844 Manuscripts* were published until the collected works of Marx and Engels began to be published in 1924 the theses on Feuerbach became, at a time when Marxism was becoming an influential doctrine through the Second Socialist International, the accepted view of Marx's views on human nature. This was in some ways unfortunate as one of the theses claimed that 'the essence of man is no abstraction inherent in each single individual. In its reality it is the ensemble of the social relations.' This might imply that the concept of human nature had no place in Marxism. The context makes it certain however that what was intended was an attack on Feuerbach's abstract way of looking at the realisation of human nature in society.[120] In any event if we were to abolish the idea of human nature and human needs it would be hard to mount any effective criticism of capitalist or any other kind of society. Such critique usually rests on the claim that in some way the society does not meet human needs, a view Marx clearly took of capitalist society.

The possibilities for social psychology raised by Marx are twofold. If we look at natural human needs or instincts we can study their transformation and dynamics as in Nietzsche and Freud. If we look at species being we can investigate our attempts to objectify ourselves in labour. This is the approach Sartre takes. His development of it through the dialectic of being and nothingness is described below. We might also have expected Fromm to develop a metaphysics of species being based on caring, but he is content in *Marx's Concept of Man* to expound Marx's own thought in the manuscripts of 1844 with little elaboration. The place we find such elaboration in Fromm's work, though it is not explicitly related to the 1844 manuscripts, is in *Escape from Freedom*. There Fromm has already argued that the disruption of frameworks of orientation and devotion by scientific enlightenment and individualism has produced, among other results, the thirst for authority.

Expositions of the Young Marx of the 1844 manuscripts became popular after the second world war.[121] Here it was sometimes argued that the Young Marx had sided with liberty and individual values against the authoritarianism and historical determinism of the Marx revealed in *Capital*. On the other side of the fence Althusser claimed that Marx's sixth thesis on Feuerbach marked his earlier work, particularly the 1844 manuscripts, as 'essentialist' and non-Marxist. In this Althusser was probably right insofar as the 1844 manuscripts do present a highly abstract picture of human nature, divorced from concrete historical circumstances. However, Althusser himself felt obliged to lean on Lacan's view of human nature in his own remarks about social psychology, though these are themselves excessively schematic and abstract.

Further Reading

The Unconscious Before Nietzsche and Freud

O. Andersson, *Studies in the Prehistory of Psychoanalysis*, Smenska Bokforlaget, Stockholm, 1962.
P. Bakan, *Sigmund Freud and the Jewish Mystical Tradition*, Van Nostrand, Princeton, 1958.
S.D. Cox, *The Stranger Within Thee, Concepts of Self in Late Eighteenth Century Literature*, Uni. of Pittsburgh Press, Pittsburgh, 1980.
J. Ehrenwald, *Psychotherapy: Myth and Method*, Gune and Stratton, New York, 1966.
H.F. Ellenberger, *The Discovery of the Unconscious*, Allen Lane, London, 1970.
V. Thweatt, *La Rochefoucauld and the Seventeenth Century Concept of the Self*, Droz, Genève, 1980.
I. Veith, *Hysteria: The History of a Disease*, Uni. of Chicago Press, Chicago, 1965.
L.L. Whyte, *The Unconscious before Freud*, Tavistock, London, 1962.

Husserl

T. de Boer, *The Development of Husserl's Thought*, Nijhoff, The Hague, 1978.
M. Farber, *The Foundation of Phenomenology*, State University of New York Press, Albany, 1967, 3rd ed.
M. Farber, *The Aims of Phenomenology*, Harper and Row, New York, 1966.
J.J. Kockelmans, *Edmund Husserl's Phenomenological Psychology*, Duquesne Uni. Press, Pittsburgh, 1967.
J.R. Mensch, *The Question of Being in Husserl's Logical Investigations*, Nijhoff, The Hague, 1981.
H. Spiegelberg, *The Phenomenological Movement*, Nijhoff, The Hague, 1965, Vol. 1, Chap. 3.
E.P. Welch, *The Philosophy of Edmund Husserl*, Columbia University Press, New York, 1941.

Bergson

D.J. Herman, *The Philosophy of Henri Bergson*, Uni. Press of America, Washington, 1980.
A.E. Pilkington, *Bergson and his Influence: a Reassessment*, CUP, Cambridge, 1976.

Brentano

A.C. Rancurello, *A Study of Franz Bentano*, Academic Press, New York, 1968.
J. Srzednicki, *Franz Brentano's Analysis 'of Truth*, Nijhoff, The Hague, 1965.

Chapter 5 :
Nietzsche and Jaspers

Main Assumptions

The social condition most responsible for the emergence of Nietzsche's philosophy was the decline of Christianity, which Nietzsche believed had become outmoded and needed to be replaced by a more human-centered philosophy.

The main assumptions of his philosophy are as follows: 1a. He considered both socialisation and redemption; 1b. He admires change and fascination most, though the virtue of stability appears as an undercurrent in both his doctrines of socialisation and of redemption; 1c. He considers chiefly experienced freedom, though in his doctrine of the eternal recurrence the abstract machine-like determinism of the universe comes to the fore; 1d. Nietzsche tends to practice a form of deep interpretation in relation to the inner meaning of Christianity and other ideologies but otherwise he avoids it; 1e. There is an implicit belief in the tendency towards completion of the personality, at least among the strong, though not much of an explicit nature is said; 2. We can become conscious of instincts and the unconscious; 3a. Power and aggression are the strongest human motives, at least when we are not dominated by hunger and thirst; 3b. The repression of power and aggression are most important in the production of culture; 3c. Not much is said about how motives work, but power and aggression are sometimes seen as continuing urges, sometimes as providing amusement and entertainment; 3d. Defence mechanisms are analysed chiefly in relation to the production of ideologies like Christianity and socialism which cloak desire for revenge in the language of brotherhood and love; 4. The unconscious becomes directly conscious once we rid ourselves of Christianity and other moralising tendencies; 5. Nietzsche does not focus much on symbol interpretation, but when he does symbols reflect attitudes to instincts, particularly the will to power; 6. Christianity and other forms of decadent culture encourage the maximising of pleasure; heroic and tragic cultures emphasise triumph through sacrifice; 7. We learn about human nature by sweeping aside the mystifications of Christianity and moralism.

Nietzsche (1844-1900)

Appointed as a full professor of classical philology at the university of Basel at the age of 25, Nietzsche seemed destined for an outstanding career as a philologist. But like Schopenhauer, whom Nietzsche greatly admired in his youth, he allowed his interest in social theory and philosophy to blight his career. His first book, *The Birth of Tragedy* (1872), was less scandalous than later works, but already strays away from philology in the strict sense towards an application of Schopenhauer's philosophy to the problems of Greek tragedy.[1] Nietzsche later repudiated the argument of the book in his preface of 1886. Between these two dates he had turned traditional philosophy upside down and the traditional view of human nature and its possibilities along with it.

The Birth of Tragedy is based on the opposition the author detects in Greek culture between the Dionysian and Apollonian tendencies. Schopenhauer had considered the spatial art of sculpture as one of the best examples of beauty in art. In *The World as Will and Representation* he takes the Apollo Belvedere as a symbol for the contemplative power both of human beings and of sculpture.[2] In his discussion of the sublime he discusses chiefly the effects of nature upon our sensibilities. In the last paragraph of the discussion, however, he says that our own will may threaten us as may the wills of others, as when a man desires a woman or people hate us. The sublime character is one who is able to rise above such excitements of the will and view them with philosophical detachment.

Nietzsche's conception of the Apollonian is almost a direct translation of Schopenhauer's experience of the beautiful. The Dionysian is said by Nietzsche to be based on Schopenhauer's discussion of terror. In his discussion of tragedy Schopenhauer says that the highest poetical achievement is the description of the terrible side of life. By showing us the downfall of characters through character the tragic dramatist encourages us to adopt the outlook of the sublime in overcoming our inevitable defects through contemplation.

Nietzsche's conception of the Dionysian is just that unbridled licence we find in certain kinds of 'weak' character. Like Schopenhauer he thinks one of the achievements of Greek tragedy was to have overcome this weakness through depiction. At the same time he has rather more admiration for this licence than this might imply. In the second volume of additions to the books of the first edition of *The World as Will* Schopenhauer had discussed intoxication as a return to a state of pure will in which the 'bridle' the intellect puts upon the will is released.[3] Intoxication is said by Nietzsche to be the chief characteristic of the Dionysian state and to bring on a collapse of the principle of individuation and a return to 'the blissful ecstasy that wells from the innermost depths of man'.[4]

Schopenhauer's discussion of intoxication, significantly, had come in his additions to Book 2. *The World as Will and Representation* is structured as a ladder to salvation and the struggle of art and philosophy to subdue the passions and perfect the character appear in Books 3 and 4. Intoxication is low on this ladder. When Schopenhauer discusses Bacchanalian orgies in Book 4, it is as follows: 'The wisest of all mythologies, the Indian, expresses this by giving to the very god who symbolizes destruction and death (just as Brahma, the most sinful and lowest god of the Trimurti, symbolizes generation, origination, and Vishnu preservation), by giving, I say, to Shiva as an attribute not only the necklace of skulls, but also the lingam, that symbol of generation which appears as the counterpart of death. In this way it is intimated that generation and death are essential correlatives which reciprocally neutralize and eliminate each other. It was precisely the same sentiment that prompted the Greeks and Romans to adorn the costly sarcophagi, just as we still see them, with feasts, dances, marriages, hunts, fights between wild beasts, bacchanalia, that is with presentations of life's most powerful urge. This they present to us not only through such diversions and merriments, but even in sensual groups, to the point of showing us the sexual intercourse between satyrs and goats. The object was obviously to indicate with the greatest emphasis from the death of the mourned individual the immortal life of nature, and thus to intimate, although without abstract knowledge, that the whole of nature is the phenomenon, and also the fulfilment, of the will-to-live.'[5]

The depiction of orgies is a reminder in death that life goes on and a cause for philosophical reflection. This attitude is far from that sympathy with real orgies felt by Nietzsche, who has already travelled a considerable distance from Schopenhauer.

In turning to discuss drama itself Nietzsche reminds us that the Dionysian attitude to creation is stirring again in Europe in the poetry of Schiller - and, he might have added, in the life of Byron. This, he tells us, long after the Dionysian cults have been reduced to those vestiges of popular frenzy found in folk songs.[6] Schopenhauer's discussions of music, we learn, are the nearest he came to an understanding of the nature of the Dionysian urge, which is a revelation of will.[7]

The essence of Dionysian creation is that the poet's images are images of himself.[8] Dionysian poetry is lyric poetry, originally the unity of lyrics and music in song. Lyric poetry, from Sappho to Wordsworth, is, as Nietzsche says, an art of self-absorbtion. We may wonder if folksongs can all play this role too, but some of these songs would fall into the class of epic and narrative poetry, which Nietzsche assigns to the Apollonian mode.

In an involved discussion of the origins and staging of Greek tragedies Nietzsche argues that the chorus, situated to see part of the audience, incites the audience to Dionysian participation with their words and action. The dialogue and actors take the part of the Apollonian. The chorus tells us the action of the story, while the dialogue distances us from this action. Sometimes, as in Aeschylus' *Prometheus*, this commentary takes the attitude of the artist, sometimes, as in Sophocles' *Oedipus*, that of the holy man. At this point Nietzsche turns away from sympathy with the devil Dionysus. According to Greek tradition, the earliest tragedy had for its subject the sufferings of Dionysus. Prometheus, Oedipus and other heroes of tragic drama are only masks of the original Dionysus, who was condemned to suffer the pain of individuation.[9] At this point Nietzsche is quite ambiguous about who redeems tragedy. At some points it is said to be Dionysus, but the logic of much of the later discussion makes it seem that Dionysus has thrown himself into the cycle of suffering that follows desire and it is Apollo who rescues him from this.

Not content with his bold analysis of the birth of tragedy, Nietzsche is also much concerned by its death. From the tragic heroes of Sophocles and Aeschylus drama degenerates into the New Comedy of Aristophanes in which the characters are everyday folk, typified by Graeculus, the good-naturedly cunning house slave. We pass from 'seriousness and terror' to 'satisfaction with easy enjoyment', from extraordinary natures to the ordinary, unimportant transactions of ordinary natures. From tragedy in which triumph is by heroic efforts of will we move to comedy in which triumph is by low cunning.[10]

This admiration for the everyday does not come simply from the public, from the demands of the demos. It was infiltrated into drama by Euripides, who acted under the influence of a rationalism whose chief exponent was Socrates. The motto of this rationalism is: 'To be beautiful everything must be intelligible.' The obscurity and inconsistency of classic tragedy, which constituted the true source of its power, were swept away by the energetic broom of rational criticism and the demand for clarity. There arose the illusion that 'thought, using the thread of logic, can penetrate the deepest abysses of being, and that thought is capable not only of knowing being but even of correcting it.'[11]

Schopenhauer had sought the route to the Ideas of Platonic rationalism through art. Nietzsche is now preparing to cut this link with the past and to announce a new philosophy: redemption by getting in touch with the instincts and then overcoming them. Yet traces of Schopenhauer linger everywhere. The rationalist, Alexandrian, culture requires a class of slaves to sustain its optimism, but through its optimistic view of life it denies the need for slaves, thus preparing its own downfall in the vengeance of the slaves, who have come to believe its Utopian vision of happiness for all. Optimism, Schopenhauer had said, is a truly wicked philosophy. It is the optimism of the rationalist and scientific view of the world that brings about its own downfall. Repression, even more strongly than in Schopenhauer, is, in rationalist culture, the repression of pessimism.

The preface of 1886 added to *The Birth of Tragedy* explains how Nietzsche's thought altered in the intervening years. His early work dealt with life through the perspective of art. This is now seen as a useful gateway through which to pass on to the questions of life itself, to 'the moral interpretation and significance of existence'.[12] Yet this new moral insight is 'antimoral', and 'a pessimism 'beyond good and evil''.[13] Life is 'something essentially amoral'. Christianity involves 'condemnations of the passions, fear of beauty and sensuality'; 'life is based on semblance, art, deception, points of view, and the necessity of perspectives and error'.[14] Now Nietzsche brings clearly into the open his conflict with Schopenhauer, who says that the tragic spirit 'leads to resignation'. Nietzsche feels that in those days he was already thoroughly opposed to resignation, ready for life and the gay science. He also unwisely placed his hopes in the German spirit, which issued in reality only in Bismark and 'founding a Reich, to a leveling mediocrity, democracy, and 'modern' ideas.'[15]

The slogans of Nietzsche's later period are well known. God is dead, we must take back life and art from a failing Christianity, overcome man and proclaim the transvaluation of values.[16] Central to this later period is Nietzsche's development of the idea of the will to power. As with so many other aspects of his philosophy, what he emphasises here differs from occasion to occasion. Two relatively distinct views of the will be power can be distinguished. The concept first takes centre stage in *Thus Spake Zarathustra* (1883-92), where it is said that the fundamental human quest is for the freedom to create. The will to power is the search for the independence to make this possible.[17]

In Nietzsche's later notes, published posthumously as *The Will to Power* (1901), he sometimes takes a different tack. Here it is argued that the will to power is actually an instinct.[18] Furthermore, all animal drives are an outgrowth of an original form of the will to power.[19]

The conflict between these two views of the will to power is mirrored in two other aspects of Nietzsche's thinking on evolution and on mastering the passions. At times evolution is denounced as a fraud and it is only the achievements of great individuals that are to count.[20] At others, the superman is claimed to herald the next step in evolution.[21] At times Nietzsche talks about overcoming the passions in the sense of escaping from their tyranny; at others he talks about harnessing them in the service of the will to power.[22]

In a more consistent thinker, or at least in one who lived long enough to synthesise the disparate strands of their thinking, we could amalgamate these three oppositions into two fundamentally opposed views of the will to power. In one, evolution is bunk, the creativity of the great individual what counts and the human quest is to create. In the other, evolution is pressing forward in the service of all-encompassing forces, great individuals are the cutting edge of history and their fundamental urge is to dominate. On the issue of whether the great creator is a heroic sufferer or a 'gay monster', Nietzsche is similarly inconsistent.[23] His philosophy is a treasure trove of disparate insights, rather than a consistent argument. In view of this, having introduced some basic conceptions of his later philosophy of human nature, it will simplify matters to outline in detail only one of his later books on the subject: *The Genealogy of Morals* (1887).

For the first essay of the book he discusses aristocratic and slave morality. The etymological derivation of the word 'good' in a number of languages is said to be from the word for 'noble' or 'aristocratic'. In aristocratic morality the natural superiority of strong natures finds expression in the making of values. In slave morality the resentment of slaves and inferior classes itself gives birth to values, among which are vengefulness, silence, forgetting, waiting and cleverness. If the noble considers inferior classes 'bad', this is the casual ignorance of contempt. The man of resentment considers the nobility as 'evil' and from suppressed envy manufactures a venomous hatred more destructive than the contempt of the nobility. This breeds not only hatred of outstanding deeds or creations but also the resignation of the philosopher, who ventures to think 'it would be good if we did nothing for which we are not strong enough.'[24] Weakness is called merit, lowliness humility, subjection obedience, cowardice patience. Aquinas, 'the great teacher and saint' says 'The blessed in the kingdom of heaven will witness the punishments of the damned, so that their bliss may be more delightful.'[25] A passage in which Tertullian lasciviously expands on the torments of kings, governors, philosophers, poets, play actors and others at the day of judgement is also used.

The second essay of the book is on guilt and bad conscience. We have, Nietzsche says, a positive need to forget. This enables us to shut ourselves away from the world to gain that quietness necessary for regulation, foresight and premeditation.[26]

Our memory, particularly for contracts and promises, is a suppression of this forgetting, a forcing ourselves to remember.

Now while this in some ways reminds us of psychoanalysis, it is at bottom a different concept from Freudian repression, with which it has sometimes been compared.[27] In Freudian repression experiences are erased from consciousness. Nietzsche's forgetting is not described as permanent. It is more like absent-mindedness and daydreaming. Promises make human beings, naturally prone to these things, into creatures who can stick to timetables and schedules, who are in the right place at the right time. To persuade them to do this has required the most draconian forms of punishment and ascetic procedures. The Germans, to acquire 'trust, seriousness, lack of taste and matter-of-factness' were obliged to resort to stoning, breaking on the wheel, piercing with stakes, trampling by horses, boiling in oil, flaying alive and cutting off strips of flesh.[28] An equivalence was made, particularly in the case of those who failed to pay monetary debts, between injury to the creditor and pain; from this same relation of the debt arose the notion of a deliberate crime committed with intention, that is to say with a deliberate violation of a promise. Out of this sphere of legal obligations arose the conscience, the sense of honour that impels people to keep their promises.

The real force of the conscience is disguised and penned up sadism. The creditor extracts a recompense from the debtor in the pleasurable experience of inflicting pain. In so doing the creditor experiences a foretaste of the 'right of the masters' to despise and mistreat inferiors, a foretaste of rising in the world. In identifying with social superiority we identify with sadism. The demand for just punishment is the demand of the sadist.

The disguised sadism of conscience is however no substitute for the real thing. The open cruelties of barbaric times were one thing that made the people of those days more cheerful and lively. Christians and pagans alike envisaged gods who found entertainment in suffering, but this could never repay the loss of open, personal brutality.

Out of the relation between debtor and creditor emerged the idea of a social contract, of human beings who have agreed with the community to abide by law in return for shelter and protection. In punishment the community exhibits the same vengefulness witnessed in war. As the community grows in strength and cohesion, however, the threat posed to its existence by lawbreakers lessens and vengefulness weakens.

In our modern sentiments towards punishment we find embalmed this whole history of attitudes and changes, including the most primitive feelings of revenge. These feelings and uses 'overdetermine' our attitudes to punishment, a usage taken over by Freud to describe how a single act or dream can fulfil several motives. Behind them all lies the instinct to aggression that not only turns outwards against wrongdoers, but now, denied open expression, is diverted inwards against the self. The modern individual suffers from a bad conscience and a tendency to self-punishment because they seek to satisfy their sadistic impulses upon themselves. This race of masochists has found in religion the perfect means to systematise and sanction its love of self-inflicted pain. God becomes the ultimate device for self-torture.

The third essay, on the meaning of ascetic ideals, begins with a beguiling catalogue of the delights of self-inflicted pain: for philosophers and scholars it can mean a precondition of higher spirituality, for women 'a touch of *morbidezza* in fair flesh', for the masses a weapon against slow pain and boredom, for priests their best instrument of power. How to explain the manifold forms of this perversion, if we are to call it that?

Schopenhauer thought himself a great life-denier, yet he was also a great hater; that was the secret of his underlying love of life. Instead of turning his hatred in upon himself he shone it outwards, against Hegel, women, sensuality, the will-to-live.[29] He loved spitting out 'black-green words' against his enemies and targets and that kept him healthy and happy. Schopenhauer, as his readers have long suspected, enjoyed his pessimism too much to be truly pessimistic.

The ideal of the ascetic priest, to which Schopenhauer aspired, is a healthy response to the unhealthy sickness contained in the festering of the bad conscience among the many. While lesser natures are paralysed, numbed by the power of self-directed aggression, ascetic priests and philosophers actually feed on asceticism, turn their fury outwards and live.

The sickness of the modern majority flows into *ressentiment*. They too turn hatred outwards, but onto the 'well-constituted and victorious'.[30] Their bile is transformed into both the pity of the do-gooder and the revenge of the anti-semite. The only doctor immediately available for their sickness is the ascetic priest, who understands their suffering and pessimism and also knows how to overcome it. The ascetic priest 'alters the direction of *ressentiment*' by telling the sick sheep, falsely as it happens, 'You alone are to blame for yourself.'[31] This advice leads into a cul-de-sac. It provides consolations, both of Christianity and philosophy, but no genuine cure. In another form it offers a regime of ceaseless mechanical activity to drive suffering from consciousness in a busy, punctilious, well-ordered life. In yet another it enjoins good works as a means of gratifying the striving for superiority. This goodwill provides the cement with which the priest glues together congregations. In orgies of emotion the priest also blasts away displeasure, gloom and depression in a flood of anger, fear, voluptuousness, revenge, hope, triumph, despair or cruelty. He lets loose 'the whole pack of savage hounds in man'.[32] The dances of St. Vitus and St. John in the middle ages, hysterical states, music, public torture, witch trials, thundering sermons were all orchestrated to this effect. But most to be feared of all, the priest taught that all powers, goals, rights, men and nations, in fact all causes, only receive sanctification from the ascetic ideal.

So far we, conditioned by an intellectual world saturated by Nietzsche's thought, have little difficulty in following him. But what comes next strikes at the core of beliefs we still for the most part retain. So far we have been in the sphere of the moral, the realm of values, where we have learned to question absolutes. But Nietzsche sees the greatest incarnation of the ascetic mania for the one correct doctrine in European science. To those who would say that while Christianity is collapsing, science is healthy, he replies that science too, as an ideal to which people devote their lives, is collapsing. There may be 'modest and worthy labourers among scholars, too, who are happy in their little nooks', but science as an ideal has now become the 'hiding place for every kind of discontent, disbelief'.[33] Scientific activity has become 'a means of self-narcosis', of blotting out pain and suffering.[34] Also, in its psychology and epistemology, modern science has taken on the task of expressing the ascetic ideal through the abasement of human worth and self-contempt.[35] The 'English' psychologists are no doubt to be included under this head.

Influence

Nietzsche has become one of the most influential of all nineteenth century philosophers. His influence has been particularly great in the literary world, admirers including Bernard Shaw, D.H. Lawrence and H.L. Mencken.[36] While he has generally been construed as a philosopher of the right, Shaw thought his ideal of the superman could be adapted to include left-wing leaders, while in *Arms and the Man* he looks back with sympathy and some amusement at an ideal of the heroic warrior with obvious Nietzschean overtones.

Nietzsche's influence on philosophy has been more patchy. While he is usually recognised as one of the founders of distinctively modern trends in philosophy, adoption of his leading ideas has been less widespread, reflecting both the leftist inclinations of many twentieth century intellectuals and the continuing involvement of philosophy with religion. The genuine influence of Nietzsche can however be seen on Bertrand Russell in the introduction to his *History of Western Philosophy*, where he acknowledges the insights of the Cambridge classicist F.M. Cornford in decrying the deadening effect of excessive prudence and reason.[37] Cornford acknowledged his debt here to Nietzsche's *The Birth of Tragedy*. This positive evaluation of Nietzsche was balanced in Russell by a profound and in my view justified distrust of the irrationalist elements in his theory of knowledge.

Nietzsche's most wholehearted disciple among the more important modern philosophers was Jaspers, whose work is discussed directly. He also had a great influence on Freud, who developed a kind of love-hate relation with the Nietzsche legend, alternately quoting Nietzsche and denying all knowledge of him. Freud's sensitivity here was understandable as he undoubtedly knew *The Genealogy of Morals* well and borrowed some of its ideas.[38] Another and perhaps more important reason for Freud's sensitivity was that while borrowing some things he also rejected many others without ever publishing an explicit critique of Nietzsche. He may well have been subconsciously aware that the Nietzschean philosophy would be one of his main rivals.

Nietzsche's influence on philosophically minded sociologists in Germany was considerable, with Weber, Scheler and Spengler all coming under his spell.[39]

Weber's conception of charismatic leadership seems to owe something to the Nietzschean superman, though Nietzsche was scathing about Weber's hero Bismark.[40] Scheler devoted a whole book to exploring the sociological ramifications of a Nietzschean concept in his *Resentment*. While Spengler devotes some space at the beginning of *The Decline of the West* to making fun of Nietzsche his own cycle of the rise and fall of civilisations has obvious links with *The Birth of Tragedy*. As with Freud we may suspect a certain defensiveness here. The opening sections of *The Decline of the West* are devoted to showing that all previous historians have considered history as a forward moving sequence rather than a series of cycles. While Vico, Gibbon and Montesquieu are clear counter-examples to this thesis, Spengler may have feared his German readers would be more familiar with Nietzsche.[41]

Some philosophers are occasionally listed as having been influenced by Nietzsche when their own philosophies are really quite opposed to his.[42] The line of thinking developed by Heidegger and Sartre cuts out all reference to primordial human passions and thus to the will to power. Heidegger's book on Nietzsche is about as unNietzschean as it could be. Merleau-Ponty discusses Nietzsche in a positive light in *The Structure of Behaviour* but his borrowing extends only to a suspicion of excessive moralising.[43]

Nietzsche was notoriously influential in the formation of official Nazi ideology and after the second world war his influence declined radically.[44] Beginning in the 1960's a kind of rescue campaign was mounted among Anglo-Saxon writers to free Nietzsche from his guilt by association with the Nazis, with Kaufmann's biography important here.[45] In the 1970's he became fashionable once again in France with Glucksmann and Derrida both counterposing his individualism to the stifling embrace of the state.[46] In my view the efforts of many of these more recent commentators to absolve Nietzsche of association with Nazism are false. Nietzsche was not himself a racist, a German nationalist or an admirer of the blond beast, except perhaps in a rather indirect way. Nonetheless his philosophy argues at times that we should fulfil ourselves through the exercise of the will to power unfettered by morality. If the historical conditions are present for the building of fascist or any other form of ruthless political organisation that will give its adherents power, then Nietzsche in at least one of his voices might well advise us to join them. I return to this question in my concluding chapter.

Jaspers (1883-1969)

Jaspers began his professional career at the Heidelberg Clinic for Neuropsychiatry after training in medicine. His early papers were on psychopathology and after receiving an invitation from the publisher Ferdinand Springer to produce a textbook on psychiatry he published in 1913 his first book, *General Psychopathology*.

This attempts to synthesise the results obtained in psychiatry by the use of different methods of investigation. Such synthesis was to remain a lifelong passion with Jaspers, who inherited from his contacts with Max Weber the idea that only by reviewing results obtained from as many perspectives as possible can one begin to approximate a picture of the whole.

At the request of Springer the book was later entirely rewritten for the fourth (1942) edition and aspects of Jaspers' later work, particularly his study of Nietzsche, are included in this. The general plan of the book was not however altered. The following comments are based on the seventh and last edition.

Jaspers begins with a study, in Part 1, of the phenomenology of mental life generally, with particular attention to morbid phenomena. This paves the way

116

for two more analytic parts in which he deals with meaningful psychic connections and causal psychic connections. This arrangement was strongly influenced by the ideas of Rickert and Weber, who stressed the need to study both the inner subjective meaning of human action and causal laws stating what, from a factual point of view, leads to what.[47] Thus it is a fact that suicide increases in the Spring, but this factual law relating to the graph of suicides can also be supplemented by an attempt to understand the kinds of inner reasons, such as distress at feeling left out of the quickening of life in the Spring, that lead to suicides at this time.

In Parts 4, 5 and 6 Jaspers presents three ways in which a synthesis of these approaches can be achieved: through the study of disease entities (like paranoid schizophrenia) and biography; through the study of social and historical aspects of psychiatric disorders; through studying 'the human being as a whole', which seems to mean through further philosophical reflection on the previous material.

In dealing with the phenomenology of mental life in Part 1 Jaspers leans heavily on traditional perspectives. We are conscious of objects, of space and time, of the body, of feelings, of urges, drive and will. In psychopathology we meet the abnormal manifestations of these things in distorted perceptions of and beliefs about the real world, inappropriate feelings, uncontrollable urges and in the loss of will of compulsive acts and the excessive faith in personal will of paranoid delusions of grandeur.

At the same time some novelties also appear. The form of mental life is distinguished from its content. This distinction comes from Husserl but in the psychiatric context takes on a new meaning. 'Hypochondriacal contents, whether provided by voices, compulsive ideas, overvalued ideas or delusional ideas, remain identifiable as content.'[48] The content of a psychiatric illness may also be fear of persecution, fear of dirt, fear of open spaces, belief in a special mission from God and so forth. These are the aspects of such illness that Freud called the dominating ideas. The form of their expression may vary by their being revealed in voices, in ideas compulsively circulated through the head, in compulsively repeated actions or in fear of doing certain things.

The distinction between form and content is further developed in the discussion of self-reflection, which Jaspers tells us is one ability that separates us from the animals.[49] In animals and very young children the influence of drives and instincts follows the natural, unreflected course of elementary existence. 'What is elementary is primarily without content and gains this only secondarily, but whatever has been evolved conceptually starts from content and operates in reverse.'[50] It is typical of morbid psychic phenomena that they have reverted to the elementary state without having regained its benign character.

The examples given of such disturbances in self-reflection are certain kinds of compulsion, of which compulsive beliefs and compulsive urges are the most clearly described. In compulsive beliefs 'A struggle ensues between conviction and knowing the opposite to be true.' The disturbance has arisen from the inability to get rid of the conviction once it is known to be false. The example is given of a young woman who thought two men might have assaulted her in hospital and she might be having a baby. Despite renewal of her periods and other evidence to the contrary she proved unable for a long time to rid herself of this compulsive idea, though herself thinking it to be false.

In compulsive urges, an urge repeatedly arises which is felt as foreign to the person's nature. The urge may arise to move chairs or to swear out loud. These can be partly understood as arising from the same source as compulsive beliefs, namely inability to get rid of a false conviction, as when a person repeatedly washes themselves for fear of a contamination they know on one level to be illusory. Acts designed to defend against such eroneous beliefs can also become compulsive, as when a man who believed he had given a promise he could not fulfil repeatedly asked for a written certificate that he had not given the promise.

Part 1 also deals with the psychology of human performance, with psychosomatic effects and with meaningful objective phenomena. Only this last topic need concern us here.

The most interesting questions raised in this connection concern the psychology of the personal world and of creativity. In his discussion of this first topic Jaspers suggests that we create a meaningful world for ourselves through such things as room arrangement and dress. Mental patients often do this, though in a way we regard as abnormal, arranging their personal treasures into strange patterns.[51]

The transformation of world experience that occurs in schizophrenia is centrally related to the content of the delusion. Whereas in compulsion the delusion is on one level of the personality felt to be mistaken, in schizophrenia the delusion is held to with full conviction, whether it be 'of catastrophe, cosmic delusions, delusions of reprieve, ... of persecution, of jealousy, of marriage, etc.'[52]

In his discussion of creative expression Jaspers concentrates on the idea that through speech and writing schizophrenics and other psychiatric patients are sometimes, though he admits this is not all that common, able to give expression to the formation and transformation of their delusions in the development of theories and cosmic and metaphysical systems. Sometimes such individuals can come to exert considerable influence through their writings, as in the cases of Holderlin and Swedenborg.[53]

In Part 2 Jaspers deals with meaningful psychic connections. He begins with a review of the problem of understanding the meaning of other people's actions. The problem is described as follows:

'In the natural sciences we find causal connections only but in psychology our bent for knowledge is satisfied with the comprehension of quite a different sort of connection. Psychic events 'emerge' out of each other in a way which we understand. Attacked people become angry and spring to their own defence, cheated persons grow suspicious. The way in which such an emergence takes place is understood by us, our understanding is genetic. Thus we understand psychic reactions to experience, we understand the development of passion, the growth of an error, the content of delusion and dream; we understand the effects of suggestion, an abnormal personality in its own context or the inner necessities of someone's life. Finally, we understand how the patient sees himself and how this mode of self-understanding becomes a factor in his psychic development.'[54]

Meaningful connections between psychic events are immediately self-evident and cannot be doubted. Thus Nietzsche saw that 'awareness of one's weakness, wretchedness and suffering gives rise to moral demands and religions of redemption, because in this roundabout way the psyche can gratify its will to power despite its weakness ...'[55] This does not mean that Nietzsche was necessarily right in discerning this process in Christianity. To prove that we must look at facts about 'verbal contents, cultural factors, people's acts, ways of life and expressive gestures'.[56] The meaningful connection is self-evident, but to find out if the various elements so connected are actually present in a situation we must look to the facts. Jaspers is particularly interested in such genetically understandable connections. He also recognises that more everyday kinds of meaningful connection are made when we interpret another person's ideas, motives or feelings.

Understanding can be divided into three major categories. In cultural understanding we have the understanding of mental content generally: ideas, images, symbols, obligations and ideals. This is a relatively easy kind of understanding and corresponds to one aspect of the everyday understanding mentioned above.

In existential understanding we meet a more difficult and remote kind of comprehension. This itself is composed of two aspects: the ununderstandable as given to causal inquiry and the ununderstandable in its existential aspect. The former includes chiefly 'instinctual drives, biological, somatic facts and supposed specific extra-conscious mechanisms'.[57] The latter 'presents itself as a freedom, which discloses itself in free decisions, in a grasp of absolute meanings, and .... that marginal point where we are raised from ordinary existence into autonomous selfhood'.[58]

In metaphysical understanding we attempt to unite cultural or psychological understanding with existential understanding in a complete system, generally related to the concept of being.

Meaningful connections are now outlined under the following headings: instinctual drives, the individual in the world, symbols, patterns formed from these and self-reflection. In this list of topics we have outlined the two clearest tendencies in Jaspers' thinking on the individual. The transformation of instincts, ideals and ideas takes place not, as Freud thought, chiefly through repression, but through genetic reactions that are comprehensible in their own terms. Jaspers here leans on the writings of Kierkegaard and Nietzsche and explicitly attacks Freud for vulgarising their discoveries.[59] At the same time he thinks that self-reflection produces further peculiarly human characteristics.

A drive is defined as 'instincts which we experience, that is, functions carried out as the result of an urge without conscious awareness of content or aim but in such a way that complex purposeful activity finally reaches its end by being moved towards it'.[60] Drives can however also be considered as purposes objectively achieved (as survival is the purpose of hunger), physical urges and as occasions for creative production (as in erotic ideas). While the achievement of pleasure and the avoidance of pain are related to instincts, the urge to achieve a particular goal may over-ride these considerations.

Three types of drives are distinguished. The somatic sensory drives include such things as sex, hunger, thirst, sleep. The vital drives include three sub-groups. The vital drives for existence are a succession of opposites: the will to power and to submit, to assert and to surrender, to self-will and to social life, courage versus fear, self-importance versus humility, love versus hate. The vital psychic drives include curiosity, protection of the young, wandering, ease and possession. The vital creative urges include those to express, demonstrate, make tools, work and create.

The third major group includes the drives of the human spirit, including the religious, aesthetic, ethical, epistemological and metaphysical. Jaspers betrays his Christian heritage when he says that the common factor in this group is the drive for immortality.

We now turn to the relation of the individual to reality. Jaspers here approves of Kretschmer's distinction between those who feel superiority and those who feel inferiority, to the world and the people in it. He adds to this the tendency to work on some continuing whole versus that to treat life as an adventure and experiment.

In self-deception we may deny reality. Alternatively we may accept symbolic substitutes for reality, as do those who lavish their love on pet animals instead of people. Another possibility is the creation of a fantasy world.

In marginal situations, such as those in which we confront disorder and death, the individual approaches the borders of the incomprehensible, but the insightful therapist may, even so, be able to offer at least authentic concern.

The relation of the individual to reality is further explored in symbols. These function, as Kant had said, to point the way to realities that can be apprehended neither through concrete experience nor through pure conceptual thought.[61] Thus a body with a soul may be a symbol for monarchy, a machine a symbol for dictatorship. The exploration of symbols takes place in myths, fairy-tales and sagas and we should study these as well as commentaries to get practice in understanding them, though ultimately the element of personal insight will be indispensable. The writings of Klages and Jung are mentioned in this respect, though Jaspers prefers the former to the latter.

The movement of the psyche is grasped through understanding the conflict of meaning that takes place when opposing drives, instincts and tendencies are pitted against one another. These conflicts take three forms. In reversal one emotion or drive such as grief or love changes into its opposite - cheerfulness or hate. In a battle of opposites the two remain present at the same time, as when wandering is balanced by stability or self-will by social life. In a choice the individual chooses one of these alternatives permanently. Jaspers feels the synthesis of psychic opposites is more constructive than permanent choice.

In self-reflection we reflect upon the symbols that are given to us as the encapsulation of a certain relation to the world, such as those of Christ on the cross or of the national flag. This frees us from accepting given relations to the world and leads to the extinction of the unconscious and the separation of the individual from the grounds of instinctual life. In this separation there is the danger of losing both meaning and the grounds for life. Only by continually reaching back to the roots of life can we remain part of life.

In self-reflection we try to understand ourselves. We can observe ourselves quite successfully, but self-understanding is endless and relative. Only in extreme situations and acts of personal commitment can we finally come to understand and know ourselves.

Self-reflection throws into full relief the contrast between the intended and the unintended. When the unintended and instinctual takes over we may enter a trance or a seizure. Domination by the unintended is experienced in morbid phenomena such as compulsion. Sometimes the attempt to regain conscious control actually frustrates its own aim, as when we try too hard to go to sleep and remain awake with insomnia.

This is followed by a new chapter on 'Meaningful connections and their specific mechanisms'. Here Jaspers is particularly interested in those mechanisms that lie outside consciousness that we are obliged to hypothesise in order to explain meaningful connections that exist within consciousness. Here he leans explicitly on Nietzsche for the three mechanisms of symbolic gratification, inadequate discharge and sublimation. He notes that Freud took over these ideas, but again charges him with vulgarising them. In symbolic gratification a symbol is taken as the object of the drive. A common form of inadequate discharge is where a person reproaches others instead of themself, as when a person dissatisfied with themselves wreaks this dissatisfaction on others. In sublimation 'lower' drives assume a 'higher' form as when sexual love is converted into platonic or religious love.

Jaspers then discusses the mechanisms of dream formation and techniques for their interpretation. His mechanisms and methods are not very dissimilar to Freud's and he cites Freud with some approval on this topic, though he mistrusts associations as clues for analysis and would rather relate the dream to contemporary wants in the dreamer's life. Confirmation of the interpretation is to be sought from the patient.

Two other normal mechanisms are discussed, those involved in suggestion and hypnosis. This is followed by a discussion of abnormal mechanisms, which include the fixation of ideas and actions into complexes, understood in an essentially Freudian sense. In dissociation part of experience and personality becomes divorced from the rest. In 'switching' a person shifts from a normal state of consciousness to something approaching dreaming or a hypnotic trance. This can occur in hysteria or psychosis. Of all these mechanisms Jaspers frankly says 'we neither know nor understand any one of them'.[62] Our theories only grapple with the puzzle.

The remaining chapters in Part 2 deal with the patient's attitude to the illness and attempts to define character types. This is followed by a discussion in Part 3 of scientific methods for observing and establishing causal connections. This includes a discussion of the effects of time of day and season, poisons, illness, brain physiology and heredity. This is followed by a comparison of the physiological theories of Wernicke and Freud. The latter is criticised for having engaged in speculative physiology when his real innovations lay in the field of establishing meaningful connections.[63] On the whole Jaspers is distrustful of pseudo-physiological explanation, though he recognises that studies of heredity have produced some interesting results.

Part 4 is titled 'The Conception of Psychic Life as a Whole'. Here the basic propositions already outlined are put to work in the areas of psychiatric classification and biography. He also discusses 'eidology', which is intended as a study of sexual and racial constitution that unifies both the method of analysis into factors, such as intelligence or fortitude, and the use of ideal types. Jaspers claims the latter are more closely connected with the method of understanding.

Part 5 deals with 'The Abnormal Psyche in Society and History'. In addition to treating such topics as the influence of work, education and political events on the type and incidence of psychiatric disorder, this also discusses a number of topics in social psychology. He follows Le Bon in seeing the mass psychology of riots and certain kinds of rallies as leading the individual into a state similar to hypnosis or psychosis in which acts of great cruelty or heroism can be performed by a lowering of both normal responsibility and caution. The increased pace and restless searching for pleasure without religious or philosophical grounds characteristic of modern life is seen as leading to a state of neuraesthenia, or generalised neuroticism.

The concluding Part 6 contains a summary of previous material and observations about the professional practice of the physician and psychiatrist.

In his major writings after *General Psychopathology* Jaspers concentrates upon metaphysics as an area in which we come to understand meaning as a confrontation with existence that leads us beyond instinct.[64] Both in this respect and in his claim that we have a will to submit to oppose the will to power, a will to surrender to oppose the desire to assert and to social life to oppose self-will Jaspers offers us a more conciliatory version of Nietzsche. He also offers a more conciliatory attitude to conventional religion.

Influence

Like Nietzsche, Jaspers is a writer who is mentioned more often than imitated. His greatest influence has been through his *Psychopathology*, which is frequently mentioned in psychiatric literature.[65] Lacan uses the term 'genetically understandable connection' in his early writing, borrowed from this source.[66] Binswanger, R.D. Laing and David Cooper were all influenced by its general conception that phenomenological method could be applied to psychiatry.[67] Lacan however is far more influenced in the content of his ideas by Freud; and Binswanger, Laing and Cooper by the metaphysics of being of Heidegger and Sartre.

Further Reading

Nietzsche

A good introduction to Nietzsche's ideas can be had from reading *The Birth of Tragedy* and *The Genealogy of Morals*. *Thus Spake Zarathustra* and *The Will to Power* are longer but should be read for a fuller understanding. There are many bad books about Nietzsche, who has suffered from both excessive hostility and excessive enthusiasm. The main problem with the better recent books is that in avoiding what Kaufmann calls the 'blood red' Nietzsche of earlier enthusiasts they fail to give the reader who has not read him the necessary reality: Nietzsche was a blood red thinker. The recent works listed below can certainly be recommended for their efforts to ascertain the facts about Nietzsche's much-mythologised life. Kaufmann's English editions of his writings are to be commended for their textual accuracy as well as their scrupulous translations.

R. Binion, *Frau Lou: Nietzsche's Wayward Disciple*, Princeton Uni. Press, Princeton, 1968

P. Bridgwater, *Nietzsche in Anglosaxony*, Leicester Uni. Press, Leicester, 1972.

F.C. Copleston, *Friedrich Nietzsche, Philosopher of Culture*, Search Press, London, 1975.

A.C. Danto, *Nietzsche as Philosopher*, Macmillan, New York, 1965.

R. Hayman, *Nietzsche; a Critical Life*, Weidenfeld and Nicolson, London, 1980.

E. Heller, 'Burckhardt and Nietzsche', 'Nietzsche and Goethe' and 'Rilke and Nietzsche'. In E. Heller, *The Disinherited Mind*, Dufour and Saifer, Philadelphia, 1952.

R.J. Hollingdale, *Nietzsche; The Man and his Philosophy*, Routledge. London, 1965.

R.L. Howey, *Heidegger and Jaspers on Nietzsche*, Nijhoff, The Hague, 1973.

W. Kaufmann, *Nietzsche: Philosopher, Psychologist, Antichrist*, Princeton Uni. Press, Princeton, 1968.

J.P. Stern, *Nietzsche*, Fontana, London, 1978.

J.P. Stern, *A Study of Nietzsche*, CUP, Cambridge, 1979.

D.S. Thatcher, *Nietzsche in England 1890-1914*, Uni. of Toronto Press, Toronto, 1970.

Jaspers

C.F. Walraff, *Karl Jaspers, An Introduction to his Philosophy*, Princeton Uni. Press, Princeton, 1970.

L. Ehrlich, *Karl Jaspers - Philosophy as Faith*, Uni. of Massachussetts Press, Boston, 1975

O. Schrag, *Existence, Existenz, and Transcendence*, Duquesne Uni. Press, Pittsburgh, 1971.

S. Samay, *Reason Revisited*, Uni. of Notre Dame Press, Notre Dame, 1971.

A.M. Olson, *Transcendence and Hermeneutics, An Interpretation of the Philosophy of Karl Jaspers*, Nijhoff, The Hague, 1979.

Chapter 6: Freud and his Followers

Main Assumptions

Freud's role in the history of psychiatry was to be one of the first to develop a non-Christian, secular approach to therapy. The French psychiatrist Pierre Janet also accomplished this task quite independently of Freud at the end of the nineteenth century, though his work declined in influence rapidly after his death in 1947. Previous to the time of Freud and Janet psychotherapy conducted by the laying on of hands and other methods had been widely practiced by Christianity under the rubric of casting out devils and spirits. Such therapy naturally had a strongly theological underpinning.

Freud's main assumptions were: 1a. Freud considered socialisation through his theory of the Oedipus complex and attempted to reduce redemption to a derivative; 1b. He admired social stability; 1c. He ignored the problem of freedom; 1d. He engages in deep interpretation, particularly in relation to dreams and neurotic symptoms; 1e. In his last writings Freud talked about the life force Eros as a constructive force building up the personality opposed by the destructive urge Thanatos; 2. We can become conscious of instincts and the unconscious; 3a. Freud was not greatly interested in the relative strength of motives; 3b. Sex is the most important motive repressed in the production of culture; 3c. He thought the libido or generalised sex drive was like a reservoir trying to empty itself; 3d. Freud wrote intermittently about the interaction of motives in defence mechanisms such as identification, projection, reaction-formation, denial, repression and regression. His views on this were later systematised by his daughter Anna Freud; 4. The unconscious communicates with consciousness primarily through dreams, personal relationships, slips of the tongue and neurotic symptoms, all of which can only be understood using psychoanalysis; 5. Symbols are formed by elaborate mechanisms designed to disguise them from the censor or conscience; 6. The unconscious id acts to hallucinate immediate gratification; the ego or conscious self acts to maximise pleasure by rational means; 7. We find out about human nature through psychoanalysis.

Of the post-Freudians dealt with in this chapter Reich and Marcuse differed with Freud chiefly by arguing that irrational restrictions on self-gratification were responsible for considerable personal and social neurosis (issue 6). They also admired social revolution (issue 1b). The American ego-analysts, not dealt with here, were chiefly distinguished by their reduction of emphasis upon the Oedipus complex and the repression of sex and their increased emphasis on adaptation to existing social reality (issues 1a, 1b and 3b). Fromm, dealt with here, differs from Freud in the same respect as the American ego analysts, except that he is in favour of social revolution and believes the most important repressed motives in the modern world are caring and belonging (issue 3b). Fromm also reintroduces an interest in traditional metaphysical routes to salvation into his philosophy (issue la). Lacan, also dealt with later in the chapter, was most notable for his introduction of discussions of traditional metaphysics and his belief that the repression of narcissism is more important than the repression of sex (issue 3b). Lacan is also interested in metaphysical routes to salvation (issue la).

Sigmund Freud (1856-1939)

Freud perfectly captured the change in mood that began to influence secular thought at the end of the nineteenth century and intensified following the first world war. Nineteenth century belief in social progress was increasingly called into question.[1] Freudian pessimism provided an appealing alternative. Freud was of course a Jew, but his cultural background could be best described as that of a European intellectual with Jewish influences. While an atheist with little specific interest in the pessimistic theological tradition, Freud would have been familiar with the view of the human condition common to that tradition and to pessimistic currents within humanism both of which stress the infinity of human desires. He was particularly interested in European literature and would certainly have found this approach to personality in one of his favourite writers, Shakespeare, as well as in the everyday culture around him.

Another important influence on Freud was nineteenth century German academic psychology, particularly the work of Fechner. At key points in *The Interpretation of Dreams* and *Beyond the Pleasure Principle* Freud refers his ideas to those of Fechner. Particularly significant for Freud was the stress that Fechner had already laid on unconscious mental processes.

Freud's development of these traditions was based on a new interest in the motivation of particular actions. This was necessary for Freud the therapist engaged in trying to understand his patients' actions. Both Christian and Jewish traditions had evolved approaches to the cure of the mentally 'ill' that used religious assumptions.[2] They used notions like possession by devils and departure of the spirit from the body borrowed from the general theological vocabulary, though these approaches had not had any great impact on the mainstream of theological thinking.

Freud provided a secular theory for a secular practice of psychotherapy, one often couched in pseudo-physiological language. The general process of secularisation of the European intellectuals and upper middle classes made such a shift necessary and rendered the physiological idiom fashionable if not universally accepted.

Freud, the theorist of secular therapy, was to become the twentieth century's most influential commentator on the relation between personality and society. His message became, after the holocaust of the first world war, as bleak as the century he was to speak for. Perhaps the only hopeful thing he did was to show that even a secular view of human personality could make it appear mysterious and fascinating. The Freudian mind with its layers of defence mechanisms and ranks of esoteric symbols could recapture some of the flavour of religion. When

Weber complained that science was disenchanting the world, he was not thinking of Freud, whose science was every bit as mysterious as the religion it claimed to replace. Nor did it use the rather tedious procedures of normal science; something his opponents never tired of rehearsing.[3]

For the rest Freud rose to the challenge that the defenders of normal science were, for a long time, too conventional or too cowardly to meet. Hope in the afterlife had, for many, been removed by science. Hope in this life was being removed by events. Freud thought the crust on the boiling lava of human nature might be reinforced and ultimate catastrophe avoided by a scientific understanding of human nature. But any Utopia was certainly impossible.

Freud's first great work was *The Interpretation of Dreams*, published in 1900. In his previous *Studies on Hysteria*, with Breuer, Freud had come to the conclusion that the symptoms of neurotic patients were the disguised expression of forbidden wishes. In *The Interpretation of Dreams* he sought a more refined route to such forbidden wishes in the analysis of his own dreams.

Freud's method of dream interpretation was to divide the dream into its component incidents and then ask the dreamer, in this case himself, to adopt a relaxed and uncritical attitude and say what each incident suggested to them.[4] Reflection upon these associations to the dream would then yield the suppressed wishes that the dream was concealing. According to Freud's own account, this method was adapted from traditional methods of dream analysis.[5] Paul Bakan has suggested Freud's procedure may also have derived from the Jewish mystical tradition of Samuel Abulafia, a thirteenth century Kabbalist whose method of meditation was strikingly similar to the Freudian method of interpretation. Such mysticism still had exponents in Freud's Vienna.[6]

It had long been recognised that dreams are sometimes able to awaken previously lost memories of childhood. Freud goes a step further in assuming that a large proportion of dreams express wishes from childhood. In assessing the most common childhood wishes, however, Freud does not rely solely on the analysis of dreams. He is very careful to base his descriptions of typical childhood wishes that lead to 'typical dreams' upon first-hand observation of children.[7] Like Augustine before him, he is struck by the selfishness of young children, their willingness to do anything to get their own way and their violent fits of anger and jealousy. Children will often wish brothers, sisters or parents who anger them dead.

From these commonplace if rather jaundiced observations about children we move straight into what was to become the heartland of Freudian territory - the Oedipus complex. We can explain children's hostility to their brothers and sisters as the result of rivalry for their parents' attention. But, says Freud, we need a different explanation for the death wishes children direct against their parents. This is to be explained as a result of the wish of the little boy for sexual intercourse with the mother and the removal of the father. With little girls things are the other way round.

The only real piece of evidence Freud brings forward for this is his claim that men direct death dreams against their fathers and women against their mothers.

However, as he retracted this claim in a footnote added in 1925, it means little.[8]

One motive Freud had in emphasising the sexual side of the Oedipal situation was his general stress on sexual motivation. Sex was by no means discovered by Freud, but he became identified with a widespread social movement to encourage the freer expression of sexual impulses.[9]

Freud's emphasis on the sexual side of the Oedipus complex was also prompted by his overall theory of motivation. The enthusiasm for biological explanations of the mind typical of a certain kind of nineteenth century thinking had infected Freud through his teacher Brücke, a physiologist.[10] Freud liked to think that the physiological drives of hunger, thirst and sex were in some way primary. Without the tension produced by these drives the organism would remain inert. Activity was, Freud thought at this time, a route to the reduction of tension and the release of 'nervous excitation'.[11] For someone with these views the sexual impulse had a kind of solid respectability as an explanation. Yet even in *The Interpretation of Dreams* Freud hints at other explanations for the wish to displace the parent of the same sex: 'An eight-year-old girl of my acquaintance, if her mother is called away from the table, makes use of the occasion to proclaim herself her successor: 'I'm going to be mummy now. Do you want some more greens Karl? Well, help yourself, then!'[12] The child is rehearsing an adult role. This kind of explanation for the Freudian insights was given by some later schools of psychoanalysis.[13] For Freud, however, such explanations would have seemed hollow; all motives involve the quest for pleasure (tension-relief) or the instinct for self-preservation.

Freud stressed a sexual motive for the child's wish to displace the parent of the same sex. He also thought sexual jealousy the motive for death wishes against the parents. As Freud points out, children are often hostile towards a parent who punishes them or is overbearing.[14] 'But', he says, 'it does not help us in our endeavour to explain dreams of a parent's death in people whose piety towards their parents has been unimpeachably established.'[15]

This statement gives an impression of a certain lack of familiarity with child-rearing, which is reinforced when Freud remarks that he 'neglected the opportunity' for observing jealousy among his own children.[16] Had he had more contact with his own children Freud would perhaps have given more weight to the role of anger at punishment in creating death-wishes to the parents. As it is we cannot help but feel that Freud's stress on hostility towards the same sex parent itself has some hidden motive.

Speculation about Freud's personal motives in devising the theory of the Oedipus complex would have little interest were it not that such speculation can throw some light on the tremendous impact of Freud's writings. Freud may have been so successful because his problems were those of many others.

From the death of his father in 1896 until the completion of *The Interpretation of Dreams* in 1899, Freud underwent a period of neurotic suffering. In 1897 he wrote to his friend Fleiss that 'the main patient who keeps me busy is myself'.[17] This suffering appears to have been due both to the loss of his father and to the frustration of Freud's unquenchable desire for fame through scientific discovery. In 1896 he was 40 and the recognition he had hoped to receive for his work with

Breuer on hysteria was receding. They had traced hysteria back to the seduction of the patient as a young child. This explanation now appeared incorrect and all that remained to Freud was his method of interpreting dreams and his continuing interest in childhood sexuality.[18]

In this situation the discovery of the Oedipal feelings must have seemed deeply significant to Freud. Here he was, a man who needed to come into maturity to achieve his great goal in life and to step into his father's shoes. But he experienced difficulty in doing so because the shoes he had imagined for himself were so big. His ambition knew few limits. The Oedipal theory explained why this was so. Little boys fear to take their father's place because they imagine that they will first have to kill the father.

In explaining his own problem in this way Freud was able to explain more generally the problems of men in adjusting to work or of women in adjusting to a domestic role. Such difficulties are difficulties in replacing the father or the mother. For men we may well feel these are often created by the inordinate ambition aroused by modern social life.

There was also the sexual element of the Oedipal conflict, which is not so easy to relate to Freud's immediate problems. But here again the theory provided a general explanation for the sexual difficulties of adults, which according to the Oedipal theory are often due to the unconscious equation of sex with incest.

In the last chapter of *The Interpretation of Dreams* Freud gives a sketch of his general personality model arising out of his work on the neuroses and on dreaming. This includes the unconscious, containing chiefly infantile memories and wishes that are acceptable to the moral code or censor; and the preconscious, containing memories and wishes that are not prevented from entering consciousness by the censor. The unconscious is regulated by the 'primary process' that hallucinates the immediate satisfaction of wishes, while the 'secondary process' uses thought and voluntary movement to achieve real satisfaction.[19] To give an example, when the baby is hungry, it hallucinates the breast. Repetition of this hallucination fails to bring complete satisfaction, so the baby begins to learn methods of obtaining the real breast (like crying and later how to prepare food.)

What interests Freud is how the three systems (unconscious, preconscious and moral censor) interact together to allow the disguised expression of unconscious wishes. Such disguised expression results both in neurotic symptoms and in dreams.

An example of the expression of a wish in a neurotic symptom is given as follows:

'I was called into a consultation last year to examine an intelligent and unembarrassed-looking girl. She was most surprisingly dressed. For though as a rule a woman's clothes are carefully considered down to the last detail, she was wearing one of her stockings hanging down and two of the buttons on her blouse were undone. She complained of having pains in her leg and, without being asked, exposed her calf. But what she principally complained of was, to use her own words, that she had a feeling in her body as though there was something 'stuck to it' which was 'moving backwards and forwards' and was 'shaking' her through and through: sometimes it made her whole body feel 'stiff'. My medical colleague, who was present at the examination, looked at me; he found no difficulty in understanding the meaning of her complaint. But what struck both of us as extraordinary was the fact that it meant nothing to the patient's mother - though she must often have found herself in the situation which her child was describing. The girl herself had no notion of the bearing of her remarks; for if she had, she would never have given voice to them. In this case it had been possible to hoodwink the censorship into allowing a fantasy which would normally have been kept in the preconscious to emerge into consciousness under the innocent disguise of making a complaint.'[20]

Freud's analysis of the formation of dreams is complex, due to the need to explain why dreams are so complicated and to explain why they take the form of visual hallucinations. This last fact is explained on the grounds that unconscious wishes cannot be expressed directly in thoughts as these belong to the preconscious and this is largely asleep. Thus the unconscious wishes are re-routed into a fourth system, called the perceptual system (Pcpt.) which produces the hallucinatory images of the dream under the joint impact of the unconscious, preconscious (Pcs.) and censor:

'The situation is this. Either residues of the previous day have been left over from the activity of waking life and it has not been possible to withdraw the whole cathexis (investment) of energy from them; or the activity of waking life during the course of the day has led to the stirring up of an unconscious wish; or these two events have happened to coincide. (We have already discussed the various possibilities in this connection.) The unconscious wish links itself up with the day's residues and effects a transference on to them; this may happen either in the course of the day or not until a state of sleep has been established. A wish now arises which has been transferred on to the recent material; or a recent wish, having been suppressed, gains fresh life by being reinforced from the unconscious. This wish seeks to force its way along the normal path taken by thought-processes, through the Pcs. (to which, indeed, it in part belongs) to consciousness. But it comes up against the censorship, which is still functioning - and to the influence of which it now submits. At this point it takes on the distortion for which the way has already been paved by the transference of the wish on to the recent material. So far it is on the way to becoming an obsessive idea or a delusion or something of the kind - that is, a thought which has been intensified by transference and distorted in its expression by censorship. Its further advance is halted, however, by the sleeping state of the preconscious. (The probability is that that system has protected itself against the invasion by diminishing its own excitations.) The dream process consequently enters on a regressive path, which lies open to it precisely owing to the peculiar nature of the state of sleep, and it is led along that path by the attraction exercised on it by groups of memories; some of these memories themselves exist only in the form of visual cathexes and not as translations into the terminology of the later systems. In the course of its regressive path the dream-process acquires the attribute of representability. (I shall deal later with the question of compression.) It has now completed the second portion of its zigzag journey. The first portion was a progressive one, leading from the unconscious scenes or fantasies to the preconscious; the second portion led from the frontier of the censorship back again to perceptions. But when the content of the dream-process has become perceptual, by that fact it has, as it were, found a way of evading the obstacle put in its way by the censorship and the state of sleep in the Pcs. It succeeds in drawing attention to itself and in being noticed by consciousness...

'I must assume that the state of sleep makes the sensory surface of consciousness which is directed towards the Pcs. far more insusceptible to excitation than the surface directed towards the Pcpt. systems. Moreover, this abandonment of interest in thought-processes during the night has a purpose: thinking is to come to a standstill, for the Pcs. requires sleep. Once, however, a dream has become a perception, it is in a position to excite consciousness, by means of the qualities it has now acquired. This sensory excitation proceeds to perform what is its essential function: it directs a part of the available cathectic energy in the Pcs. into attention to what is causing the excitation. It must therefore be admitted that every dream has an arousing effect, that it sets a part of the quiescent force of the Pcs. in action. The dream is then submitted by this force to the influence which we have described as secondary revision with an eye to consecutiveness and intelligibility. That is to say, the dream is treated by it just like any other perceptual content; it is met by the same anticipatory ideas, in so far as its subject-matter allows. So far as this third portion of the dream-process has any direction it is once again a progressive one.'[21]

In 1905 Freud published his *Three Essays on Sexuality*. In this he outlines his view of the development of sexuality prior to the Oedipal conflicts, which occur in the period 3 to 5 years. (In later years Freud altered this to include the period 2 to 5 years.)[22] The nursing infant derives pleasure chiefly from the mouth, termed the oral or cannibalistic phase. The infant in the second year of life begins to control its bowel movements prior to toilet training and this results in an interest in anal pleasure. This is assisted by the child's speculations on the nature of sexual intercourse, which is often thought to be anal. Children who witness sexual intercourse generally interpret it as ill-treatment. This results in a tendency for anal sexuality to be connected with sadism.[23] During the Oedipal phase the child finally adopts a major interest in the genital zones as sources of sexual pleasure. The existence of the two 'pregenital' phases of organisation gives rise, Freud thinks, both to love play and to sexual 'perversions', which are the remnants of these earlier phases in adult life.

Freud's writings up to the first world war were chiefly devoted to his clinical work and the problems of interpreting the disguised wishes expressed in symptoms, dreams, jokes and other activities. By the end of the war Freud was a figure of international renown. He began to turn his attention increasingly to broader questions of social philosophy and the relation of the individual to society. This new phase was inaugurated in 1913 with the publication of *Totem and Taboo*, an attempt to apply Freud's Oedipal theory to the study of tribal society. Later he expanded his speculations about the social significance of the Oedipus conflict to problems of contemporary social philosophy. Along with the application of old ideas there also emerged new ones designed to broaden the application of his basic concepts. This new phase of Freud's activity was both successful and significant. He had become the first of a new breed of psychoanalysts who were also social commentators, social theorists and social prophets. As social behaviour became increasingly irrational, with the disaster of the first world war, the rise of fascism and the Stalinist purges, the specialists in irrationality could expect a wide audience.

The first important work of this new period is *Group Psychology and the Ego*, published in 1921. This summarises and applies two ideas Freud had been working on previously. One was that the aggressive instincts are just as self-sustaining as other instincts. They have an energy source of their own and will inevitably seek an outlet. In Freud's prewar publications only two groups of instincts had appeared - the sexual instincts, which seek pleasure, and the instinct for self-preservation. In *Beyond the Pleasure Principle* (1920) he added another group of instincts, the death instincts, which are responsible for the tendency to repeat painful experiences and actively seek death. The social significance of the reservoir of aggressive impulses is explained in *Group Psychology and the Ego* when Freud discusses a novel based on the premise that Christianity has ended and as a result there is a great increase in crimes and acts of violence. Christianity, Freud feels, has traditionally channelled aggressive impulses into foreign wars and acts of aggression against outsiders:

'The phenomenon which accompanies the dissolution that is here supposed to overtake a religious group is not fear, for which the occasion is wanting. Instead of it ruthless and hostile impulses towards other people make their appearance, which, owing to the equal love of Christ, they had previously been unable to do. But even during the kingdom of Christ those people who do not belong to the community of believers, who do not love him, and whom he does not love, stand outside this tie. Therefore a religion, even if it calls itself the religion of love, must be hard and unloving to those who do not belong to it.

'Fundamentally indeed every religion is in this same way a religion of love for all those whom it embraces; while cruelty and intolerance towards those who do not belong to it are natural to every religion. However difficult we may find it personally, we ought not to reproach believers too severely on this account; people who are unbelieving or indifferent are much better off psychologically in this matter of cruelty and intolerance. If today that intolerance no longer shows itself so violent and cruel as in former centuries, we can scarcely conclude that there has been a softening in human manners. The cause is rather to be found in the undeniable weakening of religious feelings and the libidinal ties which depend upon them. If another group tie takes the place of the religious one - and the socialistic tie seems to be succeeding in doing so - then there will be the same intolerance towards outsiders as in the age of the Wars of Religion: and if differences between scientific opinions could ever attain a similar significance for groups, the same result would again be repeated with this new motivation.'[24]

The other feature of *Group Psychology and the Ego* is its focus on the Oedipus complex as the most important factor in group psychology. From the time of his unpublished 'Project' in 1895 Freud had used the term 'ego' to mean roughly the same thing as the 'preconscious' of *The Interpretation of Dreams*. In his later work the term 'ego' takes over. Likewise the 'moral censor' of *The Interpretation of Dreams* was first replaced by the term 'ego ideal' and finally by 'superego'. In *Group Psychology and the Ego* 'ego ideal' is still preferred. This change in terminology is accompanied by a widening of the functions of the 'ego ideal' which now include 'self-observation, the moral conscience, the censorship of dreams, and the chief influence in repression'.[25] In addition the ego ideal has enormous significance for social psychology because group leadership is a process of replacing the ego ideal by the group leader. This replacement then triggers off a revival of the Oedipal situation. The man (Freud is chiefly interested in male groups) behaves towards the leader like a father and treats the other members of the group as brothers.

The idea that in men the ego ideal might be the internalisation of the father was foreshadowed in his study of Leonardo da Vinci, published in 1910. He suggests that in a homosexual like Leonardo, at the time of puberty part of his ego is replaced with the image of his mother. It was not until *Group Psychology and The Ego* that Freud took the further step of asserting that in the heterosexual male the father replaces part of the ego during the resolution of the Oedipus complex, becoming the model for the ego ideal.

In his discussion of social groups Freud concentrates upon the church and the army, both male institutions at that time:

'It is to be noticed that in these two artificial groups each individual is bound by libidinal ties on the one hand to the leader (Christ, the Commander-in-Chief) and on the other hand to the other members of the group. How these two ties are related to each other, whether they are of the same kind and the same value, and how they are to be described psychologically - these questions must be reserved for subsequent enquiry. But we shall venture even now upon a mild reproach against earlier writers for not having sufficiently appreciated the importance of the leader in the psychology of the group, while our own choice of this as a first subject for investigation has brought us into a more favourable position. It would appear as though we were on the right road towards an explanation of the principal phenomenon of group psychology - the individual's lack of freedom in a group. If each individual is bound in two directions by such an intense emotional tie, we shall find no difficulty in attributing to that circumstance the alteration and limitation which have been observed in his personality.'[26]

To explain the ties of the followers to the leader and of the followers to one another Freud assumes that these are a revival of the relations between the father and his sons and of the relations among the sons. This explains the attitude of slavish obedience that followers adopt to their leader:

'The uncanny and coercive characteristics of group formations, which are shown in the phenomena of suggestion that accompany them, may therefore with justice be traced back to the fact of their origin from the primal horde. The leader of the group is still the dreaded primal father; the group still wishes to be governed by unrestricted force; it has an extreme passion for authority; in Le Bon's phrase, it has a thirst for obedience.'[27]

The revival of brotherhood explains the attitude of comradeship and cooperation between group members:

'The elder child would certainly like to put his successor jealously aside, to keep it away from the parents, and to rob it of all its privileges; but in the face of the fact that this younger child (like all that come later) is loved by the parents as much as he himself is, and in consequence of the impossibility of his maintaining his hostile attitude without damaging himself, he is forced into identifying himself with the other children. So there grows up in the troop of children a communal or group feeling, which is then further developed at school. The first demand made by this reaction-formation is for justice, for equal treatment for all. We all know how loudly and implacably this claim is put forward at school.'[28]

Group psychology thus involves a revival of childhood. But it also involves a revival of the earliest experiences of the human race. Not only does the individual relive experiences in the family, but also those in the 'primal horde':

'In 1912 I took up a conjecture of Darwin's to the effect that the primitive form of human society was that of a horde ruled over despotically by a powerful male. I attempted to show that the fortunes of this horde have left indestructible traces upon the history of human descent; and, especially, that the development of totemism, which comprises in itself the beginnings of religion, morality, and social organization, is connected with the killing of the chief by violence and the transformation of the paternal horde into a community of brothers.

'Thus the group appears to us as a revival of the primal horde. Just as primitive man survives potentially in every individual, so the primal horde may arise once more out of any random collection; in so far as men are habitually under the sway of group formation we recognize in it the survival of the primal horde.'[29]

Freud devoted considerable attention to religion in his later years. We have already seen how the authoritarian organisation of the Christian churches was thought to stem from a re-enactment of the Oedipal situation. In *The Future of an Illusion* (1927) he goes further and argues that the religious veneration of God is a revival of the young child's veneration of the parents, particularly of the father. Confronted by the pains and perils of life and menaced by the forces of nature, adults seek refuge in a childish belief in an all-powerful and all-knowing parent-God who will protect them. Freud was evidently aware that this explanation applies more obviously to Judaism than to Christianity and in one of his last writings, *Moses and Monotheism* (1934-8), he sets out to show how veneration for the father eventually came to involve worship of the son. Once again the Oedipus theory and the notion of the primal horde are central.

'The re-establishment of the primal father in his historic rights was a great step forward but it could not be the end. The other portions of the prehistoric tragedy insisted on being recognized. It is not easy to discern what set this process in motion. It appears as though a growing sense of guilt had taken hold of the

Jewish people, or perhaps of the whole civilized world of the time, as a precursor to the return of the repressed material. Till at last one of these Jewish people found, in justifying a politico-religious agitator, the occasion for detaching a new - the Christian religion - from Judaism. Paul, a Roman Jew from Tarsus, seized upon this sense of guilt and traced it back correctly to its original source. He called this the 'original sin'; it was a crime against God and could only be atoned for by death.

'With the original sin death came into the world. In fact this crime deserving death had been the murder of the primal father who was later deified. But the murder was not remembered: instead of it there was a fantasy of its atonement, and for that reason this fantasy could be hailed as a message of redemption (evangelium). A son of God had allowed himself to be killed without guilt and had thus taken on himself the guilt of all men. It had to be a son, since it had been the murder of a father.'[30]

In Civilisation and its Discontents (1930) Freud turned to the problem of happiness. Civilisation leads to greater unhappiness rather than less. This, says Freud, is due to its increasing emphasis upon order, cleanliness, use of higher mental powers and insistence on kindliness towards others.

To achieve these things civilisation must dam up both the sexual instincts and the aggressive instincts. The sexual instincts must be dammed because order, cleanliness and the use of the higher mental powers depend upon sublimated sexual energy. Sexual energy, when prevented direct expression, is converted into a new form, by 'sublimation', and can then be used for other activities. In *The Future of an Illusion* Freud had previously adopted a similar argument about the energy necessary for work. The reason that civilisation leads to unhappiness is that it suppresses the direct expression of the instincts, thus violating the 'pleasure principle'.

Despite his rejection of the evolutionary optimism of the nineteenth century, Freud was not an unreserved pessimist. Augustine had confined the possibility of progress to the few inhabitants of the City of God. Luther was even more insistent that secular society was becoming progressively more decadent. Freud began from a nineteenth century tradition of scientific optimism. He became progressively disillusioned with this tradition, but despite the shock of the first world war and later the rise of fascism in Germany he retained a faith in science that was his legacy from this tradition. Faced with the political and social disasters of the twentieth century scientists have often opted for faith in science and a scientific elite that will lead the masses out the impasse. In Freud this tendency received one of its earliest and most extreme expressions. References to the stupidity and uncontrollable passions of the masses abound in his later writings. The happiness of individuals is being reduced; the suppression of aggression within the nation state is leading to its diversion into wars between the states. He has no faith in the Soviet experiment and abominates fascism. But, surprisingly, Freud sometimes strikes a hopeful note. He never quite loses his faith in reason. This comes out strongly in *The Future of an Illusion* when he discusses his hope that people will give up their illusions in religion:

'Education freed from the burden of religious doctrines will not, it may be, effect much change in men's psychological nature. Our god *Logos* is perhaps not a very almighty one, and he may only be able to fulfil a small part of what his predecessors have promised. If we have to acknowledge this we shall accept it with resignation. We shall not on that account lose our interest in the world and in life, for we have one sure support which you lack. We believe that it is possible for scientific work to gain some knowledge about the reality of the world, by means of which we can increase our power and in accordance with which we can arrange our life. If this belief is an illusion, then we are in the same position as you. But science has given us evidence by its numerous and important successes that it is no illusion.'[31]

Freud thinks that by applying the scientific knowledge gained through psychoanalysis a form of society more in keeping with the real instinctual needs and necessary mental structures of the human race can be evolved. Yet little hint is given of how the scientific elite are to implement this plan for a new society.

At other times Freud's hopes for deliverance take on a more mystical tone, derived from his embryonic philosophy of history. The development of the human species is the struggle between the life instincts and the death instincts:

'The fateful question for the human species seems to me to be whether and to what extent their cultural development will succeed in mastering the disturbance of their communal life by the human instinct of aggression and self-destruction. It may be that in this respect precisely the present time deserves a special interest. Men have gained control over the forces of nature to such an extent that with their help they would have no difficulty in exterminating one another to the last man. They know this, and hence comes a large part of their current unrest, their unhappiness and their mood of anxiety. And now it is to be expected that the other of the two 'Heavenly Powers', eternal Eros, will make an effort to assert himself in the struggle with his equally immortal adversary. But who can foresee with what success and with what result?'[32]

In trying to evaluate Freud we can separate two aspects of his doctrines. First there is the general claim that childhood wishes are repressed and seek disguised expression in adults through neurotic symptoms, dreams, slips of the tongue and so forth. This is an interesting and potentially illuminating development of traditional ideas about personality and as a general presupposition has entered Western culture to such an extent that few question it. Allied to this claim is the notion of defence mechanism, which was developed by Freud in an *ad hoc* way and later systematised by his daughter, Anna Freud.[33] These are methods used by the ego to control anxiety. Two of the most important are repression, which prevents childhood memories and wishes from becoming conscious and so causing anxiety, and identification.

Identification is a mechanism of enormous importance for social psychology, as Freud points out in the following passage from *The Future of an Illusion*:

'The narcissistic satisfaction provided by the cultural ideal is also among the forces which are successful in combating the hostility to culture within the cultural unit. This satisfaction can be shared in not only by the favoured classes, which enjoy the benefits of the culture, but also by the suppressed ones, since the right to despise the people outside it compensates them for the wrongs they suffer within their own unit. No doubt one is a wretched plebeian, harassed by debts and military service; but, to make up for it, one is a Roman citizen, one has one's share in the task of ruling other nations and dictating their laws. This identification of the suppressed classes with the class who rules and exploits them is, however, only part of a larger whole. For, on the other hand, the suppressed classes can be emotionally attached to their masters; in spite of their hostility to them they may see in them their ideals; unless such relations of a fundamentally satisfying kind subsisted, it would be impossible to understand how a number of civilizations have survived so long in spite of the justifiable hostility of large human masses.'[34]

This passage bases identification upon narcissism. By valuing a cultural ideal highly people value themselves. This contrasts rather sharply with the account of leadership given in *Group Psychology and the Ego*, where we are told that the leader revives the father-son relation with the followers. Freud does discuss the significance of narcissism for group formation in *Group Psychology*, but this is only to say that the hostility to group outsiders is a form of narcissism that must be suppressed within the group.[35] This amounts to the same thing as asserting that the group ideal of uniformity is narcissism, but this more positive application has little prominence. Instead we are given an account of identification that stresses the Oedipus complex, though he does mention that individuals may identify with those they love as well as with those they hate and fear.[36] He also adds a mention of the traditional concept of 'sympathy' between individuals who recognise they are alike and so 'catch' feelings from one another.[37]

So from these two sources alone we have assembled four different explanations for identification. If we feel bewildered by the combined operation of these four mechanisms that is probably due more to the complexity of social psychology than any special defect of Freud's way of approaching it.

Yet there are defects in Freud's psychology. Perhaps foremost among these is his tendency to overemphasise the Oedipal conflicts. He uses the Oedipus complex as a general explanation for what it is to be human, but never presents any real evidence that the Oedipal conflicts have the deep, lasting and virtually all-encompassing impact upon human life that he claims. Nor have subsequent investigations revealed such evidence.[38]

The social significance of Freud's stress on the Oedipal conflicts is transparent. If men in particular are continually seeking to revive a situation in which the father (leader) exerts authoritarian rule over his children (followers), then social life will inevitably follow an authoritarian pattern. It is no good our imagining that a more democratic family life might lead to a more democratic social life, for Freud has prepared two elaborate lines of defence against this. In the first place, the Oedipal conflicts are the result of the irrational fantasies of children not of anything actually done to the child. In the second place these fantasies have become ingrained in our hereditary makeup. We could of course argue that democracy will inevitably fail through the violence and stupidity of human nature. Freud simply offers us a roundabout route to this commonplace conclusion.

The other very questionable aspect of Freud's personality theory is his view of instincts. We would be hard put to prove either that the energy for civilised activity is sublimated sexual energy or that there is a self-fuelling drive towards aggression. Yet even here, where Freud's assertions are at their most ideological, we feel his greatness. He gives expression to two facts about modern social life that were avoided by those who clung to a shallower optimism: its domination by war and personal unhappiness.

In addition to founding a school of orthodox followers, Freud also attracted an extraordinary number of disciples who later became disillusioned with the teachings of the master.[39] To list these 'schismatics' in chronological order; Adler abandoned orthodox Freudian theory in about 1911; Jung in 1913; Reich, Horney and Fromm had all developed considerable divergences with the orthodox theory by about 1930. Except for Reich all these well known 'post-Freudians' developed versions of psychoanalysis that did away with or relegated to a minor role the fundamental Freudian doctrine of the Oedipus complex. Psychoanalysis had become a broad cultural movement and it was only natural that its adherents would find themselves attracted to traditions other than that within which Freud worked. Other traditions exerted a particular fascination where they were in accord with the personality and interests of the analyst. Thus Adler was attracted to a modified version of the empiricist tradition, and emphasis on the striving for superiority, Jung to mysticism, Horney to cultural analysis that verged on a philosophy of history and Fromm to a metaphysical emphasis. After the second world war both Marcuse and Fromm developed sociological versions of psychoanalysis, while the French analyst Jacques Lacan developed a marriage with semiotics that has been widely influential. The work of Reich, Marcuse, Fromm and Lacan is described in the remainder of this chapter.

Reich (1897-1957)

At first sight it appears strange that orthodox Freudian theory, whose founder was both a pessimist and a conservative, should have attracted so much attention from the left. This interest has been particularly strong in the period since the second world war. Reich's writings, which were progressively anathematised by the communist left in the 1930s and ridiculed by liberals and the right, have enjoyed a renaissance among the non-communist and even the communist left since the war.

The reason for this increased attention to Reich has been that he was tackling a problem in the 1930s that has occupied the attention of the left in the post-war period. This is the problem of social control within capitalism in non-crisis periods.

In the nineteenth century Marx and Engels had expected that either through economic crisis or through military adventures capitalist society would enter repeated periods of acute crisis. These economic and military crises would cause the working class to revolt against the system and create socialism. For this reason they stressed that social order was maintained in periods of crisis through 'armed bodies of men', namely the army, the police and gangs of vigilantes.[40]

This outlook was taken over by Lenin and the Communist International and amply vindicated by the events of the first world war and the great depression.[41] These crises did not however lead to the revolutions in Europe that socialists had expected. Following the second world war capitalist governments began using Keynesian methods to avoid economic depression and held back from a great power war for fear of atomic weapons. This meant that the left had to develop strategies designed to counter the widespread acceptance of capitalism by the masses in the resulting period of affluence. Marx and Engels had been only too aware during the long booms of the nineteenth century that the masses will accept capitalism in a boom period, but they had not sought to analyse this fact or do anything about it.

It was probably also true, as Reich argued, that in the nineteenth century booms had simply made the masses apathetic, while in the twentieth century they produced a positive admiration of the upper classes and authority that were in the case of the working class barely shaken by crisis; and in the case of the lower middle class were actually increased by crisis.[42]

Other problems also impelled the left to seek an analysis of social control in the post-war period. After Kruschev's 'secret' speech in 1956, it became respectable to admit that Stalin had imprisoned and killed millions in his purges. Thus it appeared that the 'economic base' of a nationalised economy was not sufficient to ensure a humane form of socialism. The 'political and ideological superstructure', which was now generally thought to include the motives, attitudes and personality dynamics of the population, needed some independent attention. It was no longer enough to nationalise the economy and neglect or play down problems of the superstructure. In addition, Reich had run foul of Stalinist orthodoxy in the 1930s and this entitled him in some quarters to the status of a minor saint.

It could be asked why the left chose to express its interest in the 'superstructure' of personality through the pessimistic Freudian tradition, rather than through other traditions. In fact the enthusiasm for Freud was only one of three similar lines of inquiry that developed in the period after the second world war. In the work of Fromm and Sartre an effort was made to understand social personality through the existentialist tradition. Somewhat later Habermas, in the 1960s, began to apply the Kantian tradition to the same problem. Other traditions had little to offer. Behaviourism gave small attention to social psychology or social values; the ethological tradition could only be used for strictly conservative purposes; the mystical tradition tended to neglect social affairs; the philosophy of history was precisely what the left was reacting against, for in the extreme Hegelian philosophy history could never take a wrong turning. Stalin had justified his policies in terms of the long term interests of the Soviet state and the long term interests of humanity, which were assumed identical. The question that dissidents were now asking was: How long can we postpone judgement on the Soviet or any other experiment? When it came to judging human interests in the present, some standard had to be applied, such as were the members of the society happy or did they feel their lives to be meaningful? This meant turning to some view of human nature to approach these questions. The idea that history was always inevitable and right had become a monster from which socialist theory needed to be delivered.

Reich himself was not, in the 1930s, tackling the problems of social control in a non-crisis period. He was chiefly concerned with the mass acceptance of fascism in Germany. After the war, however, his findings continued to appear relevant to those who thought that the propaganda methods and character structure of fascism were being perpetuated in the West behind a democratic facade.

In *Character Analysis* (first edition 1933) Reich outlines a number of differences with Freud. He believes the Oedipus complex is a result of childrearing in the authoritarian family and is produced by the sexual repressiveness of such families, often accompanied by threats of castration to boys.[43] This contrasts with Freud's view that the Oedipus complex is a product of fantasies that are partly biologically determined. The chief results of the Oedipus complex in the authoritarian personality are for Reich an identification with authority and a weakening of ability to manage one's own affairs and think for oneself.[44] Freud thought that suppression of sexual energy was involved in the Oedipus conflicts when the parents discourage the child's incestuous and other sexual inclinations. For him this was the only way a large amount of energy could be made available for higher mental processes and thinking. For Reich sexual energy is naturally channelled into thinking and it is through sexual repression that this natural channelling is blocked and the helpless authoritarian character emerges, dependent upon a *Fuhrer* or leader to think for them. By these means Reich turned the tables on Freud's view of the Oedipal conflicts. Rather than dwelling on the need to learn to live with the effects of the Oedipus complex he can now emphasise the need to abolish the authoritarian family and get rid of the Oedipus complex and the authoritarian personality. As might be expected Reich also argues that Freud's death instinct is 'supposed to explain biologically facts which are derived from the structure of present day society' (i.e. tendencies towards self-punishment and war).[45] Reich accordingly rejects the death instinct.

Character Analysis also contains an ambitious programme for studying the production of the various kinds of reactionary character:

'The result of character formation is dependent upon: the phase in which the impulse is frustrated (i.e. oral, anal or Oedipal); the frequency and intensity of the frustrations; the impulses against which the frustration is chiefly directed; the sex of the person chiefly responsible for the frustrations; the contradictions in the frustrations themselves.'[46]

The formation of five such character types is outlined: the aristocratic; the hysterical; the compulsive; the phallic-narcissistic; and the masochistic. In addition *Character Analysis* devotes considerable attention to Reich's notion of 'character armour'. This includes all habitual behaviour which individuals use to 'absorb dammed-up psychic energy', including typical posture, muscle tone and manner of speech. Among the examples given are those of two men suffering from ejaculatio praecox (premature ejaculation):[47]

'Let us further assume that the *ejaculatio praecox* of the two male patients has the same unconscious meaning: fear of the (paternal) phallus assumed to be in the woman's vagina. On the basis of the castration anxiety which lies at the root of the symptom, both patients produce a negative father transference in the analysis. They hate the analyst (father) because they perceive in him the enemy who limits their pleasure, and each of them has the unconscious desire to dispose of him. While the phallic-sadistic character will ward off the danger of castration by means of vituperations, disparagements, and threats, the passive-feminine character will become more and more confiding, more and more passively devoted, and more and more accommodating. In both of them the character has become a resistance: the former wards off the danger aggressively; the latter gets out of its way by compromising his standards, by deceptiveness and devotion.'[48]

In 1933 Reich also published *The Mass Psychology of Fascism*. Here he was concerned to explain two things: the mass adherence of the German lower middle class to fascism; and the failure of the German working class, particularly the Social Democrats, to stop them. The refined distinctions between different character types are largely abandoned. Instead Reich concentrates on showing how the authoritarian personality with its helplessness and admiration for authority is produced both in the family and in the social environment of the adult. His argument is that both these factors are important in producing the social attitudes of the adult, with the family having a slightly greater role.[49]

The social attitudes of the lower middle class are a joint product of an upbringing within the authoritarian family and their position as adults within the economic system. The influence of the latter is described as follows:

'The answer to this is supplied by the social position of the lower- and middle-class public and private officials. The economic position of the average official is worse than that of the average skilled industrial worker; this poorer position is partially compensated by the meagre prospect of a career, and in the case of the government official by a lifelong pension. Thus dependent upon governmental authority, a competitive bearing towards one's colleagues prevailed in this class, which counteracts the development of solidarity. The social consciousness of the official is not characterized by the fate he shares with his co-workers, but by his attitude to the government and to the 'nation'. This consists of a complete identification with the state power; in the case of the company employee, it consists of an identification with the company. He is just as submissive as the industrial worker. Why is it that he does not develop a feeling of solidarity as the industrial worker does? This is due to his intermediate position between authority and the body of manual labourers. While subordinate to the top, he is to those below him a representative of this authority and enjoys, as such, a privileged moral (not material) position. The arch personification of this type in the psychology of the masses is to be found in the army sergeant.

'Butlers, valets and other such employees of aristocratic families are a flagrant example of the power of this identification. By adopting the attitudes, way of thinking and demeanour of the ruling class, they undergo a complete change and, in an effort to minimize their lowly origin, often appear as caricatures of the people whom they serve.'[50]

The family upbringing of the social democratic worker is described as follows:

'When psychoanalysts unversed in sociology try to explain social revolution as an 'infantile revolt against the father', they have in mind the 'revolutionary' who comes from intellectual circles. This is indeed the case there. But it does not apply to the industrial worker. The paternal suppression of children among the working class is not less severe, indeed, it is sometimes more brutal than it is among the lower middle class. This is not the issue. That which specifically distinguishes these two classes is found in their modes of production and the attitude towards sex which derives from these modes. The point is this: Sexuality is suppressed by the parents among the industrial workers also. But the contradictions to which the children of industrial workers are subjected don't exist in the lower middle class. Among the lower middle class it is only sexuality that is suppressed. The sexual activity of this class is a pure expression of the contradiction between sexual drive and sexual inhibition. This is not the case among the industrial workers. Along with their moralistic ideology the industrial workers have their own - in some cases more and in others less pronounced - sexual views, which are diametrically opposed to the moralistic ideology. Moreover, there is the influence exercised by their living conditions and their close association in their work. All of this runs counter to their moralistic sexual ideology.

'Accordingly, the average industrial worker differs from the average lower middle-class worker by his open and untrammelled attitude towards sexuality, no matter how muddled and conservative he might be otherwise. He is incomparably more accessible to sex-economic views than the typical lower middle-class worker is.'[51]

The economic position of the worker thus encourages social solidarity, a belief in socialism and the international brotherhood of the working class. This is however counteracted by the partially repressive nature of the worker's upbringing, which encourages passivity and respect for the wisdom of the social democratic leaders.

Just as he is able to give an account of authoritarianism that includes the effect of childhood experiences, the economics of sexual energy and the economic position of the adult, so Reich is able to relate these factors to religion. The mysticism of normal religions becomes, in fascism, part of the mysticism of blood and *Volk* encouraged by Hitler's propaganda. Reich describes the influence of sexual energy, economic development and childhood experiences upon religion as follows:

'I do not want at this point to make a thorough investigation of religious feeling. I would like merely to summarize what is already known. At a certain point there is a correlation between the phenomena of orgastic excitation and the phenomena of religious excitation, ranging from the simplest pious surrender to total religious ecstasy. The idea of religious excitation is not to be confined to the sensations that are wont to arise in deeply religious people while attending a religious service. We have to include all excitations that are characterized by a definite psychic and somatic state of excitation. In other words, we also have to include the excitation experienced by submissive masses when they open themselves to a beloved leader's speech, and the excitation one experiences when one allows oneself to be overwhelmed by impressive natural phenomena. Let us begin by summarizing what was known about religious phenomena before sex-economic research.

'Sociological research was able to show that religious forms and also the contents of various religions were dependent upon the stage of development of socio-economic conditions. For example, animal religions correspond to the mode of life of primitive peoples who lived from hunting. The way in which people conceive of a divine supernatural being is always determined by the level of the economy and of the culture. Another very important sociological factor in determining religious conceptions is man's ability to master natural and social difficulties. Helplessness in the face of natural forces and elemental social catastrophes is conducive to the development of religious ideologies in cultural crises. Thus, the sociological explanation of religion refers to the socio-economic soil from which religious cults spring. It has nothing to say about the dynamics of religious ideology, nor does it give us any clue as to the psychic process that takes place in the people who come under the influence of this ideology.

'Thus, the formation of religious cults is not dependent upon the will of the individual. They are sociological formations, which originate from the interrelations between man and man and the relation of man to nature.

'The psychology of the unconscious added a psychological interpretation to the sociological interpretation of a religion. The dependency of religious cults upon socio-economic factors was understood. Now one began to study the psychological process in the people who came under the influence of these objective religious cults. Thus, psychoanalysis was able to show that our idea of God is identical with our idea of father, that the idea of the Mother of God is identical with the mother of every religious individual. The triangle of father, mother and child is directly reflected in the trinity of the Christian religion. The psychic content of religion is drawn from early childhood familial relationships.'[52]

In his later years Reich thought he had found a means of isolating and controlling mental energy by physical means (the orgone box). This claim has generally been greeted with scepticism, but it did correspond to a vital need within Reich's view of politics. In his earlier work he had complained that the analysis of individual patients could not hope to treat enough people to bring about a social transformation: 'only a thorough turnover of social institutions and ideologies, a turnover that will depend upon the outcome of the political struggles of our century, will create the preconditions for an extensive prophylaxis of neurosis.'[53] His later position was that a radical politics would have to begin from changes in the personality of the individual. Orgone research seemed to provide the necessary hope of mass application.

Whatever the vagaries of his later work *The Mass Psychology of Fascism* remains one of the first and most successful of the attempts that have been made to combine psychoanalysis with sociology and social psychology. Its defect is one of those difficulties found in Freud himself, the overemphasis on sexual repression. For the sexual revolution advocated by Reich has largely come about, yet the improvement in human character hoped for has not.

There are two ways of taking this. One is to acknowledge that the repression of aggression was more fundamental than that of sexuality for the problems approached by Reich. This would take us back to Nietzsche and the difficulty of reinventing tragic culture. Another possibility, taken up by Marcuse and others, is to argue that the release of sexuality has taken place in an unconstructive way. Marcuse, while relying heavily on Freudian theory, also argues that the release of aggression has occurred in a similarly reactionary way. On this last point there can be no argument, but to acknowledge it we hardly need to buy into the Freudian myths about sexuality as Marcuse does.

Marcuse (1898-1977)

Like Fromm, Marcuse had belonged to the Frankfurt Institute for Social Research in the 1930s. Unlike Fromm he remained relatively uninterested in the application of psychoanalysis to the understanding of social psychology until after the second world war. During the war most members of the Institute migrated to the United States. After the war Marcuse remained in America. Here he began to feel that although formally democratic governments ruled in the West, a new type of individual had appeared who was incapable of true dissent. By the manipulation of public opinion powerful interests were able to gain democratic assent to whatever they wished. In *Eros and Civilisation* (1955) Marcuse used Freud's ideas to point a way out of this situation. Like Reich, Marcuse argues that, with only slight modification, Freudian theory can be turned from conservatism to radicalism. He thinks Freud's greatness lies precisely in his pessimism. This enabled Freud to recognise the severity of the general social crisis that began with the first world war. It also enabled Freud to shatter the enlightenment myth of progress: that increasing civilisation leads to increasing happiness. Freud argues that increasing civilisation means greater instinctual repression and thus potentially greater misery. The more individuals have to renounce immediate satisfaction in favour of delayed and substitute gratifications the more miserable they become. But this, Marcuse argues, is not a necessary state of affairs. He distinguishes between 'surplus-repression' ('the restrictions necessitated by social domination') and 'basic repression' ('the modification of the instincts necessary for the perpetuation of the human race in civilisation').[54] If surplus-repression can be removed then the helplessness and submission to authority of the authoritarian mind will be weakened.

But to understand the new form of authority-worship we must extend Freud's analysis of the Oedipal situation to take account of the post-war form of managed society. Here the family is no longer the decisive instrument of personality formation. Its place has been taken by education and mass entertainment. Freud's view of the impact of the Oedipus conflicts on the child had been true, but is now obsolete:

'The superego is loosened from its origin, and the traumatic experience of the father is superseded by more exogenous images. As the family becomes less decisive in directing the adjustment of the individual to society, the father-son conflict no longer remains the model-conflict. This change derives from the fundamental economic processes which have characterized, since the beginning of the century, the transformation of 'free' into 'organized' capitalism. The independent family enterprise and, subsequently, the independent personal enterprise cease to be the units of the social system; they are being absorbed into large-scale impersonal groupings and associations. At the same time, the social value of the individual is measured primarily in terms of standardized skills, and qualities of adjustment rather than autonomous judgment and personal responsibility.

'The technological abolition of the individual is reflected in the decline of the social function of the family. It was formerly the family which for good or bad, reared and educated the individual, and the dominant rules and values were transmitted personally and transformed through personal fate. To be sure, in the Oedipus situation, not individuals but 'generations' (units of the same genus) faced each other; but in the passing and inheritance of the Oedipus conflict they became individuals, and the conflict continued into an individual life history. Through the struggle with father and mother as personal targets of love and aggression, the younger generation entered societal life with impulses, ideas, and needs which were largely their own. Consequently, the formation of their superego, the repressive modification of their impulses, their renunciation and sublimation were very personal experiences. Precisely because of this, their adjustment left painful scars, and life under the performance principle still retained a sphere of private non-conformity.

'Now, however, under the rule of economic, political, and cultural monopolies, the formation of the mature superego seems to skip the stage of individualization: the generic atom becomes directly a social atom. The repressive organization of the instincts seems to be collective, and the ego seems to be prematurely socialized by a whole system of extra-familial agents and agencies. As early as the pre-school level, gangs, radio, and television set the pattern for conformity and rebellion; deviations from the pattern are punished not so much within the family as outside and against the family. The experts of the mass media transmit the required values; they offer the perfect training in efficiency, toughness, personality, dream, and romance. With this education, the family can no longer compete. In the struggle between the generations, the sides seem to be shifted: the son knows better; he represents the mature reality principle against its obsolescent paternal forms. The father, the first object of aggression in the Oedipus situation, later appears as a rather inappropriate target of aggression. His authority as transmitter of wealth, skills, experiences is greatly reduced; he has less to offer, and therefore less to prohibit. The progressive father is a most unsuitable enemy and a most unsuitable 'ideal' - but so is any father who no longer shapes the child's economic, emotional, and intellectual future. Still, the prohibitions continue to prevail, the repressive control of the instincts persists, and so does the aggressive impulse.'[55]

The sexual liberation of the modern era is phoney for two reasons: it is calculated and manipulated gratification; and it confines sexual gratification to a single area of life. The 'pleasure principle' involves spontaneity, while today 'in their erotic relations they 'keep their appointments' - with charm, with romance, with their favourite commercials'.[56] In a truly liberated society sexuality would infuse the whole of life:

'These prospects seem to confirm the expectation that instinctual liberation can lead only to a society of sex maniacs - that is, to no society. However, the process just outlined involves not simply a release but a transformation of the libido: from sexuality constrained under genital supremacy to erotization of the entire personality. It is a spread rather than explosion of libido - a spread over private and societal relations which bridges the gap maintained between them by a repressive reality principle. This transformation of the libido would be the result of a societal transformation that released the free play of individual needs and faculties. By virtue of these conditions, the free development of transformed libido beyond the institutions of the performance principle differs essentially from the release of constrained sexuality within the dominion of these institutions. The latter process explodes suppressed sexuality; the libido continues to bear the mark of suppression and manifests itself in the hideous forms so well known in the history of civilization; in the sadistic and masochistic orgies of desperate masses, of 'society elites', of starved bands of mercenaries, of prison and concentration-camp guards. Such release of sexuality provides a periodically necessary outlet for unbearable frustration; it strengthens rather than weakens the roots of instinctual constraint; consequently, it has been used time and again as a prop for suppressive regimes. In contrast, the free development of transformed libido within transformed institutions, while eroticizing previously tabooed zones, time, and relations, would minimize the manifestations of mere sexuality by integrating them into a far larger order, including the order of work. In this context, sexuality tends to its own sublimation: the libido would not simply reactivate precivilized and infantile stages, but would also transform the perverted content of these stages.'[57]

The frustration of the modern individual is increased by the general ignorance of those social forces that control events behind the scenes:

'Happiness involves knowledge: it is the prerogative of the animal rationale. With the decline in consciousness, with the control of information, with the absorption of individual into mass communication, knowledge is administered and confined. The individual does not really know what is going on; the overpowering machine of education and entertainment unites him with all the others in a state of anaesthesia from which all detrimental ideas tend to be excluded.'[58]

Like Freud, Marcuse retains a considerable faith in the power and usefulness of reason.

The final result of these modern forms of repression and unhappiness is an inability to revolt, to espouse ideals or think for oneself. This is often accompanied by outbreaks of mass paranoia and regression to the sado-masochistic or anal phase of development.

'The discrepancy between potential liberation and actual repression has come to maturity: it permeates all spheres of life the world over. The rationality of progress heightens the irrationality of its organization and direction. Social cohesion and administrative power are sufficiently strong to protect the whole from direct aggression, but not strong enough to eliminate the accumulated aggressiveness. It turns against those who do not belong to the whole, whose existence is its denial. This foe appears as the archenemy and Antichrist himself: he is everywhere at all times; he represents hidden and sinister forces, and his omnipresence requires total mobilization. The difference between war and peace, between civilian and military populations, between truth and propaganda, is blotted out. There is regression to historical stages that had been passed long ago, and this regression reactivates the sado-masochistic phase on a national and international scale. But the impulses of this phase are reactivated in a new, 'civilized' manner: practically without sublimation, they become socially 'useful' activities in concentration and labour camps, colonial and civil wars, in punitive expeditions and so on.'[59]

Marcuse's political beliefs underwent a number of transformations. From the dire pessimism of *Eros and Civilisation* he moved on to become in the 1960s the spokesman for youth revolution and the struggle of developing nations to free themselves from capitalism. In *An Essay on Liberation* he projects these as the new forces able to topple the military-industrial complex in the United States. His analysis of them remained however largely descriptive. His belief that youth was the vanguard of the future was certainly not a new one, though it was novel for a self-proclaimed Marxist to abandon the class criterion in this way.

Marcuse's work as a whole presents an unusual difficulty. Unlike most other commentators on Freud he sees quite clearly that radical social change must involve a qualitative break with the deadening quality of modern repression enshrined in Freudian theory. At the same time he is unwilling to question many other doubtful aspects of Freudian ideology, particularly the sometime impact of the Oedipal conflicts on attitudes to authority and the Freudian view that sadism is mainly derived from sex. In general we might anticipate that even more genuine sexual liberation than that seen so far would have less carryover to other aspects of social life than Marcuse thinks. He is, in addition, forced to paint a rather exaggerated picture of the failures of sexual liberation in order to convince us that such side benefits might still be possible in the future.

Fromm (1900-1980)

Fromm was born into an intensely religious German Jewish milieu. He was later to describe how at the ages of twelve and thirteen he was deeply touched by the prophetic writings of Isiah, Amos and Hosea, with their vision of the 'end of days' and the coming of universal brotherhood.[60] This combination of Utopian socialism with religious feeling was to stay with him throughout his career. In the early 1920s he obtained psychoanalytic training at the Berlin Psychoanalytic Institute and in 1926 began to practice clinically. In 1929 he joined the newly founded Frankfurt Psychoanalytic Institute, which had sympathetic connections with, and partly owed its foundation to, the Frankfurt Institute for Social

Investigation that was later to become identified with the names of Horkheimer and Adorno. From this time until the late 1930s Fromm became a de facto member of the nascent 'Frankfurt School', though this close working relationship was later to change to a mutual suspicion.

In the early 1930s unions of Freud and Marx were a daring novelty. Reich's work had met with hostility from communist orthodoxy. Stalin had decreed Pavlov the official psychologist of the party line.[61] Freud himself presented a pessimistic view of human nature quite at variance with traditional Marxist optimism. But by the same token the degeneration of Stalinism opened the road to a pessimistic Marxism that argued for sinister and conservative forces within the human psyche that dragged down revolutions and required a revolution within as well as without. The Frankfurt school had generally become sympathetic to this stance, but were as yet uncertain how to rework Freud.[62] Ultimately both they and Marcuse were to opt for the view that the quasi-biological libido theory was materialist and radical. The 'adventures' of the libido served to introduce the social dimension. The Oedipal theory was a realistic analysis for a now vanishing situation - the patriarchal, repressive, father-dominated family.

From the early 1930's, before this alternative approach had appeared, Fromm was radicalising Freudian theory along different lines. In 1931 he published *The Development of the Dogma of Christ*.[63] Here he argued that the first-century view of Christ as man become God represented a revolutionary hope that human beings could assume control of their destiny. The later, fourth century, idea of God becoming man reflected the extinction of such hopes and acquiescence in the powers that be. Human beings now had to hope like children for divine forgiveness and grace.

Subsequently Fromm became interested in Briffault's book *The Mothers* and in matriarchal theory generally. Such interest in matriarchal theory had a considerable precedent in Engels' *The Origin of the Family*. Here Engels adopted Bachofen and Morgan's view that there had been an original 'stage' of matriarchal society. For Fromm one of the appeals of such views was to stress, against Freud, that men are not always and inevitably dominant.[64]

In 1935 he contributed the important essay 'The social relativity of psychoanalytic therapy' to the Frankfurt Institute's house organ *Review of Social Inquiry*. Here he argues that the function of Freudian theory within the therapeutic situation is to divert attention away from the repressive social values of the analyst on to the mythical aggression of the Oedipal situation. This was a position that Fromm consistently defended thereafter, arguing in an essay on the Oedipus Complex published in 1970 that in his case of Little Hans Freud had distorted his clinical material. 'Freud, influenced by his bias in favour of parental authority and of male superiority, interpreted the clinical material in a one-sided way and failed to account for a number of data which contradict his interpretation.'[65]

In 1936 Fromm contributed an essay to *Studies on Authority and the Family* published in German by the Frankfurt Institute, by then largely transferred to the United States to escape Nazi persecution. Here he is ambivalent towards but still fairly supportive of Freudian libido theory. Sexual sadism still lay, for Fromm, at the heart of the authoritarian personality.

In 1939 Fromm resigned from the Frankfurt Institute, which he had joined while in America. In 1941 he published *Escape from Freedom* in English. Here the two further shifts that were to mark his later work are evident - the adoption of a sociological revision of existentialist metaphysics; and the rejection of the libido theory. In his controversy with Marcuse in the 1950s over the latter's *Eros and Civilisation* Fromm was to claim some residual attachment to the libido theory, but in his later work a non-biological interpretation of love is usually used, a tendency emphasised in the 1969 essay 'Freud's model of man and its social determinants'.[66] Here he argues that the libido theory is a disguised version of the *homo economicus* who 'enters into relations with others in order that they may mutually satisfy their needs'. Fromm had increasingly come to identify capitalism with the satisfaction of fictitious biological needs and opposition to capitalism with the satisfaction of metaphysical needs.

Escape from Freedom appeared in an America preparing to fight fascism. Its theme - the fear of freedom that leads individuals to embrace authoritarian regimes - was timely and the book made Fromm a celebrity. Together with its sequel *Man for Himself* it laid down the distinctive features of his later approach.

Like most modern metaphysicians Fromm is aware that human attitudes to metaphysical problems have altered radically in Western Europe in recent times. Unlike them, he is prepared to abandon the view that earlier metaphysicians had made some kind of mistake in subject matter or methodology. The primary reasons for the shift in Western metaphysics are seen as social.

Medieval European society, Fromm explains, was a world lacking in individual freedom. The individual was born (he quotes Burckhardt) 'as a member of a race, people, party, family, or corporation' and remained as such.[67] In sociological jargon roles were ascribed by sex and parentage rather than achieved by individual effort or flair. Beginning particularly in the Italian renaissance of the fourteenth century this began to change in all social classes to 'a passionate egocentricity, an insatiable greed for power and wealth'.[68] Even for successful members of the ruling orders 'the new freedom brought two things to them: an increased feeling of strength and at the same time an increased isolation, doubt, scepticism, and - resulting from all these - anxiety.'[69] For a few this insecurity could be assuaged by a quest for the fame that ensures immortality and a sense of security. But for the downtrodden masses and the solid middle class this outlet was remote. In the sixteenth century these classes turned to the doctrines of Luther and Calvin for refuge from this intolerable anxiety.

Luther and those to whom he appealed were powerless against the power of state, large capital and the church. This led to an ambivalent psychological attitude which combined elements of rebellion against authority (particularly that of the church) and of submission to and abasement before authority (particularly the predestinating power of God). The individual regains some feeling of self-respect and purpose by becoming an instrument in the hands of God. Following Weber, Fromm argues that the extreme emphasis on predestination in Calvin led to compulsive efforts to work and be successful in order both to channel anxiety and to obtain evidence of election to salvation.

Protestant doctrines also allowed considerable scope for the release of the pent-up aggression of the underdog. The rich and successful were, by and large, destined for the exquisite torments of hellfire. A rigid moralism enabled the lower middle class to righteously persecute those who infringed their code. In self-abasement this aggression was turned inward against the self. It is these tendencies, in an altered and now only partly religious form that have produced the modern 'authoritarian' who is prepared to surrender to a *Führer* or to the authority of public opinion and 'common sense' (here Fromm probably has the United States in mind).[70]

We should not, however, see protestant doctrines as solely destructive. They have sometimes been constructive, particularly in the eighteenth and nineteenth centuries 'when the middle class won its victories, economically and politically, over the representatives of an older order'.[71] Here the strength and dignity of the self was manifested in a positive form. Earlier Fromm has described the fallacy of equating self-love with selfishness. 'True love of self and love of others are metaphysical powers: love is a passionate affirmation of an 'object'; it is not an 'affect' but an active striving and inner relatedness, the aim of which is the happiness, growth and freedom of its object ... Love for one person implies love for man as such. Love for man as such is not, as it is frequently supposed to be, an abstraction coming 'after' the love of a specific person, or an enlargement of the experience with a specific 'object' ...'.[72] The terms are almost exactly those used by Descartes to Princess Elizabeth.

Having discussed general historical developments Fromm turns to a more theoretical analysis of personality mechanisms. The authoritarian personality uses the mechanisms of sadism and masochism, that enable the individual to escape feelings of aloneness and powerlessness. They recreate the lost solidarity of a settled society by permitting a form of close relationship compatible with the universal suspicion of modern society. 'The destruction of the world' on the other hand 'is the last, almost desperate attempt to save myself from being crushed by it.'[73] This is the origin of the widespread destructiveness in contemporary social life. In automaton conformity the individual escapes from the anxiety of insignificance by conforming in every detail to the dictates of public opinion and the mass media. In the concluding chapters Fromm puts these concepts to work in discussing the psychology of Nazism and the internal threat to democracy from the dangers of automaton conformity.

Despite Fromm's claims that *Escape from Freedom* is an analysis of personality that highlights the problem of freedom for purposes of exposition, we cannot escape the impression, reinforced by his later works, that freedom is close to the centre of his analysis. If there are other concepts of comparable importance they are the couples love - being and authority - destructiveness. These however grow out of the basic dilemma of freedom. Having become emancipated from the womb-like embrace of traditional society we may, Fromm says, turn either to fulfil our being in love or to the alternation of authoritarian/automaton rule with the destructiveness of war.

Man for Himself (1947) takes up two further problems - ethics and character types. As we might expect from the title the ethics expounded are humanistic and, like much humanistic ethics, based on Aristotelian teleology.[74] To be virtuous is to allow the full unfolding of one's inner potentialities. When we meet a section titled 'The Existential and Historical Dichotomies in Man' we may imagine such potentialities are to be generated from a Sartrean dialectic of metaphysical freedom. A footnote, however, immediately cautions us that Fromm has not read *Being and Nothingness* and is not using 'existentialism' in a Sartrean sense. Fromm's freedom has now become, rather more clearly than in *Escape from Freedom*, a homelessness - the state of the great wanderers of Western literature: Odysseus, Oedipus, Abraham, Faust. The increase of intellect and decline of instinct has deprived human beings of the natural belongingness of animals. The natural tendency is to explore routes back to this belongingness through religious and non-theistic systems of wisdom like Buddhism and Stoicism. This striving Fromm calls the need for 'frames of orientation and devotion'. He thinks Freud's libido is a creation of mechanistic dogma. The need for 'frames of orientation and devotion' is Fromm's metaphysical replacement for the mechanistic libido. It is no longer religion that springs from neurosis, but rather neurosis springs from a failure to find a satisfactory 'religion', conceived in Fromm's broad sense.[75]

There is a clear implication in this discussion of the flight from homelessness that human beings in some sense naturally tend towards the more benevolent solutions to this problem - Buddhism, metaphysical speculation - and away from the malignant solutions of dictator- and ancestor-worship. This is linked to his belief that dictator- and ancestor-worship are 'primitive', 'early' forms of belonging, while more benevolent systems appear later in social evolution. Someone who is 'blocked in his development' will 'remain on the level which mankind in its best representatives has already overcome thousands of years ago'.[76]

The discussion of character that follows is similar to that of *Escape from Freedom*, except that now a number of personality types are distinguished in an attempt to answer Freud's oral, anal, phallic and genital types.[77] While Freud argues that such types obtain libidinal gratification from different parts of the body, Fromm maintains that they obtain their sense of belonging and being loved in different ways. The receptive type (corresponding to Freud's oral type) obtains gratification from outside, taking love in a passive way, while being unwilling to give it. The hoarding type (Freud's anal compulsive type) gains security through possessions, including possession of the loved one. The exploitative type finds ideas and love outside themselves, but unlike the receptive type, must take them by force. This type appears similar to Freud's anal-sadistic type.

Like those other notable post-Freudians Marcuse and Lacan, Fromm is convinced the automaton-conformity type, which he now calls the 'marketing orientation', is the type most typical of and most fostered by the latest phase of capitalist development. The contemporary professional and executive must acquire a basic level of professional skills, but beyond this the bedside manner of the doctor, aggressive charisma of the executive or cheerful and reliable disposition of the sales assistant have also to be marketed to achieve success. The individual must market himself. Desirable personal characteristics are defined by the education system, mass media and cinema, placing the marketed individual in the power of those who control these sources of indoctrination.

Finally, corresponding to Freud's genital type, comes the productive orientation, capable of both giving and receiving love. The productive person experiences productive thinking and productive love. Productive love implies care, responsibility, respect and knowledge of the other person. Productive thinking involves the use of reason, which Fromm distinguishes from the intelligence used in practical mastery of the world. The description of productive thinking stresses the elements of viewing the totality, penetrating to the essence and care for the object of thought. We may be reminded of Hegelian 'reason' and of Heidegger. At this point however we come on a description of Buddha's reaction to age, sickness and death. By productive thinking Buddha produced his 'fourfold truth' for the achievement of salvation. We are also told that the scientific reaction of a modern physician who attempts to combat death, sickness and age by his own methods would also be 'productive thinking'. Fromm is certainly not the first modern metaphysician to have claimed a close connection between metaphysical and scientific thinking, but his mixture of the two merely creates a banal eclecticism. He wants to set the metaphysician above the scientist, but at the same time to borrow a little of the prestige of modern science.

Fromm's arguments take us back from orthodox Freudian dogma into the territory of metaphysics. Unlike Sartre this is not the metaphysics of an incomprehensible spontaneity, but of caring, a theme of Heidegger that drops out in Sartre. The doubtful area in his work is the great emphasis placed upon caring and the neglect of aggression. His erstwhile colleagues Horkheimer, Adorno and Marcuse in later years accused him of being a Pollyanna.[78] In some of his later work he attempts to meet this kind of objection.

In *The Anatomy of Human Destructiveness* (1974) Fromm takes up the issue of aggression directly. Here we come upon a problem that has not been fully discussed in dealing with previous writers. We have accepted that an 'instinct' is as both Nietzsche and Freud understood it, namely a push towards a given goal that will not go away until something satisfies it. This assumption has often been questioned in regard to aggression. Two other biologically-oriented theories have had considerable appeal. One is that aggression is something that is inherently pleasurable but has no drive attached to it.[79] The other is the 'frustration-aggression' hypothesis of J. Dollard et al, which says that frustration on the way to a goal leads to the generation of something like a drive to aggression.[80] This second possibility has considerable intuitive appeal as it corresponds to the experience we have of frustration. It can also be shown that frustration does lead to the displacement of aggression onto substitute objects that are relatively safe to attack. This second theory ends up in practice very close to Nietzsche's conception. Social life is bound to create frustrations that will then be likely to find their outlet in some form of aggression.

Fromm, however, rather than trying to develop a more adequate version of a biological theory of instinct, adopts a line of argument more in keeping with his own inclination to look towards metaphysics for an answer. Having dismissed Freud and Lorenz he then looks at the frustration-aggression hypothesis as part of a wide-ranging attack on behaviourism. His portrait of behaviourism rightly paints a black picture of this movement and its social meaning. Having scored points in his general analysis he moves on to deal with the frustration-aggression hypothesis. Here he argues that animal experiments prove little about human beings, a point that is well taken. But he then says that the experience of frustration only leads to aggression if the social situation contains a certain kind of meaning: 'If a child, for instance, is forbidden to eat candy, this frustration, provided the parent's attitude is genuinely loving and free from pleasure in controlling, will not mobilise aggression....'.[81] It is the perceived injustice rather than the frustration that produces aggression in such cases.

Whether we accept this or not will depend upon our stand in the age-old controversy as to whether human action is swayed by morality or self-seeking. Experimentation cannot resolve this, but then neither can Fromm's assertion. He goes on to discuss anthropological evidence. Some societies, he argues, are non-aggressive without the need for the repression of violence. Clearly, if true, this would establish his point. He uses the descriptions of such societies given by R. Benedict. M. Mead and G.P. Murdock.[82]

Recently considerable doubt has been thrown on this kind of claim by the publication by Freeman of a first-hand analysis of Samoan Society showing that Margaret Mead's 'classic' description of this society as peace-loving and non-repressive is incredibly inaccurate and that in fact aggression and the repression of aggression are widespread in Samoan life. If Mead's descriptions are not to be trusted then perhaps others' should be re-examined.[83]

Fromm's line of argument here can also be interpreted in the light of the history of ideas. Having repressed, like so many others, the important role of Nietzsche in elaborating the theory of aggression, he is then at liberty to pillory the instinctual view of aggression as typical either of Freudianism, of animal ethology or of behaviourism. This, along with the doubtful anthropological evidence, constitute the main lines of his argument.

We can even go further than this and suggest a little counter-interpretation. The outrageous claim that children are only aggressive when their parents fail them is nothing other than sadism. We have recently seen much of Western society caught in the guilt-trap of this attitude. Under its benign guidance children turn into little monsters and vent their spite on parents paralysed by guilt and 'psychology' into a modern breed of sick sheep. Fortunately the worst excesses of this kind of masochism are now past, though the 'reaction' is bringing a return to stoicism rather than any overcoming of the traditional alternatives.

Fromm's suggestion as to the metaphysical origin of aggression is that it stems from a distorted framework of orientation and devotion. His ideas here are generally vague, eclectic and hark back to traditional religious views of the human condition. He creates the impression that the world religions of Christianity, Buddhism and Hinduism were invitations to a sense of cosy belonging in the world, when both Christianity and Buddhism have strong world-fleeing tendencies and some aspects of Hindu thought encourage the acceptance of violence and killing.[84]

The most recent framework of orientation and devotion discussed by Fromm is the early philosophy of Marx which he tackles in more detail in *Marx's Concept of Man*. Here he provides a valuable introduction to the manuscripts of 1844. The difficulty of reading Marx is that with Feuerbach he is chiefly interested in what separates human beings from the animals. There is little said about what we have in common with the animals, particularly as regards aggression. I suspect that had he worked out his ideas on this topic more fully he would have given more emphasis to the social transformation of our instinctual heritage than we are offered by Fromm.

Lacan (1901-1981)

Lacan belonged to the intellectual movement known as semiotics. This is generally defined as the science of signs, signs being understood as social symbols conveying a meaning or a message, such as traffic signs, badges of office, emblems of status or speech. In social theory there has been a considerable American semiotic or semiological tradition stemming from the work of Morris.[85] Presently however the French tradition is more dominant both internationally and within the United States itself. The dominance of structural-functionalism within American sociology in the 1950's in effect prevented the full flowering of the tradition there.

French semiotics traces its ancestry back to the French linguist Ferdinand de Saussure. Within social theory the first important use of semiotics was by the great French anthropologist Claude Levi-Strauss.[86] Other key figures in its later development have been the sociologist Jean Baudrillard and the psychoanalyst Jacques Lacan.

The French semiotic movement unites two curiously opposed tendencies. On the one hand the rhetorical vocabulary of semiotics gives it a scientific image. Culture and consciousness, it argues, were traditionally studied in an intuitive way by philosophers but the science of signs has brought a new scientific rigour. We find quite conflicting styles and assumptions in the theories, but we might perhaps put that down to the inevitable confusions of a fledgling science.

Yet there is a unifying theme in much of the semiotic tradition. It is the Rousseauan argument that the culture of tribalism was a rich and meaningful one, while the culture of abstract modern societies has dislocated traditional culture patterns in the quest for indefinite adaptability and the arbitrary recombination of cultural elements. Human beings are now forced to be things they were never meant to be.

We cannot be surprised at this emphasis. It is also a central theme in Parsons and has become one of the dominant concerns of advanced industrial societies.[87] Yet there is something a little curious in this caution against the indefinite extension of modernism and the modernistic, 'scientific' language in which it is delivered. The French have always loved paradox, especially one that confounds the dim-witted Anglo-Saxon!

While I have for convenience sometimes referred to semiotics as a method, in Lacan and Baudrillard it is more like a slogan and source of vocabulary. It remains true that this movement gives quite varied answers to questions about human nature.

From 1927 to 1932 Lacan studied medicine and psychiatry in Paris under Clerembault. In 1932 he received his doctorate for a thesis on *Paranoid Psychosis and its Connections with Personality*. This comprises a theoretical preamble followed by an analysis of the case of 'Aimée'. Lacan concludes that 'We can explain the most obvious clinical correlations in the personality of this case as mechanisms of self-punishment produced, according to Freudian theory, by a particular developmental fixation of the psychic energy called libido.'[88] Having thus embraced Freudian libido theory he was to spend much of his later career denouncing it. Lacan's later work concentrates on returning psychoanalysis to the early Freud who interpreted meanings, assailing Freud's later writings as the product of mechanistic philosophy, with their talk of a fictitious mental energy or libido. The Freud Lacan was later to admire was the author of *The Interpretation of Dreams*, *The Psychopathology of Everyday Life* and *Jokes and the Unconscious*.

There are nonetheless interesting intimations of the later Lacan in *Paranoid Psychosis*. Already we find the problems of the unity of the self and of meaning are uppermost. A central place is given to the concept of 'relations of comprehension': 'Jaspers made these 'relations of comprehension' an essential criterion of psychological and psychopathological analysis... Furthermore, for him personality does not extend to the totality of relations of comprehension, but only to what is particular to the individual among the totality of comprehensible genetic relations.'[89]

Of all the European countries France resisted Freud's teaching most strongly. Until after the second world war French psychoanalysis remained weak and divided, associated chiefly with the surrealist movement. During the 1930s Lacan was close to surrealism and published a number of poems in surrealist magazines. The above quotation shows that in addition to this surrealist influence he also used notions of interpretation and understanding borrowed from the philosophy of Karl Jaspers.

Lacan feels quite differently towards Sartre. In Sartre's *Being and Nothingness* we find the isolated consciousness struggling to resolve its internal problems. This metaphysical analysis of the isolated consciousness was later denounced by Lacan in favour of his own 'structuralist' version of the personality, in which the individual is precisely 'what is particular to the individual among the totality of comprehensible genetic relations'. The metaphysics of the isolated consciousness is attacked as 'individualist ideology'.[90] We are to understand that the individual is constituted by insertion into a social system of relations and meanings. Individuality appears only at the margin of this process. Such a conception already appears in *Paranoid Psychosis*: 'Every human manifestation should thus imply, so that we may relate it to personality:

1. a biographical development, which we define objectively by a typical evolution and the relations of comprehension inscribed there. Construed for the subject

by the affective modes under which he lives his life (*Erlebnis*);

2. a conception of self (soi-même), that we define objectively by central attitudes and the dialectical progress that one can discern there. - Construed for the subject by more or less 'ideal' conscious images of himself;

3. a certain *tension in social relations*, that we defined objectively by the pragmatic autonomy of conduct and the bounds of ethical participation that reorient themselves there. - Construed for the subject by the typical value he feels when faced by another person.'[91]

These three entities within the personality can be roughly summed up as feeling-meaning, the ego-ideal (in a more or less Freudian sense) and the conscience. The development of this scheme appears in Lacan's later writings. Note that within it the id (Freud's reservoir of instinctual feelings) has been replaced by feeling-meaning (relations of comprehension) while there are, as in Freud, two agencies for socialising these tendencies - the ego-ideal and the conscience or agency of repression. There is no ego to play the roles of rational spectator and essential self. Lacan was later to severely castigate belief in this rational spectator, who became by the 1950s the hero of American 'ego psychology'.[92]

In 1934 Lacan, following a training analysis, joined the Paris Psychoanalytic Society. In 1936 he presented a paper on his theory of the 'mirror stage' to the Fourteenth Congress of the International Psychoanalytic Association at Marienbad. He was becoming a big fish in the small pond of French psychoanalysis. But after the depredations of the war years the Paris Psychoanalytic Society, the chief French association, had only eleven members in 1945, the same number as at its foundation in 1926. Its response was an aggressive membership drive and by 1951-2 it had seventy analysts in training. The decline of religion and increasing affluence and perplexity were making the secular priesthood of psychoanalysis successful, a popularity that would mushroom in the 1960s. This expansion and popularity posed problems of direction for French psychoanalysis. Some of the original members were, like Lacan, iconoclasts and apostles of permanent surrealist revolution. Others, led by Sacha Nacht, wanted to see psychoanalysis become respectable, as it had in America. They admired the quasi-medical elements of physiological speculation in Freudian theory and wanted in the early 1950s to limit admission to qualified medical practitioners, an approach that ran counter both to Freud's own wishes and to the 1949 training statutes of the Paris Society, written by Lacan, providing for non-medical analysts.[93] At this time Lacan's introduction of short sessions for the training analysis was attacked by his opponents as 'the speedy manufacture of little carbon copies of himself'.[94] By January 1953 Lacan had to promise to provide the standard one hour sessions, though his opponents claimed he broke the agreement. This failed to settle matters. In June 1953 Lacan, Lagache and others resigned from the Paris Psychoanalytic Society to form the French Psychoanalytic Society. The International Psychoanalytic Association, led by Heinz Hartmann and Anna Freud, both 'ego analysts', soon made it clear that Lacan and his co-thinkers would forfeit their membership of the International

Association. In September 1953 Lacan delivered his 'Discourse of Rome' to a group of analysts in Rome, establishing psychoanalysis as a linguistic rather than a medical science. It should be stressed, however, that this was to have little in common with academic linguistics.

Many members of the French Psychoanalytic society still wanted membership in the International Association. They were concerned to legitimate their practice in France and to break out of their international isolation. After a long process the French Society split in 1963 and the majority group re-affiliated to the International Association in 1965. In 1964 the group around Lacan decided upon an experiment with a new kind of society that would be open to anyone interested in psychoanalysis. After attending as many courses as they wished and undergoing as much training analysis as they liked a person could, in this Freudian School, authorise themselves to be a trained psychoanalyst. Under French law the term 'psychoanalyst' has no legal status and legally even a completely untrained person could take the decision to become an analyst and set up in practice. A rather similar situation has existed in England regarding the profession of 'psychotherapist'.

However, like all schools, the Freudian School soon acquired a hidden curriculum, for while anyone could authorise themselves to analyse, to 'do research' you needed a 'pass', which involved examination both by others training for a pass and by a committee of senior analysts that always included Lacan. Thus a new criterion of being 'officially successful' was introduced, once again involving judgement from the top. This fuelled the continuing allegations that Lacan preached the democracy of scientific discovery while covertly engaging in bureaucratic manipulation. He was also increasingly accused of claiming scientific objectivity while practising theatre for the benefit of the media. Within the Freudian School, aided by his growing status as a media cult figure, Lacan began to assume the powers of a philosophical dictator. Incredibly, when the school put out its own journal *Scilicet*, in 1968, only articles by Lacan were signed.

In 1966 Lacan published a large collection of his writings under the title *Écrits*. This became the 'bible' of Lacanian doctrine. While nearly all the pieces are occasional and bear the marks of his long history of bureaucratic in-fighting, there is, mercifully, a 'Rational Index to Major Concepts' by the prophet's son-in-law Jaques-Alain Miller. This index has Lacan's blessing as a codification of his theory and will be used in what follows to outline his position in 1966. It should be added that *Écrits* begins, after the introduction, with a lengthy section 'On Our Antecedents', containing Lacan's early writings. His 1966 views appear chiefly in the sections 'Now to Our Topic' and 'A Project'.

No introductory comments on Lacan would be complete without a complaint about his style. Lacan and his supporters claim that his rambling, multilingual, jargonised, allusive and fragmentary texts speak the language of the unconscious. It seems that the unconscious is highly educated. They also claim that if the meaning eludes the reader or listener a dream will occur later to clarify things. Many people forget these dreams.

One philosophical position is of particular importance in understanding *Écrits*. Lacan belongs to the epistemological school of Bachelard and Althusser.[95] He denies the theory of Aristotle and common sense that a proposition or theory is more or less true depending on how well it corresponds with reality. Between common sense (which is always a kind of ideology) and science lies an 'epistemological break'. This view emphasises the extreme difficulty we have in breaking out of an established way of thinking. Once this grips us, nothing short of a radical break can shock us out of it. For Althusser Marx achieved this break with bourgeois ideology when he adopted the concept 'mode of production' to replace bourgeois theories of society based on the essence of the individual or the essence of historical periods.

We should not be tempted to relate this epistemology to any peculiarly French passion for dogma. Recent Anglo-Saxon and German philosophy have arrived at somewhat similar philosophies of science in the doctrines of Kuhn and Popper.[96] One probable reason for the popularity of this kind of philosophy of science is that physics and chemistry have now reached a stage at which research is heavily dependent upon theory. The entities met with in theory (fundamental particles, types of radiation) are not directly encountered in everyday life and only rarely in industrial processes. To detect these entities and to manipulate them requires instruments and apparatus guided by theory.

Turning to Miller's conceptual index of the *Écrits* we find three main headings dealing with the relation of the individual to society: the symbolic order; the *moi* and the subject; desire and its interpretation. The term *moi* (I) will be left untranslated. The nearest equivalent in English usage would be *ego*, but Lacan dislikes the connotations of the Freudian ego - its independence and rationality.

The section of the index on the symbolic contains three main topics: the supremacy of the signifier; the defiles of the signifier; the chain of signification. The problem dealt with throughout is the insertion of the individual into the symbolic social order.

The distinction between signifier and signified is, Lacan tells us, taken from the academic linguist Ferdinand de Saussure.[97] The signifier is the symbol or sign - picture, word, dream image, gesture. The signified is the thing referred to by these things. Neither traditional thought nor academic linguistics were able to correctly assess the relation between the two. Only psychoanalysis could show that it is not the rational order of an outside world that structures the way we picture, talk about, dream of and indicate the world. Rather it is the collision between the individual and the symbolic order that structures the way we understand and feel. The signifiers (the pictures, words, dreams, gestures) dominate the signified (the world). This is what Lacan means by the supremacy of the signifier:

'Only psychoanalysis is in a position to bring home this primacy (of the signifier over the signified) in showing that the signifier does without all thought, however unreflective, to achieve indubitable regroupings in the significations that enslave the subject; and to manifest itself in him by alienating intrusion, whose psychoanalytic concept of symptom takes on an emergent sense: the sense of the signified that connotes the relation of the subject to the signifier.'[98] The symptom, Lacan is saying, symbolises the relation between the signifier and the signified.

It is the gesture of despair we make on finding ourselves imprisoned within the cage of the languages that surround us in words, gestures, kinship systems.

Also under the topic of 'supremacy of the signifier' we find 'structure - the symbolic, the imaginary, the real'. The symbolic means primarily the structure of kinship systems, supported by the all-important taboo against incest. The Oedipus complex achieves its importance as the means by which the child is inserted into this symbolic order of kinship.[99] The little girl must learn that she is a daughter and not a wife - she must learn to give up her ambition to marry her father just as the little boy must abandon his ambition to marry his mother. But for both sexes it is the name of the father, the symbol of symbols, that symbolises the law of kinship relations. It is the father who exercises authority in the family. To this one might object that women have great influence in the family and have historically had an interest in maintaining marriage as a safeguard for their children. Lacan does not seem to regard these points as telling. An explanation of the terms 'the imaginary' and 'the real' is given later.

The topic 'defiles of the signifier' brings us to the heart of Lacanian theory with the genesis of the *moi* and the subject. The *moi* is formed through 'imaginary identification', while the subject is formed through 'symbolic identification'. In these two concepts we re-encounter respectively the 'conception of the self' (self ideal) and the 'tension in social relations' of *Paranoid Psychosis*.

The *moi* is formed at the mirror stage. Between about six months and eighteen months infants enjoy looking at themselves in a mirror, delighted both by the realisation that this is themselves and by their ability to move arms and legs and see the movements in the mirror. Previous to this the young infant imagines the various parts of its body as separable. Lacan follows Melanie Klein in thinking that prior to the unification of the self the infant engages in aggressive and incorporative fantasies of omnipotence and paranoia involving both its own body parts and those of the mother and father.[100] Klein pictures the infant in imagination swallowing, biting and tearing to pieces parts of the parents.

Lacan, however, is more interested in what happens after the formation of the *moi* - the self image:

'The time of the mirror stage inaugurates, by identification with the *imago* of others and the drama of primordial jealousy (so well emphasised by the school of Charlotte Buhler in the facts of infant *transitivism*), the dialectic that henceforth connects the ego to elaborate social situations.

'This is the moment that decisively overturns all human knowledge through mediation by the desire of the other, constitutes its objects in an abstract equivalence by the agreement of another, and makes of the je an apparatus for which all instinctual strivings will be a danger, even though they are products of a natural maturation - even normal human maturation will henceforth depend on a cultural mouthpiece: so that the child may see itself as a sexual object in the Oedipus complex.'[101] Lacan is as usual unwilling to base himself primarily on a biologically maturing sex drive.

The drive that inserts the child as *moi* into a world of selves is above all narcissism - a term whose origin in the myth of Narcissus admiring his reflection is congenial to Lacan. This is intimately linked to aggression. Lacan attacks Freud's theory of aggressive or 'death' instincts as a biological fiction.[102] The young child's relations with other small children, between the ages of six months and two and a half years, are governed by an uncanny empathy. The child who hits another says he has been hit, while to see another child fall produces tears.[103] 'By the same token in an identification with another he experiences the whole gamut of reactions of swagger and display, his behaviour showing the structural ambivalence of the slave identified with the despot, the actor with the spectator, the seduced with the seducer.'[104] Envy for what other children have consumes the small child (he cites Augustine's remarks here). By wanting what the other child wants the child is asserting his narcissism, his wish to take the object of desire and be looked at with it by the child who now has it. Like adults, children can be very aggressive in seizing toys and possessions.

There follows a section on the role of aggression in 'the modern neurosis and the malaise of civilisation'.[105] The general encouragement of narcissism and the resulting aggression in modern capitalism is discussed here. Presumably a more complete analysis would also discuss the fantastic flowering of aggression in medieval and ancient civilisations, though these are not mentioned. Plato is praised for having shown that city life erodes both the superego and the ego-ideal. This erosion is for Lacan, as for Marcuse, one of the prime causes of the high level of aggression in modern capitalism.

Lacan also accuses our concept of space of precipitating the century of total war. Here we find one of his clearest statements on the development of 'the real':

'We will say that it is the subjective possibility of the projection of such a spatial field in the field of the other that gives the human species its originally 'geometric' structure, a structure that we willingly call kaleidoscopic. Such at least is the space in which the imagery of the moi develops, and which abuts the objective space of reality. But does it give us a place of repose? Already from the ever more tightly packed 'living space' in which human competition develops, an observer on another star would conclude we needed to avoid working alone. But the conceptual space to which we think we have reduced the real, isn't it already breaking down in theoretical physics? So as to have penetrated the foundations of matter, this 'realised' space that makes the great spaces of the imaginative creations of the ancient sages seem illusory, won't it too be made to disappear in a foundational catastrophe?'[106]

This is the stuff of metaphysical speculation - dark hints of a crack in the foundations of our world-view that will open new possibilities. Dante's creation of the imaginary spaces of heaven, hell and purgatory is mentioned in the continuation: though Dante inspired morality through the pains and pleasures of his regions rather than through the metaphysics of space. The ever-present picture of nuclear annihilation stands before us in our own 'realised' space. Perhaps it is our terrifying eagerness to embrace this annihilation that persuades Lacan there must be a deeper problem. At any event we receive little more than hints of what this might be.

We now turn to the production of the subject; Lacanian terminology for the production of the conscience as an instrument for the suppression of 'immoral' ideas and impulses. Here the 'name of the father' acts as a symbol for the insertion of the subject into the symbolic order of kinship. This involves a 'secondary identification' that introjects the *imago* of the parent of the same sex.[107]

'The energy for this identification is given by the first biological surge of genital libido. But it is clear that the structural effect of identification with the rival only comes from the self on the level of fable, and could not be conceived unless prepared by a primary identification that structures the subject as a rival to himself.'[108] Rivalry and envy are the essence of the child's narcissistic relations with its peers at the mirror stage. The child has now so to speak discovered that someone like him (father for the boy) has an even better toy (mother for the boy). It is this education in rivalry that unleashes the fury of the child's hostile impulses towards the same sex parent. If little children say they will kill for toys, then they will imagine killing for sexual possession.

We are now in a position to better understand the distinction between the imaginary, the real and the symbolic. The imaginary relates to the mirror games of narcissistic envy that occur at the mirror stage, the symbolic to the insertion within kinship structures that occurs with the Oedipal phase. The original emergence of the real is from the empathic struggles of the imaginary. Above all this establishes our idea of 'real space'. Later, however, both the real and the imaginary are structured by 'the supremacy of the symbolic over the real and the imaginary'.

If two people both hate the same particular thing, perhaps a dog that has bitten them both, they do not need to communicate their common dislike in language.[109] Both of them show fear and dislike in the presence of the dog and this binds them together. This is similar to the gestures and grimaces of infants at the mirror stage, who directly empathise with one another. Symbolic communication in language, however, presupposes at least a 'general narrator'. This general narrator is not, however, anonymous. In one of his most extended discussions of 'the signifying chain' that establishes the supremacy of the signifier over the signified Lacan deals with 'The Stolen Letter', a story translated into French from English by Baudelaire. This involves a compromising letter stolen from a queen. One of the things that interests Lacan here is that we are never told just how the letter compromises the queen with her king: 'A love letter or a letter of conspiracy, accusatory or instructive, summons or letter of distress, we only know one thing, that the queen would not wish to bring it to the knowledge of her lord and master. But these terms, far from retaining the discredited sense that they have in bourgeois drama, become highly appropriate to designate her sovereign, to whom she is bound by broken faith; and that in two ways, since her position as consort does not relieve her of her duty as subject, but rather teaches her to defend the power legally incarnated in royalty: which is known as legitimacy. Henceforth, whatever sequels the queen might have chosen to find for the letter, it remains that this letter is the symbol of a pact, and that, even if its recipient does not enter into this pact, the existence of the letter situates her in a symbolic chain different from that to which she owes allegiance.'[110]

By a trick the letter is later hidden. This, says Lacan, is a representation of the imaginary, that would like 'to see in order not to be seen, to misrecognise the real situation where he (the protagonist) is seen in order not to see. And what did he fail to see? Precisely the symbolic situation that he knew quite well how to see, and where now he is seen seeing himself not being seen.'[111] This is not, however, the triumph of the imaginary over the symbolic. For even while hidden, the letter (the symbolic) continues to determine the roles of the various participants in the story. They are playing the parts of worrying about the letter, hiding it, looking for it.

This story is a parable of the disguised expression of wishes in symbols - the heart of the Freudian theory of symptom formation. The imaginary gets hold of the symbolic and recodes it, which is actually how the letter is hidden in the story. We may well object that Lacan only offers an 'imaginative' solution to the question of how messages are recoded by the unconscious. The presence of the term 'mirror' in the phrase 'mirror stage' makes us think of recodings by reflection in mirrors. But young children don't recode messages in mirrors. They like seeing without being seen, but again the connection with the recoding of unconscious messages in dreams is largely by cleverly phrased analogy. Lacan has in effect produced a kind of interpretation squared, though this was admittedly begun by Freud. The first level of interpretation is that involving the decoding of dreams, gestures, slips of the tongue into sexual meanings. Then we have the problem of how to interpret the three departments of wish, recoding and symptom. Freud, with his biological theory, could interpret these as sexual wish, transformation due to fear of 'the censor' or later 'the superego' (the introjected father) and finally disguised symptom. Freud does not give a great deal of attention to interpreting the transformation process. It is more or less a fact that the mind has certain mechanisms at its disposal for disguising symptoms. Lacan actually interprets all three departments. The wish is, in neurosis, some 'pact' or other symbolic manoeuvre against the opposite sex parent. The recoding is an intervention of 'the imaginary'. The symptomatic expression is the result of the second acting on the first.

Lacan has not, however, quite finished even his early (1955-6) version of the dominance of the symbolic over the imaginary. For in a second and more technical section of the seminar on 'The Stolen Letter' he produces 'schema L', a diagram given much prominence in *Écrits* as a whole. This is preceded by a discussion of Freud's observations of a small boy who tied a cotton reel to a piece of string and played at making the reel disappear and reappear, uttering commands to the reel as he did so. The boy imagined, said Freud, that the reel was his mother and the symbolic manipulation was a means of dealing with the emotion of loss felt when the mother left the child. The essential feature of 'schema L', reproduced below, is that it shows that in communicating with another the *moi* and the subject of each participant are involved.

Thus each has a relation at the imaginary level and a relation at the symbolic (unconscious) level. This raises the difficult question of what Lacan means by 'the unconscious is the discourse of the other', which clearly relates to schema L. He says in 'The direction of the cure and the principles of its power' (1958):

'Desire produces itself in the beyond of the demand, from that which in articulating the life of the subject to its surrounding conditions, demand prunes from desire. But also it embeds itself in its own side, as through the unconditional demand of presence and absence, it evokes the lack of being under the three emblems of nothing that are at the bottom of it; the demand for love; of the hate that tries to deny the being of the other; and of the inexpressible which does not know itself in its request...(the nothing) is less the pure passion of the signified than pure action of the signifier, that stops, the moment the living being become sign makes it insignificant/unsignifying.[112]

'This moment of rupture is haunted by the form of a bloodstained scrap: the pound of flesh that life pays to make that scrap the signifier of signifiers, as such impossible to restore to the imaginary body; it is the lost phallus of Osiris embalmed.'[113]

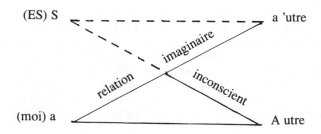

Schema L

In the continuation we encounter the case of a woman who dreamt: 'She had a phallus, she felt it under her clothes, which didn't stop her from having a vagina, nor from desiring above all that the phallus might go there... Here the opportunity is unique to elucidate the situation we describe in these terms: that unconscious desire is the desire of the Other - although the dream is made to satisfy the patient's desire beyond her request and it suggests that it might succeed in doing that. In not being a dream of the patient, it would be worthless, if in not addressing us as a patient, it speaks to her as well as the analyst could.

'This is the occasion to bring home to the patient the signifying function of the phallus in her desire. For the phallus operates in the dream to enable her to regain the use of the organ that it represents, as we shall show by the place indicated by the dream in the structure that locates her desire.'[114]

This, he continues, shows that the goal of analysis is not, as Freud thought, satisfactory genital sexual relations. It is rather to reconcile the subject in some more satisfactory manner to being a being who is dominated by the signifier.[115]

This Lacanian viewpoint must inevitably lead to different attitudes on the part of the two sexes towards the word incarnate in the laws of social, particularly kinship, organisation. In desiring the penis the woman desires to submit to the law, while in desiring the vagina the man desires to 'lay down' the law. This point has not been lost on some Lacanian feminists, who have suggested that liberation for women can only be liberation from the law of kinship organisation; family and kinship must be destroyed. This does not however seem to apply to Lacan, who admires traditional social forms based on kinship.[116]

We might gather from all this that the phrase 'the unconscious is the discourse of the other' is a description simply of the *idées fixes* of the two sexes. Yet another listing of this topic in Miller's index shows us that something more dynamic is also intended. In the 'Discourse of Rome' (1953) Lacan tells us that Freud's remarks on telepathy are some of the best discussions of this definition of the unconscious.[117] The unconscious of the subject actually picks up the current manoeuvres of the unconscious of the other.

So far we have dealt with the three topics of the first section of Miller's index (the supremacy of the signifier, the defiles of the signifier, the signifying chain) and with a topic from the second section on 'the *moi* and the subject' ('the unconscious is the discourse of the other'). The other major topics of the second section are 'the body, the *moi*, the subject', 'the function of the *moi*', 'the structure of the subject' and 'intersubjective communication'. The third section has for topics 'the formations of the unconscious', 'analytic experience' and 'the phallus'. The general place of these topics in the theory can be appreciated from the description already given.

The chief development that occurs in the treatment of these topics in the course of reading through *Écrits* is that beginning from 'On a Project' we find the influence of Hegelian themes becomes more prominent. The chief of these is the thesis that repression is due to the fear of facing the demand to enjoy oneself, forever and at the highest level. One cannot help but suspect that behind this *bouleversement* of the Freudian theory of repression as fear of punishment lies the social change noted by Marcuse in his phrase 'repressive desublimation'. The consumer society places on its subjects the advertising ethic 'you must enjoy' rather than the Old Testament 'thou shalt not'. Lacan (and Miller in his index) claim to be providing above all a theory of 'the paranoid subject of scientific civilisation' rather than a theory of an abstract human being.

Section 4 of the index concerns clinical practice, while section 5 concerns 'epistemology and theory of ideology'. Interestingly enough the claim Lacan sometimes makes that he is a 'materialist' does not appear in this index, but some discussion of it is warranted as it can be confusing to the English-speaking reader.[118]

The point at issue historically between materialism and idealism was the existence of God and the afterlife. One essential tenet of materialism was that human beings are entirely material and that this material returns to inorganic matter when we die: we cease to exist.

Lacan is at best a half-hearted materialist in this sense. His sympathies are rather with Dante's imaginary destinations for the soul. But the term 'materialist' has altered its connotations in contemporary French social theory to indicate a commitment to belief in an objective social world determining the individual. In this sense, born of the necessity to marry the French tradition of metaphysical social theory with Marxian materialism, Lacan is a materialist. This kind of materialism in no way impedes his metaphysics. The authors he cites with greatest approval and frequency in *Écrits*, leaving aside psychoanalysts, are Saint Augustine (7 times), Hegel (22 times), Heidegger (6 times), Roman Jakobson (the linguist) (6 times), Kierkegaard (5 times), La Rochefoucauld (6 times), Claude Levi-Strauss (10 times), Marx (7 times), Plato (11 times), Ferdinand de Saussure (10 times), Shakespeare (5 times), Socrates (10 times). In addition the French Hegelian Jean Hyppolite, while mentioned only four times, has an article commissioned by Lacan included in *Écrits* and plays a key role in the discussion. With the partial exception of Aristotle (mentioned 7 times), the most frequently cited authors are all metaphysicians, linguists (counting Levi-Strauss' structural anthropology here), literary figures or psychoanalysts. These bald statistics should express, even for those fashionable intellectuals who have difficulty in following arguments, the origins of Lacanian theory.

In his work after *Écrits* Lacan has developed the suggestion already made in that work that 'Human language constitutes a communication where the transmitter receives back from the receiver his own message in an inverted form.'[119] This is the collusion between individuals that is necessary for insertion in the symbolic order. This kind of solution or 'game-playing' is the basis for sexual rapport. Lacan's later work is an attempt to rework the ground covered by Laing in *Knots* and Eric Berne in *Games People Play*. Needless to say Lacan's games are more like Laing's than Berne's and more subtle than either.

The article on 'The Deaf Utterance' marks the beginning of this phase.[120] When we encounter Tiresias, the blind prophet of Greek legend, associations begin to reverberate in the mind of the reader. Any reconstruction of an underlying logic must be a reconstruction of how, if at all, the various themes fit together.

The article is evidently intended to clarify both the nature of sexual rapport and the nature of femininity. The themes trailed in front of us include: marriage versus public women; woman as the one who enjoys sex most (a judgement made by Tiresias); 'at least one' versus 'all' in logic (quantifiers); transition from a unit set to infinite sets in mathematics; various topological surfaces (torus, Moebius ring); the one and the many in Parmenides' metaphysics. The first mentioned items here are relatively 'singular', the last-mentioned relatively 'plural'. Even the case of woman as the 'one' who enjoys sex 'most' fits this description, though Lacan actually doesn't stress this verbal formula.

A clue to Lacan's intentions may be the connection he draws between the Greek 'heteros', 'etherise' and 'hetaerae' (courtesans).[121] The heterosexuals it seems are on the side of: public women; enjoying sex most; all; infinite sets; the many.

Enjoying sex most (all the time) is in Lacan's theory the origin of the fear that creates repression. The fear of this side of life thus creates the implicit homosexuality of marriage, where women (as other) enjoy sex most. Desire is the desire of the other. Men paradoxically benefit from the greater enjoyment of women. Women, we may surmise, lose out as they suffer the lesser enjoyment of men. The fear of not enjoying oneself paradoxically becomes greater in women, who are more repressed. Marriage is narcissism, thus justifying its equation with homosexuality. Out of marriage comes: woman as unique (the mystique of femininity); the unit set (perhaps woman as a poor mathematician!); the One of Parmenides (later transformed into the one God of NeoPlatonic Christianity); the torus or doughnut or vagina or space that enfolds.

The extreme difficulty of interpreting Lacan's later writings makes this imaginative reconstruction of 'The Deaf Utterance' quite provisional. Perhaps all that can be said is that if one wants to see the old Lacan in the new this is still possible.

As a whole Lacan's theory presupposes that narcissism is the primary instinct that is repressed in the production of the subject. This is just as unwarranted as Freud's emphasis upon sex. At the same time we are left with the oedipal conflicts and their wide-ranging effects virtually intact. There is a certain recognition that repression may assume qualitatively different forms in Lacan's discussions of 'paranoid-scientific civilisation'. In Lacan, as in Nietzsche, there is always a lively sense that ancient civilisations had different, and for them superior, means of socialising the individual. At the same time Lacan underplays the role of Nietzsche in the history of ideas, mentioning him only twice in *Écrits*, once to say he was 'a nova as bright as he was quickly returned to the shadows' and on the other occasion because Freud mentions him.[122] Hardly justice to the most influential philosopher of the nineteenth century (with the possible exception of Marx). In addition the Lacanian theory of repression (fear of failing to enjoy) is presented as the only mechanism of repression, rather than, as it should be, one among several.

Further Reading

Freud

Perhaps the best introduction to Freud is his own writing, particularly:
S. Freud, *Introductory Lectures on Psychoanalysis*, 1915-6, *Complete Psychological Works*, Vols. 15, 16.
Worthwhile discussions of Freud include:
P. Amacher, 'Freud's neurological education and its influence on psychoanalytic theory'. *Psychological Issues*, *4*, No. *4*, Monograph 16, 1965
S. Bernfield, 'Freud's earliest theories and the school of Helmholtz'. *Psychoanalytic Quarterly*, *13*, 341-62, 1944.
R.W. Clark, *Freud, The Man and the Cause*, Cape, London, 1980.

S. Fisher and R.P. Greenberg, *The Scientific Credibility of Freud's Theories and Therapy*, Basic Books, New York, 1977.

S. Fisher and R.P. Greenberg, *The Scientific Evaluation of Freud's Theories and Therapy*, Harvester, Hassocks, 1978.

C.S. Hall, *A Primer of Freudian Theory*, World Pub. Co., Cleveland, 1954.

M. Jahoda, *Freud and the Dilemmas of Psychology*, Hogarth, London, 1977.

E. Jones, *The Life and Work of Sigmund Freud*, Readers Union, London, 1963, abridged edition.

P. Kline, *Fact and Fantasy in Freudian Theory*, Methuen, London, 1972.

K. Levin, *Freud's Early Psychology of the Neuroses*, Uni. of Pittsburgh Press, Pittsburgh, 1978.

K.H. Pribram, 'The neuropsychology of Sigmund Freud'. In A.J. Bachrach (ed.) *Experimental Foundations of Clinical Psychology*, Basic Books, New York, 1962.

P. Roazen, *Freud, Political and Social Thought*, Knopf, New York, 1968.

A. Schusdeck, 'Freud's 'seduction theory': a reconstruction'. *Journal of the History of the Behavioural Sciences*, 2, 159-66, 1966.

D. Stafford-Cark, *What Freud Really Said*, Penguin, Harmondsworth, 1967.

W.A. Stewart, *Psychoanalysis: The First Ten Years*, Macmillan, New York, 1967.

R. Wollheim, *Freud*, Fontana, London, 1971.

R. Wollheim and J. Hopkins (eds.) *Philosophical Essays on Freud*, CUP, New York, 1982.

The Post-Freudians

Some post-Freudian writers can be approached through their own writings. Jung's *Memories, Dreams, Reflections* (Pantheon, New York, 1963, trans. R. and C. Winston) and *Psychology and Alchemy* (Routledge, London, 1966) can be recommended. Adler's *The Neurotic Constitution* (Moffat, Yard, New York, 1917) and *Understanding Human Nature* (Greenberg, New York, 1946) are also very readable, as are Reich's *The Mass Psychology of Fascism* (Farrar, Strauss and Giroux, New York, 1970, trans. V.R. Carfagno) and Fromm's *Escape from Freedom* (Farrar and Rinehart, New York, 1941). Marcuse's *Eros and Civilisation* (Vintage, New York, 1961) is turgid, but can be completed with persistence. The current literature in English on Lacan tends to be hagiographic but S. Turkle's *Psychoanalytic Politics* (Deutsch, London, 1979) provides some valuable background. Lacan's own writings require great fortitude. Useful general surveys and accounts of individual writers are:

H.L. Ansbacher and R.R. Ansbacher, *The Individual Psychology of Alfred Adler*, Harper and Row, New York, 1964.

H. Bleich, *The Philosophy of Herbert Marcuse*, Uni. Press of America, New York, 1977.

V. Brome, *Jung, Man and Myth*, Macmillan, London, 1978.

J.A.C. Brown, *Freud and the Post-Freudians*, Penguin, Harmondsworth, 1961.

J. Fry, *Marcuse, Dilemma and Liberation*, Humanities Press, New York, 1978.

N. Hale, *Freud and the Americans; the Beginnings of Psychoanalysis in the United States*, OUP, New York, 1971.

B. Hannah, *Jung, His Life and Work*, Putnam, New York, 1976.

D. Hansdorff, *Erich Fromm*, Twayne, New York, 1972.

P. Homans, *Jung in Context, Modernity and the Making of a Psychology*, Uni. of Chicago Press, Chicago, 1979.

J. Jacobi, *The Psychology of C.G. Jung*, Yale Uni. Press, Yale, 1962, (trans. R. Manheim).

B. Katz, *Herbert Marcuse and the Art of Liberation, An Intellectual Biography*, Verso, London, 1982.

A.C. MacIntyre, *Marcuse*, Fontana, London, 1970.

R.L. Munroe, *Schools of Psychoanalytic Thought*, Hutchinson, London, 1957.

P. Roazen, *Freud and his Followers*, Knopf, New York, 1975.

M. Sharaf, *Fury on Earth, A Biography of Wilhelm Reich*, Deutsch, London, 1983.

P.J. Stern, *C.G. Jung, The Haunted Prophet*, Braziller, New York, 1976.

A. Storr, *Jung*, Fontana, London, 1973.

D. Weyes, *Psychoanalytic Schools from the Beginning to the Present*, Jason Aronson, New York, 1973.

Chapter 7 : Heidegger and Modern Metaphysics

Main Assumptions

The main social condition responsible for the appearance of the varieties of metaphysics discussed in this chapter is once again the decline of Christianity. The philosophies of Heidegger and Sartre are in many respects a simple inversion of Christian metaphysics. While Christian philosophy strove to attain fullness of being and thus everlasting life, Heidegger and Sartre raise the possibility that we are more fundamentally beings that lack being. Having turned their backs on a God above to search for one within they discover nothingness, though this nothingness is often so fascinating that we can almost forgive it for not being more.

The main assumptions used by Heidegger and Sartre are as follows: 1a. They consider primarily the problem of redemption; 1b. They admire change and fascination; 1c. They consider experienced freedom to be abstract freedom; 1d. All the writers in this tradition engage in a deep interpretation of consciousness in the sense that they sometimes locate being and nothingness in places we would not immediately think to find them; 1e. There is a drive towards the completion of personality, both in Heidegger and the later Sartre; 2. Consciousness is not influenced by instincts or the unconscious: Sartre is more consistent in asserting this than Heidegger; 3a. In Sartre the struggle between motives is replaced by that between being and nothingness; 3b. Motives are not repressed; 3c. In so far as motives exist for Sartre they are rationalisations for actions that have already been decided upon; 3d. Defence mechanisms exist for Sartre in the sense just mentioned as defences against the realisation that we are nothingness; 4. The unconscious does not communicate with consciousness; 5. Symbols are a representation of various forms of interaction between being and nothingness; 6. Beliefs about the management of pleasure and pain are all attempts to achieve being by adopting a consistent rule to guide behaviour; 7. We learn about human nature through phenomenology.

Both Merleau-Ponty and Baudrillard differ somewhat from Heidegger and Sartre on the above issues. Merleau-Ponty is more inclined to amalgamate psychoanalysis and phenomenology by arguing that we experience being in the world through our body and thus through sex. Baudrillard amalgamates psychoanalysis and Sartre by claiming that at one time human nature was described by psychoanalysis but now has been altered by social change to Baudrillard's version of the Sartrian viewpoint.

It is hard not to see some connection between the politics of the four writers dealt with in this chapter and their view of human nature. Of the four, all were at some period in their careers avowed Marxists and the two who were most extreme in their views about human nature - Sartre and Baudrillard - are also the most radical in their politics. Like Marcuse, Baudrillard sometimes strikes attitudes that appear more conservative than left wing, but his entire intellectual stance is motivated by the same smouldering resentment found in Heidegger and Sartre. Heidegger's brief Nazi period shows that he was not averse to other philosophies of resentment. From this point of view the campaign against instincts mounted by these writers seems to arise from a none too secret hatred of life and desire to cut off the enjoyment of others. This aspect of their doctrine has reached its full flowering in its popularisers, who write about such topics as education and child rearing in a manner that encourages the maximum sense of guilt on the part of teachers and parents if they are unable to meet the inevitable tests put to them by children with the love and understanding demanded by the secret sadism of the experts.

It should be added that there is no mechanical correlation between Marxism and the extreme metaphysical approach to human nature. It remains true that the attention of Marxists has been divided between the unholy trinity of Pavlov, Freud and Sartre. When one contrasts this with the views both of traditional Christianity and of Nietzsche we cannot avoid the common denominator of the Marxist approaches: exaggeration. Whether searching in the heights of Sartrian idealism or the depths of Pavlovian stupidity Marxism has found it impossible to achieve balance. This no more spells historical eclipse than the violent excesses of early Christianity prevented the old educated classes from synthesising them. Marxism, unlike Christianity, had the good fortune to be founded by a highly educated man with little time for self-mortification. While it has fallen into the hands of the ignorant and the masochistic, that has reflected the peculiar combination of its triumph in developing countries and the current poor prospects of success in the West.

Heidegger (1889-1976)

Heidegger's greatest influence was through his *Being and Time* (1926). Although dedicated to Husserl, with whom he had close contacts, *Being and Time* is quite unlike Husserl's own writings. Instead of the phenomenological bracketing we have a determined attempt at ontology (the investigation of being) through a philosophical hermeneutics, or uncovering of hidden meaning. In these respects Heidegger undertakes an independent development of Brentano's neo-scholasticism rather than a continuation of Husserl's methods. The first philosophical book to have excited Heidegger's interest was Brentano's *On the Multiple Meanings of Being in Aristotle*.[1] His *Privatdozent* thesis at the University of Freiburg in 1915 was on *Duns Scotus' Doctrine of Categories and Meanings*. Here too was an indication of the kind of interest Heidegger had in being. He wanted to know its meaning. *Being and Time* investigates *Dasein*, or the being of humans. This was preparatory to an investigation of being as such. Much as Aquinas thought the mind of man provided an analogy to God, so the being of humans provides an analogy with being in general. Heidegger wants to restore philosophy to its fundamental concern with the meaning of human existence. Like Husserl he is alarmed by the meaninglessness of modern life: the disease is the same, the cure is different.

'The essence of human being (*Dasein*) lies in its existence.'[2] We are free to choose different ways of existence and this constitutes our essence. Such ways of existing are always constituted in time, within the lived time of history and of human projects. Like Husserl and Bergson, Heidegger is deeply suspicious of all attempts to see time as uniform and abstract, like a geometrical space. Descartes is once again blamed for popularising this misleading idea of time.[3]

Yet human being is intimately bound up with existence in space, to be in the world is to be 'there'.[4] Such being 'there' is not spatial in the usual sense, it is to have a mood.[5] By interpreting mood Heidegger hopes to illuminate existence. Modern consciousness sees in moods the mysterious evidence for a 'yonder', a dimly guessed meaning in life. Heidegger, with his uncanny use of language, suggests this to us: 'In having a mood, *Dasein* is always disclosed in a mood as that entity to which it has been delivered over in its Being ...'.[6] We normally resist this disclosure of the real meaning of our moods. Bad moods, for instance, reveal that 'the circumspection of concern gets led astray'.[7] One of the chief characteristics of being in a world is to feel concern for it. When such concern is wrong-circuited we have bad moods. Nor is this so hard to believe when we reflect on being in a good mood. We often call this a sense of well-being, or say 'things are going well'. We don't mean that something independent of us is developing satisfactorily. We mean that our care for our world is being satisfactorily expressed. This may be active, as in 'looking after' something, or purely a contemplative attitude.

'The fundamental ontological characteristics (of everyday Being-in-the-world) are existentiality, facticity and Being-fallen.'[8] We have already seen that the choice of an existence is fundamental to being in the world. Such an existence makes us into a 'something', a fact. To fall in the world is the opposite of being thrown. Falling is the 'being which belongs to everydayness'.[9] In everyday life we are 'tranquilised' out of facing up to the problems of existence. We engage in 'idle talk, curiosity and ambiguity' and in 'hustle' to avoid ourselves. In idle talk we 'enter the given view of the world entertained by others in a mode of groundless floating'.[10] In this state of alienation and inauthentic being our own inmost 'potentiality-for-Being' is hidden from us.[11]

In falling we flee from ourselves and this produces anxiety, so we flee from our apprehension that we are 'nothing and nowhere'.[12] Our 'ownmost potentiality-for-Being' is to be free to take hold of our lives and choose what we are. Fleeing from this we sense the uncanny but cannot take hold of it.

Being thrown on the other hand means 'to be ahead of oneself'. Our potentialities unfold themselves in life. To be ahead of ourselves means to be oriented to what we can become. Thrownness is not however simply the opposite of falling. Heidegger always talks about being thrown, or thrownness (*Geworfenheit*), not about throwing or 'throwingness'. Thrownness is not a recovery of our power of choosing, a shift to 'throwing ourselves into things'.[13] Being ahead of oneself actually includes falling. It means accepting one's destiny;

being ahead of oneself is being absorbed in the world of our concern. To realise our potential we must become absorbed in concern for a world. Concern, in Heidegger's terminology, actually belongs to falling.[14] 'Care' on the other hand is a much more general phenomenon , which includes 'care' in the narrow sense and 'solicitude', as well as 'willing', 'hankering', 'addiction' and 'urge'. Willing is the expression of our potentiality-for-being. Here that possibility which is ahead of us is disclosed to us and we will ourselves towards it. But in everyday life we are usually tranquilised out of real willing into an acceptance of 'the familiar, the attainable, the respectable' as defined by other people. This is not a complete extinction of our potentiality-for-being, but its modification into wishing. In wishing we hanker after possibilities. 'Such hankering *closes off* the possibilities; what is 'there' in wishful hankering turns into the real world.'[15] We might think that hankering after our wishes leads us into a realm of mental possibilities somehow richer than the real world. Not so, says Heidegger. *Dasein* becomes addicted to 'becoming 'lived' by whatever world it is in', the world of wishes for which we hanker becomes a world that lives us. We become addicted to our wishes. From this follows the 'urge' that crowds out all other possibilities.

It seems that in moving from willing to wishing, hankering, addiction and finally urge we might have run outside the realm of 'thrownness', of potentiality-for-being, altogether. But towards the end of the dicussion Heidegger reminds us that even the urge is also a kind of being-ahead-of-oneself. The opposites are the trifling 'concern' and 'solicitude' that belong to the inauthentic realm of being-alongside-ourselves, falling and anxiety. Being-ahead-of-ourselves includes being-alongside-ourselves, falling and anxiety; but it includes them as part of its projection of its own potentialities in the activities of willing, wishing, hankering, addiction and urge. This is not surprising. In completing any project that we have willed or wished we often encounter flat moments where anxiety and doubt take over, where it is all routine slog.

Having discovered something of human being, in Division Two Heidegger turns to a more fundamental analysis. His first thought is that the full expression of our potentiality-for-being, the full working out of our possibilities, is only discovered in death, when we make the final summing up of a person's life.[16] But we must beware of substituting our ideas about other people's deaths for our ideas of our own death. It is much easier to assess other people's lives after they are dead - the lives of Napoleon or Julius Caesar - than to assess how we live towards our own death. Heidegger wants to know what life is like from the inside, how we live our own lives, not how we assess those of other people.

In assessing our own end in death we might think of natural processes like the ripening of fruit. But we are not pears, falling when ripe. We may fulfil ourselves before we die, or we may die unfulfilled.[17]

To understand our end we look at everyday postures in the face of death. In falling we face death inauthentically, we ignore it, divert it, divert ourselves, say it won't happen yet. In authentic being-towards-death we have 'an impassioned freedom towards death ... factical, certain of itself, and anxious'.[18] Initially we only recognise authenticity by a denial of the inauthentic.

Authentic being is disclosed to us in the call of conscience. This alerts us to our possibilities. This is similar to the religious idea of a 'calling'. God calls us to take our place in his plan, he tells us our proper ends. This is not what Heidegger means, but it is a good introduction to what he means. For him the voice of conscience is a fact, not standing in any need of 'proof'. His conscience is the religious calling without God. It is a fact, explained by ontology, that conscience calls us to our goal in life.

The true voice of conscience is not a series of orders, such as those received by Joan of Arc. 'The call discourses in the uncanny mode of keeping silent.'[19] When we listen to this silence we are alerted to our own possibilities for being. How can we know that the particular possibilities suggested to us by the call are the right ones? Heidegger disclaims any intention of telling us the answer to this. The call 'gives no information about events'. Having set out to find something more definite about the authentic realisation or our potentialities the way is again blocked.

Heidegger does not mean to cheat our expectations. The call does say something, it calls us back to ourselves. 'When the call gives us potentiality-for-being to understand, it does not give us one which is ideal and universal; it discloses it as that which has been currently individualised and which belongs to that particular *Dasein*.'[20] Now we can understand why Heidegger used 'being thrown' (*Geworfenheit*) rather then 'throwing' to describe the authentic realisation of our possibilities. For it is not we who are the origin of what we will become. We give ourselves up to our own inner unfolding, though the self can never get its own basis into its power. We can say that we are the basis of our potentiality-for-being. 'But 'Being-a-basis' means *never* to have power over one's inmost Being from the ground up.'[21] Being thrown can best be described as active participation in a life whose basis is beyond our control.

If this is so, why is the message of conscience always 'You are guilty'? One reason is that we ourselves are the basis for other people's lacks. This makes us feel 'lacking in some way' and thus guilty. On a deeper level we are conscious that we are the basis for nullity. We must be a particular possibility and not others. We are conscious of not being those possibilities that we are not: this produces guilt.

Conscience summons us to an awareness of guilt and thus of our potentiality-for-being. This discloses *Dasein* to us as 'discourse, state-of-mind and understanding'.[22] The anxiety of conscience is soundless, negating the 'loud, idle chatter' of other people through which we slip into inauthentic existence. The disclosedness of conscience is called 'resoluteness', which is the authentic truth of *Dasein*.

Having disclosed being-towards-death we are able to take a step further and investigate our potentiality-for-being-a-whole revealed in our existence in time. This temporal existence takes four forms: understanding, state-of-mind, falling and discourse.

Understanding is not a definite kind of cognition. It is a kind of sight, in which we are 'looking around' or 'just looking'. Through understanding we discover our own potentialities-for-being. We know when these are being disclosed because of the resoluteness of understanding - its involvement in the anxiety and uncanniness of conscience. 'The inauthentic future has the character of awaiting.'[23] In an inauthentic understanding we wait for things to happen.

Understanding is always accompanied by a *state of mind* or mood produced by our being thrown. Paradoxically, the role of moods is to bring us back to events in the past. In fear we forget our way around in the environment, our thrownness is cut off and we go back to the past. In anxiety we feel that the everyday world no longer 'says' anything. We are anxious that authentic experiences may be repeated as inauthentic ones, that the meaningful present will become by repetition a meaningless future experience. This in turn upsets our faith in the past.

Moods are connected with thrownness, or rather with interferences to it. Anxiety is peculiar in this respect because while it emerges from such an interference it liberates us from inauthentic possibilities and allows us to become free. As it mounts it can emerge as the revelation of authentic *Dasein*.

Falling finds its meaning specifically in the present, while *discourse* makes things present to us.

Could the unfolding of the *Dasein* of the individual be part of a larger unfolding, that of history? What could authentic history be? Here we return once again to the question that has puzzled us all along - what it is that the anxiety of conscience calls us to. 'Those possibilities of existence which have been actually disclosed are not to be gathered from death.'[24] We find out about the authentic purposes of history from historiology, the study of history.[25] Here the discussion is only carried on in general terms as Heidegger is not certain whether prevailing historical knowledge is authentic or not. Rather he wants to establish that there could be such a thing. Dilthey and Count Yorck are particularly commended as having made a start.

Heidegger's later career provides an ironic commentary on his uncertainty over specific historical analyses. In the early 1930s he became an enthusiastic and widely publicised supporter of Hitler's National Socialism. Before long this led to disillusion and withdrawl from politics. Later, in his open letter on humanism in 1947, he announced the relative superiority of the Marxist interpretation of history on the grounds that it recognised the alienation and homelessness of modern life.[26] While this was a period when the Young Marx of the 1844 manuscripts was being enthusiastically rediscovered, this announcement was a little surprising as it was Nietzsche, Kierkegaard, Jaspers and Heidegger himself who had done more to announce this to the European public of previous decades.

Heidegger's own later philosophy is fragmentary and aphoristic. Increasingly the mysteries of being were approached through poetry rather than philosophy.[27] Heidegger had, in *Being and Time*, taken great pains to make his language as suggestive as possible and this route to understanding appealed to him increasingly. None of these later writings contains a systematic presentation of the human situation. Heidegger had become disillusioned with systems.

Influence

Heidegger's academic following among German philosophers and sociologists was perhaps greater than that of any other German phenomenologist, including Becker, Brecht, Brocker and Gadamer.[28] While Sartre departed from Heidegger in some respects, he agrees with him on the key issue of the primacy and inexplicability of spontaneity. Merleau-Ponty is sometimes claimed as closer to Heidegger then Sartre but on this central point this is not so. It is however true that Merleau-Ponty resembles Heidegger in his positive assessment of the possibility of achieving being and it is clear that like Sartre he was much influenced by Heidegger's general notion of a phenomenological investigation of human being.

Sartre (1905-1980)

Sartre studied in Germany from 1932 to 1934, part of the time under Heidegger at the University of Freiburg, where Husserl was still working in retirement. Like his friend Merleau-Ponty, Sartre claimed these two thinkers as the chief starting point for his philosophy. This was a surprising shift of emphasis for French philosophy to take, particularly as Heidegger is in some respects a rather similar philosopher to Bergson, both stressing the mystery of the contact between the individual and the historical-evolutionary process. Yet during the 1940s and 1950s Sartre and Merleau-Ponty succeeded in establishing this German view of contemporary philosophy as a dominant current in France.

It is unlikely that the reason for this shift of allegiance was Bergson's lack of attention to the philosophy of science and mathematics. Husserl's work, particularly in the philosophy of mathematics, gave the German tradition a solidity in these spheres that Bergson lacked. Yet Sartre in particular broke early with Husserl, preferring to develop a philosophy closer to that of Heidegger in *Being and Time*. If Sartre had a basis for legitimating his philosophy that lay outside philosophy itself it was his own output of plays and novels.

This shift is all the more surprising when we consider that Sartre always remained firmly on the left. Merleau-Ponty began on the left, but drifted rightwards in the 1950s.[29] When Sartre studied under Heidegger the latter was issuing some of his most spirited appeals on behalf of the Nazi regime. Nor could Husserl and Heidegger's commitment to investigating the meaning of subjective human experience explain things. Bergson was every bit as committed to this as his German counterparts. Furthermore, for philosophers interested in politics, as Sartre and Merleau-Ponty always were, Bergson, in *Morality and Religion*, offered a quasi-socialist political analysis of far more real interest then the vague intimations of Husserl and Heidegger. Nor can we explain the shift as a result of Bergson's Catholicism. Sartre and Merleau-Ponty began their break with Bergson in the mid-1930s when a Nazi must have appeared far more repugnant than a Catholic. After the war when Heidegger had recanted his Nazi beliefs and the cold war had begun things might have appeared different, but that was not the period of the original interest in the two Germans.

If any explanation can be given for French interest in Husserl and his descendants it seems likely to lie in an unexpected direction. Perhaps it was the very vagueness of Husserl and Heidegger on the relation of the individual to history and on the nature of the historical process that attracted Sartre and Merleau-Ponty. From 1930 to 1945 Sartre's chief political preoccupation was the political non-joiner. The chief protagonist of *The Age of Reason* (1945) has withdrawn from political commitment. Sartre himself, as described by his companion Simone de Beauvoir, was in this situation in the 1930s.[30] It was experience of the resistance during the war and of cold war politics after the war that drove Sartre to adopt definite political postures. But by that time he had become France's best known intellectual, a man who could lend himself to causes without joining parties, or at least without remaining in them for long.[31] In a sense Sartre always remained a non-joiner. To many that was his chief message - only the permanently uncommitted can remain responsible. It may be that, in seeking to escape the dogmatic interpretations of history of Stalinism, Sartre and Merleau-Ponty were attracted to the preliminary character of Husserl and Heidegger's view of history. Here was history as matter for investigation, rather than as doctrine to be applied. Another aspect of Heidegger's philosophy that undoubtedly recommended itself was its scepticism about established values. Bergson had always remained within a liberalised Christianity, while Heidegger questioned traditional Western values in a far more fundamental manner.

The Transcendence of the Ego (1936) begins with an incisive paragraph:

'For most philosophers the ego is an 'inhabitant' of consciousness. Some affirm its formal presence at the heart of *Erlebnisse*, as an empty principle of unification. Others - psychologists for the most part - claim to discover its material presence, as the centre of desires and acts, in each moment of our psychic life. We should like to show here that the ego is neither formally nor materially in consciousness: it is outside, in the world. It is a being of the world, like the ego of another.'[32]

Here Sartre sums up the difference between the traditional ego, which is identified as the will - the 'centre of desires and acts' - and the modern consciousness that we do not live our own lives; they are lived by the world, by forces beyond our control.

Towards the end of the same work he describes the situation as follows:

'A young bride was in terror, when her husband left her alone, of sitting at the window and summoning the passers-by like a prostitute. Nothing in her education, in her past, nor in her character could serve as an explanation of such a fear. It seems to us simply that a negligible circumstance (reading, conversation, etc.) had determined in her what one might call 'a vertigo of possibility'. She found herself monstrously free, and this vertiginous freedom appeared to her *as the opportunity* for this action which she was afraid of doing. But this vertigo is comprehensible only if consciousness suddenly presented to itself as infinitely overflowing in its possibilities the I which ordinarily serves as its unity.

'Perhaps, in reality, the essential function of the ego is not so much theoretical as practical. We have noticed, indeed, that it does not bind up the unity of phenomena; that it is limited to reflecting an ideal unity, whereas the real and concrete unity has long been effected. But perhaps the essential role of the ego is to mask from consciousness its very spontaneity. A phenomenological description of spontaneity would show, indeed, that spontaneity renders impossible any distinction between action and passion, or any conception of an autonomy of the will.'[33]

Interestingly Sartre quotes Rimbaud as the first to have correctly posed the problem: 'I is an other.'[34] What disturbs him about Husserl's method of bracketing is that having bracketed the natural-scientific attitude we still end up with the ego as an object: 'I cannot conceive Peter's consciousness without making an object of it.'[35] For Sartre the reality of our transcendental nature is 'infinitely overflowing in its possibilities.' Like Husserl he thinks this nature is immediately obvious to us if only we will look. But unlike Husserl he equates this 'going to look' more with a kind of psychiatry - with Janet's investigations of the unconscious - rather than with Husserl's bracketing. Our conversion of our mental states and ourselves into things - a young bride, a prostitute - is a kind of defence mechanism. We use this defence to avoid facing the terrifying reality of transcendental spontaneity. Sartre, like Heidegger and Bergson, is a philosopher of spontaneity, not of freedom. His philosophy, like Heidegger's, is often presented as showing human *angst* in the face of our ability to choose our own lives.[36] But what the young bride glimpses as she passes from bride to prostitute is the spontaneity of her life as it emerges from outside herself. This passage continues: 'But it is a necessity on the level of essence that one cannot tell the difference between voluntary spontaneity and involuntary spontaneity.'[37]

While 'existential psychoanalysis' was a term Sartre came to use, he remained suspicious of the idea of an unconscious.[38] *Sketch for a Theory of the Emotions* (1939) contains a critique of psychoanalytic views of emotion as unable to remedy the problems of traditional theories. It is not that Sartre objects to interpreting the hidden meaning of behaviour. He would like to do this in his own theory. What is objectionable is the claim that there are unconscious mental processes and that these cause our behaviour. An unconscious mental process is for Sartre, as it was for Brentano and Husserl, a sort of contradiction in terms, which Brentano originally ridiculed as 'unconscious consciousness'. The chief reason Sartre distrusts such processes is that they are held to 'cause' behaviour. We 'understand' consciousness, we do not explain its causes. Sartre would like to see a kind of psychoanalysis, incorporating some of the results of Freudian psychoanalysis, that understands consciousness by showing how it 'constitutes itself by symbolisation.'[39] If in a dream entry into a carriage signifies the sexual act, both the sexual act and the carriage are to be thought of as part of consciousness. This is not just renaming the unconscious as conscious. It is taking a vital further step and emphasising, as Dilthey and Heidegger had done, that consciousness can only be understood, not explained by causation.[40]

Conduct that is not the result of conscious reflection is 'unreflective', not unconscious.[41] Its way of being 'conscious of self is to transcend and apprehend itself out in the world as a quality of things.'[42] Then follows a suggestive description of zombie-like 'automatic consciousness': 'One might compare this world to one of those pin-tables where for a penny in the slot you can set the little balls rolling: there are pathways traced between hedges of pins, and holes pierced where the pathways cross one another. The ball is required to complete a predetermined course, making use of the required paths and without dropping into the holes. This world is difficult. The notion of difficulty here is not a reflexive notion which would imply a relation to oneself. It is out there, in the world, it is a quality of the world given to perception (just as are the paths to the possible goals, the possibilities themselves and the exigencies of objects - books that ought to be read, shoes to be resoled, etc.), it is the noetic correlate of the activity we have undertaken - or have only conceived.'[43]

Sartre hints that the humdrum everyday world is a meaningless illusion. In emotion we penetrate the veil of this illusion. But with his background in Husserlian phenomenology he cannot put it like this. The everyday world has its own noematic meaning just as do the worlds of emotion, dreams and madness.[44] He dramatises the shift from a world with one group of objects and meanings to another by saying that to do this we must pass through the infinite. In such a shift the objects in a world acquire different qualities - Sartre's transcription of *noema*. An everyday object can suddenly appear horrible. The reader is reminded of the roots of the chestnut tree in *La Naussée* (1938), that Roquentin perceives as 'beastly' and 'frightening'.[45] Roquentin also suddenly experiences the existence of the roots: 'Even when I looked at things, I was miles from dreaming that they existed: they looked like scenery to me.'[46] His horror is aroused by the realisation that 'to exist is simply to be there'. Here Sartre is expressing an idea of Heidegger that has not yet appeared in his own theoretical writing - that mood or emotion reveals *Dasein*, literally 'being there', or our being-in-the-world. *Sketch for a Theory of the Emotions* resembles some earlier sections of Heidegger's *Being and Time* where mood and emotion are used as a starting point in the analysis. Sartre knows what Heidegger's end result was, but as yet he has not revealed his own end result, his own ontological analysis of being. *Sketch* establishes only the idea of emotion as a change of worlds resulting from the disruption of normal life.

The Psychology of Imagination (1940) takes us a step nearer the reality behind emotion. The book is mainly taken up with an attempt to define more clearly than Husserl how objects are posited in the imagination. Images, Sartre argues, are a kind of thought based on the attempt to possess objects. Images assist thought to take possession of objects. In images objects are posited as unreal.[47] Such positing is a magical attempt to possess that which one desires.[48]

Sartre wants to know how our ability to imagine relates to the general nature of our consciousness. He begins by appealing to 'phenomenological reduction', which we may be tempted to equate with Husserl's bracketing. But the result of Sartre's reduction is not objects, but a world: 'the very structure of the transcendental consciousness implies that this consciousness is constitutive of a world.'[49] Like the Heidegger of *Being and Time*, Sartre believes that phenomenology reveals being-in-the-world. It is immediately obvious from our 'reflective inspection of the essence 'consciousness'' that imagination is part of this essence.[50] He prefers, so as not to outrun his French readers, as yet untutored in phenomenology, to argue from the nature of imagination to the nature of consciousness.[51] 'There is a two-fold requisite if consciousness is to imagine: it must alike posit the world in its synthetic totality, and, it must be able to posit the imagined object as being out of reach of this synthetic totality, that is, posit the world as a nothingness (*néant*) by means of the image'.[52] Sartre can appeal to Heidegger's authority in arguing that 'nothingness is the constitutive structure of the existant'.[53] It is part of the structure of consciousness to be able to imagine the unreal. Freedom is the choice that consciousness can make to withdraw from the world into this world of unreality.[54] Freedom here is not choice of action.

Despite their agreement that the unreality of nothingness is essential to being-in-the-world, Heidegger and Sartre drive towards different ends. The key experience for Heidegger is the call of conscience that reveals thrownness into destiny. Sartre's key experience is that of Roquentin: the horror of existing, of being something in particular, of pinning down consciousness under concepts and labels. According to de Beauvoir this experience hit Sartre in the same way - as a fear of the fixity of social life. At one period Sartre himself also had the opposite fear that inanimate objects would become alive.[55] In her classic *The Second Sex* (1949) de Beauvoir extends this notion to men's attitudes towards women. Men fear women because they are less intellectual (in men's eyes), less imaginative and so nearer the world of the actual. Perhaps fittingly it was here in de Beauvoir's hands that Sartre's early philosophy became most historical and most concretely political. After the painful actualisation of the imaginary world of classical Marxism in Soviet Russia there was one last imaginary world to be conquered - the emancipation of women.

A further introduction to *Being and Nothingness* appears in the essay *Cartesian Liberty* (1945-7).[56] Here Sartre quotes Descartes' words: 'A great clarity that was in my understanding followed a great inclination in my will.'[57] The human mission, for Descartes, is to understand God's creation. 'Descartes persists in calling this irresistible following of the evidence free...' Human freedom is the unfolding of the inner human necessity to understand without outside interference.[58] We only escape this destiny through error, by misunderstanding God's creation, which makes us non-existent, as nothingness (*neant*).[59] Finite and limited creatures fall into error, become non-existent. But Descartes had a basic intuition of his own freedom that went beyond this purely negative freedom. 'Little tells us that he was constrained by his epoch, as by his point of departure, to reduce human freedom to a purely negative power to refuse just that to which eventually it gives in, abandoning itself to divine care; little tells us that he hypostatised in God this original and constituting liberty whose infinite existence he seized in the *cogito* itself...'[60] Two centuries of crisis were necessary, Sartre tells us, before these truths about Descartes' doctrines could be realised and human beings could regain 'creative freedom'. For Descartes God is free in his creation of the world and of

creatures. Creatures only regain positive freedom by subordinating their wills
to that of God in understanding his creation. In understanding creation we re-
enact decisions taken by God; our only true freedom comes in subordinate re-
enactment of these decisions. The atheist Sartre wants to set us free from this
outlook.

Sartre is constructing a misleading version of the history of ideas here. It is
only for metaphysicians, as seekers after God, that Descartes constructs human
freedom along the lines indicated by Sartre. In describing our ordinary decisions
in everyday life, Descartes allows us the experience of freedom as much as most
traditional thinkers. The idea that everyday life is actually metaphysical (or
ontological, as Sartre would prefer to say) is relatively recent. The experience
of fate, of being lived by an eternal decree, that traditional metaphysicians assigned
to unique moments of metaphysical insight, has now moved into everyday
experience. In so doing its mood has changed from the ecstasy of traditional
metaphysics to the flatness of Heidegger's 'falling' and the calm of Sartre's pinball
machine. In modern metaphysics, particularly in Bergson and Sartre and to a lesser
extent in Heidegger, the metaphysical insight reveals not the marvel of total
determinism but rather the pain of metaphysical spontaneity.

So we arrive at Sartre's first *magnum opus*, *Being and Nothingness* (1945).
This begins with the observation that certain kinds of modern philosophy have
dispensed with the 'thing-in-itself' lying behind appearances altogether,
substituting 'the manifest law that presides over the succession of (the existent's)
appearances.'[61] Sartre claims, in my view incorrectly, that this was what Husserl
meant by essences. Certainly both Husserl and Heidegger had retained the core
of Aquinas' potency-act metaphysics, in which potency contains, and can be
intuited as containing, more than has yet been manifested. In the case of regularly
occuring developments, such as the physical growth of plants and animals, the
potency-act viewpoint could easily be converted into a law that specifies regular
stages of growth. But in Husserl and Heidegger's philosophies of history we intuit
the future realisation of historical potencies that have never previously manifested
themselves. Sartre cuts this out with his claim that the new philosophy eliminates
the potency-act metaphysics and that essences are only known in their
manifestations.[62] Rather Sartre seems to be thinking of certain modern
philosophies of science. The controversy between Poincaré and Duhem is
mentioned and Duhem is one source of Sartre's new philosophy of laws of
appearance.[63]

The novelty of the analysis of being presented in *Being and Nothingness* is
that Sartre is going to apply this philosophy of laws of appearance to moods. Being
is now to be simply the laws of appearance of moods: 'Thus there must be for
it (being) a *phenomenon of being*, an appearance of being, capable of description
as such. Being will be disclosed to us by some kind of immediate access -
boredom, nausea, etc., and ontology will be the description of being as it manifests
itself; that is, without preliminary.'[64] This view that being is manifested in moods
is derived from Heidegger's claims that moods are a manifestation of *Dasein* and
that being (*Sein*) can be approached through *Dasein*.

In Sartre's new ontology we are to distinguish the existence of phenomena, that is of the immediate contents of consciousness, from the being revealed in moods. We might be tempted to think therefore that various views of a tree reveal its existence, while the feeling it arouses reveals its being. But Sartre rules this out. Objects, he says, do not possess being: 'Being is simply the condition of all revelation.'[65]

The tree has an infinity of appearances, some experienced and some not. The existence of the tree is this infinity of appearances. Such existence, Sartre argues, needs a basis upon which it can be revealed, which is being. This is called the 'being of phenomena'. The being indicated by moods is called the 'phenomenon of being'.[66] His problem is to relate them. This is a classic statement of two modern intuitions about life. We cannot go beyond appearances: being is the condition for appearances, which it is impossible to investigate. But we feel the compulsion to go beyond appearances through moods.

Now we come upon a key argument. Having banished Husserl's objects of consciousness, which are known immediately, Sartre brings them back. We are immediately conscious of objects like chairs and trees. This seems to contradict the idea that these objects are the laws of their infinite appearances; we are conscious of objects as something outside consciousness as objectively existing in the world. From this Sartre concludes that the object is distinguished by non-being or nothingness: 'If being belongs to consciousness, the object is not consciousness, not to the extent that it is another being, but that it is non-being.'[67] Thus the kind of being that is the condition for appearances turns out to be non-being or nothingness.

The being of this consciousness of objects is called being-for-itself (*l'être pour soi*) and is distinct from the being of phenomena, being-in-itself (*l'être en soi*).[68] This celebrated distinction thus codifies the conflict between two distinct philosophies - modern philosophy of science represented by Duhem which bases itself upon appearances (phenomena) and whose being is phenomena (being-in-itself); and Husserl's positing of objects directly in consciousness, whose being is rather beyond appearances and lies in the objects themselves. Sartre's innovation is to wish to study the states of mind represented by these two philosophies as modes of being. For this reason he can take over the definition of being as phenomena from the former philosophy, but must now speak of the positing of objects in consciousness as a new kind of being - 'being-for-itself'. The relevance of the third kind of being so far encountered, the 'phenomenon of being', found in moods, should be evident. The moods associated with the scientific attitude are widely claimed to be different from those found in traditional philosophies of insight like that of Husserl.

We can summarise Sartre's argument as follows. He begins from Duhem's idea that only appearances (phenomena) and laws governing appearances are real and have being. But all traditional realist philosophy and Husserl in particular assume that objects, as distinct from their appearances, are presented directly in consciousness. If appearances are the standard of being, such objects can only stand outside being as they are not appearances. Thus such objects are non-being or nothingness.

The 'if' is very important here as Sartre is in reality setting up an argument he wants to destroy. What he requires from this argument initially is just some recognition that even from an apparently 'scientific' philosophy we can reach 'nothingness' very quickly. He really wants to develop notions of being and nothingness that are adequate to describe being-in-itself, being-for-itself and their interconnection. In the course of doing this he will overturn appearances as the standard of being and reinstate the objects of consciousness as being.

So far we have considered only the introduction. In the first section of the main text Sartre considers a number of ways in which being-in-itself relates to being-for-itself. The first is the question. He takes as his model for this his own activity in asking questions about being. He argues that to question is not to know the answer to the question and thus to hover in a state of indetermination, of nothingness.[69] We are reminded here of the activity of imagining, which posits objects as not-existing and thus is also a kind of nothingness.

To question being is to admit that what we are questioning about might be non-being. It is also to ask for a truth, which is only defined by what is untrue. In these activities we are faced with the indeterminacy of nothingness. It is different when we have found the answer to a question. In that state we know an answer, which may be that something is being. But before we reach that answer we hover between possibilities, which are not considered as actual. This is a state of nothingness. By positing possibilities in consciousness we posit them as not existing.

A second way of positing objects as not existing is in the negative judgement. If I judge that Pierre is not here in this café, where I had expected him, we say 'I suddenly saw that he was not there.'[70] We mean by this that Pierre was not existing there.

Next Sartre tells us that he wants to know where nothingness comes from.[71] It cannot emerge from itself, but can only emerge from being. This position, which is stated as obvious, is denied by certain kinds of NeoPlatonist metaphysics, which argue that being was 'attacked' by a nothing existing as an independent principle, dragging unchanging being into the flux of matter.[72] Ironically the view that nothing can only be produced by being is a specifically Christian conception, predicated on the omnipotence, omniscience and eternality of God, which make the possibility of an equal rival of being (God) unthinkable. In an oddly Christian manner Sartre argues that in creating nothingness being must at the same time annihilate it, to avoid being overwhelmed by it.[73] In the case of the question, the questioning process presupposes an answer that abolishes the nothingness of questioning and re-establishes being (the answer).

When human beings question they do so freely. As we saw in the case of imagination, our ability to question is an ability freely exercised.[74] We are immediately warned that such freedom is not the freedom of the human individual as agent. In answering the arguments of psychic determinism, the claim that mental states are caused by unalterable laws of causation, Sartre says that the 'cleavage' between one psychic state and the next is 'nothingness'.[75] Here there is a further ambiguity in the term 'nothingness'. So far we have, in *Being and Nothingness*, met nothing as the description of objects posited in consciousness as existing. Even being aware of 'a tree' posits the object in consciousness as nothingness because it is outside appearances and laws of appearances. Then we met the attitude of questioning as a kind of nothingness. Now we have nothingness as a cleavage between successive mental states. This third kind follows on from the second. For if we were to actually live our consciousness as if every state were determined by the previous one we would never get into the state of questioning. We wouldn't mean 'Is this true?' but rather be waiting expectantly for an answer to follow automatically from some prior state, in which we might say 'Is this true?' but would not mean it. To mean 'Is this true?' we must believe we are really questioning, not just waiting for inevitable processes to take their course. 'We wish simply to show that by identifying consciousness with a causal sequence indefinitely continued, one transmutes it into a plenitude of being and thereby causes it to return into the unlimited totality of being ...'[76] Like Bergson, Sartre wants to take determinism, the viewpoint of an omniscient and eternal God, and find out what happens if we try to live it out. We transmute consciousness into 'a plenitude of being', that is into the attitude of being-in-itself, in which appearances and their laws are considered as existent. This, at least, seems the only plausible interpretation of 'a plenitude of being' - it must be what we get when we abolish the first two kinds of nothingness, namely objects posited directly in consciousness and attitudes like questioning and imagination that posit objects as non-existent. Sartre is not of course arguing that human beings could not live without real questioning or imagination - he makes it all too clear that they often do. He wants to know how they are ever able to do these things.

Next Sartre returns to his earlier promise to relate moods and emotions ('the phenomenon of being') to his other two kinds of being. He does this in a preliminary way by relating anguish to freedom and nothingness. In the face of freedom and nothingness we experience anguish.[77] We look into the future and find that, because of our freedom, our future conduct is grounded on nothing, which provokes anguish. More interestingly, we can feel anguish about the past. A reformed gambler approaches the gambling table. Traditional moralists say there is a struggle of reason with the passions.[78] For Sartre the anguish of the gambler is that in becoming conscious of his previous resolution not to gamble he becomes aware that he is still free to choose. There is *nothing* to stop him from altering his resolution.

Sartre is completely radical in his exposition of the nothingness of our freedom: 'It follows that my freedom is the unique foundation of values and that *nothing*, absolutely nothing, justifies me in adopting this or that particular value, this or that scale of values.'[79] 'Psychological determinism, before being a theoretical conception, is first an attitude of excuse, or if you prefer, the basis of all attitudes of excuse.'[80] Through it we tell ourselves what we must be and protect ourselves from the realisation that there is no reason for being anything. This attitude of psychological determinism is the attitude of being-in-itself. 'If man adopts any particular behaviour in the face of being-in-itself ... it is because he is *not* that being.'[81]

In denying what we really are, our real freedom, we enter the realm of bad faith, of all those dodges and excuses we find to deny ourselves. The life of bad faith is not the life of being-in-itself, which we had provisionally equated with the life of automatic consciousness. Bad faith is a human being dressed up as being-in-itself. Being-in-itself exists as a theoretical entity, but it is not what we are. We are conscious, being-for-itself. To dress up as being-in-itself, to pretend that 'we are what we must be', requires the subterfuge of bad faith.

Bad faith is only one particularly important way in which we deny what we are. Becoming a guardian of 'morality' and 'law'; Scheler's 'man of resentment' who resents anyone who is anything; the use of irony to retract beliefs in the moment of asserting them; these are alternative forms of denial. One kind of bad faith is the illusion of romantic and Platonic love.[82] Here we both acknowledge the sexual, selfish and physical nature of our love - otherwise we would call it friendship - and at the same time deny it. Sartre insists that we are conscious of the physical nature of Platonic love at the same time that we deny it. Psychoanalysis is criticised for attempting to overcome this kind of sexual bad faith by asserting that we are not normally conscious of the sexual element in such love.[83] Psychoanalysis is also in bad faith for asserting that the unconscious contains things like the Oedipus complex that we are not conscious of at all.[84] It does this in the name of 'psychological science', one of the chief purveyors of bad faith. Sartre's reply is that there could not be an unconscious that we are unconscious of. We would be more correct to speak of the 'half conscious'. We are half conscious that Platonic love is also sexual; we are not conscious at all of some of the more extreme Freudian claims about the Oedipus complex. Anything we are completely unconscious of must be outside consciousness and therefore cannot affect it.

Other examples of bad faith are the café waiter who plays at being a waiter and the homosexual who insists he is not a homosexual. Sartre would be the last to say that the waiter is a waiter and the homosexual is a homosexual. They are both beings-for-themselves. But the waiter, by continuing to carry out the actions of a waiter, is almost a waiter at the same time that he imagines he is not really a waiter, just someone playing at one. Likewise the homosexual goes on acting as a homosexual, denies that he is a homosexual and actually asserts that he is something else - an individual who restlessly searches for a refined conception of the beautiful.[85] There is also the suggestion in the case of the homosexual that this other person who the homosexual really is exists as a fixed and determined entity - as a being-in-itself.[86]

This completes the first section of *Being and Nothingness*, which is concerned chiefly with the third kind of nothingness - the nothingness of choice that occurs at every instant of our life. We have glimpsed how this is connected to the nothingness of questioning and imagination in the structures of bad faith. By imagining that they are not what they are people live in bad faith. By becoming 'a questioner' or 'a quester' they mysteriously reconvert the nothingness of questioning into a kind of being. Sartre's philosophy has now travelled to the opposite pole from that of Heidegger, despite their joint commitment to the study of being. It is beginning to look as though anguish reveals only nothingness as the possibility for good faith. Heidegger had revealed the call to destiny behind the anxiety of conscience; we are called to be something. Sartre is in danger of calling us to be nothing.[87] Yet he says in introducing his second section that we must escape 'from instanteity toward the totality of being which constitutes human reality.'[88] To do this we are to examine the 'pre-reflective cogito' that is consciousness before it reflects upon itself. Such consciousness does not posit objects in itself.[89] Yet it contains belief, and this belief witnesses itself.[90] Belief, Sartre claims, cannot just be in consciousness. It must believe that it is belief, thus troubling itself, creating a 'game of reflections'.[91] These beliefs that belief has about itself are 'the self'. This 'fissure' or instability of the pre-reflective consciousness introduces nothingness.

In reaching outside its immediate instant of time the self reaches towards both values and possibilities. To desire something is a value that indicates a lack of something in the self, thus relating itself both to what is lacking and to the totality that would arise when the self is united to what it desires.

Traditional thinkers like Descartes had described the desire for perfection - for a completeness similar to that discussed by Sartre. Both physiological needs and the desire for spiritual - and perhaps narcissistic - perfection could be explained as end-directed processes. The natural ends of human life are determined by human rationality. We are both a rational being seeking the perfection of God and an animal seeking the completion of its appointed ends in the world - self-maintenance and procreation. But Sartre has done away with end-directed potencies. He is equally hostile to physiological explanations for desire.[92]

Here he is not wholly consistent. For while rejecting potencies he accepts Descartes' second proof - that 'imperfect being surpasses itself towards perfect being.'[93] He calls this human transcendence. But the altered name cannot conceal that this is indeed an end-directed process, though the end is now not fixed but generalised. The perfection that Sartre's desire seeks is not the perfection of a changeless God, who for Sartre is the apotheosis of the in-itself. Rather desire seeks the in-itself, though never finding it. We want to be a waiter or a homosexual, but always end up playing at them.[94] This relation of the for-itself to the in-itself that it lacks is permanent and inescapable, part of being human.

If there were and, in some parts of the world, still are societies that arouse the unsatisfied circle of the in-itself and the for-itself to a lesser degree than modern society, these societies must have fostered some alternative relation between the in-itself and the for-itself. Nor would we find it difficult to invent one though this matter is not investigated in *Being and Nothingness*.[95] Where the necessities of food and shelter bear more directly on the population they do not play at hunting and building when they are hungry and cold. They are hungry and cold and do become hunters and builders. In this state of mind the for-itself disappears into the in-itself to emerge again out of hours as games and rituals about hunting and building.

Yet in order to shock his readers out of their usual way of thinking, in dealing with human possibilities Sartre goes out of his way to say the exact opposite. To drink to get rid of thirst or to go to brothels to satisfy sexual desire is, he says, 'late and reflective'.[96] The natural attitude is to cling onto desire, to remain in the unsatisfied circuit of the in-itself and the for-itself. The possible is thus 'a real lack of being' - that for which we are always searching and never find.

Sartre next turns to our relations with our own past, present and future. We have a dual relation to our past. As an in-itself we 'are', unalterable and fixed. At the same time we dissociate ourselves from it by saying 'I was it' not 'I am it'.[97] Yet the past, as past, remains in-itself. It is only by moving into the present that we dissociate ourselves from the past and say 'I am not what I was'. The present is for-itself, it is that instance of nothingness that we discovered earlier. At last, in the analysis of the present, we reach the positing of objects in consciousness, now wonderfully transfigured.

Since Brentano it had been common to say that objects are present to consciousness, or present 'in' consciousness. As with so much else Sartre daringly reverses this commonsense idea. Rather the for-itself (consciousness) makes itself 'presence' to the in-itself. 'The presence of the for-itself is what makes the in-itself exist as a totality.'[98] A chair and a table and all the other objects we may see are present to us, not to each other. By making them present to us we give them presence. They are in our presence. Again the chestnut roots making themselves present to Roquentin dog us. With a flourish that is significant even against Sartre's lively writing he says: 'Beings are revealed as co-present in a world where the for-itself unites them with its own blood by that total ekstatic sacrifice of the self which is called presence.'[99] *Ekstasis* means literally 'standing out from' in Greek. We now have the first of the three *'ekstases'* by means of which the self 'stands out' from itself, through the game of the in-itself with the for-itself. It appears that the self must sacrifice itself as for-itself, for the in-itself of the objects in the world to exist. The for-itself makes itself present to the objects in the world and this gives them their present. The self does not produce the objects in the world, but it gives them their present.

Sartre of course rejects any idea that the future is determined. The future 'announces to me what I am from the standpoint of where I shall be.'[100] If we say to ourselves that we are 'completing a task', this task defines what we are in terms of what we will be - a completer of a task. Thus the future 'is what I would be if I were not free'.[101] But this hanger-of-a-picture-on-the-wall that we will be as we complete our task is not an in-itself, like the past. It projects the for-itself, that can never become in-itself. The future is another of the games of the self.

The next game or *ekstasis* is that of reflection. This is an attempt by the self to look at itself and take itself in at a glance.[102] In such a summary the self hopes to pin itself down once and for all, finally becoming a for-itself. But all such efforts are bound to fail. The goal of the summary always eludes the act of reflection. We never know ourselves.

The analysis of the present gave us a glimpse of how objects are present to consciousness. Now follows a more extended discussion under the heading of 'transcendence.' Here we see that knowing about objects is more like questioning than answering and this explains the fascination of the known for the knower. The known can never be finally pinned down, although the known has being, while the knower is nothing.[103] Sartre refers us to Rousseau's description of his being melting into the world and his sudden understanding of the pure 'being there' of the world. It turns out that it is the knower whose nothingness is revealed in such an experience, whereas previously we had considered the object of knowledge as a nothingness. This reversal measures the distance we have travelled from the philosophy that appearances are the standard of being. We must now recognise that it is the objects of consciousness that have being, at least when presented in the illumination of a metaphysical insight.

The third *ekstasis* of the self is in being-for-others. Here we experience ourselves as we appear to other people. Sartre criticises traditional theories for assuming that we experience another person's body directly and use this as evidence for discovering their mental states. Just as we experience objects directly, so we experience other people's consciousness directly when they look at us.[104]

Such a look can turn us into an object. In shame or pride we are not so much concerned with the discreditable or creditable action the other person has seen but with the fact of having been seen and made into an object.[105] Once again this effort of the for-itself of my own consciousness to become the in-itself of a thing seen by another is bound to fail. We are inevitably aware of the other's freedom.[106] We cannot predict what the other will see in us. This thrusts us back into our own freedom and nothingness. The two formal ways of looking at other people are by 'objective' science and by 'understanding'. The behaviourists are wrong, says Sartre, to think that they can erect an objective science of people in isolation from understanding them.[107] As soon as we reach out to predict other people they baffle us by their unpredictability. Even knowing what other people are thinking about is bound to fail. We reach out to grasp what they are thinking and it slips away. Once again we fail to objectify ourselves.[108]

We can take two directions in this game of being looked at by another. Either we seek to make an object of the other who is making an object of us; or we seek to accept as valid the other's view of ourselves as object.[109] The first attitude means that we try to take over the other person, to absorb them in love, language or masochism. The second attitude produces indifference, desire, hate and sadism. Neither of these strategies is ever successful and as one breaks down we adopt the other, alternating love and hatred, language and silence, masochism and sadism. In love we want to turn the other person into a mirror in which we can read ourselves given as objects. To do this the loved one must swear eternal constancy and fidelity, must cease to be a person and become an object. In masochism we insist on being treated as an object to be used.

Love is bound to fail. Having turned the loved one into an object, a mirror that has no freedom of its own, we find that the loved one can no longer really look at us. The image the other now has of us is no longer that truly human look we require. Love turns into desire, in which we desire another person as a body. We become absorbed in our own being as a body in order to become involved with the being of another as a body. The physiology of sex takes over and at last we have achieved that perfect physical, objective interaction with another that we required.[110] But the worm is in the apple. Desire is realised as sexual pleasure, which is no longer a form of relatedness, but already a relation with ourselves. In horror the lover becomes a sadist, desperately reclaiming his or her own freedom by attacking the body of the other. Now the other person has become an object to which we make ourselves known through pain; the sadist tries to take hold of another person's freedom, to force them against their will. Yet the other is really a willing victim, who could leave if they wanted to. A game is played between the sadist and the victim as to how long the pain will last, acted out as a conflict of wills in which each struggles to be the one who decides when the pain is unbearable.[111]

Inevitably the victim looks at the sadist and with that look destroys the sadist's illusion of having stolen the victim's freedom. Now all illusions are past and the for-itself must recognise it has failed to become the in-itself. Love may end in hatred based on this disillusion. Sartre does not mention that the usual outcome is 'I don't want to see you again' rather than hatred. We may speculate that hatred appears when the two must go on seeing each other - they work together or are married. Alternatively hatred may represent an effort to blame the other person for the failure of the relationship. If we punish someone there must have been a crime. Sartre does not explore these possibilities, content to remark that this is a preliminary analysis.

Particularly through communal work we reach a less unstable state of 'being-with' other people. In the class struggle both the workers and the bourgeoisie talk about 'them' and 'us'. Here 'we', the workers, see ourselves united by the disparaging view that the bourgeoisie takes of us. The workers' view of the bourgeoisie and their view of the workers takes us through much of the agonised territory of lovers. But as individuals united by the view the bourgeoisie takes of them workers don't have to look at each other. Their feelings of class solidarity therefore proceed more smoothly than those of the bourgeois.

In the final section of *Being and Nothingness* Sartre turns to action and possession. He claims that motives do not cause action as some traditional thinkers supposed. 'It is impossible to find an act without a motive but this does not mean that the motive causes the act; the motive is an integral part of the act.'[112] He also denies that the will is free and the passions subject it to causal determinism: the view of Descartes.[113] He argues that both 'voluntary' acts of will and acts based on passion are free. The difference is in how we look upon our actions. We may commit murder in cold blood, 'voluntarily', or we may commit it as a crime of passion, 'involuntarily'. The difference is in our attitude to the action, not in our freedom or in the nothingness on which it is founded.

In all action we find cause (the money for which we murder), motive (our avarice) and end (our having the money). Motive is the self-consciousness of cause.[114] Cause, motive and end project us towards possibilities. The projection of the self into possibilities (in this case becoming rich) is one of the futile attempts of the for-itself to become in-itself. Both involuntary and voluntary action is of this kind, but in voluntary action we reflect on our motives.[115] The action, Sartre says, has actually already been decided when we deliberate about motives, when we ask whether our love of money outweighs our fear of prison. To choose to deliberate in this way is to choose not the project as means and end but how we are to look upon ourselves as we engage in the project. We may think either 'I have done what I wished to do' or 'I was made to do it by some cause'.[116]

When we see people acting in the world we should not ask only about causes and motives but also about meanings. Someone who complains of being tired on a hike and sits down may be annoyed with themselves because they are becoming thing-like, determined by bodily physiology when they wished to be thought 'a good hiker' by their companions.[117] To be 'a good hiker' is to become a thing, an in-itself, in a different way from a person dominated by fatigue. Another person might have welcomed fatigue as a means of becoming purely physical, 'being one with nature'. Both 'being one with nature' through fatigue and 'doing the right thing' conjure up different cultural world-views that Sartre would like to explore further, but feels space is insufficient in an introductory treatment. He thinks that from the analysis of such everyday acts as that of the hiker we could 'proceed from there to richer and more profound meanings until we encounter the meaning that does not imply any other meaning and which refers only to itself.'[118]

Common sense tends to think that the individual is in reality a prisoner of the situation. Sartre replies to this that the situation only exists in relation to our projects. A crag may be 'not scalable' to the mountain climber but 'beautiful' to the aesthete. The crag is real and given in both cases, but what is real or given about it is produced by our projects which are freely chosen.[119] We may object to this that other people have determined for us by their meaning-generating activity the ways of existing as 'mountain climber' and as 'aesthete'. But the ferocious and unstable dialectics of the relations we have with other people's views of what we 'are' precludes Sartre from taking seriously our protestations that we are what others have made us. We come into an already established social world only in the sense that we find techniques ready to hand: walking, grasping, speaking, telling truth from falsehood, etc.[120] In speech we find syntax and sounds ready organised into the rules of language. But what we choose to express in our meanings is entirely our own free creation.[121] Even the rules themselves are in some sense freely agreed to. Sartre does not give the example of the schizophrenic who chooses not to abide by the rules of syntax, but this seems to illustrate his meaning.

Productive techniques are also like language and Marx is mentioned here in passing.[122] Little systematic discussion is given of the Marxian conception of ideology, but he remarks that the working class is generally defined by 'production, consumption or a certain type of *Weltanschauung* (world-view) springing out of an inferiority complex'.[123] Some people think that from these 'techniques for the elaboration or the appropriation of the world' the 'simple, well-marked oppositions of the 'proletarian' universe are formed'.[124] The worker is poured into a world like plaster into a mould. But this, Sartre tells us, is like confusing the syntax and sounds of a language with its meaning. 'Each for-itself, in fact, is a for-itself only by choosing itself beyond nationality and race just as it speaks only by choosing the designation beyond the syntax and morphemes. This 'beyond' is enough to assure its total independence in relation to the structures which it surpasses; but the fact remains that it constitutes itself as *beyond* in relation to *these* particular structures.'[125] We may be reminded of Engels' 'We make our own history ... but under very definite presuppositions and conditions.'[126]

The other great unalterable in life is death, which for Sartre is the loss of being human and is as such undiscoverable. He opposes Heidegger's theory in which anxiety about death reveals the call of destiny. Death is rather outside us, our limit.[127]

It seems on the surface that the three main categories of human existence are doing, having and being.[128] I desire to write a book, to have a picture or to be a scientist. But Sartre denies that people ever do things for the sake of the act of doing alone. They are sometimes aiming at some kind of possession of what they have produced, though this may be of a subtle kind. Play and sport represent to us our own freedom precisely through their lack of any possessed outcome and are thus a kind of being.

Doing, for Sartre, can always be analysed as a variety of having or as a variety of being. Even the activity of knowing is compared to violent sexual possession. These two kinds of existence remind us of the two forms of being-for-others. There we sought to make an object of the other who makes an object of us; or to accept as valid the other's view of ourselves as object. In having we seek to possess people or things as in-themselves; in being we seek to become an in-itself.[129] Both projects are of course bound to fail.

Having can be defined as a legal relation, but that only explains how we decide who owns what, not what relation people have to things they own. Ownership is not the same as right of use or of destruction. We often use things like the crockery in a café without owning them. Roman slave owners were forbidden to destroy them. The relation of possession is nearer to that of creation, from which it originated historically. In possession the possessor fancies that the object possessed is maintained in existence by being possessed. At the same time the possessor by possessing imagines they have escaped out of freedom and nothingness into being what they support in existence, their possessions.[130]

Now we are in a position to appreciate why certain qualities of objects can appear to have a profound personal meaning, a fact already explored in *La Nausée*. By appropriating these qualities and 'possessing' them, even if only by seeing or touching them, we are appropriating our own attempts to project ourselves as an in-itself. The example taken is 'the slimy', one that had also figured in Roquentin's experiences.

Sliminess is like the liquidity that fascinated Poe. A liquid is both a thing and not-a-thing. It has a shape, but this is always changing. It is solid, but slips through our fingers. It symbolises 'a possible fusion of the for-itself as pure temporality and the in-itself as pure eternity'.[131] The for-itself is here the ever-changing quicksilver quality of the liquid that persists through the changes. Liquidity is a symbol of the for-itself, of consciousness. On the other hand solid objects like tables and chairs represent the fixity of the in-itself. The slimy is threatening because in its viscosity we find the fluidity of the liquid mixed up with the solidity of the solid object. Slime is consciousness on its way to becoming object, for-itself being overwhelmed by in-itself.

Being and Nothingness as a whole resembles a kind of metaphysical martial arts. We are astonished not only by the violence of the blows but also by the accuracy with which they are delivered. Established masters are called out in turn to receive a lightning trouncing. The difficulties faced by the reader are produced by the virtuoso character of the attacks; Sartre's assumption that readers have something like his own intimate acquaintance with Western metaphysics; and his practice of changing the rules as he goes along. It is this last that creates the greatest difficulty. Sartre is not out to prove he is a greater virtuoso than Aquinas and company, though he cannot resist the temptation of some showing off. He wants to show that his new style, his new rules, are better than the old. It is in vain for his opponents to complain he is making illegal moves. It is these illegal moves he wants to demonstrate and then legalise. So as to lead us out of the old style into the new he begins by accepting contemporary metaphysics, showing its problems, exhibiting new problems and then moving forward from viewpoint to viewpoint, from style to style.

As finally revealed the basis for Sartre's attacks on traditional metaphysics are his insistence on the standpoint of consciousness and his belief that within consciousness there is an ontological priority of nothingness over being.[132] The first shift was made independently by Husserl and Bergson. Much of what Sartre says against Husserl amounts to the accusation that Husserl did not go far enough in adopting the standpoint of consciousness. It is the second shift, the affirmation of freedom based on nothingness, that marks the revolutionary departure of *Being and Nothingness*. Both Heidegger and Bergson had thought we could get in touch with an historical or evolutionary force that would give meaning and value to our lives. Sartre denies this without quite falling into complete nihilism. Meaning comes to us from our vain attempts to become in-itself. But while vain in one sense these attempts are in another absolutely necessary. It is the nature of the for-itself to strive to become in-itself. Sartre toys with nihilism, but in the end draws back from it. His later writings, particularly *Critique of Dialectical Reason*, move even further from it.

Sartre was by 1950 the most famous living French intellectual. He had in the 1930s had sympathy for the French Communist Party, but had never joined. While Althusser criticised the party's revisionism from within, Sartre, who was considered an ultraleftist by the party, assailed its reformism from without.

He had long been interested in Marxism and was evidently dismayed by the fierce criticism of *Being and Nothingness* by Marxists. At the same time the war and subsequent cold war made him more sympathetic to political commitment. The basic problem with *Being and Nothingness* from a Marxist standpoint is that it fails to relate consciousness to the social organisation of production. One way to remedy this difficulty would be to say that in the production of the necessities of life the conscious for-itself becomes the thing-like in-itself. The farmer becomes the activity of farming. In *Being and Nothingness* itself Sartre resolutely sets himself against this. Yet in his next and final major theoretical production, *Critique of Dialectical Reason* (1960), he overhauls his theoretical apparatus in a far more fundamental manner. The Sartre revealed in *Critique of Dialectical Reason* is a summariser of Marxism who wants to elaborate a social psychology based on the discoveries of *Being and Nothingness*. *Critique* contains much already discussed by Lukacs, Trotsky, Marc Bloch and the Frankfurt School, extended by a discussion of social psychology relating free consciousness to being. The most surprising thing about this project is that the related arguments of Fromm in *Fear of Freedom* (1941) are not mentioned. The key concepts in *Critique* are those of *praxis* and *totalisation*. Praxis is the activity of changing the world to achieve an end. Totalisation is a view of all the conditions relevant to achieving an end through praxis. The original form of praxis was the use of tools by the individual to transform the world through individual praxis in the activities of production. This original form of praxis can only be distinguished as a theoretical entity and is not a distinct historical 'stage'. It contained the problem that actions often have unforseen consequences. Chinese peasants for centuries cleared trees to assist agriculture, but their efforts created a problem of erosion that threatened agriculture.[133] This creation of unintended effects gives rise to the notion of a material world upon which labour acts and which has an existence and functioning independent of the labourer.

In uniting to labour with others in joint projects two kinds of relations can arise - reciprocity and reification. In reciprocity several people combine in a project that they all regard as a unitary project, not as the activities of separate individuals.[134] In reciprocity we regard the others as being the same as ourselves. Here Sartre seems to have in mind the practice of many hunter-gatherer peoples of sharing available food supplies equally in time of famine. At the same time it is famine and scarcity that are one major source of reification, a term Sartre borrowed from Lukacs but which he gives an extra dimension.[135] The form of reification produced by scarcity is the 'Manichean' view of the world that perceives life as dominated by inhuman forces of good and evil. By 'Manichean' Sartre has in mind something much broader than the historical religion of Manicheanism. He includes all those religions like Christianity that base themselves on the struggle of good and evil. In Manichean wars, for instance, each side attempts to exterminate the other as the source of the principle of scarcity. The other group becomes not just human beings trying to eat, which could be dealt with by giving them food, but the incarnation of the principle of famine.[136] This means that they must be eradicated rather than fed. Much of Sartre's discussion of the role of scarcity as it acts in all known forms of human society, including the preliminary stages of socialism as seen in the USSR, recall Trotsky's analyses in *Revolution Betrayed*.[137]

Reification is also found in the 'alienated objectification of individual and collective praxis', by which Sartre understands something close to the 'commodity fetishism' of Marx. He cites with approval Marx's statement 'In the form of society now under consideration (i.e. commodity producing society), the behaviour of men in the social process is purely atomic. Hence their relations to each other in production assume a *material* character independent of their control and conscious individual action.'[138] Sartre approves this quotation as it describes the transformation of people into matter through commodity fetishism, thus condemning materialist psychology. In such reification the social whole is seen as the alien result of 'totalising addition'.[139] Consciousness inevitably aims at totalisation, but in objective reification the result is an external addition of factors resulting in objective forces and laws, particularly those of economics, that must be obeyed. This approaches Lukacs' concept of reification in *History and Class Consciousness*.[140]

Most of the remainder of the book is taken up with an analysis of the opposition between the ossified and inert activity of individuals in 'collectives' as opposed to their dynamic and free activity in 'groups'. In the former, individuals are subject to 'reification', while in the latter they are able to engage in totalising praxis of a more genuine kind. The paradigm for these two forms of organisation are the mass political and trade union organisations of the working class (collectives) and the operation of small radical groups (groups). Sartre's own history as a member and supporter of the latter in opposition to the bureaucratic inertia of the former is clearly written here.

In addition to reification, individuals in collectives also suffer from 'seriality', which is in effect a new name for bureaucracy. Seriality arises when a number of individuals form a queue to receive some service or good, like a bus ride. Sartre opposes a meritocratic view of bureaucracy where individuals within the bureaucracy struggle to come out on top, the most able and energetic succeeding. His prolonged use of the example of a bus queue enables him to present a very different view in which the individual is rewarded depending upon time of waiting in the queue. Sometimes bus queues break down and there is a struggle, but generally individuals wait passively to find out how many empty places there are on the bus.

The discussion of seriality introduces a number of topics in the social psychology of the masses - the passivity of radio audiences, the feeling of impotence engendered by the free market, the Great Fear during the French Revolution and the French proletariat. Generally the attempt to relate these topics to seriality is unconvincing and the effect is rather a summary of existing Marxist sociology.

So far we have dealt with Book I, titled *From Individual Praxis to the Practico-Inert*. Book II is called *From Groups to History* and is intended to explain how active history-making groups emerge from the routine relations of class serialities. The treatment moves through various types of group - the fused group, the statutory group, the organisation, the constituted dialectic, the militant, the institution.

The fused group is a group constituted by a common threat. The chief example given is of the inhabitants of the Saint-Antoine district of Paris storming the Bastille during the French revolution of 1789 to obtain arms to defend themselves against a possible massacre by troops. An oblique reference is also made to the constitution of such groups in the Spanish Civil War.[141]

The fused group may find it necessary to organise and prolong its struggle by swearing a pledge to continue to struggle towards a given goal.[142] Here the individual gives up their freedom and mandates the group the right to organise praxis.[143]

The organisation develops the notion of a fixed aim by assigning groups and individuals within itself roles and functions in the pursuit of that aim.[144] In pursuit of the aim of winning at football, for instance, footballers are given the functions of forwards, goalkeeper, etc. The consciousness of organisation members tends to be technocratic; the individual perceives his mastery over techniques as sovereignty, as an extension of individual praxis.[145]

But groups also require an overall direction, which is the province of 'constituted dialectic'. Here Sartre gives an indication that in the group inertia plays a role similar to the in-itself of *Being and Nothingness*, while innovation and decision play the role of the for-itself. Thus 'It simply shows that the group is *constructed* on the model of free individual action and that it produces an organic action without itself being an organism; that is a machine for producing non-mechanical reactions and that inertia - like every human product - constitutes both its being and its *raison d'être*.'[146] The problem is how to think that the group produces inertia as its real aim, though one that can never be achieved, without falling into the error of supposing that the organisation is a kind of super-organism with its own aims, processes and laws of functioning that have no basis in the individual. American functionalist sociology in the persons of Lewin, Kardiner and Moreno is tersely rebuked for this error.[147]

Sartre reminds us of the discoveries of *Being and Nothingness*, where we found that the conscious for-itself, lost in freedom and nothingness, strives unceasingly for being as an inanimate in-itself, one of whose forms is the organisational functionary. The individual is not 'ground down' or 'bureaucratised' into becoming a functionary - a judge or a policeman. The individual desperately strives to become an in-itself, only to be endlessly undermined by the impossibility of completely discarding all freedom.

The organisation is the dialectical unity of the struggle for inertia and the innovation of leadership, which appears in one form as the consciousness of the militant, concretised for Sartre by the militants of the Communist Party. This consciousness affirms 'the party line' as that which is necessary to counter external threat. 'But it remains schematic and the more it identifies him with the group, the more it cuts him off from reality.'[148] Thus the fact that group consciousness is achieved, in this initial form, by reference to the external threat of 'the Others' means that such consciousness is initially schematic and cut off from reality. Once again we are back in the territory of *Being and Nothingness*, for 'this structure … represents in everyone his Being in the milieu of the Other…'.[149] After the attempt to realise being in the inertia of the organisation, we now meet the attempt to find being in the eyes of the Other by a concerted campaign against those opposed to the organisation.

Finally we meet the level at which this conflict becomes institutionalised. Sartre says of this: 'Being-in-the-group, in interiority, is manifested through a double, agreed failure: it is being unable to leave and also unable to integrate oneself into it; in other words, being either unable to dissolve it in oneself (pledged inertia), or to dissolve oneself in it...'[150] 'Interiority' here refers to the viewpoint of the individual, who sees life 'from the inside' and is thus possessed of freedom. 'Pledged inertia' refers both to the pledge of the individual to give over their freedom to the group and to the effort of the individual to achieve the being of complete inertia by adopting a stereotyped role or function.

The fiction that the individual can become completely absorbed within the group through a pledge of allegiance always threatens to become apparent. Thus purges and institutionalised terror arise to preserve this fiction. In the Convention, from 1793 on there was a rising tide of distrust based on the purge of May 31st. The purging of the twenty-nine most prominent Girondins was intended to re-establish homogeneity within the National Assembly, but this could only be fictitious as so many Girondins remained. Terror arose as the means of restoring a fictitious unity. Terror leaves a group given over to institutionalised inertia. Within this group the activity of leadership passes over to a 'great leader' - a Napoleon or a Stalin. This leader takes over from individuals their suspicion of the traitor which has been aroused during the terror and organises it. It is important that the leader rise from the ranks, representing 'just anyone', as was the case with Napoleon and Stalin. One feature of this type of leadership is that it can only arise from the impotence and inertia of the mass of the institution. The sovereign freedom of the membership is paradoxically returned to them through the sovereign freedom of the leader, who must pursue activist and idiosyncratic policies to gratify the needs of those who are inert and uniform.[151]

We must realise here, as throughout, that the order in which different types of social organisation are described is based on Sartre's dialectical logic, not upon a theory of historical cycles or stages. So while the relation between sovereign and institution can arise in revolutionary periods along roughly the lines already indicated, this sequence is by no means uniform and the description of the relations between sovereign and members in an institution can also apply to the relation between sovereign and people in a state, whether the sovereign be a monarch or a collection of state institutions. In class societies this creates the contradiction that the state must both pursue the objectives of the ruling group of classes and appear as the 'sovereign of all', as their representative and their freedom. In a revival of the terminology of *Being and Nothingness* Sartre says 'This position of autonomy, and heterogeneity of structure, and these possibilities of manoevre, lead it to *posit itself for itself*, as the nation itself...'[152]

Mass conformity is easily manipulated by leaders to turn individuals into zombies by mass propaganda but ultimately this is bound to fail because individuals are not zombies, however much they might like to become them. The particular contradiction Sartre mentions here is that between the serial organisation of bureaucracies and the market and the need for the sovereign to produce 'totalising action'. This problem for political leaders has become more acute since Sartre wrote *Critique*, providing an impressive confirmation of his ideas. The political leader must be a 'machine politician' utilising rational bureaucratic and economic techniques to produce rational ends. At the same time the leader must provide the charisma of leadership, engaging in free 'totalising' actions that may run counter to institutional rationality. This problem remained in abeyance whilst leaders had the charisma of a war record to fall back upon, though in the second world war conflicts between charisma and rationality also occurred, as between Churchill and some British generals. The war fever promoted in the United States from 1978 to 1981 has often been ascribed to the need for both actual and potential Presidents to demonstrate their 'powers of leadership'. The drama and unified action of war provide a form of 'totalisation' difficult to achieve through peacetime methods. These examples are not of course mentioned by Sartre who refers rather to the Stalinist 'cult of the personality'. He also discusses top ten records, racism and anti-Semitism. He stresses the dangers for those who promote racism as a means of manipulating the masses. A racist act against a passive population, as in the looting of undefended shops, may end as an administered act 'in cold blood'.[153] This revives the spectre of the administrative rationality that condemns the totalising irrationality of the pogrom. The art of this kind of government is to 'extract organic actions from the masses without disturbing their statute as non-organised'.[154]

The project of other direction has always existed, though it takes on a more obvious character in modern society. Like other human projects to attain being, it is contradictory and bound to proceed through crises. Against this form of existence we must consider the praxis-process of social classes, particularly the working class and bourgeoisie. Here Sartre wants to avoid the simplification of supposing that in revolutionary upheavals the working class becomes directly conscious of its historical mission. So he says that 'the transformation of a class into an actualised group has never actually occurred, even in revolutionary periods'.[155] He also tells us that at this point we have left the realm of theoretical abstractions. Now, by uniting the abstractions into a total picture, we can 'reach the concrete at last', which is the world of the class struggle.[156]

As a preliminary to understanding class praxis we must realise the consciousness that the bourgeoisie attempts to inculcate in the working class: 'The contradiction therefore is to recognise that the worker is free and to introduce him by compulsion into a system in which it is *also* recognised that he will be reduced to a sub-human level.'[157] The worker is both free and 'unintelligent, sub-human'. Nineteenth century bourgeois humanism asserted that the operation of the 'iron laws' of free market economics was responsible for the inhumanity and suffering produced by the system. At the same time the individual was asked to freely assent to abide by those 'laws' because they produced a greater social product. The benefits of such enrichment were intended to be limited to the privileged classes.[158] Liberal free-market economics was carried to an extreme by Malthus, who asserted that the deaths through starvation produced during capitalist economic crises were beneficial to society as a whole as they reduced the population to a more appropriate level, thus benefiting the survivors.[159] The

Malthusians also pursued a policy of increasing the productivity of large scale industry in France without increasing production, thus reducing the demand for labour while endeavouring to retain a constant market without seeking overseas outlets. This led to rising wages for those workers with jobs - a necessity if the home market was to be sustained with a contracting labour force; less workers paid more took the place of more workers paid less.[160] Workers are thus defined in seriality against other workers - a worker with a job is taking the place in the queue of one without. At the same time working class women become through the practice of abortion the instrument of Malthusian limitations on population.[161]

Yet Sartre is as aware as anyone else that even in France, notorious for its class antagonisms, Malthusianism was eventually replaced in part by 'the paternalist idea of that memorable mystification which would a hundred years later (than the revolutions of 1848) be called 'class collaboration'....'.[162] In France this occurred particularly slowly as the French bourgeoisie founded their consciousness of themselves on the two 'memorable massacres' of workers in 1848 and 1871.[163] In 'those countries that have experienced class oppression without civil war', 'paternalism, neopaternalism and 'human engineering''have become the dominant praxis-processes of the bourgeoisie.[164] (Presumably this really means 'working class oppression without working class insurrection' and is intended to include Britain as well as the United States.) Sartre feels such paternalism has not, by 1960, advanced far in France and his intention of concentrating upon France and of using Malthusianism as an illustrative example of bourgeois praxis-process prevents him from exploring other varieties of rule.

The praxis-process of the French bourgeoisie created, by the mid-nineteenth century, its mirror image within the French working class, which saw itself as inhuman and adopted an antihumanism in opposition to the humanism of the bourgeoisie.[165] The bourgeoisie defined itself as free, sovereign and human, the working class as unfree, servile and inhuman. The working class adopted this as a 'totalising conception of society'.[166] The 'bad worker' who is animal-like and inhuman is at the same time faithful to his class.[167]

At this point Sartre is clearly aware of the accusation his fellow-Marxists have made against his own philosophy of freedom - that it is a philosophy of the bourgeoisie. Now he turns the accusation back upon his accusers, by pointing out that the humanism of the bourgeoisie is not real humanism. The working class radical must adopt a 'true and positive humanism' to avoid the twin dangers of accepting the bourgeois definition of the worker as inhuman and of deserting the working class for bourgeois humanism.[168] Sartre assigns the petty bourgeois intellectual an important role in the elaboration of such a true humanism.[169]

The truly humanist dialectic of the proletariat aims at a totalising form of praxis to oppose the 'atomising rationality of positivism'.[170] This is produced in proletarian combat groups. The chief problem here is 'of predicting a freedom which is itself predicting this prediction'.[171] The difficulty both of uniting with one's allies and of opposing one's enemies is that they too are free consciousnesses. No doubt the mass of a given class at a given period adopts Malthusianism or proletarian antihumanism as a given solution to the dilemmas of freedom. But in the proletarian combat groups and the think tanks of the bourgeoisie decisions are made to actively change the complexion of mass class consciousness. The difficulties that can be encountered here have already been mentioned in considering the leadership problems of the Western countries. Such difficulties are perhaps particularly acute in France due to the long tradition of working class intellectualism and Marxism which render 'mass manipulation' even more uncertain than elsewhere, though Sartre does not mention this aspect of the problem.

In the reciprocal action of struggle there is a continued oscillation between regarding self as object and the opponent as free subject and the reversal in which self is subject and opponent object. In attempting to outwit the other by predicting their action we aim to make the opponent a predictable object.[172]

Here, for the first time, we clearly see the profound gulf that separates *Critique* from *Being and Nothingness*. It had always been difficult to determine whether the flight of freedom into being was more powerful than the reverse tendency, but in *Being and Nothingness* the former was certainly portrayed as the more dominant human activity, perhaps because of the hopelessness of the latter. Now, in *Critique*, Sartre has realised the success of the bourgeois project of turning the working class into a predictable object. This is now the greatest threat and the struggle for freedom the dominant theme. 'Here in fact one can see, against the background of scarcity, the profound threat which mankind presents to itself. The human is the Being by whom (by whose praxis) another human is reduced to the state of a haunted object…'.[173]

The praxis of the proletarian combat group does not, however, simply aim at reversing the situation by turning the bourgeoisie into an object. Rather it aims to remove the 'background of scarcity' against which the struggle presently takes place. It is this that produces the vicious dialectic of reification, engulfing both those who fancy themselves free and those who fancy themselves objects.[174]

In his last two pages Sartre claims that he has now laid the groundwork for a dialectical view of history that avoids the Lukacsian error of supposing the existence of classes as subjects, that is as actors on a historical stage. This at least seems to be the meaning of 'totalisation without a totaliser'.[175] We now have the abstract concepts necessary for historical analysis but not their use in the actual analysis of history. This is the reason we have been offered only historical examples, rather than a concerted analysis of any particular historical development. Yet because most of the examples belong to French history since 1789 he has in fact been able to build up a picture of French historical development. Perhaps for this reason Sartre felt the completion of the projected second volume of *Critique* to be less urgent than those other studies that engaged his attention after 1960. The promised second volume has not appeared.

Throughout *Critique* Sartre scrupulously avoids mentioning Weber, that notorious inspiration for his arch-enemy Aron. Yet the analyses of *Critique* amount to a new view of Weber's problem of the alternation of bureaucratic and charismatic leadership in modern society. The aim, socialism, may be Marxist, but the means, charismatic leadership, is definitely Weberian. What is new is the detailed analysis of leadership problems in different kinds of groups and the attempt to relate these problems to the overall theme of the for-itself becoming in-itself.

During the 1960s Sartre's efforts were successfully ridiculed by Althusser and his followers as continuing to neglect the key concepts of causality and social structure, particularly the Marxist concept of the mode of production. While this is partly true, Sartre is in some ways more sensitive to the new problems of the 'society of the other' than Althusser, fixated on Lenin and an earlier phase of capitalist development.

Having looked at Sartre's exposition in *Critique*, we must now ask if it is really Marxist in the sense of developing the 1844 manuscripts, or is it just another general social psychology needed to fill a gap in Marxism, this time based on spontaneity and the refusal to interpret the instincts?

If the former is true, then the concept of species being must be fundamental to it, as the concept of natural being clearly is not. The obvious place to look for species being is in the ideas of praxis, reification and totalisation. Human beings become through praxis either reified or engaged in totalising action. The need for totalising action is clearly a translation of the need for species being. Here the all round development of ideas and practice recommended in the 1844 manuscripts and *The German Ideology* is central. To be present to ourselves as a species we must cease to be specialists engaged in atomised activity and become involved in totalising praxis.

Yet there is also a significant difference with the 1844 manuscripts. There the economic category of labour was said to be fundamental. In Sartre on the other hand labour is only a first kind of practice that later gives way to social and political practices. In this revision Sartre abandoned an unnecessary restriction in Marx's idea that both highly specialised labour and highly formalised social relations are in some sense unnatural to us. These ideas are however not specifically Marxist and were widespread in nineteenth century thinking before him.[176] His quotation from Say shows that Marx was clearly aware of this in relation to the division of labour.[177] They have also become prominent in Christian critiques of modern capitalism.[178]

Influence

Sartre's influence on French philosophy in the period immediately after the second world war was immense. While Merleau-Ponty developed in some respects a rather different philosophy he devotes the last section of his major work *The Phenomenology of Perception* to approving what he can from *Being and Nothingness*. A more straightforward use of Sartre's ideas can be found in his companion Simone de Beauvoir's feminist classic *The Second Sex* (1949).

During the 1950's Sartre moved towards a far left political stance which undermined his support in France on a political level.[179] Marxists were suspicious of the idealist metaphysics contained in Sartre's writings and in the 1960's the materialist philosopher Louis Althusser succeeded in influencing much of the more cerebral part of the French left into sympathising with his own emphasis on materialist theories of causation.[180] In the theory of the individual Althusser found Lacan's modified Freudianism a more congenial ally than Sartre's emphasis on the struggle between spontaneity and the achievement of being. At the same time his companions of the 1930's, the sociologist Aron and fellow philosopher Merleau-Ponty, put up a powerful barrage of liberal-conservative criticism against Sartre's political idealism, against his radical philosophical separation of matter from mind and against what they increasingly saw as his implicit support for totalitarian communist regimes.[181]

Oddly, or perhaps rather predictably, at the time Sartre's reputation dimmed in France it waxed in the Anglo-Saxon world, as psychologists and psychiatrists there became disillusioned with both behaviourism and medically-based psychiatry founded on physical treatments using drugs and electroconvulsion. In the United States Sartre influenced the development of 'humanistic psychology' though the chief founders of this movement, Rogers and Fromm, had originated their ideas independently of Sartre. In Britain the radical psychiatrists R.D. Laing and David Cooper borrowed more directly from Sartre's writings.[182]

In the 1970's Sartre's ideas made something of a comeback in France through the writings of Baudrillard, though in place of Sartre's leftism Baudrillard's political posture is that of a conservative anarchist.

Merleau-Ponty (1908-1961)

While Merleau-Ponty was a close associate of Sartre in the 1930's and 1940's his views and approach differed quite considerably from those of Sartre even in that period. In the 1950's Sartre moved increasingly to the left and Merleau-Ponty to the right in political terms. The greatest change in Merleau-Ponty's philosophical views however came between *The Structure of Behaviour* (1942) and *The Phenomenology of Perception* (1945).

In both books Merleau-Ponty is more academic, more clearly organised and more sympathetic to materialism than Sartre. *The Structure of Behaviour* begins with an introduction on the relations between consciousness and nature and continues with two substantial chapters devoted to conditioned reflexes, the Gestalt theory of perception, the association of ideas and the effects of brain lesions on perception and consciousness. The upshot of the discussion is to conclude that the Gestalt emphasis on form as an organised structure of wholes is correct in these areas, as well as in describing the organisation of behaviour into patterned wholes, as in Kohler's description of reasoning in apes.

Next follows a chapter on three orders of structured wholes: the physical order, the vital order, the human order. Gestalt theory is now criticised for lacking a truly philosophical theory of form, which is to take into account both the fact that all knowledge originates in perceptions that are themselves already given structures within consciousness and that the physical universe is a unified structure that any particular act of cognition, such as a scientific experiment, partially but never completely dismembers for the purpose of analysis.[183]

The structured wholes that we call organisms and human activity are then subjected to the same kind of analysis. Any perception or cognition relating to events within these orders is also immediately structured.

The section on the human order gives a phenomenological version of psychology very similar to that expounded by Jaspers in his *Psychopathology*. We are to understand this order in the light of its dialectical interplay with the physical and vital orders that surround it. There is no question here of a phenomenology that deals with an abstract consciousness removed from the physical and biological worlds.

Merleau-Ponty thinks that previous ideas about the interplay between mind and matter, particularly that of Descartes but also some of the formulations of the Neokantian philosopher Brunschvicg, have taken this relation to be external. One of the central themes of Merleau-Ponty's philosophy is that this relation can become an internal, dialectical one if we can develop a phenomenology of our immediate perception of our bodies and their actions. Such a phenomenology, he now contends, must turn to child psychology to study the direct perceptions that children have of their own bodies, of the objects they act upon and of other people. Such perceptions, he feels, must contain immediately given meanings.[184] Such meanings would correspond to Husserl's noematic meanings and Husserl's writing is referred to extensively throughout. An example of such an immediately given meaning for children is animism - the tendency to see sticks as people or faces in clouds. We might normally think that such experiences occur because one thing reminds the child of another, but Merleau-Ponty wants us to think that the experience a child has when it looks at a face is fundamentally no different from that it has when looking at a cloud; in both cases the meaning is directly present to consciousness and requires no further explanation. Kant is given credit for realising that consciousness contains an immediately given awareness of space, but he fell into the error of equating this with Euclidean space.[185] Merleau-Ponty has already been at some pains to point out that Gestalt psychology has shown that the structure of immediately perceived space, even for adults, is not that of Euclidean space.[186]

There follows an attempt to suggest how Freud's model of human action could be reformed to accord with this approach. Merleau-Ponty's line here is particularly reminiscent of Jaspers: 'Without calling into question the role which Freud assigns to the erotic infrastructure and to social regulations, what we should like to ask is whether the conflicts themselves of which he speaks and the psychological mechanisms which he has described - the formation of complexes, repression, regression, resistance, transfer, compensation and sublimation - really require the system of causal notions by which he interprets them and which transforms the discoveries of psychoanalysis into a metaphysical theory of human existence. For it is easy to see that causal thinking is not indispensable here and that one can use another language. Development should be considered, not as the fixation of a given force on outside objects which are also given, but as a progressive and discontinuous structuration (Gestaltung, Neugestaltung) of behaviour. Normal structuration is one which reorganizes conduct in depth in such a way that infantile attitudes no longer have a place or meaning in the new attitude; it would result in perfectly integrated behaviour, each moment of which would be internally linked with the whole. One will say that there is repression when integration has been achieved only in appearance and leaves certain relatively isolated systems subsisting in behaviour which the subject refuses both to transform and to assume. A complex is a segment of behaviour of this kind, a stereotyped attitude, an acquired and durable structure of consciousness with regard to a category of stimuli. A situation which could not be mastered at the time of an initial experience and which gave rise to the anguish and the disorganization which accompanies failure is no longer experienced directly: the subject perceives it only through the physiognomy that it assumed at the time of the traumatic experience. In these conditions each new experience, which in reality is not a new experience, repeats the result of the preceding ones and renders its return even more probable in the future.'[187]

As in Jaspers the central idea here is to abolish the category of the unconscious in favour of a confused or disorganised consciousness of certain things. We are half-conscious of our defence-mechanisms as we operate them, just as hysterical patients are half-conscious of the meaning of their symptoms. From such pathological solutions to the conflicts present within consciousness, Merleau-Ponty distinguishes cases in which there is a real transcendence of difficulties. True love is mentioned as one such transcendent solution. Nietzsche's analysis of the pathology of self-sacrifice is mentioned with approval as an example of a kind of failure of transcendence.[188]

Merleau-Ponty objects to the traditional empiricist view that we use reason to achieve inborn ends:

'Human action can be reduced to vital action only if one considers the intellectual analysis by which it is accomplished as a more ingenious means of achieving animal ends. But it is this completely external relation of end and means which becomes impossible from the point of view which we are adopting. It imposes itself as long as consciousness is defined by the possession of certain 'representations', for then the consciousness of the act is necessarily reduced to representation of its goal on the one hand and possibly to that of the bodily mechanisms which assure its execution on the other. The relation of means to end can be only external under these conditions.

'But if, as we have just said, representative consciousness is only one of the forms of consciousness and if this latter is defined more generally by reference to an object - whether it be willed, desired, loved, or represented - the felt movements will be linked together by a practical intention which animates them, which makes of them a directed melody; and it becomes impossible to distinguish the goal and the means as separable elements, impossible to treat human action as another solution to the problems which instinct resolves: if the problems were the same, the solutions would be identical. An analysis of the immanent meaning of action and its internal structure is substituted for an analysis of the goals of action and their means.'[189]

It should not however be thought that the influence of consciousness on life is a simple negation of instincts: 'From this new point of view one realizes that, although all actions permit an adaption of life, the word 'life' does not have the same meaning in animality and humanity; and the conditions of life are defined by the proper essence of the species. Doubtless, clothing and houses serve to protect us from the cold; language helps in collective work and in the analysis of the 'unorganized mass'. But the act of dressing becomes the act of adornment or also of modesty and thus reveals a new attitude toward oneself and others. Only men see that they are nude. In the house that he builds for himself, man projects and realizes his preferred values. Finally, the act of speaking expresses the fact that man ceases to adhere immediately to the milieu, that he elevates it to the status of spectacle and takes possession of it mentally by means of knowledge properly so called.'[190]

The Structure of Behaviour contains some isolated and little developed remarks on the possibility of relating behaviour to a philosophy of existence.[191] *The Phenomenology of Perception* develops both these remarks and earlier suggestions about exploring the phenomenology of the perception of the body and movement. The book begins once again by returning to classical analyses of sensation, association, attention and judgement. To these Merleau-Ponty once again opposes his insistence that perceptual structures and inherent meanings are directly present in consciousness. Part One then sets out an analysis of our experience of our own and other people's bodies. His concerns here are at least partly inspired by Husserl's *Cartesian Meditations*, a text Merleau-Ponty refers to repeatedly in his preface. He is concerned that we find a way back from abstract space to the lived space of the body, which contains not only fragments of non-Euclidian geometry but also immediately lived meanings: '…. our body is not an object for an 'I think': it is a grouping of lived-through meanings which moves towards its equilibrium.'[192]

The act of giving coherence and meaning to bodily experience is very fundamental to us because it is in this way we achieve a truly human existence as a being for itself rather than as a being in itself, like stones or tin cans. While these terms are the same as those used by Sartre in *Being and Nothingness*, their meaning for Merleau-Ponty is almost the opposite of that given to them by Sartre. For Merleau-Ponty we create meaning in our world at every moment by positive acts of meaning-creation which parallel what traditional philosophy called acts of will. We are in control of the meaning-giving activity we undertake in the world. This is quite different from the Sartrian view that spontaneity acts out of nothingness before so-called acts of will are fabricated to rationalise the results. In this sense Merleau-Ponty is much closer to the popular stereotype of 'existentialists' as philosophers who encourage us to take control of the overall significance of our lives.

Merleau-Ponty's view of how we give coherence and meaning to the actions of the body is well illustrated by the following passage: '… in a word, to place behind the flux of impressions an invariant which makes it comprehensible and to assemble into a form the matter of experience. But one cannot say that consciousness *has* this power, it *is* this power. As soon as there is consciousness, and for there to be consciousness, there must be something of which it is conscious, an intentional object; and it can only adopt a bearing towards this object in so far as it 'derealises' itself and throws itself into it, is wholly involved in this reference to something and is a pure signifying act. If a being is consciousness, it must be nothing but a web of intentions. If it ceases to define itself by the signifying act, it falls back to the status of a thing, a thing being just that which doesn't know, that rests in total ignorance of self and world, which is not a real self, that is a for-itself, and has only spatio-temporal individuation, that is to say existence in-itself. Consciousness does not allow of more or less. If a sick mind ceases to exist as a consciousness, it exists as a thing. Either that person's movement is movement for itself, and the 'stimulus' is not the causal agent, but the intentional object - or their movement fragments and disperses itself into existence in-itself, becoming an objective process of the body, whose phases succeed one another but do not know one another. The peculiarity of concrete movements in illness is that they are reflexes in the classical sense. The sick person's hand finds the part of the body where a mosquito has landed because pre-established neural circuits adjust the movement accordingly. In such cases (of mental disorder) trade skills are retained because they depend upon well established conditioned reflexes. They remain despite mental deterioration because they are movements in-themselves. The distinction between concrete movement and abstract movement, between *Greifen* and *Zeigen*, should be that between the physiological and the psychic, between existence in-itself and existence for-itself.'[193]

Because we build up our world of immediate perception by acting upon the world through the body, one of the most fundamental ways of experiencing our social world is through sex, which is one way in which, both in fantasy and actuality, we can directly experience the bodies of other people. Accordingly, a whole section is devoted to the body in its sexual being. Here Freud's work is emphasised, though Merleau-Ponty sets out to show that it is not sex as a biological drive that makes it so important but rather its role in our elaboration of a social world.[194]

In the course of his discussion of Freud Merleau-Ponty makes it clear that he still regards the unconscious as a misnomer for things that are really partly conscious. Thus a hysterical symptom, as in a girl who loses the power of speech after her parents make her break her engagement, is a partly conscious refusal and protest, rather than the manifestation of unconscious powers that take over.[195]

Part Two contains an elaboration of these ideas in the areas of sense experience, space, the natural world and the human world. Part Three summarises his conclusions regarding the Cartesian *Cogito*, time and freedom. The latter is the most interesting part. Merleau-Ponty refers on almost every page to Sartre's *Being and Nothingness*, which had been published two years before. Yet while Merleau-Ponty's ideas are so different from those of Sartre, he makes no mention of these differences, presumably to avoid disturbing his close personal relations with Sartre. Instead he adopts the strategy of borrowing those ideas from *Being and Nothingness* that suit him, tactfully ignoring its major thesis regarding the spontaneity that emerges from nothingness.

Merleau-Ponty is able to give hearty assent to Sartre's rejection of the role of physical causality in traditional theories of motivation. He continues: 'The alleged motive does not bear upon my decision, but on the contrary my decision lends it force. Everything I 'am' through nature or personal history - hunchbacked, beautiful or Jewish - I am never just exactly this thing for myself, as just explained. Granted I am it for the other, but I remain free to regard the other either as a consciousness whose views are damaging to my being or alternatively as a simple object. It is true that such a choice is itself a constraint: if I am ugly I have the choice to be either the source or the object of disapproval, I can be sadist or masochist but I cannot be unaware of others. This choice which is a fact of the human condition, is not one for me as pure consciousness: nonetheless it is me who makes the other exist for myself and who makes both of us exist as men. Besides which, even if being human were something imposed upon me, only my manner of being remaining chosen, making just this choice without admitting the small number of possibilities would still be a free choice. If someone were to say that my temperament inclines me to sadism or to masochism, that's just a manner of speaking, as temperament only exists for that secondary consciousness that I have of myself when I see myself through the eyes of others, which itself is something I recognise, give value to and in a sense choose.'[196]

Merleau-Ponty thus frees us from motivation not in order to hand us over to a blind and incomprehensible spontaneity but to our own freedom to choose. This freedom is exercised within situations, but is not determined by them: 'Our freedom does not destroy our situation, but is intermeshed with it: so long as we live our situation is open, which implies both that it calls for special methods of resolution and that by itself it is powerless to effect one.'[197]

Merleau-Ponty's writings after *The Phenomenology of Perception* involve the application of the views about human nature found there, though his political opinions changed considerably. In an article in *Les Temps Modernes*, which he founded with Sartre, he talks more explicitly about his disagreements with *Being and Nothingness*. The chief objection he makes to it is that it involves too great an antithesis between the for-itself and the in-itself. Only a hint is given of the objection that Sartre makes nothingness primary.[198]

Another interesting piece is 'The child's relations with others', a course given at the Sorbonne in 1960.[199] Here he makes extensive use of the child psychology of the French psychologist Henri Wallon. He is particularly interested in the period from six to twelve months of age. Wallon emphasises learning about one's own body image through observation in mirrors in this period. Merleau-Ponty would however rather follow Lacan in thinking that this is not simply an intellectual apprehension, but rather the beginning of intense feelings of narcissistic pleasure when contemplating our own body that later spill over into pleasure in being watched by others.[200] Merleau-Ponty follows both Wallon and Lacan in thinking that the jealousy and rage that emerge shortly after can be attributed to annoyance at being deprived of the pleasures of attention. He breaks with Lacan at this point and follows Wallon in thinking that the 'three year crisis' occurs because the child begins to realise more clearly that when the other looks at him it is not himself who is looking, but rather another who may steal his freedom to construe his body both spatially and emotionally. The child must now learn to live with such a dangerous potential assailant. We are not however to imagine that this phase displaces the Oedipal situations, which occur later and are still assigned the dominant position given them by Freud.[201]

Influence

Merleau-Ponty's influence has certainly been less than that of Sartre, with de Waelhens his only prominent follower in Europe.[202] His writings have however occasioned a large number of expository studies and his work continues to be widely read and discussed.

Baudrillard (1928 -)

Baudrillard is known in the English speaking world chiefly from *The Mirror of Production*, his only translated work, and from Mark Poster's introduction to that translation. In addition Poster recommends Baudrillard at the end of his *Existentialist Marxism in Postwar France* as one of the most promising forces on the current French intellectual scene.[203] Similar claims have been made in a number of articles by various authors. There is no doubt of Baudrillard's success in France itself.

Rhetoric is an important element in much French writing on social theory, even among supposedly scientific Althusserians. With Baudrillard rhetoric flowers particularly luxuriantly, often verging on poetic. Baudrillard has published a volume of poetry and like a number of modern philosophers - Heidegger and Horkheimer come to mind - he sees poetry as the only form of discourse that offers any hope of breaking out of the mental prison of false rationality within which modern society has encased us. Baudrillard has little time for Soviet Russia or for socialism as an ideal. Heidegger by conversion and Horkheimer by original conviction were nominal adherents of Marxism; Baudrillard has increasingly set out to assail Marxism even as a verbal tag, which is at least more honest than those who adopt the tag while rejecting virtually every traditional Marxist position.

The most succinct description of Baudrillard would be a French Marcuse. Like Marcuse he thinks Freud described the patriarchal personality of a social form that is now passing away. The new social type Baudrillard calls 'The Man of Arrangement' and 'The Man of Relation and Ambience'. Such people are addicted to maintaining control over their environment and by means of the techniques of 'human relations' are able to 'fit in' anywhere.[204] The parallels with Marcuse's 'One Dimensional Man' are close.

Also like Marcuse and the Frankfurt School more generally Baudrillard sees the struggle for control over nature through labour as the original source of many modern individual and collective ills, though unlike them he sees this as now replaced by control over signs. Like them be believes the Marxist distinction between economic base and political and ideological superstructure to be outmoded. Modern society is a functional interlocking machine whose chief feature is the manipulation of the masses by 'models',of which more later. While the Protestant Work Ethic and the economic law of value were responsible for producing the consumer society they have now been superceded by mass manipulation as the fundamental force in society. This is the source of Baudrillard's frequent attacks on political economy, which in his view has become a false ideology that diverts people away from the real issue of manipulation into an antiquarian pursuit.

Baudrillard however differs from Marcuse in two respects: vocabulary and attitude to socialism. His vocabulary owes much to Barthes, Sartre and Lacan, while Marcuse tended to create his own jargon. From Barthes we get an emphasis on 'discourse' and the jargon of semiotics. From Sartre we have 'anguish' and 'series', the latter a term Sartre adopted in his *Critique of Dialectical Reason* to denote the allocation of scarce resources on the basis of time of waiting in a queue or time on a waiting list. Sartre tried to implicate a wide variety of other topics in his discussion of seriality, perhaps most relevantly the passivity of radio audiences and the feeling of impotence engendered by the free market. Already in Sartre we find the term beginning to slide. The free market typically allocates scarce resources on the basis of ability to pay not by a waiting list. The problem of terms degenerating into rhetorical catch-alls that can be conveniently summoned to plug a hole in an argument is a long-standing one in French social theory. In *The System of Objects* Baudrillard defines 'series'in quite a different way. A consumer product is 'serial' chiefly on account of its built in obsolescence.[205] He cites with approval Vance Packard's summary of the three methods of limiting the durability of consumer goods: incessant technological 'innovation'; fragility or poor manufacture; incessant changes of fashion.[206] There is of course nothing wrong in redefining a term from Sartre and in this case there is some justification for it. As we shall see, 'series' does have an existential connotation, but it is not that given to the term by Sartre. Borrowing and redefining terms is a typical Baudrillard manoeuver; his way of legitimating himself. It does however create certain difficulties for the reader.

Baudrillard also borrows freely from Freud and Lacan in his use of terms. He even seems to echo Marcuse when he says in *The System of Objects* 'in this controlled convergence, in this organised fragility, in this perpetually destroyed synchrony, negativity is no longer possible'. Oddly enough Marcuse is one writer Baudrillard avoids mentioning, or perhaps hasn't read.[207]

There is however a second difference with Marcuse beyond that of terminology. For Marcuse economic revolution has assumed a distorted form in the USSR and sexual revolution has assumed a distorted form in the repressive desublimation of the West. He looked to a more complete economic revolution, particularly in the Third World, and a more complete sexual revolution. For Baudrillard 'Existing revolutions all index themselves by the immediately preceding state of the system. They all arm themselves with a nostalgic resurrection of the real in all its forms, which is to say with semblances of the second order: dialectic, use value, the transparency and finality of production, 'liberation' of the unconscious, of sensory repression (of the signifying or of the signified called desire), etc. All these liberations present themselves as an ideal content; phantoms which the system has devoured in its successive revolutions and which it subtly revives as phantasms of revolution. All revolutions are but the transition to generalised manipulation. The revolution itself is meaningless at the stage of probabilistic control processes.'[208] The 'second order' mentioned here refers to old-style capitalist society governed by political economy and patriarchy. We now live in the 'third order', which is an order of 'signs' and 'codes'. Again Baudrillard has borrowed the term 'sign' from semiotics, but has redefined it to mean the kind of meanings and values that belong to society of the 'third order'. Likewise the term 'symbol' is redefined to mean primarily the symbolic exchange of gifts in tribal societies and tribal ideology. A degenerate form of symbolism is also present within 'second order' society in Freudian symbolism and patriarchal values.

Despite all this Baudrillard does not consider change unlikely or struggle hopeless: 'Every system that approaches perfect operationality is close to being lost. When the system says 'A is A' or 'two and two make four', it approaches both absolute power and complete ridicule, which is to say that immediate subversion is probable - it needs only a slight tap to make it collapse'.[209] This means that 'the only strategy is *catastrophic*, not dialectical', which explains Baudrillard's many adverse references to dialectic.[210] Again the problem of shifting meanings plagues us. To Lenin in his *Philosophical Notebooks*, and thus to many Marxists, the value of dialectic was that it emphasised the slow buildup of changes in society leading to a flashpoint and, given the right conditions, to revolution.[211] This, with an entirely different content, is also Baudrillard's model. Baudrillard's many sallies against dialectic are directed at a gradualist interpretation of the term dialectic. It certainly isn't Baudrillard's fault that 'dialectic' has acquired more meanings than Heinz varieties: but his rhetorical style and lack of definitions do not improve the situation.

Baudrillard seems quite optimistic that the society of signs will collapse of its own accord. The model for this could well be the Festival Revolution of May 1968. At that moment the established codes cracked with unexpected rapidity and people began 'really talking to one another' in a spontaneous way. But if the system needs a push to collapse this will, Baudrillard thinks, come chiefly from the activity of theorists - Althusser's 'theoretical practice' returned in an unwelcome form. Baudrillard's suggestions for the direction of theoretical activity are however quite confusing. One suggestion is that the theorist must 'go further than the system in simulation'.[212] That is must produce a model of 'perfect operationality' even more perfect than the simulation models produced by those 'system theorists' who are also theorists for the system. If Baudrillard really means this then he himself is a very bad theorist. His own theoretical writing is suggestive and couched in original but highly ambiguous language. It certainly provides no model for 'system simulation'.

Fortunately there are two other suggestions Baudrillard makes about theorising that he is able to live up to more fully. 'Against a hyper-realist system, the only strategy is pataphysics of some kind, 'a science of imaginary solutions', which is to say a science-fiction of the system turning against itself.'[213] Pataphysics means a form of revolutionary metaphysics - Sartre again. And: 'We have only theoretical violence left. Speculation to death, of which the only method is the radicalisation of all hypotheses.'[214] These, and not 'system simulation', are the real guidelines under which he operates. Baudrillard does, however, give us a fairly clear idea of the kind of society that he believes would, or should - the two are not clearly distinguished - emerge after the cataclysmic eclipse of the society of signs. This is a society based on symbolic exchange - that is on a return to tribal ideology. Significantly enough no attention is given to the economic organisation of such a society. This reflects Baudrillard's rather astonishing position that *'There is neither a mode of production nor production* in primitive societies.'[215] He denounces Marxism 'from Engels to Althusser' for its 'scientific canonisation' of the myth that 'history is the history of modes of production'.[216] There is a clear implication that not only do tribal societies have no concept of mode of production, but that they have no concept of production. Here again a little less rhetoric and a little more serious analysis might have been helpful. Tribal societies do recognise the need for production and certainly engage in what we would regard as production - hunting, gathering, agriculture. They also use methods of production involving magic, ceremony and symbolic exchange with ancestors and powers from the spirit world. But to say this makes them doubt the need for productive activities in just our sense of the term is ridiculous. Could a society abandon everyday production entirely in favour of supernatural methods? Would the gods or ancestors really provide manna for the faithful? Baudrillard appears to think they would. These points are of course quite separate from arguments as to whether production is a dominant 'instance' in tribal society.[217]

Baudrillard's writings can be conveniently divided into three topics: the analysis of consumer objects; the attack on political economy; the description of symbolic exchange.

Consumer objects are the topic of *The System of Objects*. The discussion is divided into four sections: the functional system (objective discourse); the non-functional system (subjective discourse); the meta-and dysfunctional systems of gadgets and robots; the socio-ideological system of objects and consumption. Central to all these areas is Baudrillard's definition of consumption as : 'An activity involving the systematic manipulation of signs... To become a consumer object, an object must become a sign, that is to say in some way exterior to a relation that it does nothing but signify - thus arbitrary and not coherent with this concrete relation, but taking its coherence, and thus its sense, from an abstract and systematic relation to all the other object-signs.'[218] To understand Baudrillard's notion of object-signs we must get away from the classical distinction between necessities, which satisfy natural needs, and luxuries, which give a refined pleasure or allow the upper classes to show off. Within a truly consumer society the essential role of consumer objects is to transmit messages to form a code of signs. In itself not a particularly original thought. We are quite used to thinking of consumer objects as 'status symbols', though Baudrillard would prefer us to say 'status signs'. But he wants to go much further than this rather familiar, though very important, observation about consumer goods. Coded up in consumer objects is actually a whole system of ideology - the ideology of signs.

A sign is an arbitrary label that is part of a system of such labels. The mania for control over the world which characterised societies of the second order has now been superceded by mania for control over sign systems. Here is a further distinction between Baudrillard and the Frankfurt School of Marcuse and Horkheimer. For them the mania for control over the world was still the dominant human motive, while for Baudrillard various manias and obsessions connected with sign systems have now become dominant.

His first sign-system is exemplified by the functionalist style of interior decoration. Functional interior design has two main aspects: arrangement and ambience. The man of arrangement is keen to have a functional interior composed of modular units, each of which cleverly doubles up as kitchen table cum writing desk cum drinks cabinet or whatever. 'There is in this model of 'functional' living an obvious abstraction. Advertising wants us to believe that the modern individual really no longer has any *need* for their objects, that they only need to operate among them like an intelligent communications technician.'[219] In *The System of Objects* Baudrillard is still playing with psychoanalytic analyses of this - he suggests that the traditional relation to the house was the oral relation to the mother symbol. Functionalism encourages anal play with symbols of faeces.[220] This belief that psychoanalytic explanations can still be applied to the society of signs is less pronounced in his later work.

Ambience is also deliberately manipulated in the functional interior. Interior colours and materials can be 'warm' or 'cold'. This is used to provide an environment in which human relationships can likewise be manipulated. In a 'warm' environment people feel intimate, in a 'cold' one they feel formal. One is reminded of the joke about the American college professor who was asked what makes college girls promiscuous. 'Personally I find Mantovani works the best' was the reply.

Non-functional objects also play an important part in the consumer society because they appear to provide a safe, subjective haven away from the all-embracing message of functionalism. The crucial feature of many such non-functional objects is their age. Antique furniture, paintings and restoration of old houses give people a new kind of myth of origin. To provide this the objects must be 'authentic'. Baudrillard says that 'The functional object is the absence of being'.[221] He hints that the authenticity of the antique is what gives us back our private certainty of being. He is sympathetic to this passion for the ancient as it brings the modern functionalised individual into contact with the sterling values of the past, back to a more essential relation with our environment. But he is also suspicious of this return. It provides a safety valve for a deeply felt need that would otherwise blow apart the society of signs. The contact with the past achieved is also an emasculated one: 'Today technical civilisation has repudiated the wisdom of the ancients, but it prostrates itself before the density of old things, whose only value is sealed and sure .'[222]

Collections of objects also play an important part in modern subjective consciousness. They provide 'not just a material body that resists, but a mental kingdom where I reign, something I give meaning to, my property, my passion.'[223] Collections have above all a narcissistic function. We decide upon 'the most beautiful domestic animal' to collect as a sign of our own beauty written in the language of 'a sort of thing intermediate between beings and objects'.[224] In our perverse attitude to sex we destructure sex objects into their component parts in order to write the message of our own narcissistic control over them. Baudrillard cites a scene from the film *Le Mépris* (Contempt) by Jean-Luc Godard:

'You love my feet?' she said.

'Yes I love them'.

'You love my legs?'

'Yes'.

'And my thighs?'

'Yes', he said again, 'I love them'. (And so on, from top to bottom.)

'So you love me totally?'

'Yes I love you totally'.

'Me too, Paul', she said summing up the situation.[225]

In the meta- and dysfunctional systems we meet the robot and the gadget. Science fiction has already given us civilisations peopled by robotic machines. This, Baudrillard says, is the extrapolation of our own fascination for automatic machines. The symbolic value of robots and automatic machines is that they provide an image of a completely functionalised human being that remains sexless. This provides functionalised humanity with a vision of 'itself' as 'it' would like to be - relieved of the anguish of being human that results from sexual relations, kinship groups and symbolic exchange. Gadgets on the other hand are dysfunctional in that their inventors tend to invent not only the object to perform the functions, but the function itself - the remote control television operator, the electric carving knife. We don't actually need these gadgets; manual methods work just as well. The gadget is there to reassure us that for every function there is a gadget - even for unnecessary functions like switching channels with no hands and carving a roast without arms.

Erected on this mania for the manipulation of signs denoting functionalism is the socio-ideological system of the consumer society. Within this society the upper classes consume models and pay cash while the masses consume series and live on credit. This produces a kind of existential oppression that has replaced oppression through hard labour and deprivation of the necessities of life. Models confer on their possessors the privilege of reality because the prestige house and the prestige car are built to last; cheaper houses and cars, that Baudrillard calls series, are designed with built-in obsolescence. The masses are also unable to keep up with the fashions set by the upper classes and so never have the 'very latest' things. This feeling of not being real is intensified by the system of credit.

210

This ensures that the unreal objects possessed by the masses are not really theirs either; they belong to the hire purchase companies. To round things off advertising has created a universal if brutally simple code of '*le standing*', that is the prestige value attached to goods.[226]

In his next book, *The Consumer Society*, we come closer to an economic analysis of the contemporary social system. In discussing waste Baudrillard describes the 'potlatch perfume' of conspicuous consumption, reinforced by the great consuming heroes of television and film who live lives of ostentatious luxury and waste. By contrast we have the 'cold participation in the constraints of the economic order' of war.[227] This echoes the Marxist theory of modern war as an economically necessary destruction of capital. He was soon to dispense with such Marxian props.

He turns his attention to a critique of political economy in *Towards a Critique of the Political Economy of Signs* and *The Mirror of Production*. This critique is in reality a critique of the Marxian critique of political economy. Marxism, for Baudrillard, is tilting against a windmill in aiming to socialise the economy. The economy as such no longer exists within the consumer society, having been replaced by a total system in which both use value and exchange value are absorbed within the system of signs. Baudrillard's modernised version of political economy gives us a new kind of object: 'The object of this political economy, that is its simplest element, its nuclear element - which for Marx was the commodity - is today neither commodity nor sign, but indissociably both, where both are abolished as specific determinations, but not as forms; this object is perhaps simply the object, the *form*/object, upon which use value, exchange value and sign value converge in a complex manner which describes the most general form of political economy.'[228]

We can understand this proposition in two ways. One would take it as a statement about the culture and values of consumer society. The other as the specification of a new quantitative law of exchange to replace the Marxian claim that exchange value is proportional to the labour time socially necessary for the production of a commodity. To illustrate the second line of argument we might think of deviations from the labour theory of value produced by signs in their role as codes for social status, such as the high price of professional labour. Perhaps the professional status of doctors, lawyers and teachers has elevated the price of the products of their labour, producing a systematic deviation from the law of value. The orthodox Marxist is liable to reply that this is not relevant as doctors, lawyers and teachers operate within a kind of guild production or as part of the state. The problem is therefore to be analysed in terms of the articulation of these modes of production with the capitalist mode based on the production of commodities for a free market. But don't the manufacturers of prestige motor cars and the designers and builders of prestige houses enjoy similar privileges? Are they outside the capitalist mode of production? We could extend this second quantitative type of argument to the quantitative determination of demand and the quantitative determination of status and other sign values. These latter would be extremely hazardous enterprises and Baudrillard wisely doesn't embark upon them. Rather his emphasis is upon the arbitrary and unstable nature of value in a consumer society. For this reason he is unwilling to specify any quantitative law of exchange to replace the labour theory of exchange value. Even the topic of 'deviations' from the labour theory of exchange value is too definite. When he discusses wages and prices it is the arbitrary nature of values that comes to the fore. On wages: 'Inversely, from the moment that pay is disconnected from labour power nothing stands in the way any longer (according to the trade unions) of a maximal unlimited wage demand. For if there is a fair price for a certain quantity of labour power, there is no price for consensus and global participation.'[229] On prices: 'The price of things thus becomes essential, not any longer just quantitatively as exchange value, not just differentially as in the Veblen effect (presumably the effect of the conspicuous consumption of goods in producing distinctions of social status), but as law, as a fetishised form - the crux of the market economy and the psychic economy of value.'[230] People, he is saying, need a price on objects so as to know how to react to them, how to value them, how to desire them.

Because he abstains from proposing any new law of exchange value, Baudrillard concentrates on a generalised account of the role of the amalgamated exchange/use/sign value in contemporary culture. Here the decline and fall of the work ethic, that is of labour as a value, looms large, as does Baudrillard's contention that in leaving use value outside the scope of his analysis of the commodity Marx fell back into thinking of use value as natural usefulness.[231] While he might have given Marx a little more credit for recognising the socially produced nature of human needs, there is no doubt that use value was almost untheorised in classical Marxism.

In *Symbolic Exchange and Death* (1976) Baudrillard sets out in more detail his view that one of the chief problems of modern societies, capitalist as well as communist, is their inability to relate to death. A virtue of tribal society was its ability to include the dead in a system of symbolic exchange. In commodity producing society 'The obsession with death and the wish to abolish it by accumulation becomes the fundamental motor of the rationality of political economy.'[232] Individuals seek immortality through the creation of dynastic fortunes.

Baudrillard's view of tribal society is explicitly derived from the work of Marcel Mauss. Mauss stressed the importance of gifts between social groups within the tribe to maintain social solidarity. Baudrillard can therefore draw upon a considerable tradition in his analyses of symbolic exchange within tribal society. Significantly enough he neglects Levi-Strauss, probably because he dislikes the Levi-Straussian emphasis on classification as the basic impulse of tribal thought. Levi-Strauss' extensive analyses of the game-like recoding of classification schemes in tribal thought would be even more unwelcome to Baudrillard, who would presumably take this as an example of cultural imperialism - the reading back of the society of signs onto tribal consciousness. For Baudrillard tribal symbolism has an essential relation to the objects and processes symbolised.

Baudrillard's description of tribal views of death is quite surprising. He says

'Savages have no biological concept of death. Or rather: biological facts - death, birth or sickness - everything that belongs to nature and which we accord the privilege of necessity and objectivity, for them simply have no meaning. They (the uninitiated) are absolute disorder, because they cannot be exchanged symbolically, and what cannot be exchanged symbolically constitutes a mortal danger for the group.'[233] Drawing on R. Jaulin's *Saran Death*, he argues that initiation is the key to understanding the tribal view of death. Here 'the ancestors' 'swallow the koys' (the young candidates for initiation), who die '*symbolically*' in order to be reborn.[234] This gift of life from the ancestors marks the real moment of birth at which the youth becomes 'a social being'. In return for the gift of life the living must offer gifts to the ancestors. Death is 'to be removed from the cycle of symbolic exchange'.[235]

It would be easy to query this description of how tribal peoples view death. His analysis seems to imply that uninitiated children are viewed as being dead, which is certainly not true. Basing his analysis largely on the Sara he finds himself having to argue against even Jaulin, who thinks that the Saran opinion is 'To death and to life, which are given to them, human beings have added initiation, through which they transcend the disorder of death.'[236] Baudrillard also fails to discuss tribal peoples who do not believe in reincarnation and those who have a pessimistic view of the life of spirits after death, both of which would seem to offer him problems. Perhaps we can grant him the general point that tribal peoples have less trouble in dealing with death than we do. Ultimately that may be more crucial to his message than the details of the analysis.

Baudrillard is perhaps the most successful of recent social theorists in conveying the pessimistic hysteria of the traditional intellectual faced with an appallingly integrative, war-crazed social system. Yet his suggestion for 'insurrection against signs' remains an idealist project, without hope of success. Consumer images act to reinforce the integrative power of the system. But material, physiological affluence coupled with nationalism provide the necessary foundations for this. The decisive proof of this is the example of the Roman plebs, progressively integrated without benefit of advertising into an imperial system by handouts and war. Circuses helped to celebrate but not create these fundamental touchstones, then as today. Advertising and consumer values are certainly repellent. What matters to the realist is: when will they become offensive to the masses? The ability to deliver consumer goods adds to the state's legitimacy. The analysis of consumerism should add to the theory of legitimacy. Instead Baudrillard has taken it off on a semi-Hegelian tangent, erecting the spirit of signs as the self-destructing spirit of the system, convincing himself that its economy and value system are also about to explode. Even a local crisis of the consumer value system remains to be demonstrated, let alone such an all-embracing catastrophe.

Further Reading

Heidegger

Heidegger's writings are difficult and the student would be advised to prepare by reading some of the following:
E.G. Ballard and C.E. Scott (eds), *Martin Heidegger in Europe and America*, Nijhoff, The Hague, 1973.
J.D. Caputo, *The Mystical Element in Heidegger's Thought*, Ohio Uni. Press, Athens, 1978.
D. Halliburton, *Poetic Thinking: An Approach to Heidegger*, Uni. of Chicago Press, Chicago, 1981
M. King, *Heidegger's Philosophy*, Blackwell, Oxford, 1964.
T. Langan, *The Meaning of Heidegger*, Columbia Uni. Press, New York, 1959.
J.L. Mehta, *The Philosophy of Martin Heidegger*, Harper and Row, New York, 1971.
H. Spiegelberger, *The Phenomenological Movement*, Nijhoff, The Hague, 1965, Vol. 1.
G. Steiner, *Heidegger*, Harvester, Hassocks, 1978

Sartre

Sartre's philosophical writings also tend to require some introduction, which can be found in the following;
R. Aron, *The Opium of the Intellectuals*, Basic Books, New York, 1965.
R. Aron, *Marxism and the Existentialists*, Harper and Row, New York, 1969.
H.E. Barnes, *Sartre*, Lippincott, Philadelphia, 1973.
P. Caws, *Sartre*, Routledge, London, 1979.
A.C. Danto, *Sartre*, Fontana, London, 1975.
J.P. Fell, *Emotion in the Thought of Sartre*, Columbia Uni. press, New York, 1965.
G.J. Hayim, *The Existentialist Sociology of Jean-Paul Sartre*, Uni. of Massachusetts Press, Amherst, 1980.
J.H. McMahan, *Humans Being*, Uni. of Chicago Press, Chicago, 1971.
M. Merleau-Ponty, *Adventures of the Dialectic*, Northwestern Uni. Press, Evanston, 1973, trans. J. Bien.
J. Meszaros, *The Work of Sartre*, Harvester, Brighton, 1979.
M. Poster, *Existential Marxism in Postwar France*, Princeton Uni. Press, Princeton, 1975.

Merleau-Ponty

Both *The Structure of Behaviour* (Methuen, London, 1965, trans. A.L. Fisher) and *The Phenomenology of Perception* (Routledge, London, 1962, trans. C. Smith) are reasonably accessible, though the latter is marred by an atrocious translation. The following provide additional information and analysis:

J.F. Bannan, *The Philosophy of Merleau-Ponty*, Harcourt, Brace and World, New York, 1967.

R.C. Kwant, *From Phenomenology to Metaphysics, an Inquiry into the last period of Merleau-Ponty's Philosophical Life*, Duquesne Uni. Press, Pittsburgh, 1966.

R.C. Kwant, *The Phenomenological Philosophy of Merleau-Ponty*, Duquesne Uni. Press, Pittsburg, 1963.

G.B. Madison, *The Phenomenology of Merleau-Ponty*, Ohio Uni. Press, Athens, 1981.

S.R. Mallin, *Merleau-Ponty's Philosophy*, Yale Uni. Press, New Haven, 1979.

Baudrillard

Of Baudrillard's main writings only *The Mirror of Production* (Telos, St. Louis, 1975, trans. M. Poster) has so far appeared in English. This gives a useful introduction to his ideas. The secondary literature is at present largely uncritical.

Chapter 8: Conclusions

1. On Methodology

I have argued throughout that the origin of modern ideas about human nature lies not in the methods of investigation provided by psychoanalysis, phenomenology or semiotics but in the historical decline of Christianity, particularly in its hold over the intellectuals. My evidence for this is partly that we find like-minded thinkers like Nietzsche and Jaspers use different methods of investigation, while a single method of investigation, such as psychoanalysis, can produce thinkers as diverse as Freud, Jung and Lacan. On the more positive side clear links can be established between the contents of the doctrines of Nietzsche, Freud and Sartre and the historical decline of Christianity.

It will be relevant at this point to summarise what has been said so far about the contents of the doctrines of Freud and Sartre in particular and bring it into clearer relation with historical and cultural alterations. For this purpose I shall concentrate upon the issues I have called 1a and b : the problems of socialisation, redemption and attitudes to stability. Both Freud and Sartre used deep interpretation to create realms into which they could project their attitudes on these topics. In Freud's case this was the realm of the unconscious, ruled by King Oedipus. In Sartre's case it was the realm of being, dominated by the dialectic of being and nothingness. In neither case can we reasonably believe these writers' claims that by using a new method they were able to find a previously unknown continent. In Freud's case, several of his disciples claimed that by using the same method they discovered different continents. Both Jung and Fromm provide clear examples of this. Considering their professional standing and success it is hard to argue that they were simply incompetent apprentices. In addition, the material that Freud actually interprets in his early studies, namely the symptoms of hysterical patients and his own dreams, can and has been interpreted in quite different ways by other people.

Things are in a similar case with Sartre, where he himself later reversed his own judgement that nothing predominated over being without any methodological alterations being offered to account for this. The contrast between Sartre and Merleau-Ponty raises a somewhat different issue as Merleau-Ponty believed all along in what amounted to constructive acts of will. Thus he was entitled to be somewhat more optimistic about the ability of consciousness to realise itself in some kind of positive existence.

The differences between Sartre and Merleau-Ponty here are related to their approach to the problem of freedom. For the early Sartre freedom is not simply subjective, it is objective and realised in an objective doctrine of being. If one accepts such a doctrine it is hard to accept any limitations whatsoever on freedom and thus anything that smacks of motives or reasons for making decisions must be energetically resisted. This leads inevitably to the doctrine of blind spontaneity. Merleau-Ponty on the other hand had always wanted to find some kind of compromise between the traditional doctrine of motivation and freedom and was content to keep freedom as a subjective state of mind in order to do so. His attitude to efforts to create an absolute reality are well expressed towards the end of *The Phenomenology of Perception*.

'The absolute Idea is not something that is clearer to me than my finite spirit, it is through the latter I know the former. In other words, we are in the world: things take shape, an immense totality makes itself known, each existence understands itself and understands others. We must just hold onto these things that lie at the bottom of all our certainties. Belief in an absolute spirit or a world in itself detached from us is nothing but a rationalisation of this primordial faith.'[1]

Thus belief in the primacy of being or that of nothingness is linked by rational argument to the issue of experienced versus abstract freedom. While Sartre's later *Critique* does not explicitly repudiate his earlier enthusiasm for absolute being and absolute freedom, his implicit reliance on the 'humanism' of Feuerbach and Marx brings him closer to Merleau-Ponty on this issue.

Does this mean that beliefs about the relative priority of being and nothingness are simply an expression of willingness to consider abstract or experienced freedom? Or can they be related to fundamental social attitudes to change and permanence as I have alleged?

The answer to these questions is I think that there are tensions set up between these two realms of ideas that can never entirely be resolved. The possibility of a nihilist metaphysics that places nothingness higher than being is without any doubt due to the decline in the power of Christianity. Catholic theologians issued what anathemas they could against *Being and Nothingness*, one describing it as more dangerous to faith than '18th century rationalism or 19th century positivism.'[2] They were however no longer able to suppress its ideas.

I have suggested something further: that we now positively value freedom and change so much that we are willing at least at times to erect them into absolutes. It seems more convincing to pose the relation between our two issues in this way than to claim that they are simply quite independent choices. There is a human issue at stake here, which is whether we can endure an eternity of abstract certainty. Having tasted the real possibility of this it seems that, like Bergson, we take fright.

We can reach similar conclusions by looking at the more technical aspects of phenomenological and psychoanalytic method. In Husserl's phenomenology his method goes considerably beyond a simple demand for a return to consciousness. Husserl was concerned above everything else to resist psychologism, the belief that reality, in particular the structure and concepts of logic, are purely subjective. His defence against this was to argue that the objective reality of objects and concepts is directly given in consciousness along with the noematic meaning that accompanies them. This is a defence against the sophisticated view that what is immediately given in consciousness is sensation. The use that Heidegger, Sartre and Merleau-Ponty later made of Husserl's method was also anti-psychologistic in the sense that they claimed to find the opposition of being and nothingness directly present in consciousness. The issue of psychologism versus anti-psychologism however tells us nothing about the particular contents discovered in consciousness. Supposedly objective entities could be discovered within consciousness but considering the extent of dispute regarding what these entities were - whether being or nothing was primary and whether these were located in spontaneity or choice - it is hard to believe they are presented to consciousness with anything like the immediate certainty of an object like a tree.

In psychoanalysis the chief difficulty is that even if we accept Freud's methods for interpreting dreams and neurotic symptoms by free association, the conclusions we reach are not those of Freudian theory. Thus even if Freud himself and a considerable number of other people are indeed obsessed with Oedipal problems in their dreams this does not show that such obsessions are universal or that they are primarily sexual in origin, let alone that we have a fixed reservoir of instinctual libido.

The case is much the same with semiotics. Here we see that writers whose theoretical opinions are as different as those of Levi-Strauss, Lacan and Baudrillard can all claim to be adopting the approach. The fact is that opinions regarding the interpretation of signs and symbols, which is what is meant by semiotics, are determined by more general theoretical presuppositions. Freudians regard symbols as frequently revealing the hidden dialectics of the Oedipal situation; Sartre regards symbols as revealing the underlying struggle between being and nothingness. Among those claiming the label semiotics Lacan falls into the first category, Baudrillard into the second. Among writers on semiotics in general we can find a much broader range of opinion. Common sense as well as much traditional philosophy would suggest that social symbols often represent the wish to advertise our indulgence of certain appetites or our renunciation of them. We talk about symbols of power, status, authority and sex or of dignity, justice, professionalism or virtue. Levi-Strauss interprets symbols in this more conventional way, though his view that it is their formal combination that counts as much as their manifest reference takes him well beyond the bounds of common sense in his ultimate conclusions.[3]

2. Post-Structuralism and Irrationalism

Only one of the writers grouped under this heading (Baudrillard) has developed a systematic position on human nature that seemed worth extended treatment here. This is not to say that their writing lacks interest, but simply that they haven't said anything novel on this particular issue. As the Anglo-Saxon philosophical world is at present particularly interested in French writers on this subject some fuller outline of this movement is needed at this point.

It became fashionable for some French writers in the 1970s to assail the 'structuralism' of Levi-Strauss, Merleau-Ponty, Foucault and Lacan with a kind of anarchistic anti-structuralism sometimes called 'post-structuralism'. Deleuze and Guatari argued that the Oedipal 'structure' represented a form of social domination that could only be broken by a return to the pre-Oedipal world of the schizophrenic.[4] Derrida set out to assail the certainties of organised philosophical knowledge with his own particularly ingenious brand of scepticism.[5] Baudrillard claimed that only the most extreme forms of antirationalist metaphysics could break the prison of consumerised society. Glucksmann looked to Nietzsche's philosophy to deliver the individual from the hands of the Hegelian and Marxist states.[6]

Common to all these writers was suspicion of the way in which modern society crushes the individuality of the human personality. Contrary to what one sometimes reads, however, this is not what distinguishes them from previous authors. Levi-Strauss, Merleau-Ponty and Lacan were all equally concerned that the individual might be eclipsed by the state. One can level the accusation of complicity in such a crime at the Marxists Foucault and Althusser, both leading so-called 'structuralists', but perhaps a majority of its writers were keen to stand out against such tendencies. What distinguishes 'post-structuralism' is its equation of reason with the activities of the social system or the state and its belief that only by a turn to irrationality can we hope to oppose the state or the abstract rationality of the social system.

Irrationalism was a tendency in Nietzsche, but these writers take this tendency to a new extreme. While they don't have anything new to say about human nature their appearance is undoubtedly both significant and disturbing. Derrida it is true is concerned that Nietzsche's philosophy was easily turned to good use by the ideologues of German fascism.[7] However in my view he uses his philosophical sophistication to avoid the rather obvious connection between Nietzsche's writings and the possibility of a fascist ideology.

Nietzsche suggested in at least some of his many voices that we should use indulgence of the will to power to create an ethic beyond ethics. He admired Napoleon's achievements in this direction, as well as some of the more barbarous military practices of the ancient world. If we accept Nietzsche's premise that Christian morality is a kind of disguised self-hatred that is destined for historical decline there is only one defence against this argument. This is that setting out to rule the world is imprudent. This was the line Bertrand Russell took against Nietzsche and however unfashionable may be Russell's views on that philosopher, this element in them remains valid. Russell also thought that our sympathy for those we would crush to conquer worlds would also deter us, although this view seems much shakier. It did not, after all, deter Hitler, Mussolini, or their millions of followers for whom the criticism of weapons proved the only decisive argument.

You may be expecting that at this point I am going to conclude that post-structuralism is dangerous and incipiently fascist. In fact I conclude only that it is dangerous. Such opinions cannot be said to be incipiently fascist except when the historical conditions exist for the rise of fascism. However this is not the end of the problem as fascism is only one possible application of post-Nietzschean irrationalism. If this is or were to become the ideology of the military planners of the superpowers then things far worse than fascism are just around the corner. Fortunately a good deal of rationality and prudence still remains within such circles, but this example provides a good reason for energetic resistance to post-structuralist irrationalism.

Are we likely to be successful in such resistance, or had we better join the planners in their bunkers forthwith? Is post-structuralism the harbinger of some new era in philosophy? Is Derrida a new Kant? or even a new Hume? Or is this just the most recent fad in a country notorious for the evanescence of its intellectual life?

The five writers I have mentioned as belonging to the post-structuralist movement are all disillusioned participants of the radicalism of the 1960s. While this sounds comfortingly temporary, some of the conditions that produced the particular kind of individualistic radicalism popular in the 1960s are not, particularly the historical decline of liberalism and Marxism as philosophies likely to appeal to the young.

In a society where growing up is difficult and dangerous, where there are abundant social dislocations and nuclear annihilation is a sombre backdrop, young people need hope. They turn, as we know, to religious cults, to radical politics and to various kinds of irrationalism. When the chief ideology of official radical politics, Marxism, no longer appeals, we may expect, as observed, an upsurge in religious cults and irrationalism. Can, in that dull Weberian phrase, these forms of charisma be institutionalised?

It has been popular among Anglo-Saxon commentators on Derrida's deconstruction in particular, which represents a variety of post-structuralism, to decry its absorption into the mainstream of academic life, as if the deep commitment of the anti-Establishment thinker has an inherent romance denied their more conventional colleagues.[8] I suggest we think very carefully before giving this line of reasoning too free a rein. It is nice to have one's dull existence enlivened by young radicals at academic seminars. If there were no intellectual innovations what would we all write about? But what would happen to the world if everyone took post-Nietzschean irrationalism seriously? The result would not be at all pleasant. If the academic establishment can domesticate this tendency I for one shall applaud. This is not of course to say that the political and social status quo needs accepting, just that rational as opposed to irrational methods should be used to produce change where necessary.

3. A Summary of Issues

To be critical of some of the methodologies that have been used in the study of human nature is not to be critical of a methodical approach. On the contrary, one of the chief reasons that so many one-sided cults arise in this area is that some questions are not even raised as issues, but are prejudged. I hope that simply by listing the main areas of contention this process will be short-circuited. I must however emphasise that even among the super-sophisticated, perhaps especially among them, the prejudging of issues is rife. We have all come up against the diehard Reichians, Lacanians and followers of other cult figures. It is no good thinking this kind of thing is confined to the uneducated. One only has to look at the uncritical adulation accorded to Lacan by whole sections of the most elite strata of French culture in the 1960s to realise that super-sophistication easily becomes transformed into super-silliness. The tendency to base intellectual debate on the 'have you read the latest writers' game may be at its most virulent in the undergraduate years, but it persists among those who should know better.

la. *Do we consider primarily socialisation, redemption or both?*
lb. *Do we admire stability and safety or change and fascination?*

One of the difficulties theoreticians have encountered is that they have tended to collapse socialisation into redemption or *vice versa*. For Sartre our social existence is a cypher for an ultimate existential reality whose analysis originates from an inversion of the Christian philosophy of redemption through the attainment of being. For Freud the desire for redemption is explained away as a wish to get back to childhood.

Amongst the most important philosophers it has only been Nietzsche and, by way of dramatic contrast, Erich Fromm, who have insisted on retaining a distinction here that is surely valid. To be socialised is to be restrained and protected. Restraint and protection are certainly elements within redemption, but the fact that a whole culture, that of Christianity, could base itself on a sharp separation of the two shows that they are certainly in principle different kinds of things.

Perhaps modern culture has transcended such a distinction, or rather abolished it and passed beneath it? Yet within our selected theorists there are still a great majority in favour of retaining salvation as a key concern. It may be that mass culture will ultimately drag philosophy into its train, but any such conclusion would certainly be very premature at this point.

Something should be said about the contents of doctrines of socialisation and salvation. Consideration has already been given to the deep-interpretation doctrines of Freud and Sartre in these areas in a previous section. It remains however to adopt some positive attitude to these doctrines.

In my view this attitude should be that as such doctrines represent primarily a mythology expressing attitudes we would do best to demythologise these areas, sidestep the technical theories of interpretation that have arisen and admit frankly what our attitudes are. We may hope for social stability or social revolution and change, for everlasting permanence or the romance of creation. We need as a beginning to admit that it is these issues that interest us. Beyond this there is a wealth of factual information and theoretical argument that might sway us. In the case of socialisation this belongs to the realm of sociology and social theory; in that of redemption matters are more subjective, but arguments about the practical possibilities of implementing various spiritual disciplines under given social conditions should also play a part. In addition, in socialisation theory we must acknowledge that Freud pointed us towards the location of a central question: how are we first coaxed and bullied into becoming social? Does this have an all-embracing effect on later life or is it the gradual build-up of parental influence that counts?

The answer to the first of these two questions has I think been most satisfactorily investigated by the psychologist David Ausubel. He argues, following closely our common-sense knowledge of children, that it is the crisis of restraint at around two and a half years of age that provides the scene for the child's initial process of identification with the parents.[9] The adults attempt to impose their notions of a cultured being who does not draw on walls or go to the toilet on the carpet. The child resists at first, but then falls back on defensive identification with the parents, imagining being a powerful initiated member of the culture like daddy and mummy as a recompense for the inconvenience involved in scribbling only on paper and waiting to go to the toilet. While Ausubel sees this as a revision of Freud, a philosopher might well see it as a recreation of some of Nietzsche's doctrines about socialisation, though where Nietzsche soars and is often contradictory, Ausubel is systematic but pedestrian.

The second question, regarding the permanent effects of the initial experience of socialisation, is harder to answer. Ausubel agrees with Freud in thinking there are such permanent effects. Most of the evidence that has been gathered to test the permanent impact of the Freudian traumatic experiences of weaning and toilet training has told against the Freudian hypotheses.[10] It seems that it is the long haul of parental influence that produces the oral and anal personality types.[11] Not surprisingly, the permanent or even the initial impact of inaccessible Oedipal fantasies has proved quite resistant to research studies. Ausubel has on the other hand managed to produce a reasonable amount of evidence that the failure of early identification (sattelisation as he calls it) or the failure to de-identify during adolescence (desattelisation) have long-lasting effects. The non-satteliser becomes a minimally social outsider; the non-desatteliser becomes a dependent and gullible adult.[12] Notice that such effects are probably to be explained by the long-haul effects of such events, which like points in a railway track set the growing individual off onto a line of development that ultimately solidifies.

The early beginnings of socialisation have been discussed in detail by Lacan in particular. His emphasis on the infant's experience of looking in a mirror as the origin of its insertion into relations bound by narcissism often brings a sympathetic response as we are so familiar with the 'showing off' of the infant in the second year of life. The infant has however other needs than narcissism, particularly those for milk, solid foods, nappy changing, amusement and exploration of its motor abilities. We can better understand the infant's earliest attachment to other people through its need to communicate its needs to others. A by now classic study of Schaffer and Emerson found that it was not necessarily the person who gave the infant the bottle who was initially chosen as the object of infant bonding, but the person, perhaps a grandparent or father, who could communicate most adequately with the infant.[13] Such communication often takes place through turn-taking activities such as the game 'peep-bo'.

It appears from this that communication, even at a very young age, is partly independent of need satisfaction. It seems very unlikely however that it is ever completely so. Infants like to play games involving communication and later try to get others to gratify quite arbitrary whims because they like to feel their lifeline is in working order. It may also be that game-playing and the satisfaction of needs are more widely separated in the first year of life than they later become. At any event by two years the scene has been set for the power struggle described by Ausubel. When this occurs, it is most implausible for Lacan to say that the toddler succumbs to identification and repression because of a fear of failing to enjoy. Toddlers are rarely seen to desist from their efforts at gaining enjoyment by their own initiative; it is their parents who fail to enjoy their depredations and thus begin to put restrictions on their activities. It is adults who fear failing to enjoy, not toddlers.

It is also worth considering the specific content of ideas about salvation and transcendence. In Nietzsche we have the usual luxuriant growth of conflicting ideas. Transcendence is presented as the paternalism of a trans-moral hero who represents the next step in human evolution and foreshadows a new kind of society; as the purely individualistic flowering of the personality of a ruthless superman; as the act of creating new ethical principles to replace the old ones; as the realisation that all things recur and that the present will return in the future when all other possible states in the universe have been exhausted.

The opposition here is perhaps on a deeper level that between the ethical innovator and the individualist. In practical terms however there is considerable difference between the life of a practical innovator like Napoleon and that of a philosophical one like Nietzsche, as between the flowering of passions and the icy comfort of the eternal recurrence.

In Heidegger and Sartre transcendence is in the attainment of being. The early writings of Sartre deny that such transcendence is possible on any permanent basis, but his later Marxist view asserts this possibility. In both Heidegger and the later Sartre being is attained through social projects. This corresponds to the very ancient view that we can achieve immortality through great achievements. Fromm agrees with this view, but he sees the achievement of such goals as partly guided by the impulse to care for others.

Jaspers and Merleau-Ponty are more interested in finding some kind of transcendence through philosophy itself. Perhaps because of his greater longevity Jaspers carried this project further than Merleau-Ponty, his aim in his later philosophy being nothing less than a complete synthesis of all existing philosophy into a form of contemplative release adequate to a highly literate, cosmopolitan civilisation.

Beneath the often convoluted surface of these contemporary philosophers we find ideals of transcendence that are as old as philosophy itself: to become immortal through great achievements or through contemplation. Christianity itself had appropriated these ideals for itself and with the decline of Christianity they have been repossessed by secular philosophy. A further ideal, that of Buddhist non-existence, surfaces in Sartre's *Being and Nothingness* but has not so far proved as popular as the other two.

From this point of view the quest for transcendence can be considered as a motive. Sartre was right to consider the search for being in this way, though such a conception was at variance with his opposition to determinism. This also clarifies an aspect of Nietzsche's views. Power not only enables its possessor to satisfy base motives but also to transcend themselves through fame and enduring achievements. Yet Nietzsche's use of the concept 'will to power' tends to obscure the relation of this form of transcendence to others. It suggests that this is the only and inevitable means of transcending everyday existence.

Nietzsche was naturally somewhat at a loss to account for the fascination that Buddhism evidently held for him. He resorts to saying that it was originally the doctrine of an aristocracy.[14] Whatever the historical facts about the origins of Buddhism, this seems oddly special pleading in favour of a religion so at variance with the will to power. The hermit-like existence of Zarathustra can be justified as a necessary sacrifice on the road to the creation of new and all-powerful values, but to ascribe Buddha's asceticism to this would be sophistry.

In recent German philosophy we find a number of writers like Bloch, Jonas and Frank who are interested in furthering the process of rescuing traditional philosophy and mystical sensibility.[15] It would be fair to say that many more overtly religious philosophers such as Tillich, Buber and Marcel were also interested in this, though in them the reliance on a God-centered view of the human condition remained stronger. Bloch provides a convenient and well-known example of this in his argument that if we search the human heart we find such an unquenchable desire for hope and human progress, so many indications of Utopian longing, that any human-centered philosophy must take these transcendental desires into account. Bloch, like the other writers mentioned, emphasises the need to re-incorporate the element of cosmopolitanism found in classical and early modern writers in a future culture of transcendence, against the swim of modern popular culture, which has often capitulated to narrow nationalism. While they do not share Sartre's Marxist version of this historical quest, such writers can certainly sympathise with his attempt to get in touch with history and his cosmopolitanism. In this they side with Sartre against Camus' emphasis on the individual's attempt to find salvation in personal rebellion against everything social.

While Sartre himself had been very close to this latter posture in *Being and Nothingness*, his experience of the wartime resistance to the Nazis ultimately led him to a Marxist posture. In the 1950s the issue of individual versus social rebellion was debated between Camus and Sartre in the pages of *Les Temps Modernes*. This was not, strictly speaking, individual salvation versus social salvation as Camus' vision of the individual was heroic but bleak. It nonetheless served to highlight the possibility of individual salvation which had earlier been announced by Nietzsche.

The emphasis on the problem of achieving personal identity found in writers like Erikson and Berger and Luckmann can also be related to the quest for transcendence, though these particular authors tend to hypostatise it into a natural and normal feature of all human beings.[16] Identity generally means getting in touch with and contributing to some kind of tradition. The term has acquired a connotation that emphasises passive getting in touch with history rather than active contribution to it. It is interesting that identity is a concept favoured by sociologists, who must deal with mass forms of consciousness, while transcendence through great contributions to a tradition is favoured by philosophers, particularly those of a Nietzschean persuasion.

It is also interesting, though perhaps not surprising, that the ideal of transcendence, so neglected by the classic British empiricist writers, has been reintegrated into this tradition through Bertrand Russell. One of the chief aims of education, according to Russell, should be to enable us to distance ourselves sufficiently from the bustle of everyday affairs in order to achieve that somewhat cosmic perspective demanded by science.[17]

Another issue that has become open for discussion is how to deal with the passions in achieving these forms of transcendence. It is quite striking that few of the philosophers discussed here side with Christian asceticism. Nietzsche suggests in *Thus Spake Zarathustra* that we should actually unleash our passions to achieve transcendence, though the hermit-like life of Zarathustra contrasts oddly with this. Apart from these two extreme and contradictory suggestions most modern philosophers seem to recommend, if only by their silence, that we adopt some kind of working compromise between the needs of the flesh and those of the spirit; except for Sartre for whom the needs of the flesh are illusory.

Finally, there have been considerable differences of opinion as to the period of life at which the search for transcendence becomes a burning issue. Crudely speaking, philosophers who incline more to materialism tend to place this preoccupation later in life, while those who regard consciousness as being more sharply divided from matter will argue that the emergence of transcendence is contemporaneous with the emergence of consciousness itself. Thus for Sartre and even for Merleau-Ponty the quest for being begins in early infancy. R.D. Laing also follows this tendency when he argues that the ontological insecurity of the schizophrenic emerges very early in life, leading them to erect a protective false self.[18] On the other hand there is little sign that Nietzsche thought of transcendence as important so early in life. He claimed that philosophies were marked with the period of life in which they originated, which in the case of his own doctrines of transcendence would mean the middle to late thirties.[19] The psychologist Carl Jung has also placed the mid-life crisis in which the individual begins a search for spiritual values at this age.

Empirical psychology provides yet a third answer here. It is well established that conscious fear of a child's own death emerges around four or five years of age, often resulting in night fears.[20] As much transcendental longing stems from the desire to overcome death this might seem the appropriate period in which to locate the origin of transcendental tendencies.

Further consideration shows that some reconciliation can be achieved here. The ideas of Sartre and Merleau-Ponty are really based more on dogmatism than detailed investigation. Merleau-Ponty, who did the most to attempt such investigation, produces no real evidence that the immediately given consciousness of very young infants actually contains any reference to being.

The remaining two possibilities can be accommodated as follows. First, not all transcendental wishes are related to fear of death. The other traditional source of such desires lies in world-weariness, suffering and ennui. While young infants undoubtedly experience suffering and boredom, it would be forced to attribute philosophical remedies to them. It is more plausible to think that young children of four or five years of age come to fear their own death and that the first attempts to counter this are either denial in the form of refusal to think about the problem or denial in the form of a religious belief in an afterlife. In adolescence religious belief may be undermined in various ways and then lead to concerns about identity and/or plans for great achievements. Personal retreat from the world into contemplation as well as great interest in philosophy are sometimes also found in late adolescence.

The crisis of religious and transcendental values of the late 30s results from two circumstances. Family life and occupation are now often in a fixed pattern, or have been rejected as unwanted goals. At the same time boredom and ennui increase, death is nearer and established methods of coping with fear of death come under strain.

1c. *Do we consider experienced or abstract freedom, or both?*

Some of the ramifications of this issue have been discussed in an earlier section. Within a philosophy of being based on consciousness, concentrating on experienced freedom allows us to be more sympathetic to the idea that from the viewpoint of a generalised and impartial observer there is nonetheless adherence to causal laws. If we concentrate on abstract freedom, that is freedom from a generalised abstract viewpoint, we must oppose causal laws in any form as applied to self-conscious beings.

One argument that has often been brought to bear on this issue in recent years is the so-called closed envelope paradox.[21] This maintains that unless predictions about our behaviour based upon supposed laws are kept in a closed envelope they will fail as if we learn of the predictions we may set out to falsify them. This is held to demonstrate that we do possess real freedom. In reality, however, this argument makes no advance on what was said above. The generalised and impartial observer must be supposed to keep their predictions to themself and thus no paradox arises.

1d. *Should we engage in deep or only in minimal interpretation?*

Several points relating to this issue have already been dealt with. I have argued that deep interpretation as practiced by both Freud and Sartre leads to a projection of social attitudes into the substance of human nature. This does not however rule out the possibility that the practice of interpretation could be improved to the point at which real progress could be made. I will discuss the issue of how such improvements could be brought about under 4 and 5 below.

1e. *Is there a drive towards the completion of the human personality?*

According to the tradition that leads from Feuerbach and Marx to Sartre and Fromm such a drive or inherent regulating tendency does exist. Carl Jung has also advocated a somewhat different version of this idea.

That so many important theorists, and along with them so many ordinary people, have thought this shows that many people do feel such an impulse or tendency operating within themselves. The question is whether such an impulse has its origins primarily within the individual or the social order. The obvious place within the social order to locate such influence would be in the activities and sentiments of ruling groups or elites and within the organised opposition to them. It is a necessity for ruling groups to attain an overall qualitative evaluation of the social order in order to rule. It is also necessary for oppositional groups, such as the Bolshevik and Communist parties, to develop such an analysis. Both kinds of groups find themselves through their political and cultural activities closely connected with enough elements within the social whole to do this.

This sociological analysis fits in disconcertingly well with the political and social postures of the theorists mentioned above who tend to pronounced radicalism or conservatism. Feuerbach is perhaps the least convincing case, but he was certainly associated with liberal opposition to the ruling conservatism of the German states in the 1840s. The oppositional politics of Marx, Sartre and Fromm are too well known to require elaboration. Jung's strongly conservative political sympathies admirably fit him for the role assigned in this scheme. In addition Jung experienced a profoundly religious upbringing through his father, a Lutheran pastor. It has been as much through the church and the universities as through the state itself that the ruling orders have organised their stewardship in Europe.

Against this a Marxist sympathetic to Marx's early writings would undoubtedly reply that this distribution of sentiments is in reality established through the violation and perversion of natural human tendencies. It is through the active intervention of the ruling orders that the majority of the population are reduced to those unwitting cogs in the social machine so admired by Durkheim.

A number of things can and I think should be said against this version of events. As with so much else in Marxism this applies more to the nineteenth rather than the twentieth century. It is certainly not the case that modern state education systems set out to impose vocational narrowness on an unwilling populace. Whatever the differences from country to country, the accusation is far more often heard that the middle class teacher attempts, against considerable resistance from their charges, to inculcate the elements of a liberal-humanist general education.[22] It may be said that class hostility to the teacher plays a role here but experience also shows that sheer intellectual laziness has a greater one. The parent who values education succeeds in instiling an educational work ethic that overcomes this inertia. The burning desire for a general education is not something a majority of secondary school teachers discover at the bottom of child nature.

It should also be said against the Marxist view that uncultured fragmentation is no more the doing of the media than it is of the schools. In most advanced capitalist countries up-market or cultured newspapers and radio and television stations are freely available to anyone at zero or minimal extra cost, but they are avoided like the plague by the majority of the population.

A final Marxist argument might be that such resistance to general culture at school and in the media emanates from the stultifying and narrow conditions of work suffered by the majority of the population. But again this seems to owe more to romanticism than logic. There are plenty of sections of the upper middle class, such as physicians, physical scientists or stockbrokers, who have only a narrowly defined sphere of occupational interest but participate more in general political and cultural discussions than the majority.

A more plausible view of the impulse to develop a general culture can be found in Nietzsche, who regarded the acquisition of a generalised understanding of society as indispensable to the struggle both to retain and to attain power in society. This is a more realistic origin for the impulse to gain such rounded cultural attainments than a drive towards wholeness located purely within human nature itself.

2. *Can we become conscious of the instincts and of the unconscious?*

We are normally conscious of instinctual motives like hunger, thirst or sex when they act upon us. Sartre's ingenious arguments in favour of explaining this experience as a rationalisation for spontaneous acts of choice are a triumph of perverse cleverness. If our actions were in reality governed by spontaneity, how could we explain that such outside events as not having eaten or drunk for a long time are so reliably linked with them?

It is far more debatable that we can become conscious of the unconscious. There are two widely canvassed arguments here. One is that of Jaspers and Merleau-Ponty, which argues that the so-called unconscious is really that which is confused or divided in consciousness. According to this argument both the meaning of hysterical symptoms and the meaning of dreams can be explained as something that the person is only dimly aware of or aware of at some times but not at others. This can be described as a kind of minimal interpretation. If we assume that there is no further 'deep unconscious' then there could be no objection to such a theory. In addition, according to both Jaspers and Merleau-Ponty we can rescue much of what is worth saving from orthodox Freudian theory.

If on the other hand we believe there is a deep unconscious containing material that is permanently excluded from consciousness but nonetheless influencing it this could prove a doubtful procedure. There is some reason to take this path. There is for instance considerable evidence that in cases of shell shock the victim blots out whole passages of events from recall - so-called traumatic amnesia.[23] Thus experiences are certainly made unconscious in the Freudian sense. The debatable question is whether such events can continue to influence consciousness. Again there is reason to think this possible, as if there was not a real fear of the events being remembered why should the victim suppress them from consciousness? It could be said that the person remembers the fear while forgetting the events, but this is only a restatement of the Freudian view. For us to take the alternative view it would be necessary to be able to find some way to know about what is unconscious from what is conscious, as when we see an object half appearing round a corner in the street. Nor can we take refuge in the idea that the unconscious events are somehow permanently erased from memory. With the passage of time segments of the memories normally reappear. The only real question must be: how widespread is this kind of repression in normal childhood and how widespread are the effects of such repressed memories upon adults?

Here we must I think say frankly that the issue needs further research. One question that needs looking at is whether hysterical patients really are, as Merleau-Ponty so confidently claimed, half-conscious of the origin of their symptoms.[24] This was certainly not the way Freud and others described them. Another issue that could be looked at is whether adults are aware of the impact that childhood experiences have had upon them. Given that it is the long haul rather than the traumatic event that counts in childhood, we would expect most adults to be at least partially aware of the effect of things like a strict upbringing or identification with one parent rather than another. It is plausible in this context to think of the presence of a large quantity of permanently repressed and troublesome experiences from childhood as typical of the neurotic patient rather than the normal person. In this case, Freud may have drawn too close a parallel between 'normal' people and neurotics.

3a. *What is the relative strength of motives?*
3b. *Which repressed motive is most important for the production of culture?*
3c. *What are motives like and how do they work?*

Answers to the first two of these questions depend upon the third, the nature of motives. According to the reservoir theory there is a kind of substance behind such things as the aggressive and sexual urges. This substance, which Freud called libido, discharges itself and the urge is fulfilled. A weaker version of this theory might argue that there is only a steady push demanding the fulfilment of the drive but no substance or given amount of satisfaction required. A second major theory says that some drives are chiefly reactive, that is they are minimal until some event like a naked body or an annoying motorist arouses them. A third major theory argues that drives are chiefly cyclical, being largely determined by the time since the last meal or sexual activity. A final theory argues that some apparent drives are really things we do to give us a 'jag' of excitement to relieve boredom and sluggishness.

Motivation theory is complex because some drives or instincts probably involve several of these things. There can be little doubt that hunger, thirst and the need for air and warmth are the most pressing of our needs and that they are all chiefly of the cyclical variety, though elements of the reactive and jag theories can be found in the ways we react to the sight of food and use food and clothing to amuse ourselves. It is when we get beyond these to sex, aggression, caring and love of admiration that dispute begins.

Nowadays few people accept Freud's reservoir view of the libido or would accept such a view of aggression.[25] There is too much evidence that such drives are partly reactive and too little evidence of any quantitative amount of release needed for satisfaction.

Aggression seems to be of three kinds: instrumental, designed to get something; a reaction to frustration or threat; or done for amusement. Sex seems to be also of three kinds: designed to achieve an ulterior aim; a reaction to sexually arousing situations; or for amusement. Sex has the peculiarity that unlike aggression we normally think of sexually arousing situations as more likely to arouse after a period of deprivation. It is probably however also true that depletion of the body's energy reserves and prolonged release of hormones like adrenalin into the bloodstream brings about a kind of satiation of aggression in extreme situations like war or executive stress.

The desires to care for people, animals or environments or to belong to groups can also arise from three sources: desire for an ulterior goal; reactions to seeing animals or people in need of care or protection; and desire for amusement, usually in this case described as 'giving them something to do'. Some ethologists, basing themselves on the elicitation of caregiving reactions to the young in animals, have speculated that babies and young mammals have an especially powerful and inborn effect in calling forth such reactions.[26] As with sexually arousing stimuli it seems quite plausible that we are in some sense pretuned to such stimuli though definite evidence that this is so in human beings is lacking.

The desire for admiration can also be divided into the elements of ulterior motive, reaction to a situation where applause is likely to be forthcoming and desire for amusement or exhilaration. The most controversial question is the extent to which the reactive situations that inflame these passions are innate 'releasing mechanisms' or simply situations in which we have learned either by direct experience or by information from others that pleasurable gratification is likely to be available. A best guess answer would probably be that both are involved.

The relative strength of the groups of motives for sex, aggression, caring and admiration will be influenced by the tendency for a given style of life to allow reactive situations to inflame a particular motive. It remains the case however that in most social situations aggression and the search for power bear an asymmetrical relation to the other motives. Success in the exercise of aggression to achieve power generally leads to the ability to gratify other motives. It is true that people can be enslaved by sexual passions, but in the two areas that have most engaged the attention of theorists - politics and the child in the family - there is generally little scope for this. The repression of motives is also much influenced by social environment, though theorists have sometimes hazarded more unqualified opinions. For Freud it is the repression of sex that is most important in producing culture; for Nietzsche aggression and the urge to dominate; for Fromm it is caring and belonging; for Lacan the love of admiration.

A preliminary point here is that different kinds of culture no doubt repress different motives. However in dealing with contemporary Western society a far more crucial observation is that the repression of different motives is likely to be of different importance in different social institutions. Thus Nietzsche was particularly interested in politics and social ethics. As politics generally consists of either armed or unarmed struggle it is hardly surprising to find aggression so important. Among those who have lost out in the political and social struggle we would expect to also find the repression of aggression and the will to power. While it is plausible to think that this became incorporated within the religion of the oppressed, some of Nietzsche's most general formulations about religion are over-enthusiastic. The impulses to care and belong do exist in an independent form, something scarcely allowed when that philosopher was in a growling mood.

When we turn to the family however things are much more obscure. Freud and Lacan deal centrally with the family but they disagree quite radically about

230

what is repressed there. A commonsense answer would be that the family represses everything but caring. Young children are routinely discouraged by their parents from sex, aggression and showing off too much. This seems to represent the most balanced answer we can give at present.

Fromm's position is the most ambiguous as he deals with much the same territory as Nietzsche but inverts his conclusions. His argument is that the conditions of modern political and social life inhibit caring and belonging and the resultant insecurity is converted into aggression. In this he seems to be advocating a kind of reservoir theory of caring that has no real theoretical plausibility or justifying evidence. When Fromm tries to form an amalgam of the frustration-aggression hypothesis and the evils of behaviourism to disconnect frustration and aggression he is making very transparent propaganda.

A far more plausible version of Fromm's theory would be as follows. Modern life stimulates both the instrumental and the frustration types of aggression while the impulses to caring and belonging are disconnected from the political system and the workplace and hived off into the home and the church. The factual difference between this view and that of Nietzsche is now very small and the real area of disagreement is seen to be in attitude to such a situation. Nietzsche thought we had to say 'yea', even welcome it as a healthy return to classical brutality; others may prefer Fromm's view that other forms of society are possible.

A final point should be made about the historical course of repression. Freud's emphasis on sexual repression became popular at a time when sexual repression was lifting, and it has continued this popularity into a period when it is certainly very much reduced. In a real sense an emphasis upon the negative effects of sexual repression has been acceptable to liberal society in a way that Nietzsche's emphasis on the negative effects of repressed aggression was not. As Jaspers pointed out, Freud's philosophy was palatable to those lower down in the social order.[27] Nietzsche's philosophy has only ever been popular among elite and ruling groups; its message is too radical for others. This unpalatableness remains its greatest vindication.

3d. *How do defence mechanisms mediate the interaction of motives?*

This is an issue upon which little difference of opinion has appeared among the theoreticians covered. Nearly all agree that the fundamental Freudian mechanisms of identification, repression, denial, reaction formation, regression and projection do exist and act to reduce unpleasant anxiety. They differ widely in regard to what we defend ourselves from, but little in regard to how we do it.

4. *How does the unconscious communicate with consciousness?*

5. *How are symbols formed and how may we interpret them?*

If we include Sartre's interpretations of half-hidden meanings here, we have three fundamentally different kinds of deep interpretation: Freudian, Sartrian and Nietzschean. For Freud symbols are formed by the process of unconscious wishes striving to evade the censor and express chiefly aspects of the Oedipal situation. For Sartre they are expressions of the dialectic of being and nothingness and are interpreted by a combination of clear thinking and the phenomenological method. For Nietzsche symbols are rather various in meaning but they chiefly express cultural attitudes to the will to power and are interpreted simply by throwing off the blinkers of Christianity. My general conclusions regarding these styles of interpretation have already been given. What follows is an attempt to say something about how a more adequate style of interpretation could be developed. I have already suggested that there is a real problem of making the unavailable meaning of symbolism available and both neurotic symptoms and dreams seem to require this. Social and cultural symbolism contains less deeply hidden meanings but can also be subjected to a similar analysis.

Even critics of Freud's excessive emphasis on Oedipal myths have often agreed that his method of asking for associations to the elements in a dream is a good one.[28] Such an association helps to bring to light a meaning for the dream symbolism that is subconscious rather than unconscious. If such meanings were really unconscious in the strict Freudian meaning of the term they could not surface through the technique of association. In my experience, which is substantiated by the writings of a number of researchers in the area of dream interpretation, the combination of such associations with some knowledge of the dreamer's present and past life is generally enough to produce a fairly convincing dream interpretation.[29] Yet Freud claimed to adopt this process and revealed his own Oedipal preoccupations. This is not however a disconfirmation of this approach. The Oedipal conflicts are a very real and important element in individual psychology because they represent the power fantasies of young children, which are maintained for much of the period of childhood. The little boy is, in Ausubel's term, devalued in his power relations with his parents, and he responds to this by alternately imagining the dethronement of his father and giving obeisance. He rivals his father, just as the little girl rivals her mother, not for sexual motives but because to be grown up for a little boy is to be a father and he cannot imagine being grown up in any family other than his own. Where Freud went wrong was in attributing this rivalry to sexual motives and in overgeneralising his own case to everyone else. Other power situations may be equally or more important, such as rivalry with the opposite sex parent, brothers and sisters or other children. Jung was also I think correct in arguing that Freud was too determined to see the past in dreams and too little inclined to look for plans for the future, including those involving spiritual strivings and transcendence.[30]

In the interpretation of neurotic symptoms I would argue for the same kind of principles to be applied. Cultural symbolism raises the additional problem of how to deal with the Sartrian insight, used extensively by Baudrillard, that finds the ultimate meaning of such things as consumer goods in the dialectic of being and nothingness.

If we were to treat consumers as a dream interpreter approaches those who dream, the meaning of consumer goods would I think be revealed chiefly for what we normally think it to be - an expression of the common human passions of sex, power, belonging and admiration, coupled either with a positive, negative, playful or other attitude towards their expression. Occasionally we would also run across people who see consumer goods as the expression of a kind of spiritual striving for permanence and perhaps more who regard the game of image-building as a fascinating diversion. Baudrillard places his observation post so near this corner of the building that it comes to occupy the whole picture.

6. *What attitudes may be taken to the personal management of pleasure and pain?*

According to Christian tradition human beings naturally act to maximise pleasure and minimise pain. Both Nietzsche and Sartre questioned this. For Nietzsche hedonism was an aspect of the decadence of Christianity; for Sartre it was a form of being that could be replaced by others, such as the attitude of the hiker who wishes to overcome the limitations of nature.

In an extreme form I think we must reject both the Nietzschean and Sartrian arguments. Both animals and infants show a pre-social love of pleasure rightly emphasised by Freud. There is however certainly truth in the idea that the human quest for transcendence, whether in the Christian, Nietzschean or Sartrian versions, often leads people to non-hedonistic approaches to the management of pleasure and pain. Once again it is Sartre who misconstrued this issue most radically through his attempt to erect a sharp division between human self-consciousness and animal life.

Heidegger and Sartre rejected hedonism because their exclusive emphasis on the metaphysical discouraged any attention to our lower nature. Christianity had been able to argue that in seeking metaphysical salvation human beings seek a higher happiness, which is at least in general conception similar to the quest for base pleasures. Nietzsche turned away from this because of his emphasis on great achievements as a form of salvation, only achievable through self-sacrifice. In theory however we should weigh up the fear of death and loss of self against this sacrifice. This makes possible a revised form of hedonism similar to that found in Christianity.

7. *How do we acquire knowledge about human nature?*

Modern theory of the individual has been much concerned with the interpretation of the unconscious and of being. Although our acquisition of knowledge about human nature is a wider question, the answers given to the problem of interpretation by psychoanalysis, phenomenology and semiotics have often been extended to cover the wider issues. The arguments already canvassed against thinking of these methods as providing the kind of knowledge about human nature they have claimed also apply to these wider issues. We acquire more securely grounded understanding by a careful separation of the various distinct questions that have been asked about our constitution and an attempt to bring the results of common observation, historical experience and empirical psychology to bear upon them. Cautious use of the Freudian method of interpretation using free associations provides a partial exception to this general conclusion, but we need to be a lot more careful about our use of confirmatory evidence from other sources than Freud himself.

Translations

The source of translations is indicated in footnotes. Where the note is to the original the translation is my own, except in the case of the writings of Augustine, where all translations are my own.

Standard Editions

Where references appear in the notes without an edition the following standard edition is intended. Sometimes a standard English edition of the works of an author in another language exists but this does not include some works. In such cases the titles of translated works are given in English, those of untranslated works in the original.

Aquinas, Saint Thomas
Summa Theologiae, Eyre and Spottiswoode, London, 1964, trans, T. Gilby et al.
Aristotle
Aristotle's Works, Oxford University Press, Oxford, 1931, ed. W.D. Ross.
Augustine, Saint Aurelius
The Works of Aurelius Augustine, T. and T. Clark, Edinburgh, 1972, ed. M. Dods.
Sancti Aurelii Augustini Opera Omnia, Apud Gaumes Fratres, Paris, 1838.
Bonaventura, Saint
The Soul's Journey into God, The Tree of Life and The Life of St Francis, S.P.C.K., London, 1978, trans. E. Cousins.
Opera Omnia, Collegii, Quaracchi, 1883-1902.
Descartes, René
Oevres et Lettres, Gallimard, Paris, 1958.
Duns Scotus
God and Creatures, Princeton University Press, Princeton, 1975, trans. F. Alluntis and A.B. Wolter.
Elyot, Sir Thomas
Gouernour, Dent, London, 1937.
Fourier, Charles
Oevres Complètes, Anthropos, Paris, 1966-8.
Freud, Sigmund
Complete Psychological Works, Hogarth, London, 1955, trans. J. Strachey.
Hincmar
Patrologiae Cursus Completus, Garnier Fratres, Paris, 1878-90.
Hobbes, Thomas
Leviathan, Blackwell, Oxford, 1954.
Kant, Immanuel
Gesammelte Schriften, de Gruyter, Berlin, 1961.
Leibnitz, Gottfried Wilhelm
Philosophical Papers and Letters, University of Chicago Press, Chicago, 1956, ed. L.E. Loemker.

New Essays Concerning Human Understanding, University of Chicago Press, Chicago, 1916, trans. A.G. Langley.
Locke, John
Works, Clarendon, Oxford, 1979.
Maine de Biran
Oevres, Alcan, Paris, 1920.
Mill, John Stuart
Collected Works, University of Toronto Press, Toronto, 1963.
More, Sir Thomas
The Workes of Sir Thomas More Wrytten by him in the English tonge, Microcard Foundation, Middleton, 1957.
Ockham, William of
Opera Plurima, Gregg, Farnborough, Hants, 1962. Vol. 4 contains his *Reportatio Super IV Libros Sententiarum*.
Quodlibeta Septem, Editions de la Bibliothèque S.J., Louvain, 1962.
Pascal, Blaise
Oevres, Hachette, Paris, 1904-14, eds. L. Brunschwicg and P. Boutroux.
Plato
The Collected Dialogues of Plato, Bollingen, New York, 1969, ed. E. Hamilton and H. Cairns.
The Republic of Plato, Clarendon, Oxford, 1941, trans, F.M. Cornford.
Plutarch
Plutarchi Operum Volumen I-V, Didot, Paris, 1841-55.
Suarez, Fernando
Opera Omnia, Vives, Paris, 1963.
Wolff, Christian
Gesammelte Werke, G. Holms, Hildesheim, 1962.

Notes

Chapter 1

1. J. Boswell, *Boswell's London Journal*, Heinemann, London, 1950, p.285.

2. See for instance *The Will to Power*, Weidenfeld and Nicolson, London, 1967, trans. W. Kaufmann. The fragments arranged under the heading 'perspectivism' (pp.272-6) speak in favour of moderate perspectivism; those under the heading 'judgement' (pp.286-93) in favour of.the extreme view. The discussion of Socrates on pp.235-7 also favours moderate perspectivism.

3. On intellectual balance and the landed aristocracy see *The Will to Power*, pp 40-48, pp.235-7.

4. See 'Entretiens avec Jean-Paul Sartre' in S. de Beauvoir, *La Cerémonie des Adieux*, Gallimard, Paris, 1981.

5. There is a long tradition of American social criticism that has taken the higher education system to task on this score. See A. de Toqueville, *Alexis de Toqueville on Democracy, Revolution and Society*, University of Chicago Press, Chicago, 1980; T. Veblen, *The Higher Learning in America*, Hill and Wang, New York, 1957; H.L. Mencken, *The Vintage Mencken*, Vintage, New York, 1955; P. Rieff, *The Triumph of the Therapeutic*, Harper and Row, New York, 1966.

6. See J.C. Flugel, *A Hundred Years of Psychology*, Methuen, London, 1964, 3rd Edition, Part III, Chap 2. The distinction between actions performed by reason and those due to animal instinct (*instinctus*) is clearly given by Plutarch in his *Moralia*, in the essay on 'The Natural Love or Kindness of Parents...', para. 1. Philemon Holland's translation of this essay published in 1603 already uses the English word 'instinct' in this sense (*Plutarch's Moralia*, Dent, London, 1911, trans. P. Holland).

7. In the sixteenth century the English word instinct was already used in the sense of a natural impulse by both Sir Thomas More (*Works*, p. 521) and Sir Thomas Elyot (*Gouernour*, Bk iii, Chap. 3, Para. 5). In the eighteenth century we find Johnson and Hume using the term in this sense (*Boswell's Life of Johnson*, Oxford University Press, Oxford, 1980, pp. 363, 422; *Treatise of Human Nature*, Oxford University Press, Oxford, 1978, Book II, Part 3, Sects. 3, 9; Book II, Part 1, Sect. 5).

8. C. Darwin, *The Descent of Man*, Murray, London, 1883, 2nd edition, pp. 131-2.

9. A.R. Wallace, *Darwinism*, MacMillan, New York, 1905, p. 462.

10. W. McDougall, *An Introduction to Social Psychology*, Methuen, London, 1908, 1st edition.

11. D. Morris, *The Naked Ape*, Cape, London, 1967, pp. 94-5.

12. An example is R. Ardrey, *The Territorial Imperative*, Collins, London, 1967.

13. In Strachey's vocabulary for translators of psychoanalytic works we find *Trieb* translated as 'instinct, drive, impulse or urge' (A. Strachey, *A New German-English Psychoanalytical Vocabulary*, Baillière, Tindall and Cox, London, 1943).

14. For instance, *Nietzsche Werke*, Gruyter, Berlin, 1968, Vol. VI, p. 96.

15. F. M. Cornford, *From Religion to Philosophy*, Arnold, London, 1912, p. xi.

16. B. Russell, *A History of Western Philosophy*, Allen and Unwin, London, 1946, p. 18.

17. T. Parsons, *The Structure of Social Action*, Free Press, Glencoe, 1949.

18. *Ibid*, pp. 60-1.

19. See Chapter 3.

20. *Ibid*, p. 64.

21. Parsons has an unusually extended definition of utilitarianism and discusses Locke, Hobbes, Adam Smith, Ricardo and Malthus under this head (*Ibid*, pp. 95-106). Of these Hobbes and Smith wrote quite explicit treatises on the motives of individuals (see Chapter 3). Bentham and J.S. Mill, who can be considered as the central representatives of utilitarianism in its usual, narrower, sense both followed earlier writers in discussing the occasions for specific pleasures and pains. Bentham gives a minute analysis of this in Chapter 3 of *Introduction to the Principles of Morals and Legislation* (in *A Fragment on Government, etc.*, Blackwell, Oxford, 1967). Mill is less explicit in his *A System of Logic* but refers readers to the psychological writings of Hartley, James Mill, Bain and Spencer for a fuller analysis (*Collected Works*, Vol. VII, pp. 853-6).

22. *Ibid*, p. 63.

23. *Ibid*, pp. 65-6.
24. *Ibid*, pp. 459-60.
25. *Ibid*, p. 721.
26. M. Weber, *Wirtschaft und Gesellschaft*, J.C.B. Mohr, Tubingen, 1976, pp.1-30.
27. H. Stuart Hughes, *Consciousness and Society*, Knopf, New York, 1958, pp. 33, 63-4.
28. *Ibid*, p. 36.
29. *Ibid*, pp. 33, 38-9.
30. *Ibid*, pp. 40-1.
31. *Ibid*, pp. 43-53.
32. R.S. Peters, *The Concept of Motivation*, Routledge and Kegan Paul, London, 1960, second edition, p. 5.
33. *Ibid*, p. 6.
34. *Ibid*, p. 143.
35. *Ibid*, Chap. 5.
36. *Ibid*, p. 16ff and Chap.5.
37. *Ibid*, pp. 1, 12. See Also D.W. Hamlyn, 'Behavior', *Philosophy, 28*, 132-145, 1953.
38. P. Rieff, *The Triumph of the Therapeutic*, Penguin, Harmondsworth, 1966, p. 59.
39. *Ibid*, p. 48.
40. P. Rieff, *Freud, The Mind of the Moralist*, Gollancz, London, 1959, p. 340.
41. H.F. Ellenberger, *The Discovery of the Unconscious*, Allen Lane, London, 1970, p. 886.
42. *Ibid*.
43. *Ibid*, p. 887.
44. *Ibid*. pp 887-91
45. *Ibid*, pp. 158-70.
46. See 'Obsessions and phobias: their psychological mechanism and aetiology.' *Complete Psychological Works*, Vol. III, p. 81.
47. See V. Thweatt, *La Rochefoucauld and the Seventeenth Century Concept of the Self*, Droz, Genève, 1980, especially Chap. VII.
48. W. Kaufmann, *Discovering the Mind*, Vol. 3, McGraw-Hill, New York, 1980, p.449.
49. *Ibid*, Vol. 1, p.15.
50. *Ibid*, Vol. 3, p.437.
51. *Ibid*, p. 438.
52. *Ibid*.
53. *Ibid*, pp. 438-9.
54. *Ibid*, pp. 464-9.
55. F. Nietzsche, *Basic Writings*, Modern Library, New York, 1968, trans. W. Kaufmann, p. 460.
56. In Condillac's thought this appears with his *Traité de Sensations*, 1754, where Locke's joint use of sensation, innate ideas and reflection is replaced by the analysis of sensation alone. His 'statue' however develops by the comparison of sensations that reveal similarities and differences rather than by the blind 'hooking-up', or principle of contiguity, which came to dominate behaviourism. See R.S. Peters (Ed.) *Brett's History of Psychology*, Allen and Unwin, London, 1953, pp. 465ff. Taine's contribution in *Les Philosophes Classiques du XIXe Siècle en France*, 1856, was to recommend a return to the views of Condillac. His own *De l'Intelligence*, 1870, shows the 'lascivious taste for the grotesque' with its entertaining treatment of dissections and asylums.
57. This motive was particularly clear in the *idéologues* Cabanis and Destutt de Tracey, who saw materialism and sensationalism as means to bait the Catholic church. It can be found also in Taine (see R.S. Peters (Ed.) *Ibid*, pp. 465ff).
58. J.B. Watson, *Ibid*. See also D. Cohen, *J.B. Watson, the Founder of Behaviourism*, Routledge and Kegan Paul, London, 1979.
59. This movement, sometimes known as 'behaviour theory', gained the upper hand in the 1930s in the work of Hull, Skinner and Tolman. Skinner and his followers attempted to meet the challenge of relevance after the second world war, particularly in the area of educational psychology (see B.F. Skinner, *The Technology of Teaching*, Appleton-Century, New York, 1968).
60. K. Lorenz, *King Solomon's Ring*, Methuen, London, 1952 and D. Morris, *The Naked Ape*, Cape, London, 1967.

61. L. Kohlberg, 'From is to ought'. In T. Mischel (ed.) *Cognitive Development and Epistemology,* Academic Press, New York, 1971; L. Kohlberg, 'Moral stages and moralisation'. In T. Lickona (ed.) *Moral Development and Behaviour,* Holt, Rinehart and Winston, New York, 1976.

62. See C.G. Jung, *Psychology and Alchemy,* London, Routledge, 1966.

63. A. Schutz and T. Luckmann, *The Structures of the Lifeworld,* Northwestern University Press, Evanston, 1973; E. Goffmann, *Frame Analysis,* Harper and Row, 1974; P. Berger and T. Luckmann, *The Social Construction of Reality,* Penguin, Harmondsworth, 1971.

64. Berger and Luckmann say that primary socialisation means learning what people of a particular kind, such as a three year old boy, should do. This is described both as something the person is expected to do and as something regarded as part of their identity. The first possibility provides a motive, though a single one for nearly all action, in love of approval. The second, which is more prominent in their treatment, effectively removes the problem of motivation and reduces action to 'knowing what to do'. (P. Berger and T. Luckmann, *The Social Construction of Reality,* Doubleday, Garden City, 1967, pp.129-162).

65. J. P. Sartre, *Critique of Dialectical Reason,* NLB, London, 1976, trans. A. Sheridan-Smith, pp.551-2.

66. E. Durkheim, *Moral Education,* Free Press, Glencoe, 1961, especially Chap. 9; M. Weber, *Wirtschaft und Gesellschaft,* J.C.B. Mohr, Tubingen, 1976, 5th ed., Kap. 1.

67. As Rossi has pointed out in his essay on Levi-Strauss' notion of the unconscious, although Levi-Straus himself occasionally claims to have been influenced by Freud, his interpretation of the unconscious structural meaning of myth is really based on a constructivist version of Kant. See I. Rossi, 'Intellectual antecedents of Levi-Strauss' notion of the unconscious'. In I. Rossi (ed.) *The Unconscious in Culture,* Dutton, New York, 1974.

Chapter 2

1. *On Nature and Grace,* Chap. 33.
2. *Ibid.*
3. *Sermo,* CXXV, 11.
4. *Ennarationes in Psalmos, XXXIX, 7.*
5. *Ibid.*
6. *The City of God,* Book VII, 3.
7. *Ennarationes in Psalmos,* CXIII, 3.
8. *Confessions,* Book IX, IV, 10.
9. *On Christian Doctrine,* Book 1, Chap. XXIII, 23.
10. *Ennarationes in Psalmos,* 1, 1.
11. *The City of God,* Book V, 13.
12. *Ibid,* Book XV, 5.
13. *Ibid,* Book V, 19.
14. *De Nuptiis et Concupiscentia,* Liber 1, 7.
15. *Confessions,* Book 1, VII, 11.
16. *Ibid,* Book 1, 11, 2.
17. *On Christian Doctrine,* Book 1, Chap. XXVI.
18. *On the Gospel of St. John,* Tractate VI, 25-26.
19. *The City of God,* Book IV, 4.
20. *Ibid.*
21. *Confessions,* Book XIII. For the origins of his doctrine of free will see M. T. Clark, *Augustine, Philosopher of Freedom,* Desclée, New York, 1958.
22. See J. O'Connell, *Augustine's Early Theory of Man,* Belknap, Cambridge, 1968, pp. 1-30.
23. A.O. Lovejoy, *The Great Chain of Being,* Harvard University Press, Cambridge, 1936.
24. *Timaeus,* 29E.
25. See B.A.G. Fuller, *The Problem of Evil in Plotinus,* Cambridge University Press, Cambridge, 1912.
26. A.O. Lovejoy, *Ibid.*

27. The Christian revision of NeoPlatonic doctrine had previously, in Justin and Irenaeus, decided that the Logos of St. John was to be equated with the NeoPlatonic World-Soul (see M. Werner, *The Origins of Christian Doctrine*, pp. 228-9). Augustine alters this to equate God the Father with the Being of the second hypostasis and God the Son (Logos) with the Ideas of the second hypostasis. The Holy Spirit is equated with morality and justice. This at least is the argument of *The City of God*, Book XI, 25-6. In *On the Trinity*, Book XV, Chap. XXI he alters this so that Father, Son and Holy Spirit are reflected in memory, understanding and will respectively. This shift seems to be an attempt to find a better expression for the Christian idea that God the Father is the greatest member of the trinity, who created the Son before time. Memory in Augustine is a very global category owing to his belief that time is an illusion and that memory reveals an ever-present reality (*Confessions*, Book XI). Thus memory can be said to contain both Being and Ideas. The Ideas contain the prototypes for the creation both of intellectual understanding and morality, thus explaining the priority of God the Father. In both schemes Being remains primary, though other details alter. Augustine continually says in *On the Trinity* that he is struggling to apprehend mysteries that may be beyond human understanding.

28. The definition of God as fullness of Being is a way of saying that God is immutable. In seeking to participate in fullness of Being we seek to participate in this immutable state (see J.F. Anderson, *St. Augustine and Being*, Martinus Nijhoff, The Hague, 1965, p. 13).

29. *De Perfectione Iustitiae Hominis*, 44.

30. e.g. P. Brown, *Augustine of Hippo*. Faber, London, 1967, p. 366; J. Pepin, *Mythe et Allegorie*, Études Augustiniennes, Paris, 1976: P. Rieff, *Freud, the Mind of the Moralist*, Doubleday, Garden City, 1961.

31. This is particularly blatant in *Confessions*, Books XI and XII.

32. For Freud's debt to Jewish mysticism see P. Bakan, *Sigmund Freud and the Jewish Mystical Tradition*, Van Nostrand, New York, 1958.

33. This is contrary to H. Pirenne's thesis that trade remained relatively untouched by the earlier invasions (*Mahomet and Charlemagne*, Allen and Unwin, London, 1939). More recent research shows this is to be in error. See S.C. Easton and F. Wieruzowski, *The Era of Charlemagne*, Anvil, Princeton, 1961, p. 49ff.

34. For the transformation of social relations under Charlemagne see S.C. Easton and F. Wieruszowski, *Op. Cit.*, pp. 69-73; J. Boussard, *The Civilisation of Charlemagne*, McGraw-Hill, New York, 1968, trans, F. Partridge, pp. 43-56.

35. E. Troeltsch, *The Social Teaching of the Christian Churches*, Allen and Unwin, London, 1931, trans. O. Wyon, pp. 218-9.

36. J. Pelikan, *The Christian Tradition*, *Vol 3*, University of Chicago Press, Chicago, 1973, p. 101.

37. *De Praedestinatio*, 19.

38. Notably Bradwardine and Gregory of Rimini. See G. Leff, *Bradwardine and the Pelagians*, Cambridge University Press, Cambridge, 1957; H.A. Oberman, *Archbishop Thomas Bradwardine, a Fourteenth Century Augustinian*, Kemink and Zoon, Utrecht, 1957; G. Leff, *Gregory of Rimini: Tradition and Innovation in Fourteenth Century Thought*, Manchester University Press, Manchester, 1961.

39. On Luther's views see E. Iserloh et al *Church history*, *Vol 5*, Burns and Oates, London, 1980, Chap. 13; M. Werner, *Erasmus und Luther: Glaube und Aberglaube*, Haupt, Bern-Stuttgart, 1957; J. Boisset, *Erasme et Luther*, Presses Universitaires, Paris, 1962. On Augustinism in the Catholic church see E. Iserloh et al, *Ibid*, Chap. 41.

40. The scholastic revival of the sixteenth century was most notable for the return to Aquinas both as regards human nature and in general theology. See E. Iserloh, *Ibid*, Chap. 41; W. Weber, *Wirtschaftsethik am Vorabend des Liberalismus*, Aschendorff, Munster, 1959.

41. *Works*, Vol. 1, pp. 60-1.

42. *Works*, Vol. 2, p. 7.

43. *Works*, Vol. 2, p. 165.

44. On Calvin's doctrine of human nature see B.B. Warfield, *Calvin and Augustine*, Presbyterian and Reformed, Philadelphia, 1956; L. Smits, *Saint Augustine dans l'Oevre de Jean Calvin*, Van Gorcum, Assen, 1957-8; Th. F. Torrance, *Calvin's Doctrine of Man*, Lutterworth, London, 1949.

45. *Institutes of the Christian Religion*, Westminster Pren, Philadelphia, 1960, trans, F.L. Battles,

p. 273-4.

46. See L.E. Elliott-Binns, *The Decline and Fall of the Medieval Papacy*, Archon, New York, 1967; L. von Pastor, *History of the Popes from the Close of the Middle Ages*, Routledge and Kegan Paul, London, 1938-67, trans. F.I. Antrobus et al.

47. See S. Iserloh, *Ibid*, Chap. 14; F. Schmidt-Clausing, *Zwingli*, de Gruyter, Berlin, 1965; W. Köhler, *Huldreich Zwingli*, Koehler, Stuttgart, 1952, 2e Aufl.

48. H. Bornkamm, *Phillipp Melanchthon*, Vandenhoek, Göttingen, 1960; W.H. Neuser, *Der Ansatz der Theologie Phillipp Melanchthons*, Moers, Neukirchen, 1957.

49. Hay, D. 'Schools and Universities'. In *The New Cambridge Modern History, Vol. 2*, Cambridge University Press, Cambridge, 1968, p. 431.

50. *The New Cambridge Modern History, Vol. 2*, p. 211.

51. *The New Cambridge Modern History, Vol. 2*, pp. 116, 383.

52. See H. Porter, *Reformation and Reaction in Tudor Cambridge*, Cambridge University Press, Cambridge, 1958; N. Wood, *The Reformation and English Education*, Routledge, London, 1931.

53. *The New Cambridge Modern History*, Vol. 2, p. 430.

54. *Ibid*, p. 431.

55. On Arminius see C. Bangs, *Arminius*, Abingdon, Nashville, 1971; G.O. McCulloch, (ed.), *Man's Faith and Freedom : the Theological Influence of Jacobus Arminius*, Abingdon, New York, 1962. On the Arminian movement in Britain see G. F. Nuttal, 'The influence of Arminianism in England', in G. O. McCulloch, (ed.), *Ibid*.

Chapter 3

1. For fuller details see E. Gilson, *La Philosophie de Saint Bonaventure*, J. Vrin, Paris, 1953, pp. 292-3.

2. *Sentences*, 1, d 3, p 1, dub. 1.

3. *Ibid*, IV, d 49, p 1, un. 2, fa 1-2.

4. *Ibid*, III, d 24, dub. 3.

5. For fuller details see J.F. Quinn, 'The moral philosophy of St. Bonaventure.' In R.W. Shahan and F.J. Kovack (eds.) *Bonaventure and Aquinas*. University of Oklahoma Press, Norman, 1976.

6. *The Soul's Journey into God*, IV.

7. Effort in scholasticism was understood to be towards good works rather than good work in an economic sense. On the changes in attitude that occurred at the reformation see W. Weber, *Wirtschaftsethik am Vorabend des Liberalismus*, Aschendorff, Munster, 1959.

8. M. Weber, *The Sociology of Religion*, Methuen, London, 1965, trans. E. Fischoff, p. 2.

9. *Summa Theologiae*, Prima Pars, Qu. 83, Art. 2, Reply.

10. *Ibid*, Qu. 81, Art. 3, Reply.

11. *Ibid*, Secunda Secundae, Qu. 91, Art. 2, Reply.

12. *Ibid*, Prima Secundae, Qu. 105, Art. 2.

13. On Aquinas' metaphysics see J. de Finance, *Être et Agir dans la Philosophie de Saint Thomas*, Presses de l'Université Gregorienne, Lille, 2e Ed, 1965; H. Meyer, *The Philosophy of Thomas Aquinas*, Herder, Freiburg, 1944, trans. F. Eckhoff; F.C. Coppleston, *Aquinas*, Penguin, Harmondsworth, 1955.

14. For opposing views of this see J.C. Doig, *Aquinas on Metaphysics*, Nijhoff, The Hague, 1972; R.J. Henle, *Saint Thomas and Platonism*, Nijhoff, The Hague, 1956.

15. *Summa Theologiae*, Secunda Secundae, Qu. 180.

16. *Summa Theologiae*, Pars Prima, Qu. 2, Art. 3.

17. *Ibid*.

18. *Ibid*, Qu. 12, Art. 12.

19. *Ibid, Qu. 93, Art. 2*.

20. *Ibid*, Qu. 14, Art. 2.

21. *Ibid*, Qu. 93, Art. 7.

22. *Ibid*.

23. *Ibid*, Qu. 45, Art. 2.

24. *Ibid*.
25. J. Pelikan, *The Christian Tradition*, *Vol. 1*, University of Chicago Press, Chicago, 1973.
26. *Summa Theologiae*, Secunda Primae, Qu. 82, Art. 3.
27. *Ibid*, Qu. 74, Art. 3.
28. *Ibid*, Secunda Secundae, Qu. 47, Art. 15.
29. *God and Creatures*, Qu. 18.
30. A. von Harnack, *History of Dogma*, Williams and Norgate, London, 1899, trans. N. Buchanan, Vol. VI, p. 302n.
31. See F. Copleston, *A History of Philosophy*, Burns Oates, London, 1950, Vol. 2; C.R.S. Harris, *Duns Scotus*, Humanities Press, New York, 1959, 2 vols.; E.H. Gilson, *Jean Duns Scot*, J. Vrin, Paris, 1952.
32. See F. Copleston, *Ibid*, p. 527.
33. F. Copleston, *Ibid*, p. 532.
34. *Nicomachean Ethics*, Book III, Ch. 5, Para. 11.
35. *Reportatio*, III, Qu. 12, K.
36. *Quodlibeta Septem*, III, Qu. 10.
37. *Nicomachean Ethics*, Book VII., Ch. 9, Para. 5.
38. F. Copleston, *Ibid*, Vol. 3, p. 84
39. F. Copleston, *Ibid*, Chap. 6.
40. F. Copleston, *Ibid*, p. 94.
41. J. A. Robson, *Wyclif and the Oxford Schools*, Cambridge University Press, Cambridge, 1961.
42. S. D'Irsay, *Histoire des Universités*, Picard, Paris, 1931, Vol. 1.
43. G. Leff, *Paris and Oxford Universities in the Thirteenth and Fourteenth Centuries*, Wiley, New York, 1968, p. 190ff.
44. *Ibid*, pp. 240-3.
45. See G. Leff, *William of Ockham*, Manchester University Press, Manchester, 1975, p. 494.
46. J. A. Robson, *Ibid*.
47. *Works*, Vol. 1, pp..60-1.
48. See A. von Harnack, *Ibid*, Vol VI, p. 59.
49. A von Harnack, *Ibid*, pp. 87-88.
50. L. Cognet, *Le Jansenisme*, Presses Universitaires, Paris, 1961; L. Cognet, in W. Muller et al, *History of the Church*, *Vol. 6*, Burns and Oates, London, 1981, Chaps. 2 and 3.
51. H. Jedin, in S. Iserloh, *Ibid*, Chap. 41; J. Brodrick, *Robert Bellarmine, Saint and Scholar*, Burns Oates, London, 1966, 2nd Edition.
52. A. von Harnack, *Ibid*, p. 104.
53. W. Muller, in W. Muller *et al, Ibid*, Chap. 28.
54. See H.R. Fox Bourne, *The Life of John Locke*, Vol. 1, Henry King, London, 1876, Chap. 1; G. Compayré, *Historie Critique des Doctrines de l'Éducation en France depuis le Seizième Siècle*, Saltkine, Paris, 1879, pp. 195-7.
55. H.R. Fox Bourne, *Ibid*, p. 45.
56. See R. Briggs, *The Scientific Revolution of the Seventeenth Century*, Longmans, Harlow, 1969; A. R. Hall, *From Galileo to Newton*, Collins, London, 1963.
57. F. Bacon, *The Advancement of Learning*, Dent, London, 1973, XXXV, Paras. 16, 20.
58. On the growing separation of science and religion in Britain in the sixteenth century see C. Hill, *The Intellectual Origins of the English Revolution*, Oxford University Press, Oxford, 1965, especially Chap. 3.
59. On Descartes' relation to Plato and Augustine see H. Gouhier, *La Pensée Metaphysique de Descartes*, Vrin, Paris, 1962; E. Gilson, *Le Rôle de la Pensée Mediévale dans la Formation du Système Cartésien*, Vrin, Paris, 1951.
60. F. Suarez, *Disputationes Metaphysicae*, Disp. 25, Sec. 1.
61. On seventeenth century mechanism see E.J. Dijksterhuis, *The Mechanisation of the World Picture*, Clarendon, Oxford, 1961.
62. On the reading public in the seventeenth and eighteenth centuries see W.H. Barber, *Leibniz in France, From Arnauld to Voltaire*, Clarendon, Oxford, 1955; C.B. O'Keefe, *Contemporary Reactions to the Enlightenment*, 1728-1762, Saltkine, Genève, 1974. For a tendentious but informative view of

the fiction reading public see Q.D. Leavis, *Fiction and the Reading Public*, Chatto and Windus, London, 1932.

63. On the rationalism of Shaftesbury and Clarke see S. Grean, *Shaftesbury's Philosophy of Religion and Ethics*, Ohio University Press, Athens, 1967; E. Cassirer, *The Platonic Renaissance in England*, Gordian Press, New York, 1970, trans. J.P. Pattegrove, especially Chap. 6; H.C. Alexander, *The Leibniz-Clarke Correspondence*, University of Manchester Press, Manchester, 1956; J. P. Ferguson, *The Philosophy of Dr. Samuel Clarke and its Critics*, Vantage, New York, 1974.

64. On Leibniz' project for a universal church see J. Baruzi, *Leibniz et l'Organisation Réligieuse de La Terre*, Alcan, Paris, 1907.

65. Thus L. Goldmann has Descartes, Leibniz, Locke and Hume as the classical representatives of 'individualism' (*Kant*, New Left Books, London, 1971, trans. R. Black, p. 51). Kant is excepted from this list as showing a greater concern with community, though his concern is in reality not much greater than that of Leibniz or Locke. J.R. Kantor introduces a different but equally dubious theory of individualism, which he grounds in Hume's statement that mind is 'nothing but a heap or collection of different perceptions' (*Treatise of Human Nature*, Book I, Part 4, Sect. 2.). This 'atomistic' view of mind is said to have been produced by 'the British Islanders, with their individualistic institutions ...'. Yet the popularity of corpuscular and atomic theories more obviously originates from their popularity in physical sciences, an influence that was stronger in Britain because of the greater attention paid to such sciences (J.R. Kantor, *The Scientific Evolution of Psychology*, Principia, Chicago, 1969, Vol. 2, pp. 123, 120).

66. C.B. MacPherson, *The Political Theory of Possessive Individualism*, Oxford University Press, Oxford, 1961. Another valid sense in which we can speak of individualism is the removal of 'causae secundae' from political theory in the sixteenth and seventeenth centuries. See: P. Honigsheim, 'Zur Soziologie der Mittelalterlichen Scholastik', in M. Palyi, (ed.), *Hauptprobleme der Soziologie: Erinnerungsausgabe für Max Weber*, Duncker und Humbolt, München, 1923; M. Scheler, *Problems of a Sociology of Knowledge*, Routledge and Kegan Paul, London, 1980, trans. M.S. Frings, pp. 87-88.

67. *Summa Theologiae*, Pars Prima, Qu. 75, Art. 5.

68. See S.T. Hall, *History of General Physiology, 600 B.C. to A.D. 1900*, University of Chicago Press, Chicago, 1969.

69. *Oevres Philosophiques*, Vol. 1, p. 396ff.

70. *Ibid*, p. 448-449.

71. *Ibid*, p. 441ff.

72. *Ibid*, p. 448-449.

73. *Ibid*, p. 450.

74. *Ibid*.

75. Thus Bain says 'States of pleasure are concomitant with an increase, and states of pain with an abatement, of some, or all, of the vital functions.' (A. Bain, *Mental Science*, Longmans Green, London, 1875, p. 75.) Pavlov complicated this idea considerably with his demonstration that stomach activity is influenced by tasting and swallowing independent of the actual digestion of food (I.P. Pavlov, *The Work of the Digestive Glands*, Charles Griffin, London, 1902, trans. W.H. Gantt.) It was later shown that animals found tasting and swallowing rewarding even when food was prevented from entering the stomach, thus confirming that 'pleasure' is not always related to meeting a physiological need (C.L. Hull, et al, 'True, sham and esophageal feeding as reinforcements', *Journal of Comparative and Physiological Psychology*, 44, 236-245, 1951; see also G.A. Kimble, *Conditioning and Learning*, Methuen, London, 1961, Chap. 9).

76. *Oevres Philosophiques*, pp. 407-408.

77. *Ibid*, p. 453. He also describes something very like reflex action in explaining why we remove a hand from fire (pp. 469-470). Canguilhem claims this is not really reflex action because 'there is no homogeneity between the incoming impulse (*excitation*) and the outgoing impulse (*reaction*)' (G. Canguilhem, *La Formation du Concept de Réflexe*, Presses Universitaires de France, Paris, 1955, p. 36). This is true in that incoming impulses consist of threads and outgoing of animal spirits, but the era in which physiologists assumed incoming impulses to be always transmitted by the same mechanisms as outgoing was one that ended with the discovery of neural transmitter substances (see S.P. Grossman, *Physiological Psychology*, Wiley, New York, 1967, pp. 18-24). In this sense Descartes'

ideas resemble modern once more than those of Sherrington. The real change here is in observational techniques. In Descartes' time these were those of simple dissection, in Sherrington's day those of recording electrodes, while Dubois-Reymond and Loewi added to this the technique of transporting neurohumoral substances from one site to another. Advances in analytic chemistry were also involved (see S.P. Grossman, *Ibid*).

78. See C. Hull, *A Behavior System*, Yale University Press, New Haven, 1952; D.O. Hebb, *A Textbook of Psychology*, W.B. Saunders, Washington, 1966, Chap. 10; D.E. Berlyne, *Conflict, Arousal and Curiosity*, McGraw-Hill, New York, 1960.

79. *Oevres Philosophiques*, Vol. 1, p. 471.

80. *Ibid*, pp. 578-579.

81. R.H. Popkin, *The History of Skepticism from Erasmus to Descartes*, Van Gorcum, Assen, 1960.

82. *Discourse de la Méthode*, Prem. Part., Para. 9.

83. *Ibid*, Deux. Part., Paras. 18, 19.

84. *Les Règles pour La Direction de l'Espirit*, Paras. 383-390.

85. *Discours de la Méthode*, Quat. Part.; *The City of God*, Book XI, 26. Augustine says 'If I am mistaken (in thinking he exists), I exist. A man who does not exist can certainly not be mistaken, and if I am mistaken, therefore I exist.'

86. *Discours de la Méthode*, Cinqu. Part., Para 42.

87. *Ibid*, Trois. Part.

88. Lettre à Elizabeth, 15 Septembre, 1645.

89. Lettre à Elizabeth, 6 Octobre, 1645.

90. *Passions de l'Âme*, Art. 36.

91. *Ibid*.

92. On Spinoza see S. Hampshire, *Spinoza*, Faber and Faber, London, 1956; H.E. Allison, *Benedict de Spinoza*, Twayne, Boston, 1975; E.M. Curley, *Spinoza's Metaphysics : an Essay in Interpretation*, Harvard University Press, Cambridge, 1969.

93. W.H. Barber, *Leibniz in France, From Arnauld to Voltaire*, Clarendon, Oxford, 1955, pp. 30, 41.

94. On Malebranche see F. Alquié, *La Cartesianisme de Malebranche*, Vrin, Paris, 1974; G. Rodis-Lewis, *Nicolas Malebranche*, Presses Universitaires de France, Paris, 1963; W. Craig, *De la Recherche du Bien*, Mouton, The Hague, 1973.

95. *Specimen Dynamicum*, Part II.

96. See B. Russell, *The Philosophy of Leibniz*, Allen and Unwin, London, 1900; L. Couturat, *La Logique de Leibniz*, Baillière, Paris, 1901; G.H.R. Parkinson, *Logic and Reality in Leibniz' Metaphysics*, Clarendon, Oxford, 1965. Descartes and Malebranche knew a crude version of the conservation of momentum involved when gland H interacts with particles of animal spirits. In their theories God continually violates this law to allow the soul to interact with the body. Leibniz gave a correct statement of this law, and an approximate statement of the conservation of kinetic energy, but thought it unworthy of God to violate his laws in this way (*Pensées Critiques sur Descartes*, Part II, Art. 360.) His answer is to say 'The effect of percussion will be equally in the collision ... it suffices to derive the passion which is in one from the action which is in it, so that we need no influence of one upon the other, even though the action of one provided the occasion for the other to produce a change in itself' (*Specimen Dynamicum*, Part II, Para. 5). This happy coincidence is a preordained harmony established by God, which also applies to soul-body interaction (*Système Nouveau*, Para. 14). In effect, there are now no laws of interaction between bodies, but only those of the unfolding of destiny within bodies. When bodies interact with the soul, pre-established harmony provides the occasion for their movement.

97. J. Pelikan, *From Luther to Kierkegaard*, Concordia, St. Louis, 1950, Chaps. 1-4.

98. W.H. Barber, *Ibid*.

99. *New Essays*, Book IV, Chap. VI and J. Jalabert, *Le Dieu de Leibniz*, Presses Universitaires de France, Paris, 1960.

100. *New Essays*, Preface, Para. 4.

101. *Ibid*, Chap XXXIII.

102. *Ibid*, Para 18.

103. *Ibid*, Part 4.

104. *Primae Veritates*, Para. 2.

105. *Uber das Naturgesetz*, in G.E. Guhrauer (ed.) *Liebniz's Deutsche Schriften*, Verlag von Viet, Leipzig, 1838.

106. J. Bayle, *Dictionaire Historique et Critique*, 1697, enlarged 1702, supplemented 1704-6, entries on Manicheanism.

107. Voltaire's early writings are more optimistic in tone, e.g. *Babouc* and *Zadig* (both published in 1747), but his later writings show an increasing pessimism, e.g. *Poème sue le Désastre de Lisbonne* (1756) and the brilliant *Candide* (1759).

108. For instance in *The City of God*, Book XI, Para. 25, he appeals to the lack of perfection in creatures; for the rebellion of the angels see J. O'Connell, *Augustine's Early Theory of Man*, Belknap, Cambridge, pp. 158-9; J. O'Connell, *Augustine's Confessions*, Balknap, Cambridge, 1969, pp. 23-36.

109. *Essais de Théodicée*, Prem. Part., Para. 31.

110. *Ibid*, Preface, Paras. 5-6.

111. L.E. Loemker, *G.W. Leibniz, Philosophical Papers and Letters*, University of Chicago Press, Chicago, 1956, Introduction, p. 47.

112. *Monadologie*, Paras. 18-35.

113. *Ibid*.

114. *Ibid*, Para. 20.

115. W.H. Barber, *Ibid*, p. 57.

116. W. Arnsperger, *Christian Woolfs Verhaltnis zu Leibniz*, Habilitations-Schrift, Weimar, 1897.

117. *Psychologica Empirica*, 1732; *Psychologica Rationalis*, 1734; *Philosophia Moralis, sive Ethica*, 1750-3.

118. *Psychologica Empirica*, Para. 918.

119. See L.G. Crocker, *Nature and Culture: Ethical Thought in the French Enlightenment*, John Hopkins Press, Baltimore, 1973, Chap. 1.

120. The transformation of French metaphysics begins with Maine de Biran, whose work was not widely influential until its publication by Cousin between 1834 and 1841. This change produced an emphasis in both de Biran and Bergson upon the data of consciousness as the starting point for philosophy. This was already present in Hume and Kant, but was now interpreted in a spiritualist and romantic direction. See Maine de Biran, *Nouveaux Essais Anthropologiques*, Oevres, Tome XIV and H. Bergson, *Time and Free Will*, Allen and Unwin, London, 1910, trans. F.L. Pogson.

121. See R.S. Peters, *Hobbes*, Penguin, Harmondsworth, 1967, 2nd edition; M.J. Oakeshott, *Hobbes on Civil Association*, Blackwell, Oxford, 1975.

122. *Leviathan*, VI, Para. 1.

123. *Ibid*, Introduction.

124. *Ibid*, XIII, Para. 2.

125. *Ibid*, Para. 3.

126. *Ibid*, X, Para. 1.

127. *Ibid*, Paras. 5, 6, 7.

128. *Ibid*, XIII, Paras. 6, 7.

129. R.S. Peters, *Ibid*, p. 132.

130. *Ibid*, XIV, Para. 1.

131. *Ibid*, Para. 5.

132. *Ibid*, Para. 17.

133. *Ibid*, Para. 30.

134. *Ibid*, XIX, Para. 1.

135. *The Elements of Law*, Frank Cass, London, 1889, Chap. 9, Para. 17.

136. *Ibid*, Chaps. 7-9.

137. *Ibid*, Chap. 9, Para. 15.

138. See W.J. Ong, *Ramus, Method and the Decay of Dialogue*, Harvard University Press, Cambridge, 1958.

139. *Of Civil Government*, Dent, London, 1924, Book II, Chap. 2.

140. For Hobbes' early reception see J. Laird, *Hobbes*, Russell and Russell, New York, 1934, Part 3; J. Bowle, *Hobbes and his Critics*, Cape, London, 1951. Hobbes was accused of having caused two suicides prompted by the nihilism of his doctrine! His chief positive influence was on Ireton and Spinoza, though the latter acknowledged little of his debt.

141. *Of Civil Government*, Book II, Chap. XIX, Para. 226.

142. On Locke's reaction to the revolution of 1688 see H.R.F. Bourne, *Ibid*, Vol. 2, Chap. XI.

143. *A Treatise of Human Nature*, Oxford University Press, Oxford, 1978, Bk. III, Part 1, Sect. 1.

144. *Ibid*, Book II, Part 3, Sect. 3.

145. *Ibid*, Book II, Part 1, Sect. 1.

146. *Ibid*, Book II, Part 1, Sect. 8.

147. *Ibid*, Book II, Part 1, Sect. 5.

148. *Ibid*.

149. *Ibid*.

150. *Ibid*. Bk. II, Part 1, Sect. XI.

151. *Ibid.* Bk. III, Part 11, Sect. II.

152. *Ibid*, Bk. III, Part 11, Sect. II.

153. *Ibid*, Bk. III, Part 11, Sect. II.

154. *Ibid*, Bk. III, Part II, Sect. II.

155. On Berkeley's epistemology see A.A. Luce, *The Dialectic of Immaterialism*, Hodder and Stoughton, London, 1963.

156. *An Essay Concerning Human Understanding*, Chap. XXXIII.

157. *A Treatise of Human Nature*, Bk. 1., Part 1, Sect. IV.

158. Compare J. Mill's *Analysis of the Phenomena of the Human Mind*, Kelley, New York, 1967 and J.S. Mill's *System of Logic, Collected Works*, Vols. VIII and IX, Book IV, Chap. IV, Para. 3. Here the principle of causation is replaced by that of intensity, but otherwise their account is quite similar to that of Hume.

159. On Smith's relation to Hume and Hutcheson see D.D. Raphael and A.L. Macfie (eds.) *The Theory of Moral Sentiments*, Clarendon, Oxford, 1976, pp. 10-14.

160. *The Theory of Moral Sentiments*, p. 40.

161. *Ibid*.

162. *Ibid*, p. 50.

163. *Ibid*, p. 53

164. *Ibid*, p. 57.

165. *Ibid*, p. 58.

166. *Ibid*, p. 63.

167. Bain is an example of this (see Chapter 3, note 75). The general tendency until the advent of behaviourism, found in Bentham and J.S. Mill, was however to allow a role to the social meaning of pleasure. Bentham is inclined to give more weight to social responsibility in himself than in others: 'In my composition I happened to have a larger share of sympathy than falls often times to man's share ... Coming in a favourable age it received expansion after expansion, till it extended itself over the planet in which we live.' (Letter to Lord Erskine in 1819, cited in M.P. Mack, *Jeremy Bentham 1748-1792*, Columbia University Press, New York, 1963, p. 343.)

168. *Ibid*, pp. 111-112.

169. C.L. de Secondat Montesquieu, *Considérations sur les Causes de la Grandeur des Romains...*, Garnier, Paris, 1954.

170. *The Wealth of Nations*, Random, New York, 1937, Book 1, Chap. IX.

171. See M.P. Mack, *Jeremy Bentham 1748-92*, Columbia University Press, New York, 1963, p. 343; J.Mill, *Analysis of the Phenomena of the Human Mind*, Kelley, New York, 1967; J.S. Mill, *Utilitarianism, Liberty and Representative Government*, Dent, London, 1940; B. Russell, *A History of Western Philosophy*, Allen and Unwin, 1947; A.J. Ayer, 'The principle of utility'. In A.J. Ayer, *Philosophical Essays*, MacMillan, London, 1965.

172. B. Russell, *Human Knowledge, its Scope and Limits*, Simon and Schuster, New York, 1946; A.J. Ayer, *Language, Truth and Logic*, Gollancz, London, 1936.

173. B. Russell, *A History of Western Philosophy*, Allen and Unwin, London, 1946; A.J. Ayer, 'The principle of utility'. In A.J. Ayer, *Philosophical Essays*, MacMillan, London, 1965.

174. L.W. Beck, *Studies in the Philosophy of Kant*, Bobbs-Merrill, New York, 1965, pp. 5-7.

175. See W.C. Dampier, *A History of Science*, Cambridge University Press, Cambridge, 1961, Chaps. 3 and 4.

176. K. Ward, *The Development of Kant's View of Ethics*, Blackwell, Oxford, 1972, pp. 3 and 34.

177. See H.J. Vleeschauwer, *The Development of Kantian Thought*, Nelson, London, 1962, trans. A.R.C. Duncan.

178. *Critique of Pure Reason*, MacMillan, London, 1929, trans. N. Kemp Smith, Method of Transcendental Analytic, Chap. 3.

179. *Ibid*, Transcendental Analytic, Book 2, Chap. 3.

180. *Ibid*, Para. 19.

181. *Ibid*, Para. 24.

182. J. Piaget, *Insights and Illusions of Philosophy*, Routledge and Kegan Paul, London, 1972, trans, W. Mays, pp. 56-7.

183. *Critique of Pure Reason*, Second Part, First Division, Book 1, Chap. II, Sect. 11, 11.

184. *Ibid*, Book 11, Chap. 1. While Piaget disagreed with the importance Kant attached to counting in the formation of number concepts, in recent years the Kantian view has come back into fashion: see D. Klahr and J.G. Wallace, *Cognitive Development : an Information Processing View*, Erlbaum, Hillsdale, 1976; M.L. Lifschitz and P.E. Langford, 'The role of counting and measurement in conservation learning', *Archives de Psychologie, 46*, 1-14, 1977.

185. *Ibid*, Second Part, Second Division, Intro., 2A.

186. *Ibid*, Second Part, First Division, Chap. 2, Sect. III, II.

187. *Ibid*, Transcendental Dialectic Book II, Chap. III, Sect. 7.

188. *Ibid*, Transcendental Dialectic, Appendix.

189. *Ibid*.

190. See F.P. van de Pitte, *Kant as Philosophical Anthropologist*, Nijhoff, The Hague, 1971, Chap. 4.

191. See N. Machiavelli, *Discourses*, Routledge and Kegan Paul, 1975, trans, L.J. Walker, Book 1, Sects. 11-15; Montesquieu, C.L. de Secondat, *Considérations sur les Causes de la Grandeur des Romains*, Chap. 10, Para. 4.

192. *Critique of Practical Reason*, Bobbs-Merrill, Indianapolis, 1956, trans. L.W. Beck. Part 1, Book 1, Chap. 1, Paras. 7, 8.

193. *Ibid*, Para. 1.

194. *Ibid*, Book II, Chap II, IV.

195. *Ibid*, Part 1, Book 1., Chap. 1, Para. 1.

196. *Ibid*, Book 1., Chap. III.

197. *Schriften*, VII, pp. 267-74.

198. *Ibid*, pp. 268-9.

199. *Critque of Practical Reason*, Book II, Chap. II, V.

200. *Schriften*, VII, pp. 267, 268, 271.

201. *Ibid*, p. 272.

202. J. Boswell, *Life of Johnson*, Oxford University Press, Oxford, 1980, p. 333.

203. *Critique of Judgement*, Clarendon, Oxford, 1952, trans. J.C. Meredith, Introduction, VI.

204. *Ibid*, Introduction, III.

205. This interpretation is strengthened by Kant's final summing up, in which he reverts to the moral arguments for God and immortality as more satisfactory than the teleological argument. *Ibid*, Appendix, General remarks on teleology.

206. *Ibid*, Second Part, First Division.

207. 'Idea for a universal history from a cosmopolitan point of view', in L.W. Beck (ed.) *On History*, Bobbs-Merrill, Indianapolis, 1963.

208. See J. Passmore, *A Hundred Years of Philosophy*, Duckworth, London, 1966, 2nd Edition, Chap. 3; H.L. Ollig, *Der Neukantismus*, Metzler, Stuttgart, 1979. On more recent Kantian trends in German philosophy see F.J. von Rintelen, *Contemporary German Philosophy*, H. Bouvier, Bonn, 1970.

209. On Neokantian sociology see D.A. Martindale, *The Nature and Types of Sociological Theory*, Houghton Mifflin, Boston, 1960; K.F. Wolff, *The Sociology of Georg Simmel*, Free Press, Glencoe, 1950; T. Abel, *Systematic Sociology in Germany*, Columbia University Press, New York, 1929.

210. See J.R. Staude, *Max Scheler 1874-1928*, The Free Press, New York, 1967.

211. M. Horkheimer, *Kant und die Anfange der burgerlichen Geschichtsphilosophie*, Surkhamp, Stuttgart, 1930; M. Jay, *The Dialectical Imagination*, Heinemann, London, 1973, pp. 44-46.

212. M. Horkheimer and T. Adorno, *Dialektik der Aufklarung : Philosophische Fragmente*, Fischer, Frankfurt, 1969; M. Jay, *Ibid*, Chap. 8.

213. Habermas' Kantian assumptions appear most clearly in J. Habermas, *Zur Rekonstruktion des Historischen Materialismus*, Surkhamp, Frankfurt, 1976.

Chapter 4

1. F. Nietzsche, *The Will to Power*, Weidenfeld and Nicholson, London, 1967, trans. W. Kaufmann, pp.94, 362, 389, etc.

2. M.P. Mack, *Jeremy Bentham 1748-92*, Columbia Uni. Press, New York, 1963.

3. See for instance their appraisal of bourgeois socialism in the *Communist Manifesto*; of Panslavism in *Revolution and Counter-Revolution in Germany*; and of nationalism as the ideology of a faction of the French bourgeoisie in *The Eighteenth Brumaire* (K. Marx and F. Engels, *Selected Works*, Progress Publishers, Moscow, 1969, Vol. 1, pp. 133, 341-2, 406-7).

4. L.L. Whyte, *The Unconscious before Freud*, Tavistock, London, 1962, Chaps. 5-7.

5. L.L. Whyte, *Ibid.*, Chaps. 5, 6.

6. H.F. Ellenberger, *The Discovery of the Unconscious*, Allen Lane, London, 1970.

7. J. Miller, *The Uses of Pain*, South Place Ethical Society, London, 1974.

8. Maine de Biran, *Oevres*, Tome XIV (*Nouveaux Essais Anthropologiques*).

9. H. Bergson, *Essai sur les Données Immédiates de la Conscience*, PUF, Paris, 1965; H. Bergson, *L'Évolution Creatrice*, Alcan, Paris, 1912.

10. A. Schopenhauer, *On the Fourfold Principle of Sufficient Reason*, Open Court, La Salle, 1974, trans. E.F.J. Payne.

11. See W. Kaufmann, *Hegel*, Doubleday, Garden City, 1965, pp. 236-8.

12. *The World as Will and Representation*, Vol. 1, Dover, New York, 1969, trans. E.F.J. Payne, Introduction.

13. See T.M. Knox, 'Hegel and Prussianism', in W. Kaufmann (ed.) *Hegel's Political Philosophy*, Atherton, New York, 1970.

14. *The World as Will and Representation*, Dover, New York, 1969, Vol. 1, trans. E.F.J. Payne, Para XXV.

15. Voltaire's conversion to pessimism is outlined in Chapter 3, note 107. Johnson, who in early life endured considerable poverty, already paints a black view of human life is his poem 'London', written at age 29. Smith, like Johnson, seems to have suffered from lifelong bouts of depression. His first essay for the *Edinburgh Review* is devoted to supporting Parr's sceptical view of human nature against Godwin's 'universal philanthropy' (S. Smith, *Works*, Longman, London, 1850, pp. 1-5).

16. *The World as Will and Representation*, p. 140.

17. *Ibid*, p. 101.

18. *Ibid*, p. 105.

19. *Ibid*, p. 143.

20. *Ibid*, p. 145.

21. *Ibid*, p. 113.

22. *Ibid*, p. 129.

23. *Ibid*, p. 128.

24. *Ibid*, p. 372.

25. *Ibid*, p. 129.

26. *Ibid*, p. 169.

27. *Ibid*, p. 182.

28. *Ibid*, p. 185.

29. *Ibid*, p. 191.

30. *Ibid*, p. 199.

31. *Ibid*, p. 202.

32. *Ibid*, pp. 221-3.

33. *Ibid*, p. 230.

34. *Ibid*, p. 239.

35. *Ibid*, pp. 254-5.
36. *Ibid*, p, 257.
37. *Ibid*.
38. *Ibid*, p, 259.
39. *Ibid*, p, 272.
40. *Ibid*, p, 275.
41. *Ibid*, p, 312.
42. *Ibid*, p, 314.
43. *Ibid*, p, 315-6.
44. *Ibid*, p, 324.
45. *Ibid*, p, 328.
46. *Ibid*, p, 334-5.
47. *Ibid*, p, 334.
48. *Elemente der Psychophysik*, Breitkopf und Hartel, Leipzig, 1860, vol. 2, pp. 461-2.
49. Lettre à Elizabeth, 6 Octobre, 1645.
50. Lettre à Elizabeth, 1 Fevrier, 1647.
51. *Politics*, Book 5, Chapter 11.
52. See C. Fourier, *Oevres*, VI and XI, p. 208ff.
53. G.W.F. Hegel, *The Phenomenology of Spirit*, Sonnenschein, London, 1910, trans. J.B. Baillie, Vol. 2, p. 661: 'These individuals, who felt the fear of death (produced by absolute terror), their absolute lord and master, submit to negation and distinction once more, arrange themselves into groups and return to a restricted and apportioned task....' Hegel's view here is closer to the fear of freedom emphasised by Johnson (see note 58) and later by Fromm (see Chap. 6). F. Nietzsche, *The Genealogy of Morals*, First Essay.
54. See S. Freud. *Complete Works*, XX, p. 60. Freud here claims he read Nietzsche only after he formulated his own doctrines. The references to Nietzsche in Jones' biography of Freud, which total fifteen, are almost equally divided between occasions when Freud quoted Nietzsche and those on which he denied having much knowledge of him! In a letter to Zweig in 1934 he explains quite clearly his motives for his denials, saying that he may be biased against Zwieg's book on Nietzsche and that his reason 'may have something to do with the way in which you compare me to him. In my youth he signified a nobility to which I could not attain. A friend of mine, Dr Paneth, had got to know him in the Endgadine and he used to write to me a lot about him.' (E. Jones, *The Life and Work of Sigmund Freud*, *Vol. 3*, Hogarth, London, 1957, p. 489.) Further evidence that Freud was well acquainted with Nietzsche's writings at a relatively early date comes from his statement in 1908 that Nietzsche had a more penetrating knowledge of himself than any other man who ever lived; a strange thing to say about a man with whose inner workings you are unfamiliar (*Ibid, Vol. 2*, p.385). This remark was made immediately following Freud's claim that he had read Nietzsche but found his thinking too rich to understand. Jones points out that Freud's discussions of the superego in *The Ego and the Id* (1932) bear a remarkable similarity to those of Nietzsche's *Genealogy of Morals* which we know the Vienna Psychoanalytic Society devoted two meetings to in Freud's presence in 1908 (*Ibid, Vol. 3*, p. 306).
55. On the adulation both sought and obtained by French absolute monarchs see G. Pages, *La Monarchie de l'Ancien Regime en France*, Colin, Paris, 1928; J.B. Wolf, *Louis XIV*, Gollancz, London, 1968, Part 4 (see especially the notes to this part); M.Rouston, *The Pioneers of the French Revolution*, Fertig, New York, 1969, trans. F. Whyte, Chap. 1.
56. The idea that 'le fanatisme' (religious fanaticism) was abused by foreign monarchs was often expressed by the philosophes; D. Mornet, *Les Origines Intellectuelles de la Révolution Français*, Armand Colin, Paris, 1934, 2e edition, p. 240ff. Particularly at the height of Louis XV's popularity, they were often reluctant to level such an accusation at their own rulers (M. Roustan, *Ibid*, Chap. 1). On Hume and Gibbon's more radical attitudes see G.R. Cragg, *Reason and Authority in the Eighteenth Century*, Cambridge University Press, Cambridge, 1964, Chap. 5. For the earlier background to the British discussion see J. Redwood, *Reason, Ridicule and Religion*, Thames and Hudson, London, 1976, Chap. 3.
57. The general esteem in which officers were held gave rise in most eighteenth century services to promotion through a combination of influence (which preserved hereditary ranks) and purchase

(which undermined them). Conditions were somewhat different in the British navy, where influence and efficiency were the most powerful influences and young men of middle class origin could rise by merit (E. Robson, 'The armed forces and the art of war', in *The New Cambridge Modern History*, Vol. VII).

58. See Chapter 3, notes 162,3. Samuel Johnson also discusses the thirst for authority in the same period: 'They are glad to supply by external authority their own want of constancy and resolution, and court the government of others, when long experience has convinced them of their inability to govern themselves.' (Letter to Baretti in J. Boswell, *Life of Johnson*, Oxford University Press, Oxford, 1980, p. 258.) It seems that the lack of 'external authority' was a relatively novel experience in Britain in the eighteenth century, accounting for the small attention paid to it previously.

59. *Psychology from an Empirical Standpoint*, Routledge and Kegan Paul, London, 1973, trans. L.L. McAllister, p. 97.

60. *Ibid*, p. 103
61. *Ibid*, p. 139.
62. *Ibid*, p. 88.
63. *Ibid*, p. 197.
64. *Ibid*, p. 200.
65. *Ibid*, p. 201, 239.
66. *The True and the Evident*, Routledge and Kegan Paul, London, 1966, trans. R.M. Chisholm, p. 21.
67. *Ibid*, p. 6ff.
68. *Ibid*, p. 122.
69. *Ibid*, p. xxiv
70. *Psychology from an Empirical Standpoint*, p. 200
71. *The True and the Evident*, p. 32.
72. *Ibid*, p. 130-3.
73. On Brentano's influence see A.S. Rancurello, *A Study of Franz Brenano*, Academic Press, New York, 1968, Part 3.

74. Discussions of Husserl's supposed Platonism can be found in E. Levinas, *Théorie de l'Intuition dans la Phénomenlogie de Husserl*, Vrin, Paris, 1963, Chap. 6; M. Farber, *The Foundation of Phenomenology*, State University of New York Press, Albany, 1943, pp. 203, 244-251, 504, 522; E.P. Welch, *The Philosophy of Emund Husserl*, Columbia University Press, New York, 1941, Chaps. 5 and 6. Part of the problem seems to be that both Husserl, and some of his followers (e.g. Farber), adopt an extreme definition of Platonism in order to distance themselves from ideas Plato might well have rejected himself. Thus Farber says that Platonic ideal universals are 'unrelated to all that is subjective' (*loc cit.*, p. 504n); a quite false characterisation of Platonism. Levinas' view that Husserl developed a novel kind of transcendental idealism with some Platonic elements seems more satisfactory.

75. *Ideas*, Allen and Unwin, London, 1931, trans. W.R. Boyce Gibson, author's preface to the English translation.

76. *Ibid*, Section 31.
77. *Ibid*, Section 33.
78. *Ibid*, Section 87.
79. *Ibid*, Section 90.
80. *Ibid*, Section 91.
81. *Ibid*, Section 92.
82. *Ibid*, Sections 94, 95.
83. *Ibid*, Section 94.
84. *Ibid*, Section 100.
85. *Ibid*, Section 104.
86. *Ibid*, Section 106.
87. *Ibid*, Section 109.
88. *Ibid*, Sections 112-3.
89. *Ibid*, Section 114.
90. *Ibid*, Section 117.
91. *Ibid*.

92. *Ibid*, Section 121.

93. *Ibid*, Section 143.

94. H. Bergson, *Creative Evolution*, Macmillan, London, 1911, trans. A. Mitchell.

95. See *Cartesian Meditations*, Second Meditation and 'Philosophy and the Crisis of European Man', in *Phenomenology and the Crisis of Philosophy*, Harper Torchbooks, New York, 1965, trans. Q. Lauer.

96. *Cartesian Meditations*, Section 65.

97. *Ibid*, Section 58.

98. L.Landgrebe, 'World as a phenomenological problem', *Philosophy and Phenomenological Research*, 1, 38-58, 1940; M. Merleau-Ponty, *Themes from the Lectures*, Northwestern University Press, Evanston, 1970, trans. J. O'Neill, Chap. 11; M. Merleau-Ponty, *Phenomenology, Language and Sociology*, Heinemann, London, trans. J. O'Neill, pp. 95-110; A. Schutz and T. Luckmann, *The Structures of the Lifeworld*, Northwestern University Press, Evanston, 1973, trans. R.M. Zaner and H. Tristram Engelhardt.

99. *Husserliana*, VI, Nijhoff, The Hague, 1954.

100. *Ibid*, p. 48.

101. *Ibid*, p. 49.

102. *Ibid*, p. 52.

103. *Ibid*, p. 70.

104. *Ibid*, p. 120ff.

105. *Husserliana*, IV, V, XIII, XIV, XV, Nijhoff, The Hague, 1952-73.

106. P. Berger and T. Luckmann, *The Social Construction of Reality*, Doubleday, Garden City, 1967.

107. *The Essence of Christianity*, Ungar, New York, 1957 (1st ed. Leipzig, 1841).

108. *Ibid*, Chap. 2.

109. *Ibid*, Chap. 1.

110. *Ibid*.

111. *Ibid*.

112. See E. Kamenka, *The Philosophy of Ludwig Feuerbach*, Routledge and Kegan Paul, London, 1970.

113. K.Marx, *The Economic and Philosophical Manuscripts of 1844*, International Publishers, New York, 1964, trans. D.J. Struik, p. 114.

114. *Ibid*, p. 115.

115. *Ibid*, p. 114.

116. *Ibid*, p. 181.

117. *Ibid*, p. 182.

118. *Ibid*, p. 147.

119. *Ibid*, p. 162.

120. '...he that would criticize all human actions according to the principle of utility must first deal with human nature in general and then with human nature as modified by each historical epoch.' K.Marx, *Capital*, C.H. Kerr, Chicago, 1906, Vol. 1, p. 668.

121. See D.J. Struik's introduction to *Economic and Philosophic Manuscripts of 1844*, International Publishers, New York, 1964, trans. M. Milligan.

Chapter 5

1. For its reception see W. Kaufmann's introduction to *The Basic Writings of Nietzsche*, Modern Library, New York, 1968, p. 5.

2. *The World as Will and Representation*, Dover, New York, 1969, Vol. 1, trans. E.F.J. Payne, p. 178.

3. *Ibid*, Vol. 2, p. 203.

4. *Basic Writings*, p. 36.

5. *The World as Will and Representation*, Vol. 2, pp. 275-6.

6. *Basic Writings*, p. 53.

7. *Ibid*, pp. 51-5.

8. *Ibid*, p. 50.

9. *Ibid*, p. 73-4.

10. *Ibid*, p. 78.

11. *Ibid*, p. 95.

12. *Ibid*, p. 22.

13. *Ibid*, p. 22-3.

14. *Ibid*, p. 23.

15. *Ibid*, p. 25.

16. These ideas are all expounded in *Thus Spake Zarathustra*.

17. *Portable Nietzsche*, Chatto and Windus, trans. W. Kaufmann, London, 1971, pp.174-7.

18. *The Will to Power*, Weidenfeld and Nicolson, London, 1967, trans. W. Kaufmann and R.J. Holingdale, p.187.

19. *Ibid*, p.333.

20. *Ibid*, pp.363-4, p.344, para.3.

21. *The Portable Nietzsche*, pp. 398-407; *The Will to Power*, pp. 500-504. It is worth mentioning that the passages cited in the previous note generally belong to a later period than those in the present note, which may indicate a shift in viewpoint.

22. *The Will to Power*, pp. 206-7.

23. On the sufferings of the creator see *The Portable Nietzsche*, pp. 174-7; pp. 398-406; *The Will to Power*, pp. 501-3; p. 509. On the joy of the creator see *The Portable Nietzsche*, pp. 407-8; p. 415; *The Will to Power*, pp. 40-82. While *Thus Spake Zarathustra* stresses the pain of a long struggle followed by the joy of success, both *The Genealogy of Morals* and the opening sections of *The Will to Power* lay more emphasis on the permanent cheerfulness of the noble soul.

24. *Basic Writings*, p. 482.

25. *Ibid*, p. 485.

26. *Ibid*, p. 494.

27. For instance F. Golffing in F. Nietzsche, *The Birth of Tragedy and the Genealogy of Morals*, Anchor Books, New York, 1956, p. ix.

28. *Basic Writings*, p. 498.

29. *Ibid*, p. 542.

30. *Ibid*, p. 558.

31. *Ibid*, p. 564.

32. *Ibid*, p. 575.

33. *Ibid*, p. 583.

34. *Ibid*.

35. *Ibid*, p. 583.

36. See P. Bridgewater, *Nietzsche in Anglosaxony*, Leicester Uni. Press, Leicester, 1972.

37. B. Russell, *A History of Western Philosophy*, Allen and Unwin, London, 1946, p.18.

38. See Chapter 4, note 54.

39. In Jaspers' essay on Weber he claims the latter lacked the personal will to power of a political leader (K. Jaspers, *Leonardo, Descartes, Max Weber*, Routledge, London, 1965, p.263); for the influence of Nietzsche on Scheler see H. Mayerhoff's introduction to M. Scheler, *Man's place in Nature*, Beacon Press, Boston, 1961; for his influence on Spengler see H. Stuart Hughes, *Oswald Spengler*, Scribner, New York, 1962.

40. See F. Copleston, *Friedrich Nietzsche*, Burns Oates, London, 1942, p.9.

41. On other occasions Spengler proved more than ready to acknowledge his debt to Nietzsche. See H. Stuart Hughes, *Oswald Spengler*, Scribner, New York, 1962, pp.61-5.

42. For a cogent critique of this error see R.J. Holingdale, *Nietzsche*, Routledge, London, 1965, pp.309-311; W. Kaufmann is often in danger of falling into this error, e.g. *Nietzsche,Philosopher, Psychologist, Antichrist*, Princeton Uni. Press, Princeton, 1968, p.422.

43. M. Merleau-Ponty, *The Structure of Behaviour*, Methuen, London, 1965, trans. A.L. Fisher, p.180.

44. See C. Brinton, *Nietzsche*, Harper and Row, New York, 1965, pp. 244-50.

45. W. Kaufmann, *Nietzsche: Philosopher, Psychologist, Antichrist*, Princeton Uni. Press, Princeton, 1968; R.J. Holingdale, *Nietzsche: The Man and His Philosophy*, Routledge, London, 1965.

46. See D. Glucksmann, *Les Maitres Penseurs*, Grasset, Paris, 1977; J. Derrida, *L'Oreille de l'Autre*,

VLB, Montreal, 1982.

47. See H. Rickert, *Science and History, a Critique of Positivist Epistemology*, Van Nostrand, Princeton, 1962, trans. G. Reisman; M. Weber, *The Methodology of the Social Sciences*, Free Press, Glencoe, 1949, trans. E.A. Shils and H.A. Finch.

48. K. Jaspers, *General Psychopathology*, University of Chicago Press, Chicago, 1963, trans. J. Hoenig and M.W. Hamilton, p. 59.

49. *Ibid*, p. 131.

50. *Ibid*, p. 132.

51. *Ibid*, p. 278.

52. *Ibid*, p. 282.

53. *Ibid*, p. 292.

54. *Ibid*, p. 302-3.

55. *Ibid*. p. 303.

56. *Ibid*.

57. *Ibid*, p. 308.

58. *Ibid*.

59. *Ibid*, pp. 315, 364.

60. *Ibid*, p. 317.

61. I. Kant, *Critique of Practical Reason*, Section 59.

62. *General Psychopathology*, p. 382.

63. *Ibid*, p. 539.

64. K. Jaspers, *Philosophy*, University of Chicago Press, Chicago, 1969-71, trans, E.B. Ashton; K. Jaspers, *Von der Wahrheit*, Piper, München, 1958.

65. See Rollo May, 'The existential approach'. In S. Arieti (ed.) *American Handbook of Psychiatry*, Basic Books, New York, 1959; P.K. Benedict, 'Special aspects of Schizophrenia'. In L. Bellak (ed.) *Schizophrenia: A Review of the Syndrome*. Logos, New York, 1958; F.C. Redlich and D.X. Freedman, *The Theory and Practice of Psychiatry*, Basic Books, New York, 1966, Chap. 26; Rollo May et al (eds.) *Existence: A New Dimension in Psychiatry, and Psychology*, Basic Books, New York, 1958.

66. J. Lacan, *De la Psychose Paranoiaque dans ses Rapports avec la Personnalité*, Seuil, Paris, 1980, p. 254 (reprint of 1932 edition).

67. R.D. Laing, *The Divided Self*, Penguin, Harmondsworth, 1959, p. 27; R.D. Laing and D.G. Cooper, *Reason and Violence*, Tavistock, London, 1974, 2nd ed. pp. 35-40; L. Binswanger, 'Insanity as a life-historical phenomenon and as mental disease' and 'The case of Ellen West'. In Rollo May et al (eds.) *Existence: A New Dimension in Psychiatry and Psychology*, Basic Books, New York, 1958, pp. 233-5, 354-5.

Chapter 6.

1. See J. Passmore, *The Perfectibility of Man*, Duckworth, London 1970.

2. See H.F. Ellenberger, *The Discovery of the Unconscious*, Allen Lane, London, 1970. While this contains much valuable material on Freud it is sometimes very inaccurate, e.g. the description of Schopenhauer as a 'sexual mystic' who influenced Freud (p. 545).

3. Among the earliest criticism of Freud from this point of view was: G. Aschaffenburg, 'Die Beziehungen des sexuellen Leben zur Entstehung von Nerven- und Geisteskrankheiten', *Münchener medizinische Wochenschrift*, 53, 1793-8, 1906; A.A. Friedlander, 'Über Hysterie und die Freudsche psychoanalytische Behandlung derselben', *Monatschrift für Psychiatrie und Neurologie*, 23, 45-54, 1907; W.B. Parker (ed.), *Psychotherapy: A Course of Reading in Sound Psychology, Sound Medicine, and Sound Religion*, Centre Publishing, New York, 1909, 3 vols., particularly the essay by R.C. Cabot.

4. *The Interpretation of Dreams*, *Complete Works*, IV, Chap. 2.

5. *Ibid*.

6. P. Bakan, *Sigmund Freud and the Jewish Mystical Tradition*, Van Nostrand, New York, 1958, Chap. 10.

7. *The Interpretation of Dreams*, Chap. 5D.

8. *Ibid*, p. 256.

9. See H.F. Ellenberger, *Ibid*, pp. 291-303.

10. See H.F. Ellenberger, *Ibid*, pp. 431-3.

11. *The Interpretation of Dreams*, pp. xv-xviii.

12. *Ibid*, p. 258.

13. Most clearly in D.P. Ausubel, *Theory and Problems of Child Development*, Grune and Stratton, New York, 1980, 3rd edition.

14. *The Interpretation of Dreams*, pp. 256-7.

15. *Ibid*, p. 257.

16. *Ibid*, p. 256.

17. H.F. Ellenberger, *Ibid*, p. 446.

18. *Ibid*.

19. *Complete Works*, V, pp. 598-599.

20. *Ibid, p. 618.*

21. *Ibid*, pp. 573-5.

22. *Ibid*, VII, p. 200n.

23. *Ibid*, pp. 185-200.

24. *Ibid*, XVIII, pp. 98-99.

25. *Ibid*, p. 110.

26. *Ibid*, p. 95.

27. *Ibid*, p. 127.

28. *Ibid*, p. 120.

29. *Ibid*, pp. 122-3.

30. *Ibid*, XXIII, p. 86.

31. *Ibid*, XX, pp. 54-5.

32. *Ibid*, XX, p. 145.

33. A. Freud, *The Ego and the Mechanisms of Defence*, Hogarth, London, 1948, trans. C. Baines, 2nd edition.

34. *Collected Works*, XXI, p. 13.

35. *Ibid*, XVIII, p. 102.

36. *Ibid*, p. 107.

37. *Ibid*, p. 107.

38. For recent surveys of attempts to validate Freudian theory see P. Kline, *Fact and Fantasy in Freudian Theory*, Methuen, London, 1972; S. Fisher and R.P. Greenberg, *The Scientific Credibility of Freud's Theories and Therapy*, Harvester, London, 1976.

39. For surveys of these see R.L. Munroe, *Schools of Psychoanalytic Thought*, Hutchinson, London, 1957; D. Weyes, *Psychoanalytic Schools from the Beginning to the Present*, Jason Aronson, New York, 1973; J.A.C. Brown, *Freud and the Post-Freudians*, Penguin, Harmondsworth, 1961.

40. F. Engels, *The Origin of The Family, Private Property and the State*, Progress Publishers, Moscow, 1948; K. Marx, *Critique of the Gotha Programme*, International Publishers, New York, 1936.

41. V.I. Lenin, *The State and Revolution*, Progress Publishers, Moscow, 1965.

42. On the British working class in the booms of the nineteenth century see M. Beer, *A History of British Socialism*, Vol. 2, National Labour Press, London, 1921, pp. 200, 221-2. For Reich's views see *The Mass Psychology of Fascism*, Pelican, Harmondsworth, 1946, third edition, trans. V.R. Carfagno, pp. 105-6.

43. *Character Analysis*, Farrar, Strauss and Giroux, New York, 1948, 3rd edition, trans. V.R. Carfagno, pp. 163-4.

44. *Ibid*, pp. 157-8.

45. *Ibid*, p. 280.

46. *Ibid*, p. 163.

47. *Ibid*, p. 53.

48. *Ibid*, p. 50.

49. *The Mass Psychology of Fascism*, p. 92.

50. *Ibid*, pp. 80-1.

51. *Ibid*, p. 99.

52. *Ibid*, pp. 176-7.

53. *Character Analysis*, p. xxi.

54. *Eros and Civilisation*, Abacus, London, 1955, p. 42.

55. *Ibid*, pp. 78-9.

56. *Ibid*, p. 78.

57. *Ibid*, p. 145.

58. *Ibid*, p. 82.

59. *Ibid*, p. 81.

60. *Beyond the Chains of Illusion*, Simon and Shuster, New York, 1962, p. 5.

61. See D. Joravsky, *Soviet Marxism and Natural Science, 1917-32*, Routledge and Kegan Paul, London, 1961.

62. See M. Jay, *The Dialectical Imagination*, Heinemann, London, 1973, Chap. 3.

63. *The Dogma of Christ*, Routledge and Kegan Paul, London, 1963.

64. M. Jay, *Ibid*, pp. 95-8.

65. *The Crisis of Psychoanalysis*, Penguin, Harmondsworth, 1970, p. 110.

66. *Ibid*, p. 48.

67. *Escape from Freedom*, Holt, Rinehart and Winston, New York, 1941, p. 43.

68. *Ibid*, p. 48

69. *Ibid*.

70. *Ibid*, p. 105.

71. *Ibid*, p. 122.

72. *Ibid*, pp. 114-5.

73. *Ibid*, p. 179.

74. *Man for Himself*, Holt, Rinehart and Winston, New York, 1947, p. 13.

75. *Ibid*, p. 49.

76. *Ibid*.

77. *Ibid*, pp. 62-117.

78. M. Jay, *Ibid*, p. 108ff.

79. That aggression can be fun in itself is a point studiously avoided by most writers on the topic. It is however discussed by A. Storr in *Human Destructiveness*, Heinemann, London, 1972, pp. 19-20.

80. J. Dollard et al, *Frustration and Aggression*, Yale University Press, New Haven, 1939.

81. *The Anatomy of Human Destructiveness*, Cape, London, 1974, p. 68.

82. *Ibid*, p. 167.

83. D. Freeman, *Margaret Mead and Samoa*, Harvard University Press, Cambridge, 1983.

84. *The Anatomy of Human Destructiveness*, pp. 234-5. On the element of violence in Hindu culture see for instance C.B. Day, *Peasant Cults in India*, Chinese Materials Centre, San Francisco, 1974, pp. 30-33; A Hiltbeitel, *The Ritual of Battle*, Cornell University Press, Ithica, 1976.

85. See C.W. Morris, *Writings on the General Theory of Signs*, Mouton, The Hague, 1971.

86. On Levi-Strauss see C.R. Badcock, *Levi-Strauss, Structuralism and Sociological Theory*, Hutchinson, London, 1975; E.R. Leach, *Levi-Strauss*, Fontana, London, 1970.

87. See T. Parsons, *The Social System*, Free Press, Glencoe, 1951. Examples of universal aspects of social structure that Parsons believes are rooted in human nature are the ascription, as opposed to achievement, of first roles (p. 155); the family as a transmitter of values (p. 209); and the giving, in industrial societies, of rewards for work competence (p. 160).

88. *De la Psychose Paranoiaque dans ses Rapports avec la Personnalité*, Le Francois, Paris, 1932; Édition de Seuil, Paris, 1980, p. 254 in the latter edition.

89. *Ibid*, p. 39n. Lacan, following Kastler and Mendowne's French translation of *General Psychopathology*, uses 'comprendre' to render 'verstehen' directly into French.

90. Thus in the 'Rational Index of Major Concepts' at the end of *Écrits* (Éditions du Seuil, Paris, 1966) we find 'theory of the autonomous self' and 'humanism' listed under 'The ideology of liberty'. See also references to the main text cited there.

91. *De la Psychose Paranoiaque*, p. 43.

92. Leading figures in ego psychology were A. Freud (*The Ego and the Mechanisms of Defence*, International Universities Press, New York, 1946, trans. C. Baines); H. Hartmann (*Ego Psychology and the Problem of Adaptation*, International Universities Press, New York, 1958, trans. D. Rapaport); E. Kris (*Selected Papers*, Yale University Press, New Haven, 1975).

93. S. Freud, 'The question of lay analysis', *Complete Works*, Vol. XX, pp. 179-258.

94. S. Turkle, *Freud's French Revolution*, Burnett, London, 1980, p. 105. Information in the following two paragraphs comes mainly from this source.

95. See G. Bachelard, *Le Nouvel Espirit Scientifique*, Presses Universitaires de France, Paris, 1973, 12e édition; *L'Activité Rationaliste de la Physique Contemporain*, Presses Universitaires de France, Paris, 1965, 2e ed.; L. Althusser, *For Marx*, Allen Lane, London, 1969, trans. B. Brewster; *Reading Capital*, New Left Books, London, 1970, trans. B. Brewster.

96. T. Kuhn, *The Structure of Scientific Revolutions*, University of Chicago Press, Chicago, 1962; K. Popper, *Conjectures and Refutations*, Routledge and Kegan Paul, London, 1965, 2nd Edition.

97. *Écrits*, p. 467.

98. *Ibid*.

99. *Ibid*, p. 278.

100. *Ibid*, p. 97.

101. *Ibid*, p. 98.

102. *Ibid*, p. 101.

103. *Ibid*, p. 113.

104. *Ibid*.

105. *Ibid*, p. 120.

106. *Ibid*, pp. 122-3.

107. *Ibid*, p. 117.

108. *Ibid*.

109. *Ibid*, p. 19.

110. *Ibid*, pp. 28-9.

111. *Ibid*, p. 31.

112. The single term 'insignifiante' seems intended in this double sense of 'insignificant/unsignifying'.

113. *Ibid*, p. 629. In Egyptian legend the father/king (Osiris) is cut up (castrated) by his brother Set. Isis the wife/queen and Horus the son/king-to-be defeat Set and establish the cult of the embalmed remains of Osiris.

114. *Ibid*, p. 632.

115. *Ibid*, p. 634.

116. For instance J. Mitchell in *Psychoanalysis and Feminism*, Allen Lane, London, 1974.

117. *Écrits*, p. 265.

118. The description of Lacan as a materialist is sometimes justified by the phrase 'dialectical materialism': Lacan is more dialectical than Freud and thus more materialist. This is of course a fallacy. Examples are J. Kristeva, *Semiotike*, Seuil, Paris, 1969; R. Coward and J. Ellis, *Language and Materialism*, Routledge and Kegan Paul, London, 1977.

119. *Écrits*, p. 898.

120. 'L'Étourdit', *Silicet*, 4, 5-52, 1973. 'L'Étourdi' may mean someone who is stunned or deafened, but it also means someone who blurts things out without thinking. The inclusion of 'dit' in Lacan's neologism may mean 'deaf speaker'; it could also suggest someone who blurts things out because they are possessed.

121. *Ibid*, p. 23.

122. *Écrits*, pp. 407, 547.

Chapter 7.

1. See H. Spiegelberg, *The Phenomenological Movement*, Nijhoff, The Hague, 1965, p. 292.

2. *Being and Time*, Basil Blackwell, Oxford, 1973, trans. J. Macquarie and E. Robinson, p. 67.

3. *Ibid*, p. 124.

4. *Ibid*, p. 171.

5. *Ibid*, p. 172.

6. *Ibid*, p. 173. (translation slightly altered)

7. *Ibid*, p. 175.

8. *Ibid*, p. 235.
9. *Ibid*, p. 219.
10. *Ibid*, p. 221.
11. *Ibid*, p. 222.
12. *Ibid*, p. 230.
13. *Ibid*, p. 237.
14. *Ibid*.
15. *Ibid*, p. 240.
16. *Ibid*, p. 279.
17. *Ibid*, p. 288.
18. *Ibid*, p. 311.
19. *Ibid*, p. 322.
20. *Ibid*, p. 326.
21. *Ibid*, p. 330.
22. *Ibid*, p. 342.
23. *Ibid*, p. 386.
24. *Ibid*, p. 343 (translation slightly altered).
25. *Ibid*, p. 444.
26. *Platons Lehre von der Wahrheit*, Francke, Bern, 1942.
27. *Was ist Metaphysik?*, Klostermann, Frankfurt, 1929; *Erlauterung zu Holderlin's Dichtung*, Klostermann, Frankfurt, 1971, 4e Aufl.; *Holzwege*, Klostermann, Frankfurt, 1950.
28. See H. Spiegelberg, *The Phenomenological Movement*, Nijhoff, The Hague, 1965, Vol. 1.
29. On Merleau-Ponty's political development see A. Rabil, *Merleau-Ponty, Existentialist of the Social World*, Columbia University Press, New York, 1967.
30. S. de Beauvoir, *The Prime of Life*, Penguin, Harmondsworth, 1962, trans. P. Green.
31. See M. Poster, *Existential Marxism in Postwar France*, Princeton University Press, Princeton, 1975.
32. *The Transcendence of the Ego*, Noonday Press, New York, 1957, trans. F. Williams and R. Kirkpatrick, p. 31.
33. *Ibid*, pp. 100-1.
34. *Ibid*, p. 97.
35. *Ibid*, p. 96.
36. For instance M. Warnock, *Loc. Cit.* and E. Breisach, *Op. Cit.*, p. 155.
37. J.P. Sartre, *La Transcendence de l'Ego*, J. Vrin, Paris, 1965 (first published 1936), p. 85. The translation by Williams and Kirkpatrick (*op. cit.*) of '*necessité d'essence*' as 'essential necessity' implies that '*essence*' is qualifying '*necessité*', when it really seems to be the other way round.
38. The term appears in *Being and Nothingness*, Methuen, London, 1969, trans. H.E. Barnes, pp. 557-574.
39. *Sketch for a Theory of the Emotions*, Methuen, London, 1962, trans. P. Mairet, p. 54.
40. Heidegger is given as the source of the notion of *verstehen* (understanding of action) on p. 51.
41. *Ibid*, p. 61.
42. *Ibid*.
43. *Ibid*, p. 62.
44. See the remarks on *neosis* on p. 81.
45. *La Nausée*, Gallimard, Paris, 1938, p. 170.
46. *Ibid*.
47. *The Psychology of Imagination*, Philosophical Library, London, 1948, anonymous translation, p. 174.
48. *Ibid*, p. 177.
49. *Ibid*, p. 259.
50. *Ibid*, p. 260.
51. *Ibid*.
52. *L'Imaginaire*, Gallimard, Paris, 1940, p. 353.
53. *Ibid*, pp. 267-8.
54. *Ibid*, p. 267.

55. S. de Beauvoir, *Ibid*. p. 37ff.
56. *Situations*, 1, Gallimard, Paris, 1947, pp. 314-335.
57. *Ibid*, p. 322.
58. *Ibid*.
59. *Ibid*, p. 325.
60. *Ibid*, p. 334.
61. *Being and Nothingness*, Methuen, London, 1958, trans. H.E. Barnes, p. xxii.
62. *Ibid*.
63. *Ibid*.
64. *Ibid*, p. xxiv.
65. *Ibid*, p. xxv.
66. *Ibid*.
67. *Ibid*, p. xxxvi.
68. *Ibid*, p. xxxix.
69. *Ibid*, p. 5.
70. *Ibid*, p. 9.
71. *Ibid*, p. 22.
72. The idea that a principle of evil pre-existed that of good was proposed by Plato himself in the *Statesman*. Plutarch was a notable exponent of this doctrine (*De Animae Procreatio in Timaeo*, 6).
73. *Being and Nothingness*, p. 23.
74. *Ibid*, p. 25.
75. *Ibid*, p. 27.
76. *Ibid*, p. 26.
77. *Ibid*, p. 29.
78. *Ibid*, p. 32.
79. *Ibid*, p. 38.
80. *Ibid*, p. 40.
81. *Ibid*, p. 44.
82. *Ibid*, p. 56.
83. *Ibid*, p. 53.
84. *Ibid*, p. 51.
85. *Ibid*, p. 63.
86. *Ibid*, p. 64.
87. *Ibid*, p. 85.
88. *Ibid*, p. 74.
89. *Ibid*.
90. *Ibid*.
91. *Ibid*. p. 75.
92. *Ibid*, p. 87.
93. *Ibid*. p. 89.
94. *Ibid*.
95. The possibility of a complete synthesis of the in-itself and the for-itself is explicitly denied on p. 90.
96. *Ibid*, p. 101.
97. *Ibid*, p. 116.
98. *Ibid*, p. 121.
99. *Ibid*, p. 122.
100. *Ibid*, p. 129.
101. *Ibid*, p. 128.
102. *Ibid*. p. 153.
103. *Ibid*, p. 177.
104. *Ibid*, p. 253.
105. *Ibid*, p. 261.
106. *Ibid*.
107. *Ibid*, p. 294.

108. *Ibid*, pp. 303-360.

109. *Ibid*, p. 363

110. *Ibid*, p. 397.

111. *Ibid*, p. 403.

112. *Ibid*, p. 438.

113. *Ibid*, p. 441.

114. *Ibid*, p. 449.

115. *Ibid*, p. 451.

116. *Ibid*, p. 452.

117. *Ibid*, p. 457.

118. *Ibid*.

119. *Ibid*, p. 488.

120. *Ibid*, p. 512.

121. *Ibid*, p. 518.

122. *Ibid*, p. 519.

123. *Ibid*, p. 513.

124. *Ibid*, pp. 513-4.

125. *Ibid*, p. 520.

126. F. Engels, letter to J. Block, September, 1890. In *Marx and Engels, Selected Correspondence*, Lawrence and Wishart, London, 1934, trans. D. Torr, p. 475.

127. *Ibid*, p. 545.

128. *Ibid*, p. 576.

129. *Ibid*, p. 586.

130. *Ibid*, p. 591-2.

131. *Ibid*, p. 607.

132. *Ibid*, p. 619.

133. *Critique of Dialectical Reason*, New Left Books, London, 1976 (original French publication, 1960), trans. A. Sheridan-Smith, p. 161ff.

134. *Ibid*, p. 131.

135. *Ibid*, p. 134.

136. *Ibid*, p. 133.

137. L. Trotsky, *The Revolution Betrayed*, New Park Publications, London, 1936

138. *Critique of Dialectical Reason*, p. 307.

139. *Ibid*, p. 176.

140. G. Lukacs, *History and Class Consciousness*, Merlin, London, 1971, trans. R. Livingstone.

141. *Critique of Dialectical Reason*, p. 357.

142. *Ibid*, p. 433.

143. *Ibid*.

144. *Ibid*, p. 450.

145. *Ibid*, p. 452.

146. *Ibid*, p. 553.

147. *Ibid*, pp. 551-2.

148. *Ibid*, p. 573.

149. *Ibid*.

150. *Ibid*, p. 581.

151. *Ibid*, p. 628.

152. *Ibid*, p. 641.

153. *Ibid*, p. 653.

154. *Ibid*, p. 654.

155. *Ibid*, p. 679.

156. *Ibid*, p. 671.

157. *Ibid*, p. 740.

158. *Ibid*, p. 749.

159. *Ibid*, p. 764.

160. *Ibid*, pp. 784-5.

161. *Ibid*, pp. 782-3.
162. *Ibid*.
163. *Ibid*, p. 781.
164. *Ibid*, p. 787.
165. *Ibid*, p. 799.
166. *Ibid*.
167. *Ibid*, p. 800.
168. *Ibid*.
169. *Ibid*.
170. *Ibid*, p. 802.
171. *Ibid*, p. 807.
172. *Ibid*, p. 808.
173. *Ibid*, p. 811 (translation slightly altered).
174. *Ibid*, p. 815.
175. *Ibid*, pp. 817-8.
176. See R. Williams, *Culture and Society*, Chatto and Windus, London, 1958, Chaps. 1-4.
177. *Economic and Philosophical Manuscripts of 1844*, p. 162.
178. See for instance: G. Baum, *Religion and Alienation*, Paulist Press, New York, 1975; P. Berger, *The Precarious Vision*, Doubleday, Garden City, 1961; T.S. Eliot, *The Idea of a Christian Society*, Harcourt, Brace, New York, 1940; B.V. Hill, *Education and the Endangered Individual*, Teachers College Press, New York, 1973; R. Niebuhr, *The Self and the Dramas of History*, Scribner, New York, 1955.
179. See M. Poster, *Existential Marxism in Postwar France*, Princeton Uni. Press, Princeton, 1975.
180. See A. Callinicos, *Althusser*, Pluto, London, 1976.
181. M. Merleau-Ponty, *Les Aventures de la Dialectique*, Gallimard, Paris, 1955; *L'Opium des Intellectuels*, Calmann-Levy, Paris, 1955.
182. See R.D. Laing, *The Divided Self*, Penguin, Harmondsworth, 1960; D.G. Cooper, *The Death of the Family*, Penguin, Harmondsworth, 1972; R.D. Laing and D.G. Cooper, *Reason and Violence: A Decade of Sartre's Philosophy 1950-60*, Tavistock, London, 1964.
183. M. Merleau-Ponty, *The Structure of Behaviour*, Methuen, London, 1965, trans. A.L. Fisher, p.139.
184. *Ibid*, p.167.
185. *Ibid*, p.171.
186. *Ibid*, p.93.
187. *Ibid*, pp.177-8.
188. *Ibid*, p.180.
189. *Ibid*, pp.173-4, translation slightly altered.
190. *Ibid*, p.174.
191. *Ibid*, pp.124-8.
192. M. Merleau-Ponty, *Phénomenologie de la Perception*, Gallimard, Paris, 1945, p. 179.
193. *Ibid*, pp. 140-2.
194. *Ibid*, pp. 185-6.
195. *Ibid*, p. 187.
196. *Ibid*, p. 497.
197. *Ibid*, p. 505.
198. M. Merleau-Ponty, *Sense and Non-sense*, Northwestern Uni. Press, Evanston, 1964, trans. H.L. Dreyfus and P.A. Dreyfus, pp. 72-3.
199. M. Merleau-Ponty, *The Primacy of Perception*, Northwestern Uni. Press, Evanston, 1964, trans. J.M. Edie, pp. 96-158.
200. *Ibid*, pp. 135-6.
201. *Ibid*, p. 155.
202. See H. Speigelberg, *The Phenomenological Movement*, Nijhoff, The Hague, 1965, Vol. 2.
203. M. Poster, *Existential Marxism in Postwar France*, Princeton Uni. Press, Princeton, 1975, p. 360.
204. *Le Système des Objets*, Gallimard, Paris, 1968, pp. 32, 52.

205. *Ibid*, p. 173.
206. V. Packard, *The Hidden Persuaders*, Longmans Green, London, 1957.
207. *Le Système des Objets*, p. 184.
208. *L'Échange Symbolique et La Mort*, Seuil, Paris, 1976, pp. 9, 10.
209. *Ibid*, p. 11.
210. *Ibid*.
211. V.I. Lenin, *Collected Works*, Lawrence and Wishart, London, 1961, Vol. XXXVIII, pp. 85-244.
212. *L'Echange Symbolique et la Mort*, p. 12.
213. *Ibid*.
214. *Ibid*, p. 13.
215. *The Mirror of Production*, Telos, St. Louios, 1975, trans. M. Poster, p. 49.
216. *Ibid*, p. 48.
217. See B. Hindness and P.Q. Hirst, *Pre-Capitalist Modes of Production*, Routledge and Kegan Paul, London, 1975, Chap. 1.
218. *Le Systeme des Objects*, pp. 233-4.
219. *Ibid*, p. 32.
220. *Ibid*, pp. 35-6.
221. *Ibid*, p. 98.
222. *Ibid*, p. 101.
223. *Ibid*, p. 103.
224. *Ibid*, p. 107.
225. *Ibid*, p. 121.
226. *Ibid*, p. 228.
227. *La Societe de Consommation*, Gallimard, Paris, 1970, pp. 53-5.
228. *Pour une Critique de L'Economie Politique des Signes*, Gallimard, Poitiers, 1972, p. 179.
229. *L'Echange Symbolique et la Mort*, p. 38.
230. *Pour une Critique de L'Economie Politique des Signes*, pp. 264-5.
231. *Ibid*, pp. 154-171.
232. *Ibid*, p. 224.
233. *L'Echange Symbolique et la Mort*, p. 202.
234. *Ibid*, p. 203.
235. *Ibid*, p. 207.
236. *Ibid*, p. 204.

Chapter 8

1. M. Merleau-Ponty, *Phénomenologie de la Perception*, Gallimard, Paris, 1945.
2. M. Merleau-Ponty, *Sense and Non-Sense*, Northwestern Uni., Evanston, 1964, trans. H.L. and P.A. Dreyfus, p. 71.
3. C. Levi-Strauss, *La Pensée Sauvage*, Gallimard, Paris, 1956; *Mythologiques*, Vols. 1-4, Plon, Paris, 1964-71.
4. G. Deleuze and F. Guattari, *l'Anti-Oedipe*, Gallimard, Paris, 1970.
5. J. Derrida, *The Archeology of the Frivolous*, Duquesne University Press, Pittsburg, 1980, trans. J.P. Leavey; J. Derrida, *Of Grammatology*, Johns Hopkins, Baltimore, 1976.
6. A Glucksmann, *Les Mâitres Penseurs*, Grasset, Paris, 1977.
7. J. Derrida, *L'Oreille de L'Autre*, VLB, Montreal, 1982.
8. See C. Norris, *Deconstruction: Theory and Practice*, Methuen, London, 1982; J.D. Culler, *The Pursuit of Signs*, Routledge, London, 1982.
9. See D.P. Ausubel, *Theory and Problems of Child Development*, Grune and Stratton, New York, 1980, third edition.
10. See P. Kline, *Fact and Fantasy in Freudian Theory*, Methuen, London 1972; S. Fisher and R.P. Greenburg, *The Scientific Credibility of Freud's Theories and Therapy*, Harvester, London, 1977.
11. See note 10.
12. D.P. Ausubel, *Ibid*, pp. 184-93.
13. H.R. Schaffer, *The Growth of Sociability*, Penguin, London, 1970.

260

14. *The Will to Power*, Weidenfeld and Nicolson, London, 1967, pp. 95-97.
15. E. Bloch, *Gesamtausgabe*, Bd 5 (*Das Prinzip Hoffnung*) and Bd 16 (*Geist der Utopie*), Suhrkamp, Frankfurt, 1976; M. Frank, *Der Kommende Gott*, Suhrkamp, Frankfurt, 1982; H. Jonas, *Organismus und Freiheit*, Vandenhoek und Ruprecht, Götingen, 1973; H. Jonas, *Das Prinzip Verantwortung*, Insel, Frankfurt, 1983.
16. See Chapter 1, note 64.
17. B. Russell, *Education and the Social Order*, Allen and Unwin, London, 1932.
18. R.D. Laing, *The Divided Self*, Penguin, Harmondsworth, 1960.
19. See *Mixed Opinions and Maxims* (272) in F. Nietzsche, *The Portable Nietzsche*, Chatto and Windus, London, 1971, p. 66.
20. S. Anthony. *The Discovery of Death in Childhood*, Allen Lane, London, 1971.
21. See W.H. Davis, *The Freewill Question*, Martinus Nijhoff, The Hague, 1971, Chap. 7; R.F. Franklin, *Freewill and Determinism*, Routledge, London, 1968, Chap. 7.
22. G.H. Bantock, *Education in an Industrial Society*, Faber, London, 1963, Chap. 7; R.E. Gross, *British Secondary Education*, OUP, London, 1965.
23. See I.L. James, *Stress and Frustration*, Harcourt, Brace, Jovanovich, New York, 1971, Chaps. 1-4.
24. M. Merleau-Ponty, *Phénomenologie de la Perception*, Gallimard, Paris, 1945, p. 160.
25. See C.N. Cofer and M.H. Appley, *Motivation: Theory and Research*, Wiley, New York, 1964.
26. See H. Hass, *The Human Animal*, Hodder and Stroughton, London, 1970, pp. 121-2; R.A. Hinde 'Ethology and child development'. In P.H. Mussen (ed.) *Handbook of Child Psychology*, Vol. 2, Wiley, New York, 1983.
27. K. Jaspers, *General Psychopathology*, Uni. of Chicago Press, Chicago, 1963, trans. J. Hoenig and M.W. Hamilton, pp. 360-3.
28. J.A. Hadfield, *Dreams and Nightmares*, Penguin, Harmondsworth, 1954; N. MacKenzie, *Dreams and Dreaming*, Aldus, London, 1965, Chap. 11; M.F. De Martino (ed.) *Dreams and Personality Dynamics*, C.C. Thomas, Springfield, 1959.
29. See note 28.
30. J.A. Hadfield, *Ibid*.

Index

MARTINUS NIJHOFF PHILOSOPHY LIBRARY

1. D. Lamb, Hegel – From Foundation to System. 1980. ISBN 90-247-2359-0
2. I.N. Bulhof, Wilhelm Dilthey: A Hermeneutic Approach to the Study of History and Culture. 1980. ISBN 90-247-2360-4
3. W.J. van der Dussen, History as a Science. The Philosophy of R.G. Collingwood. 1981. ISBN 90-247-2453-8
4. M. Chatterjee, The Language of Philosophy. 1981. ISBN 90-247-2372-8
5. E.-H.W. Kluge, The Metaphysics of Gottlob Frege. An Essay in Ontological Reconstruction. 1980. ISBN 90-247-2422-8
6. D. Dutton and M. Krausz (eds.), The Concept of Creativity in Science and Art. 1981. ISBN 90-247-2418-X
7. F.R. Ankersmit, Narrative Logic. A Semantic Analysis of the Historian's Language. 1983. ISBN 90-247-2731-6
8. T.P. Hohler, Imagination and Reflection: Intersubjectivity. Fichte's *Grundlage* of 1794. 1982. ISBN 90-247-2732-4
9. F.J. Adelmann (ed.), Contemporary Chinese Philosophy. 1982. ISBN 90-247-3057-0
10. E.N. Ostenfeld, Forms, Matter and Mind. Three Strands in Plato's Metaphysics. 1982. ISBN 90-247-3051-1
11. J.T.J. Srzednicki, The Place of Space and Other Themes. Variations on Kant's First Critique. 1983. ISBN 90-247-2844-4
12. D. Boucher, Texts in Context. Revisionist Methods for Studying the History of Ideas. 1985. ISBN 90-247-3121-6
13. Y. Yovel, Nietzsche as Affirmative Thinker. 1986. ISBN 90-247-3269-7
14. M.H. Mitias (ed.), Possibility of the Aesthetic Experience. 1986. ISBN 90-247-3278-6
15. P.E. Langford, Modern Philosophies of Human Nature. 1986. ISBN 90-247-3370-7
16.
17. W. Horosz, Search without Idols. 1986. ISBN 90-247-3327-8
18. R. Ellis, An Ontology of Consciousness. 1986. ISBN 90-247-3349-9

Series ISBN 90-247-2344-2